Welcome

I wanted to draw a fun story.

Thanks for reading it!

Naoshi Komi

*Author

NAOSHI KOMI was born in Kochi Prefecture, Japan, on March 28, 1986. His first serialized work in *Weekly Shonen Jump* was the series *Double Arts*. His current series, *Nisekoi*, is serialized in *Weekly Shonen Jump*.

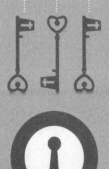

NISEKOI:
False Love

VOLUME 1
SHONEN JUMP Manga Edition

Story and Art by
NAOSHI KOMI

Translation ✐ Camellia Nieh
Touch-Up Art & Lettering ✐ Stephen Dutro
Design ✐ Fawn Lau
Shonen Jump Series Editor ✐ John Bae
Graphic Novel Editor ✐ Amy Yu

NISEKOI © 2011 by Naoshi Komi
All rights reserved.
First published in Japan in 2011
by SHUEISHA Inc., Tokyo.
English translation rights arranged
by SHUEISHA Inc.

The stories, characters and incidents mentioned
in this publication are entirely fictional.

Printed in the U.S.A.

Published by VIZ Media, LLC
P.O. Box 77010
San Francisco, CA 94107

10 9 8 7 6 5 3 4 2 1
First printing, January 2014

www.shonenjump.com

www.viz.com

NISEKOI
False Love
vol. 1: The Promise

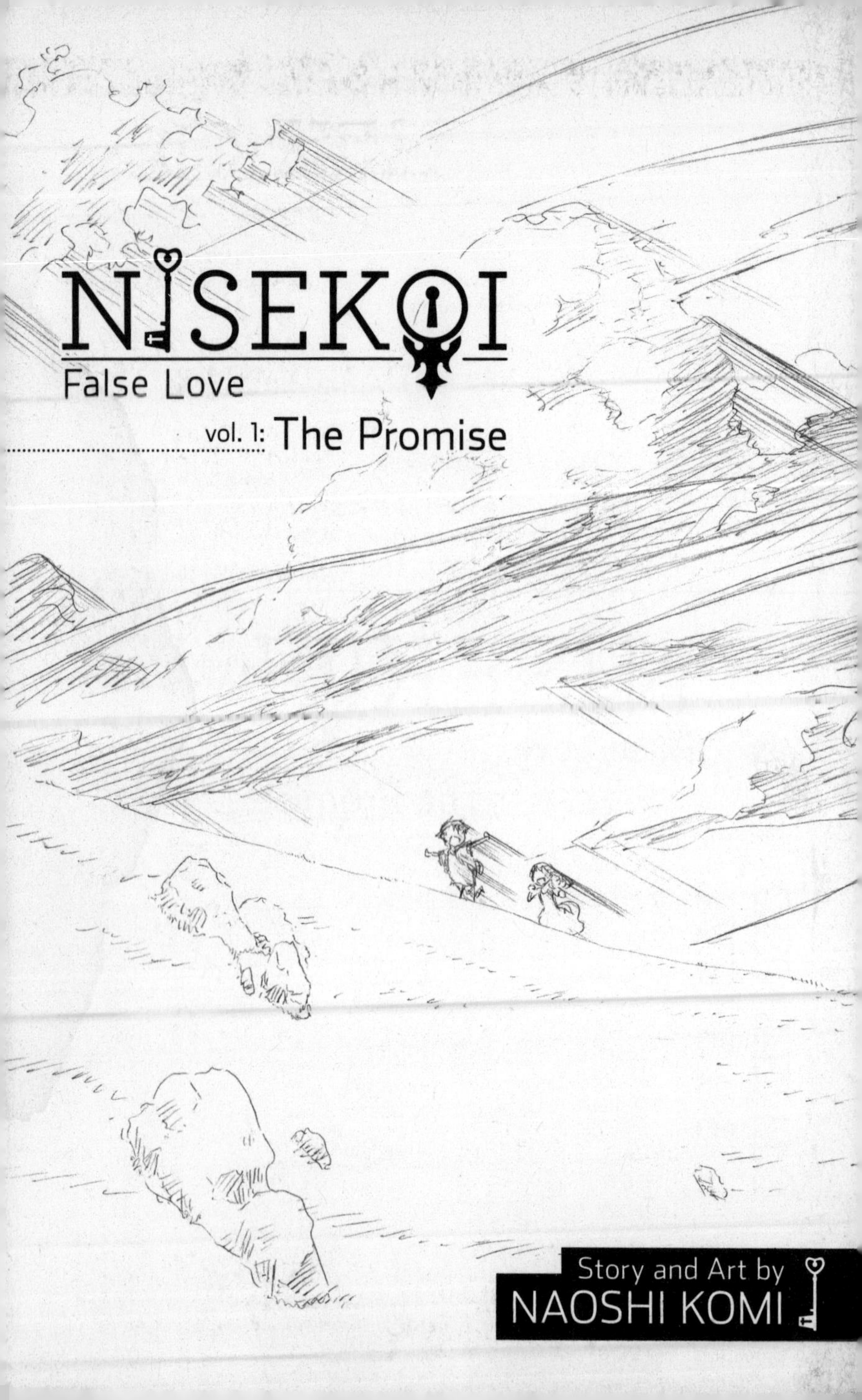

Story and Art by
NAOSHI KOMI

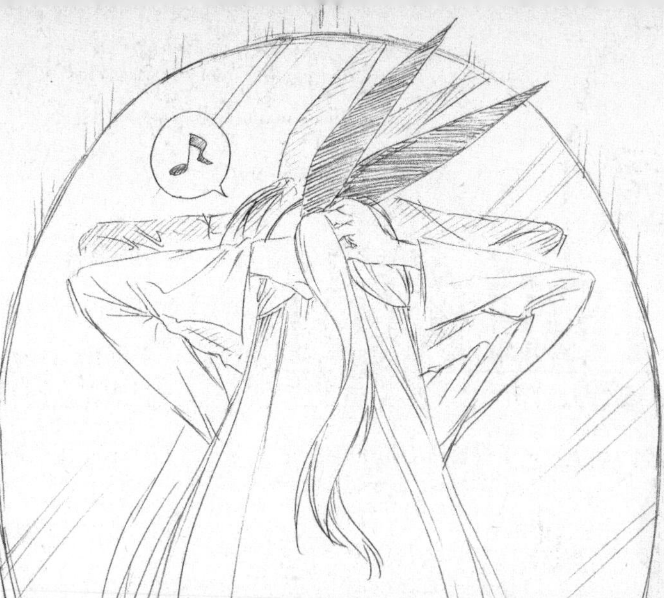

NISEKOI

False Love

vol. 1: The Promise

TABLE OF CONTENTS

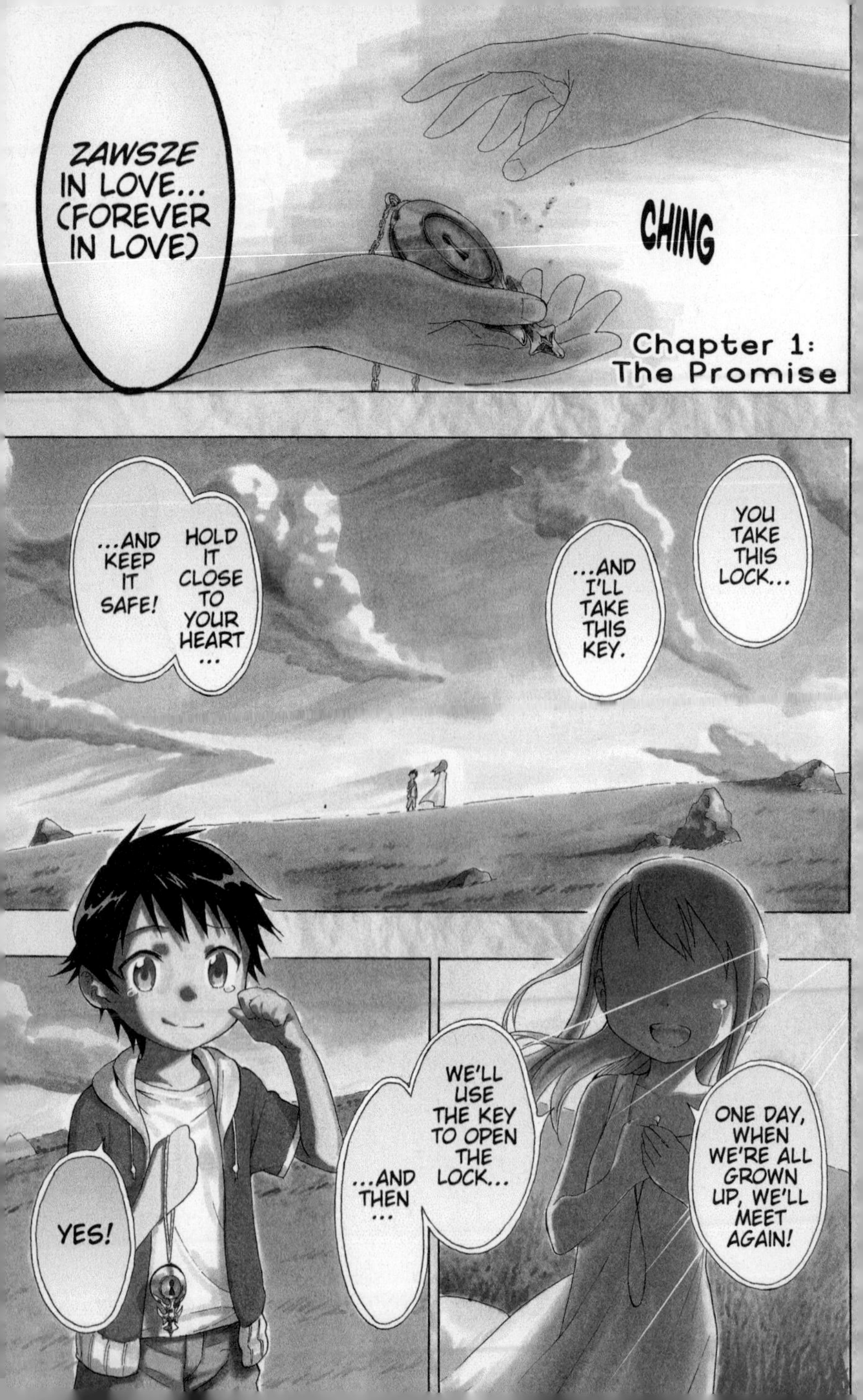
CHING
Chapter 1: The Promise
ZAWSZE IN LOVE... (FOREVER IN LOVE)
YOU TAKE THIS LOCK...
...AND I'LL TAKE THIS KEY.
HOLD IT CLOSE TO YOUR HEART...
...AND KEEP IT SAFE!
ONE DAY, WHEN WE'RE ALL GROWN UP, WE'LL MEET AGAIN!
WE'LL USE THE KEY TO OPEN THE LOCK...
...AND THEN...
YES!

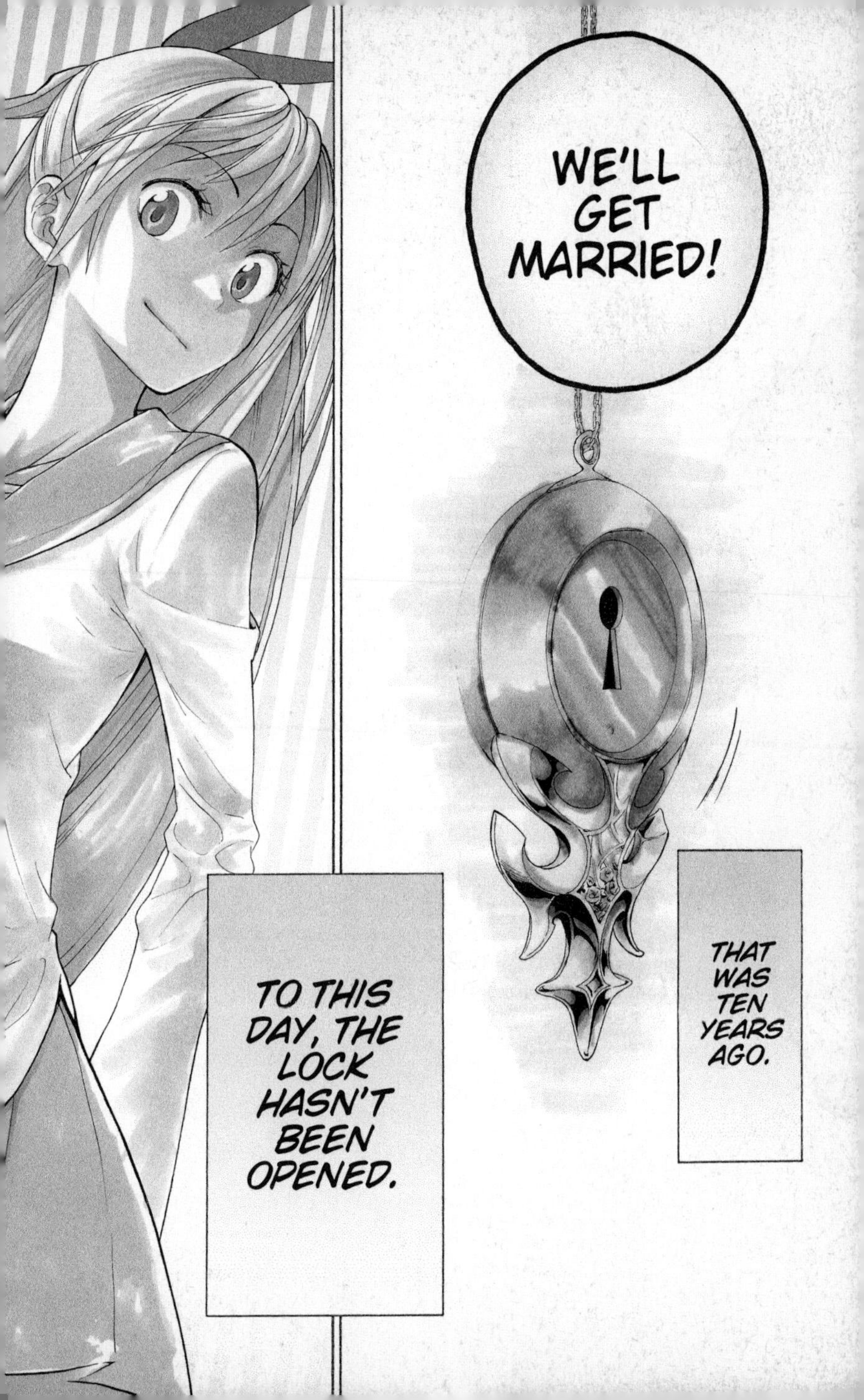
WE'LL GET MARRIED!
THAT WAS TEN YEARS AGO.
TO THIS DAY, THE LOCK HASN'T BEEN OPENED.

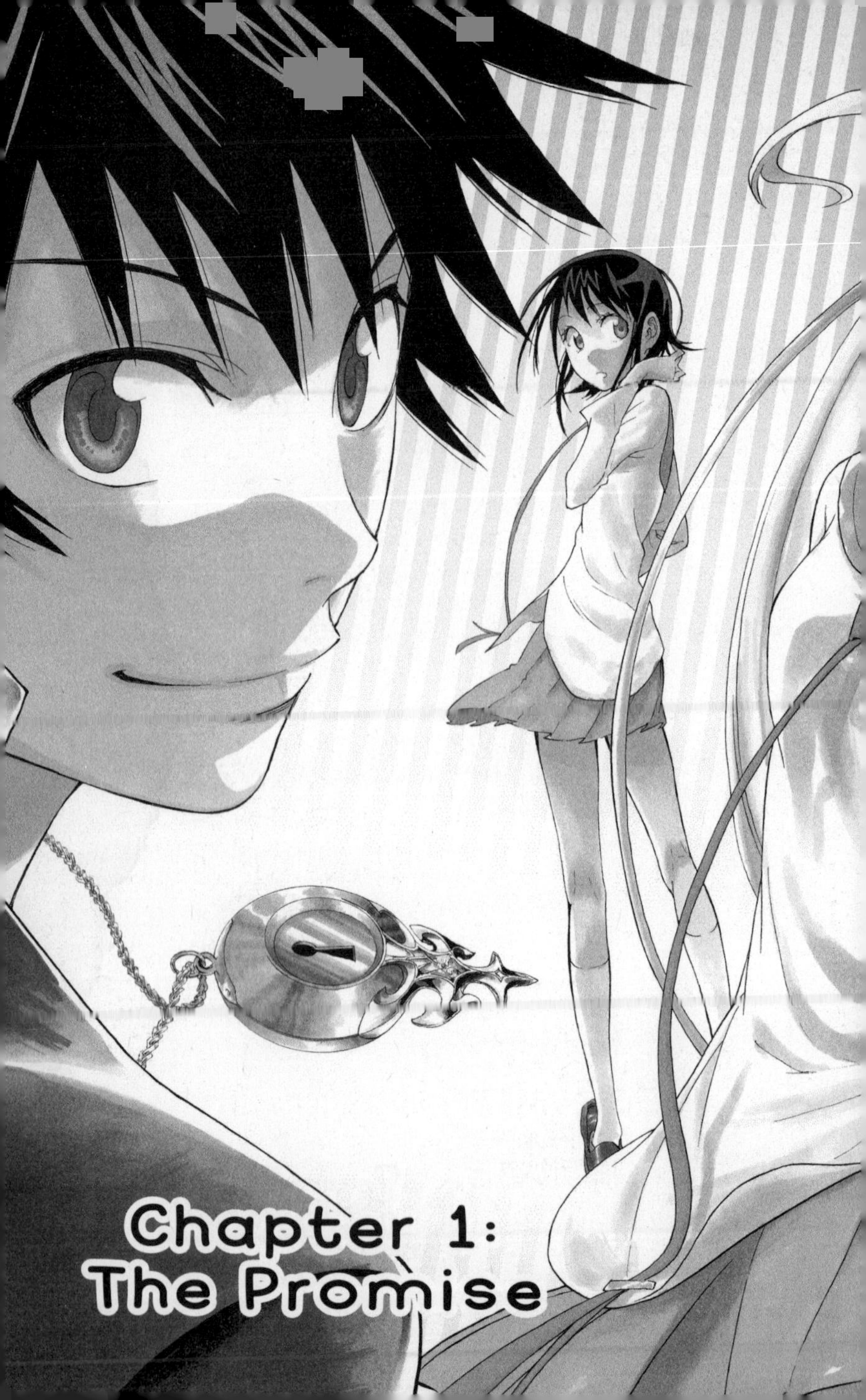
Chapter 1:
The Promise

NISEKOI
False Love

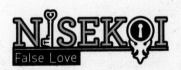

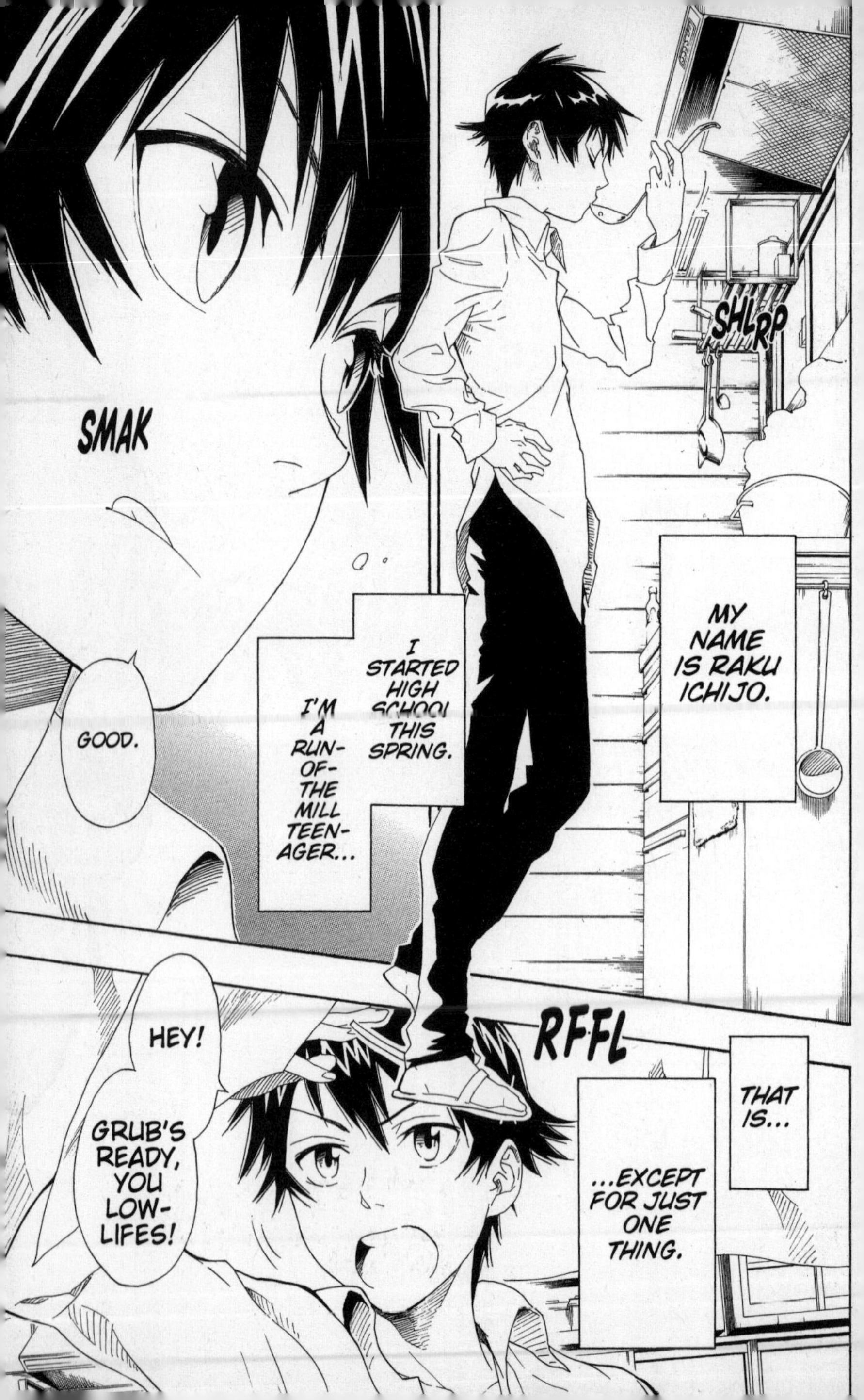
SHLRP
MY NAME IS RAKU ICHIJO.
I STARTED HIGH SCHOOL THIS SPRING.
I'M A RUN-OF-THE-MILL TEENAGER...
SMAK
GOOD.
RFFL
THAT IS...
...EXCEPT FOR JUST ONE THING.
HEY!
GRUB'S READY, YOU LOW-LIFES!

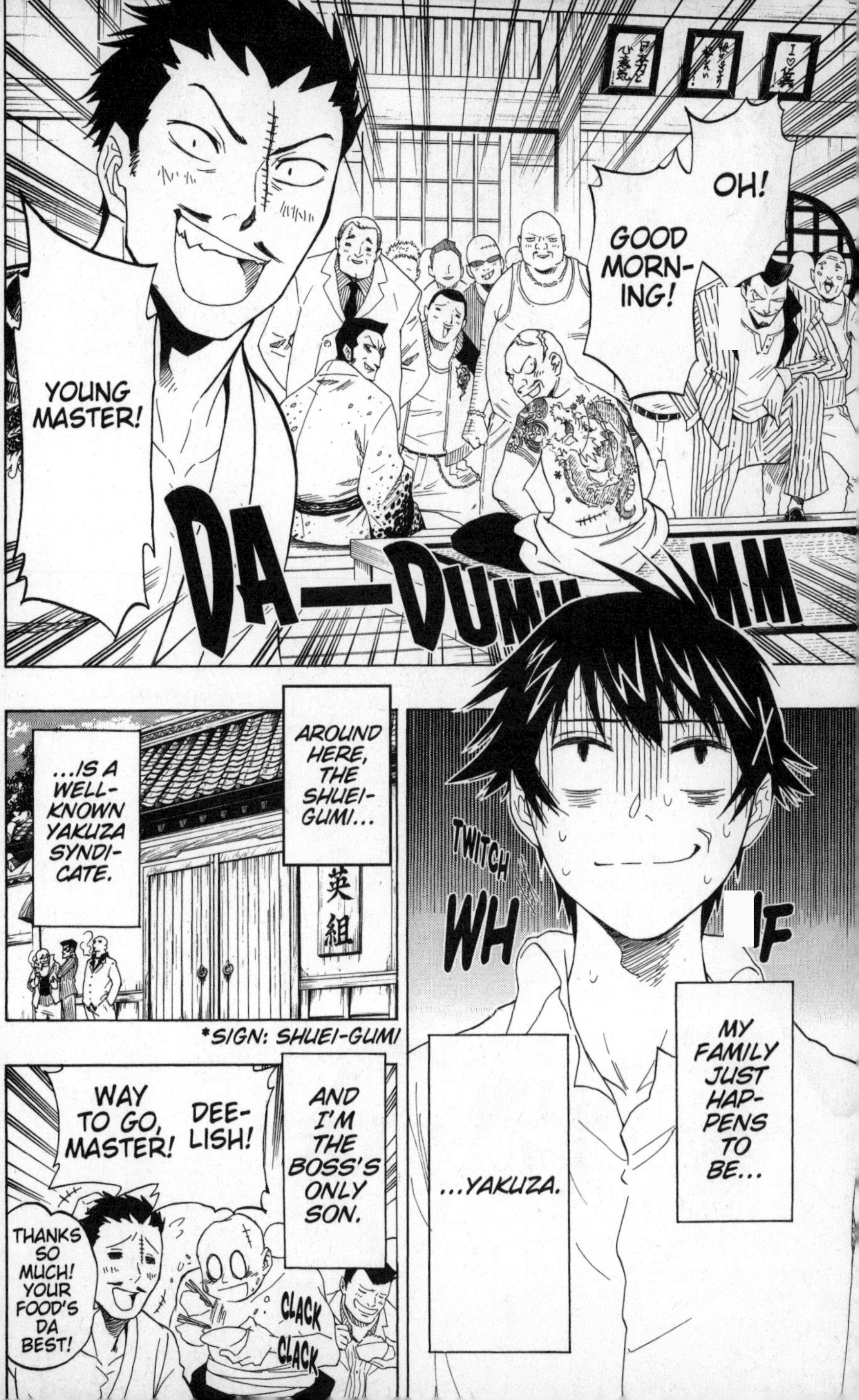
OH!
GOOD MORNING!
YOUNG MASTER!
DA—DUMM
MM
TWITCH
WH
F
MY FAMILY JUST HAPPENS TO BE...
...YAKUZA.
AROUND HERE, THE SHUEI-GUMI...
...IS A WELL-KNOWN YAKUZA SYNDICATE.
英
組
*SIGN: SHUEI-GUMI
AND I'M THE BOSS'S ONLY SON.
DEE-LISH!
WAY TO GO, MASTER!
THANKS SO MUCH! YOUR FOOD'S DA BEST!
CLACK
CLACK

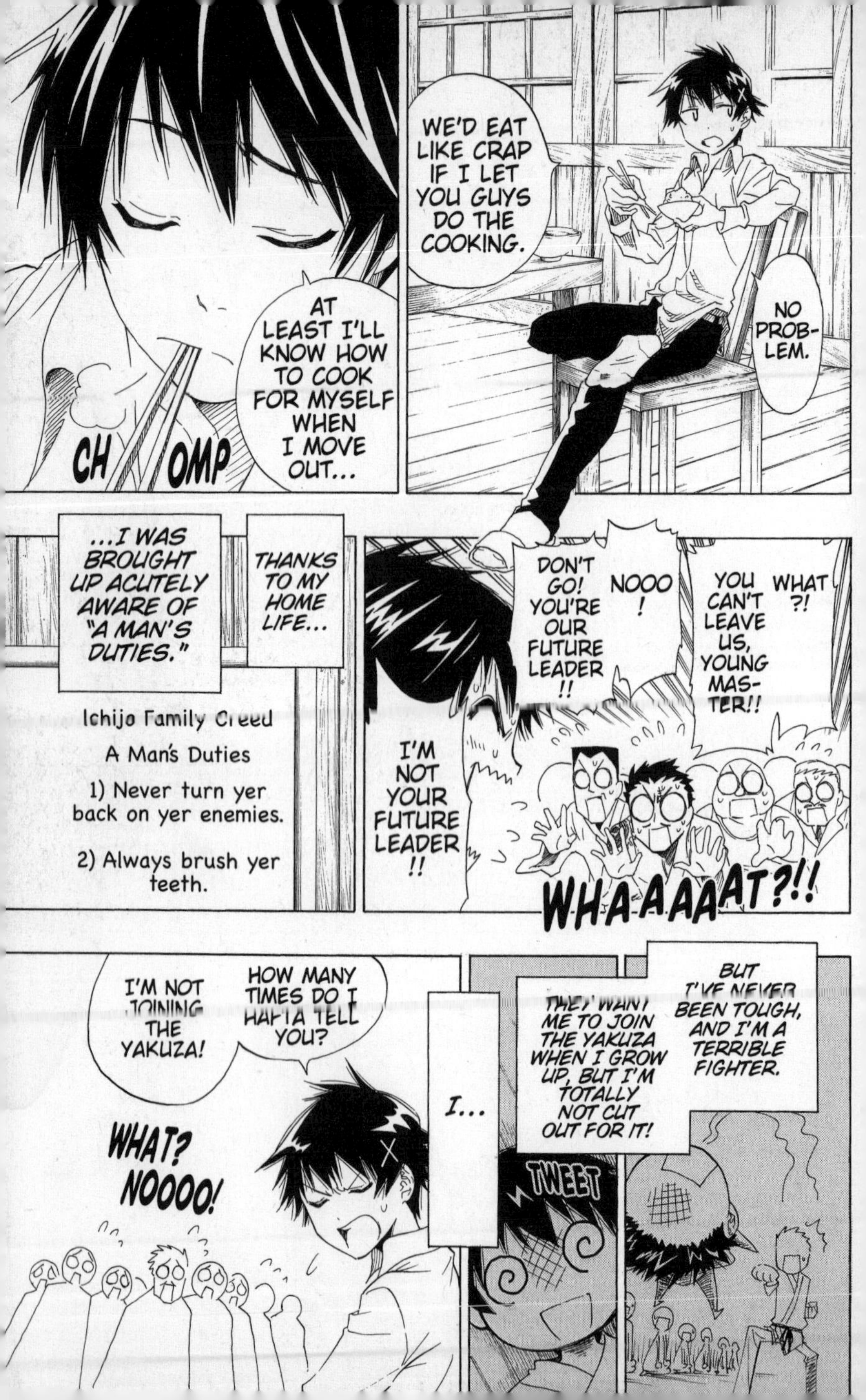
WE'D EAT LIKE CRAP IF I LET YOU GUYS DO THE COOKING.
NO PROBLEM.
CHOMP
AT LEAST I'LL KNOW HOW TO COOK FOR MYSELF WHEN I MOVE OUT...
WHAT?!
YOU CAN'T LEAVE US, YOUNG MASTER!!
NOOO!
DON'T GO! YOU'RE OUR FUTURE LEADER!!
I'M NOT YOUR FUTURE LEADER!!
WHA-A-AAAAT?!!
THANKS TO MY HOME LIFE...
...I WAS BROUGHT UP ACUTELY AWARE OF "A MAN'S DUTIES."
Ichijo Family Creed
A Man's Duties
1) Never turn yer back on yer enemies.
2) Always brush yer teeth.
THEY WANT ME TO JOIN THE YAKUZA WHEN I GROW UP, BUT I'M TOTALLY NOT CUT OUT FOR IT!
BUT I'VE NEVER BEEN TOUGH, AND I'M A TERRIBLE FIGHTER.
TWEET
I...
HOW MANY TIMES DO I HAFTA TELL YOU?
I'M NOT JOINING THE YAKUZA!
WHAT? NOOOO!

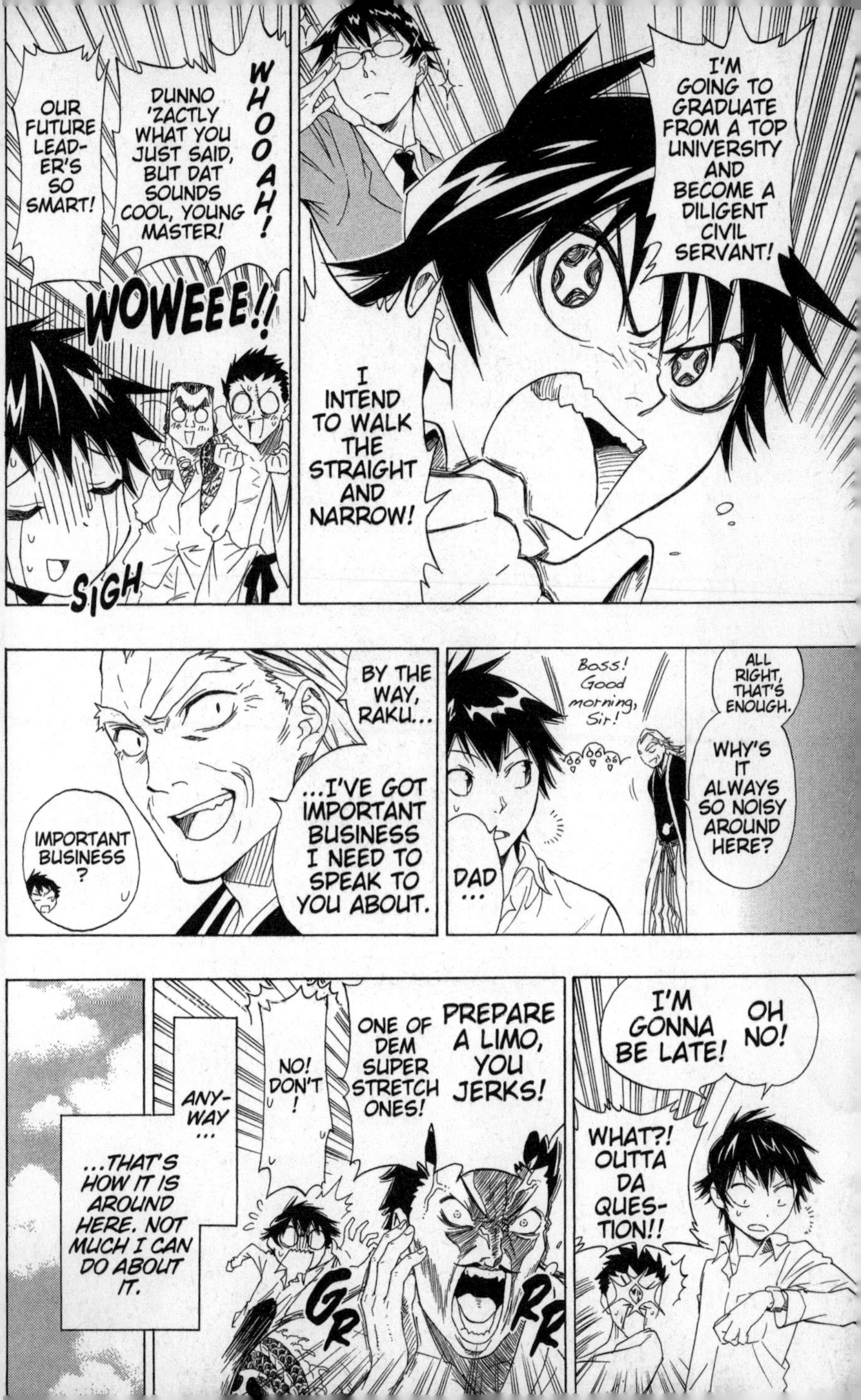
I'M GOING TO GRADUATE FROM A TOP UNIVERSITY AND BECOME A DILIGENT CIVIL SERVANT!
I INTEND TO WALK THE STRAIGHT AND NARROW!
WHOOAH!
DUNNO 'ZACTLY WHAT YOU JUST SAID, BUT DAT SOUNDS COOL, YOUNG MASTER!
OUR FUTURE LEAD-ER'S SO SMART!
WOWEEE!!
SIGH
ALL RIGHT, THAT'S ENOUGH.
WHY'S IT ALWAYS SO NOISY AROUND HERE?
Boss! Good morning, Sir!
DAD...
BY THE WAY, RAKU...
...I'VE GOT IMPORTANT BUSINESS I NEED TO SPEAK TO YOU ABOUT.
IMPORTANT BUSINESS?
OH NO!
I'M GONNA BE LATE!
WHAT?! OUTTA DA QUES-TION!!
PREPARE A LIMO, YOU JERKS!
ONE OF DEM SUPER STRETCH ONES!
NO! DON'T!
GRRR
ANY-WAY...
...THAT'S HOW IT IS AROUND HERE. NOT MUCH I CAN DO ABOUT IT.

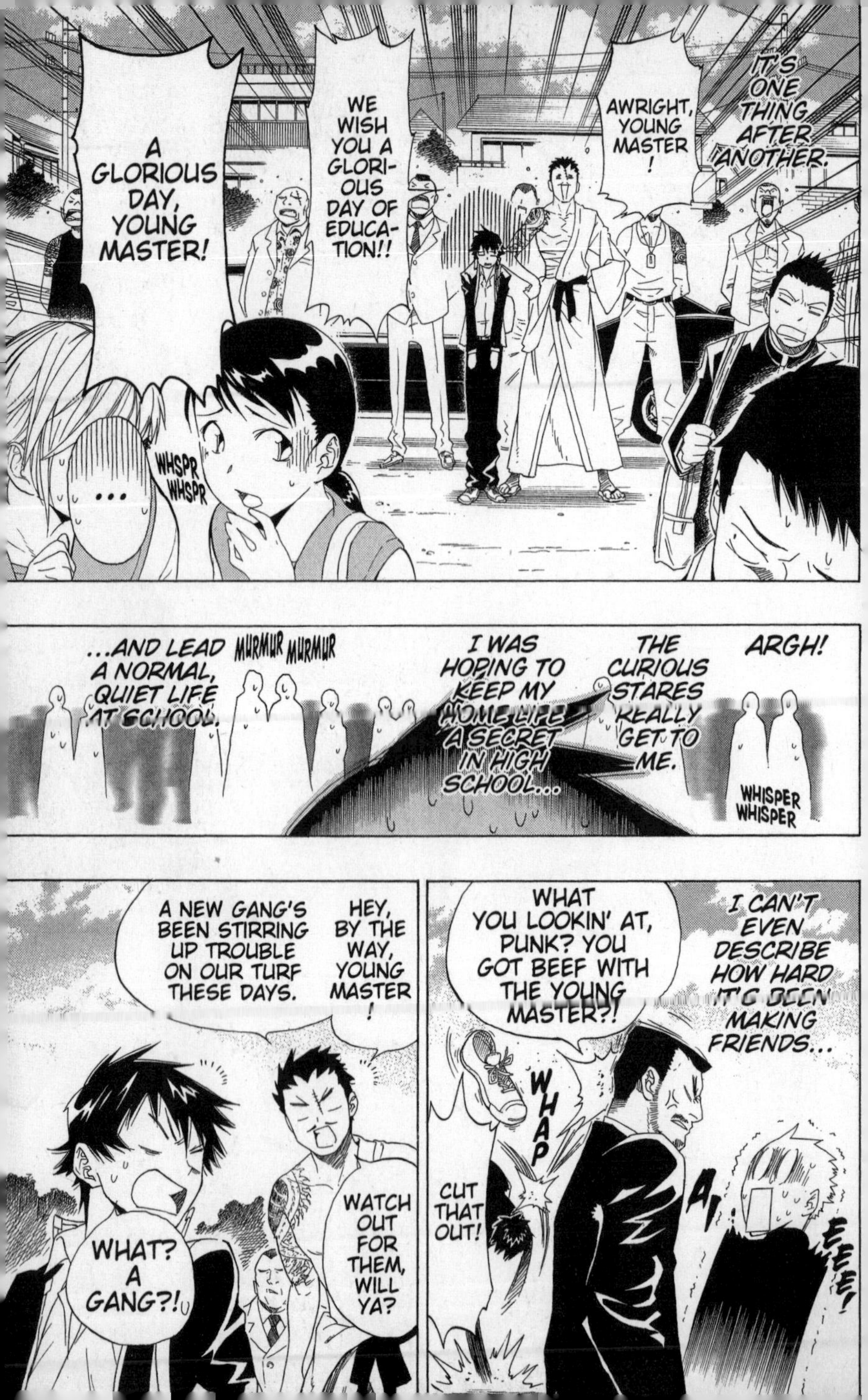
IT'S ONE THING AFTER ANOTHER.
AWRIGHT, YOUNG MASTER!
WE WISH YOU A GLORIOUS DAY OF EDUCATION!!
A GLORIOUS DAY, YOUNG MASTER!
WHSPR WHSPR
...
ARGH!
THE CURIOUS STARES REALLY GET TO ME.
I WAS HOPING TO KEEP MY HOME LIFE A SECRET IN HIGH SCHOOL...
...AND LEAD A NORMAL, QUIET LIFE AT SCHOOL.
MURMUR MURMUR
WHISPER WHISPER
I CAN'T EVEN DESCRIBE HOW HARD IT'S BEEN MAKING FRIENDS...
WHAT YOU LOOKIN' AT, PUNK? YOU GOT BEEF WITH THE YOUNG MASTER?!
WHAP
CUT THAT OUT!
AI
EEEE!
HEY, BY THE WAY, YOUNG MASTER!
A NEW GANG'S BEEN STIRRING UP TROUBLE ON OUR TURF THESE DAYS.
WATCH OUT FOR THEM, WILL YA?
WHAT? A GANG?!

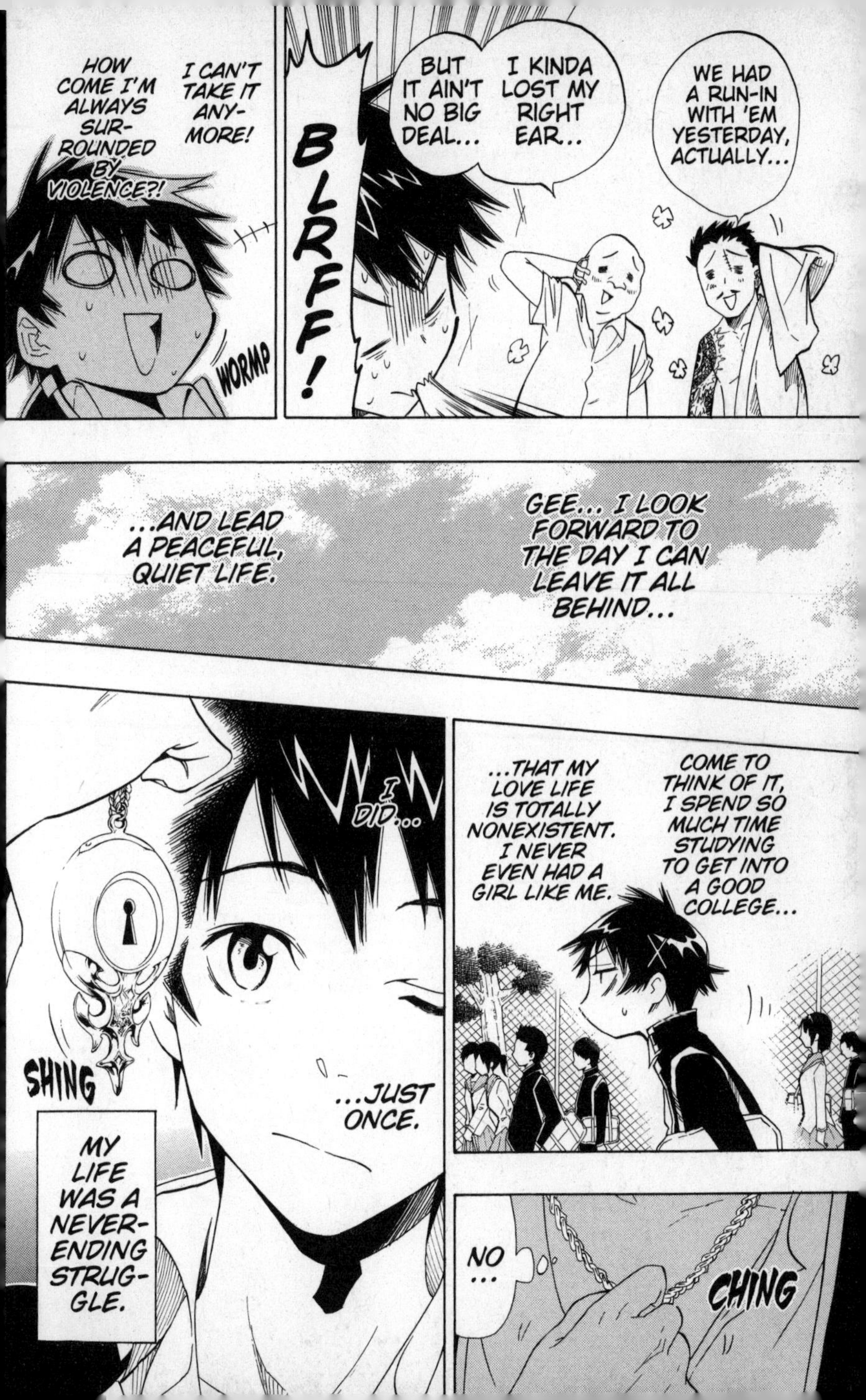
WE HAD A RUN-IN WITH 'EM YESTERDAY, ACTUALLY...
I KINDA LOST MY RIGHT EAR...
BUT IT AIN'T NO BIG DEAL...
BLRFF!
I CAN'T TAKE IT ANYMORE!
HOW COME I'M ALWAYS SURROUNDED BY VIOLENCE?!
WORMP
GEE... I LOOK FORWARD TO THE DAY I CAN LEAVE IT ALL BEHIND...
...AND LEAD A PEACEFUL, QUIET LIFE.
COME TO THINK OF IT, I SPEND SO MUCH TIME STUDYING TO GET INTO A GOOD COLLEGE...
...THAT MY LOVE LIFE IS TOTALLY NONEXISTENT. I NEVER EVEN HAD A GIRL LIKE ME.
NO...
CHING
I DID...
SHING
...JUST ONCE.
MY LIFE WAS A NEVER-ENDING STRUGGLE.

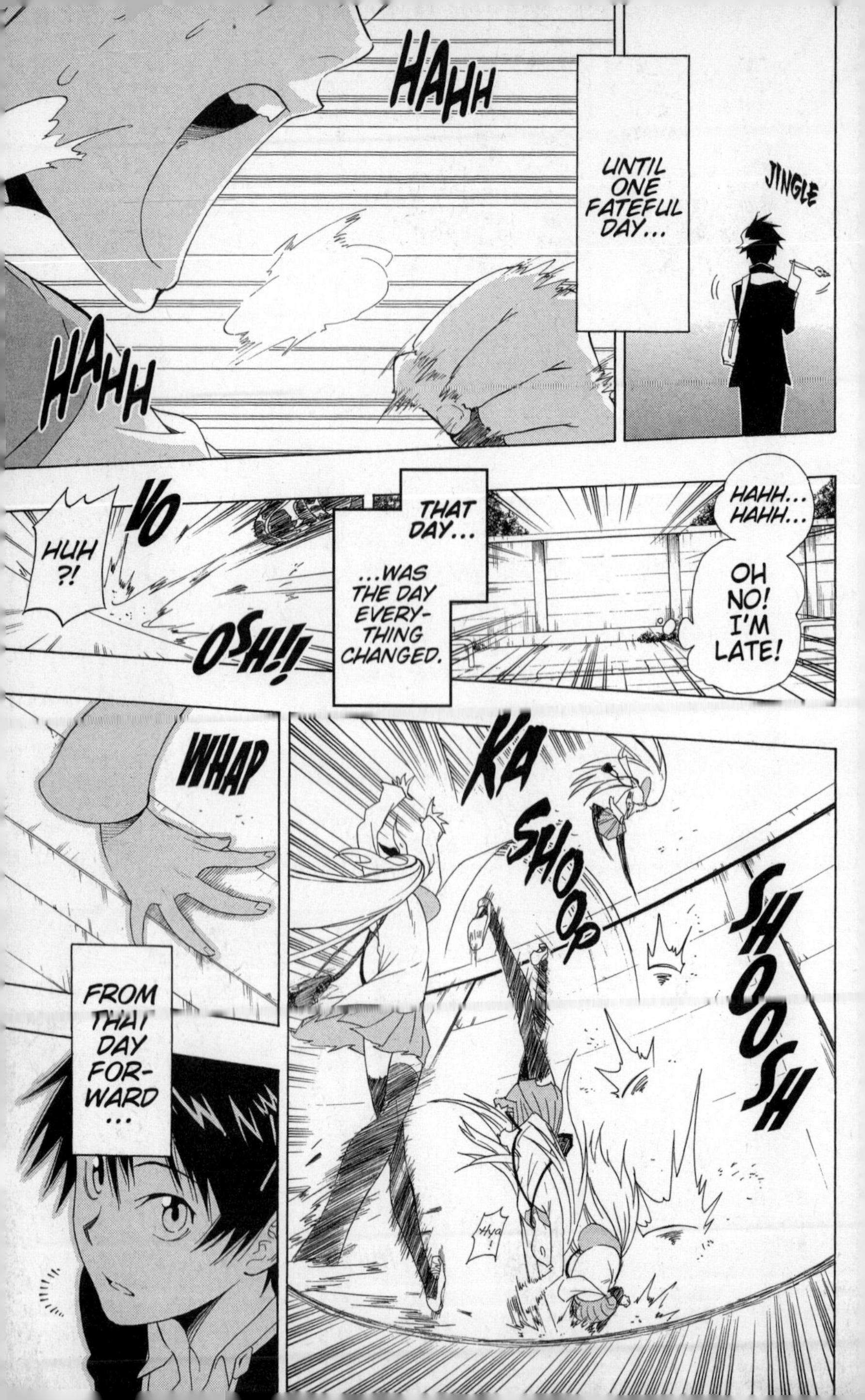
UNTIL ONE FATEFUL DAY...
JINGLE
HAHH
HAHH
HAHH... HAHH...
OH NO! I'M LATE!
THAT DAY...
...WAS THE DAY EVERY-THING CHANGED.
VOOSH!!
HUH?!
KA SHOOP
SHOOSH
Hya!
WHAP
FROM THAT DAY FOR-WARD...

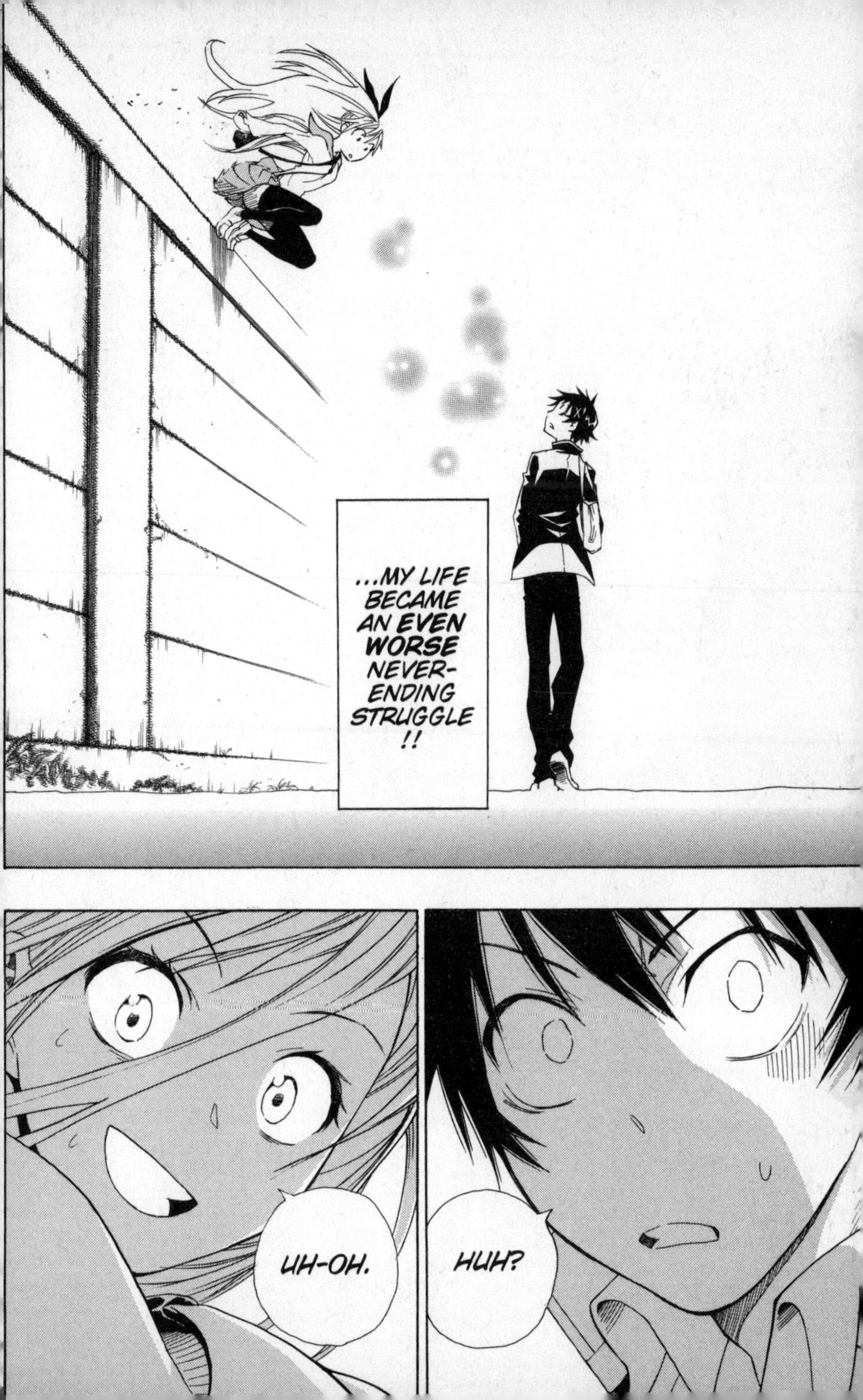
...MY LIFE BECAME AN EVEN WORSE NEVER-ENDING STRUGGLE!!
HUH?
UH-OH.

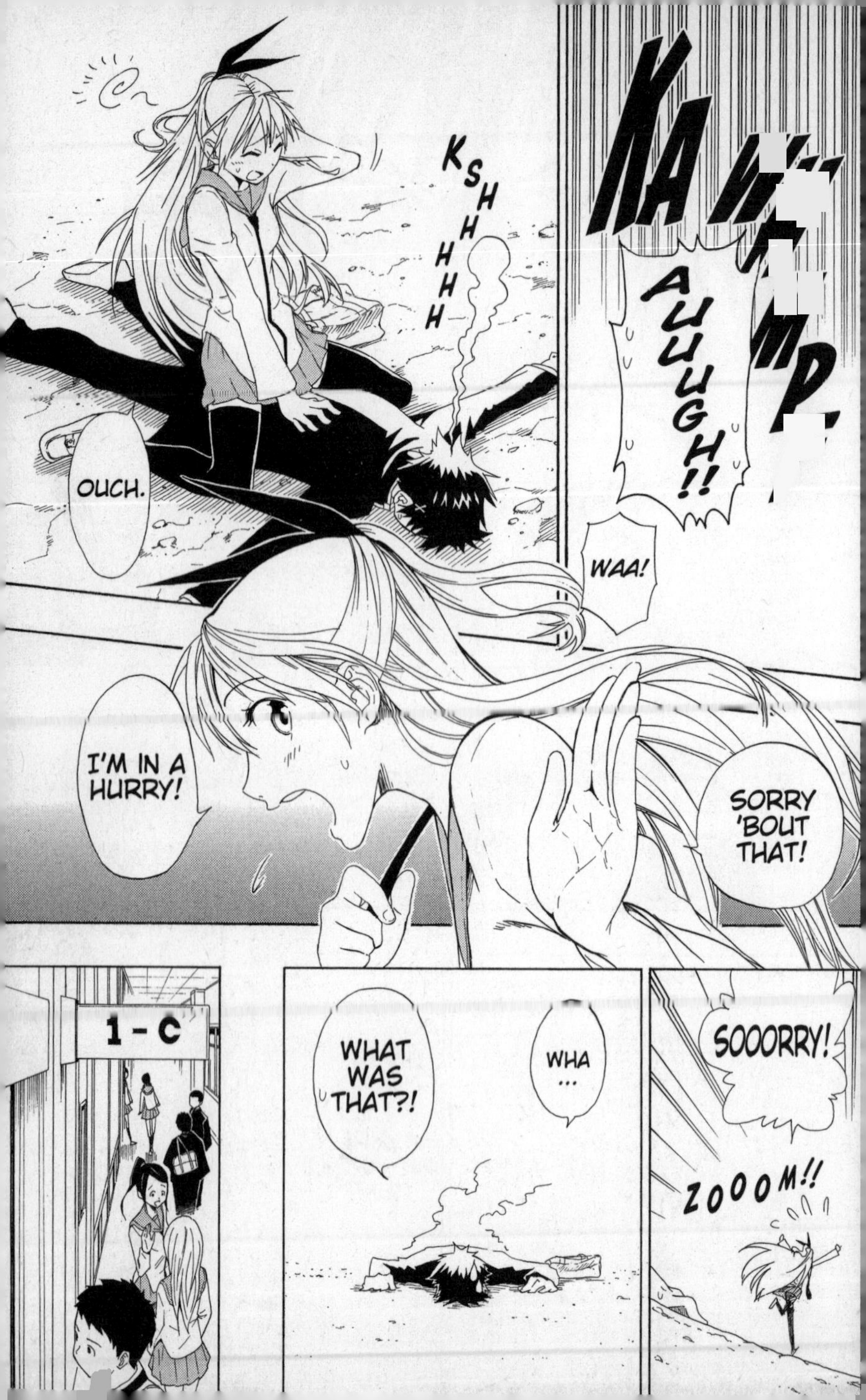
AUUUGH!!
WAA!
KSHHHHHH
OUCH.
SORRY 'BOUT THAT!
I'M IN A HURRY!
SOOORRY!
ZOOOM!!
WHA ...
WHAT WAS THAT?!
1-C

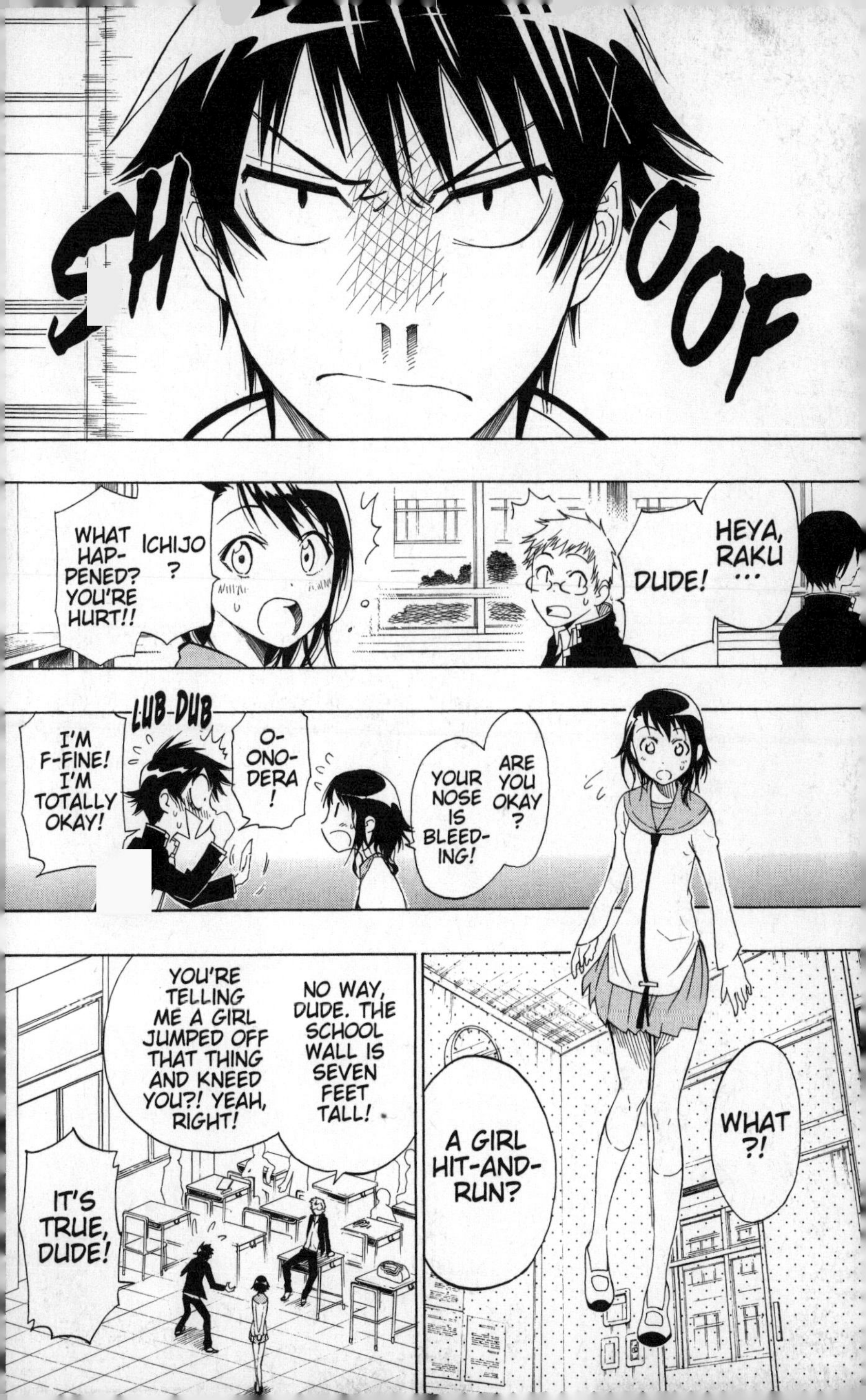
SHOOF
HEYA, RAKU...
DUDE!
ICHIJO?
WHAT HAPPENED? YOU'RE HURT!!
ARE YOU OKAY?
YOUR NOSE IS BLEEDING!
LUB-DUB
O-ONODERA!
I'M F-FINE! I'M TOTALLY OKAY!
WHAT?!
A GIRL HIT-AND-RUN?
NO WAY, DUDE. THE SCHOOL WALL IS SEVEN FEET TALL!
YOU'RE TELLING ME A GIRL JUMPED OFF THAT THING AND KNEED YOU?! YEAH, RIGHT!
IT'S TRUE, DUDE!

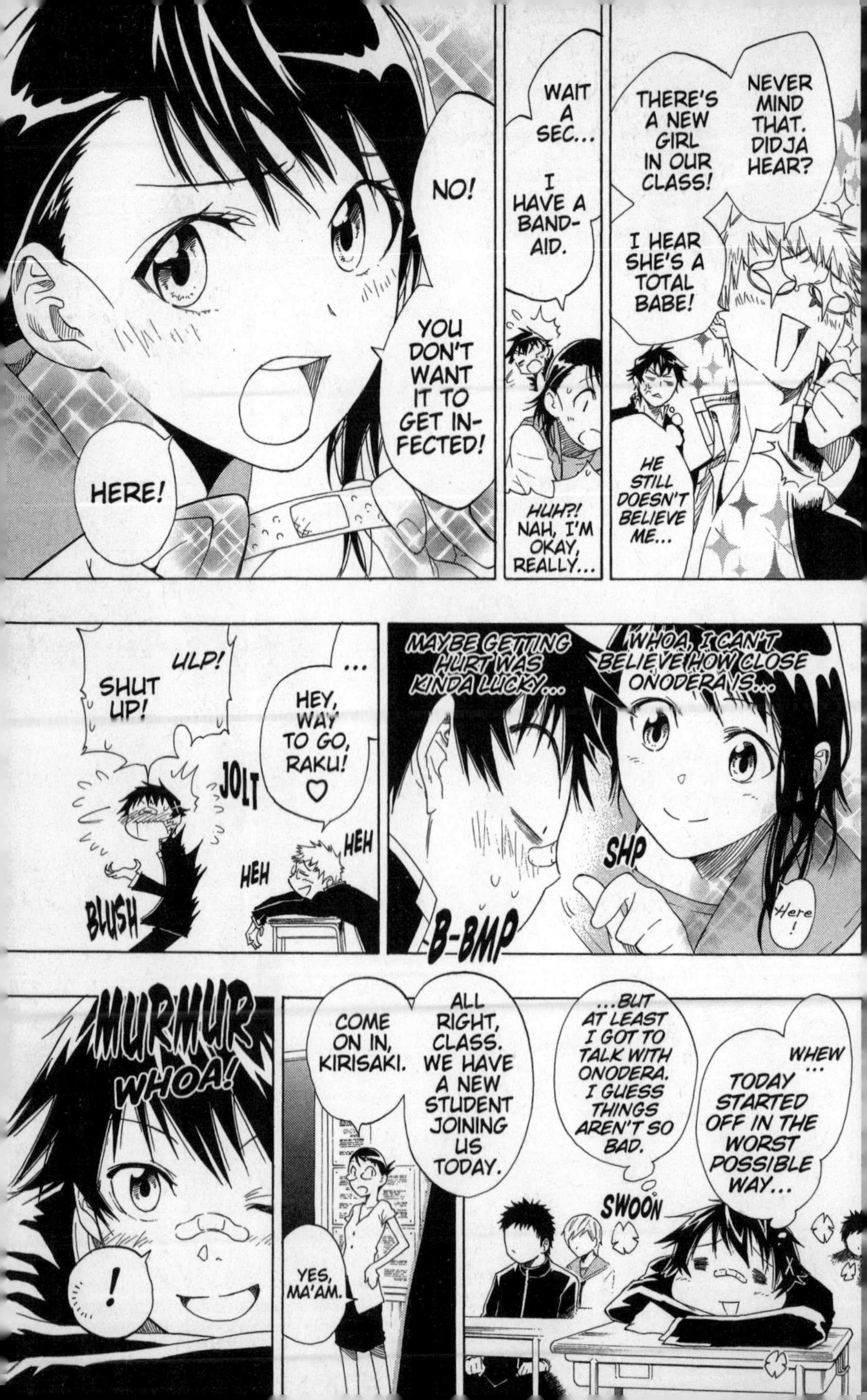
NEVER MIND THAT. DIDJA HEAR?
THERE'S A NEW GIRL IN OUR CLASS!
I HEAR SHE'S A TOTAL BABE!
HE STILL DOESN'T BELIEVE ME...
WAIT A SEC...
I HAVE A BAND-AID.
HUH?! NAH, I'M OKAY, REALLY...
NO!
YOU DON'T WANT IT TO GET INFECTED!
HERE!
WHOA, I CAN'T BELIEVE HOW CLOSE ONODERA IS...
MAYBE GETTING HURT WAS KINDA LUCKY...
SHP
Here!
B-BMP
...
HEY, WAY TO GO, RAKU! ♡
HEH
HEH
ULP!
SHUT UP!
JOLT
BLUSH
WHEW... TODAY STARTED OFF IN THE WORST POSSIBLE WAY...
...BUT AT LEAST I GOT TO TALK WITH ONODERA. I GUESS THINGS AREN'T SO BAD.
SWOON
ALL RIGHT, CLASS. WE HAVE A NEW STUDENT JOINING US TODAY.
COME ON IN, KIRISAKI.
YES, MA'AM.
MURMUR
WHOA!
!

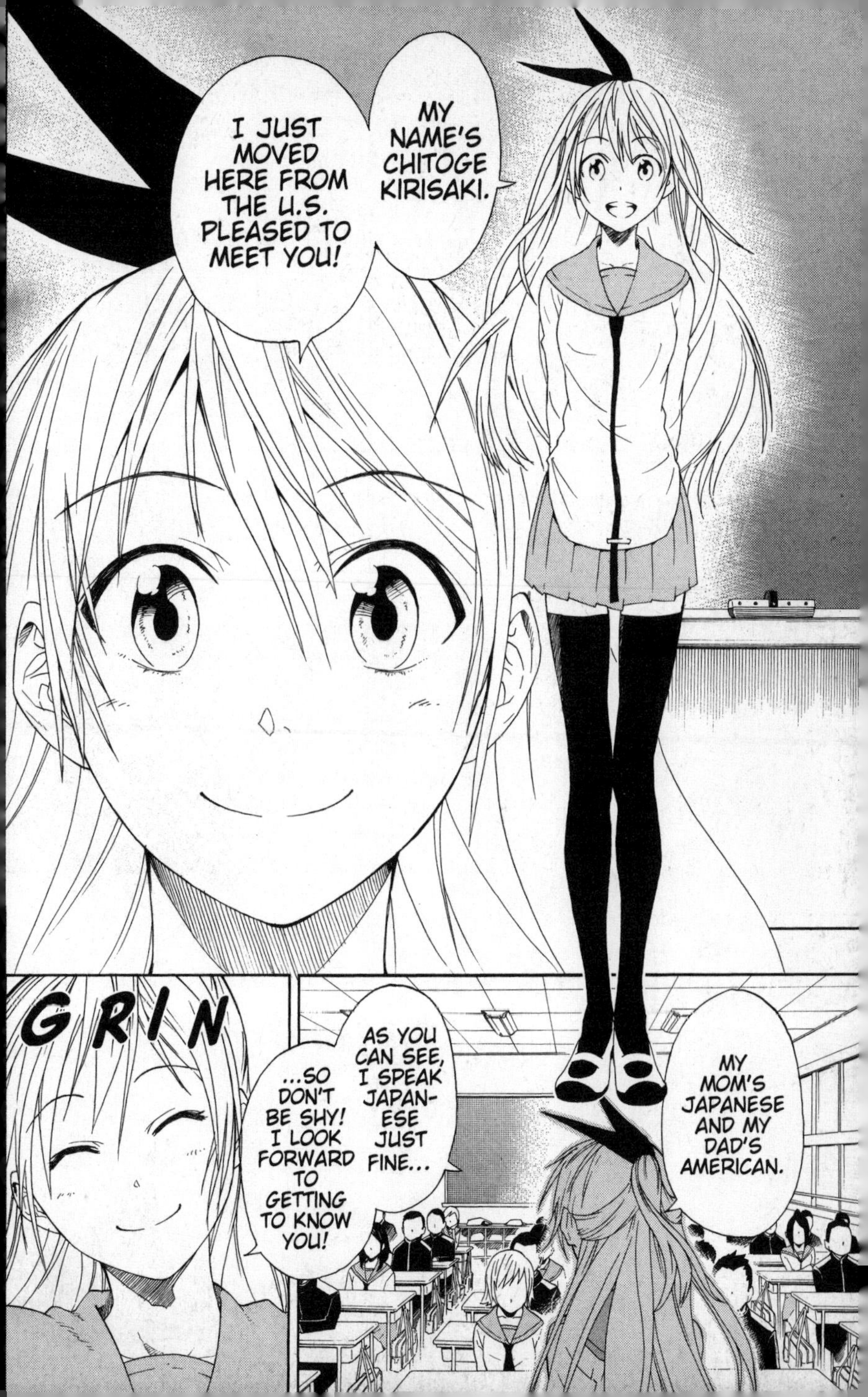
MY NAME'S CHITOGE KIRISAKI.
I JUST MOVED HERE FROM THE U.S. PLEASED TO MEET YOU!
MY MOM'S JAPANESE AND MY DAD'S AMERICAN.
AS YOU CAN SEE, I SPEAK JAPAN-ESE JUST FINE...
...SO DON'T BE SHY! I LOOK FORWARD TO GETTING TO KNOW YOU!
GRIN

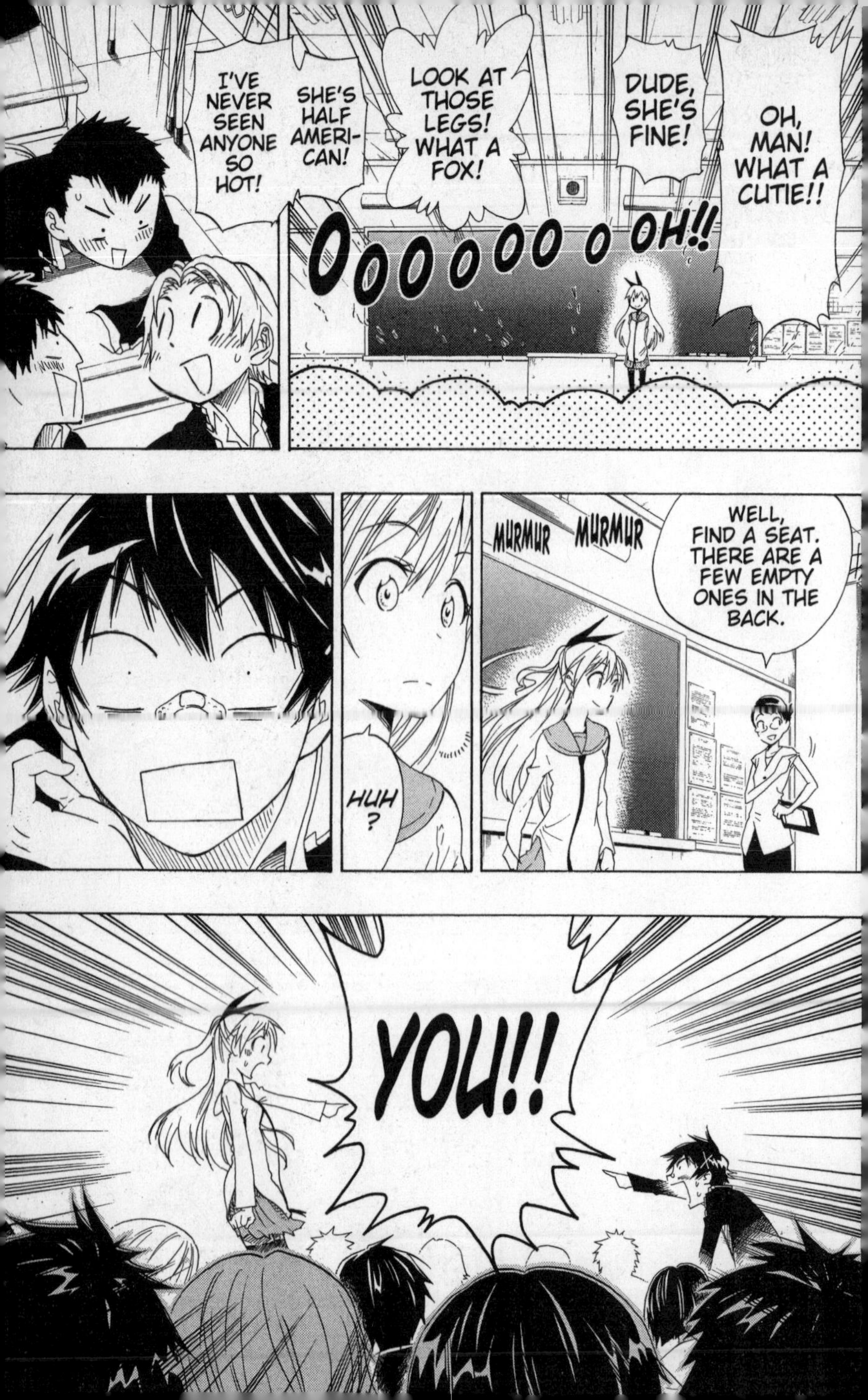
OH, MAN! WHAT A CUTIE!!
DUDE, SHE'S FINE!
LOOK AT THOSE LEGS! WHAT A FOX!
OOOOOOO O OH!!
SHE'S HALF AMERI-CAN!
I'VE NEVER SEEN ANYONE SO HOT!
WELL, FIND A SEAT. THERE ARE A FEW EMPTY ONES IN THE BACK.
MURMUR
MURMUR
HUH?
YOU!!

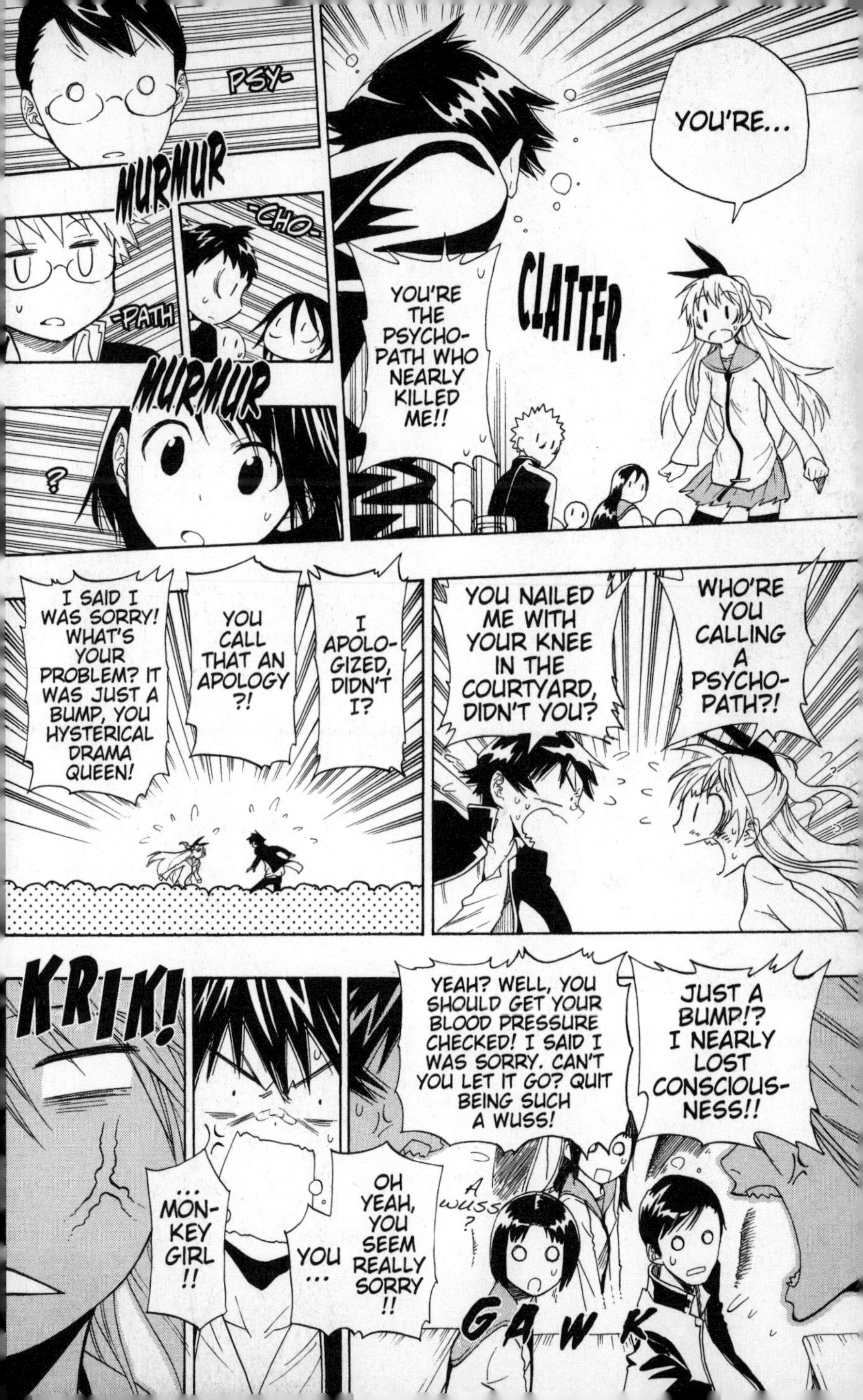
YOU'RE...
CLATTER
YOU'RE THE PSYCHO-PATH WHO NEARLY KILLED ME!!
PSY-
MURMUR
-CHO-
-PATH
MURMUR
?
WHO'RE YOU CALLING A PSYCHO-PATH?!
YOU NAILED ME WITH YOUR KNEE IN THE COURTYARD, DIDN'T YOU?
I APOLO-GIZED, DIDN'T I?
YOU CALL THAT AN APOLOGY?!
I SAID I WAS SORRY! WHAT'S YOUR PROBLEM? IT WAS JUST A BUMP, YOU HYSTERICAL DRAMA QUEEN!
JUST A BUMP!? I NEARLY LOST CONSCIOUS-NESS!!
YEAH? WELL, YOU SHOULD GET YOUR BLOOD PRESSURE CHECKED! I SAID I WAS SORRY. CAN'T YOU LET IT GO? QUIT BEING SUCH A WUSS!
A WUSS?
GAWK
OH YEAH, YOU SEEM REALLY SORRY!!
YOU...
...MON-KEY GIRL!!
KRIK!

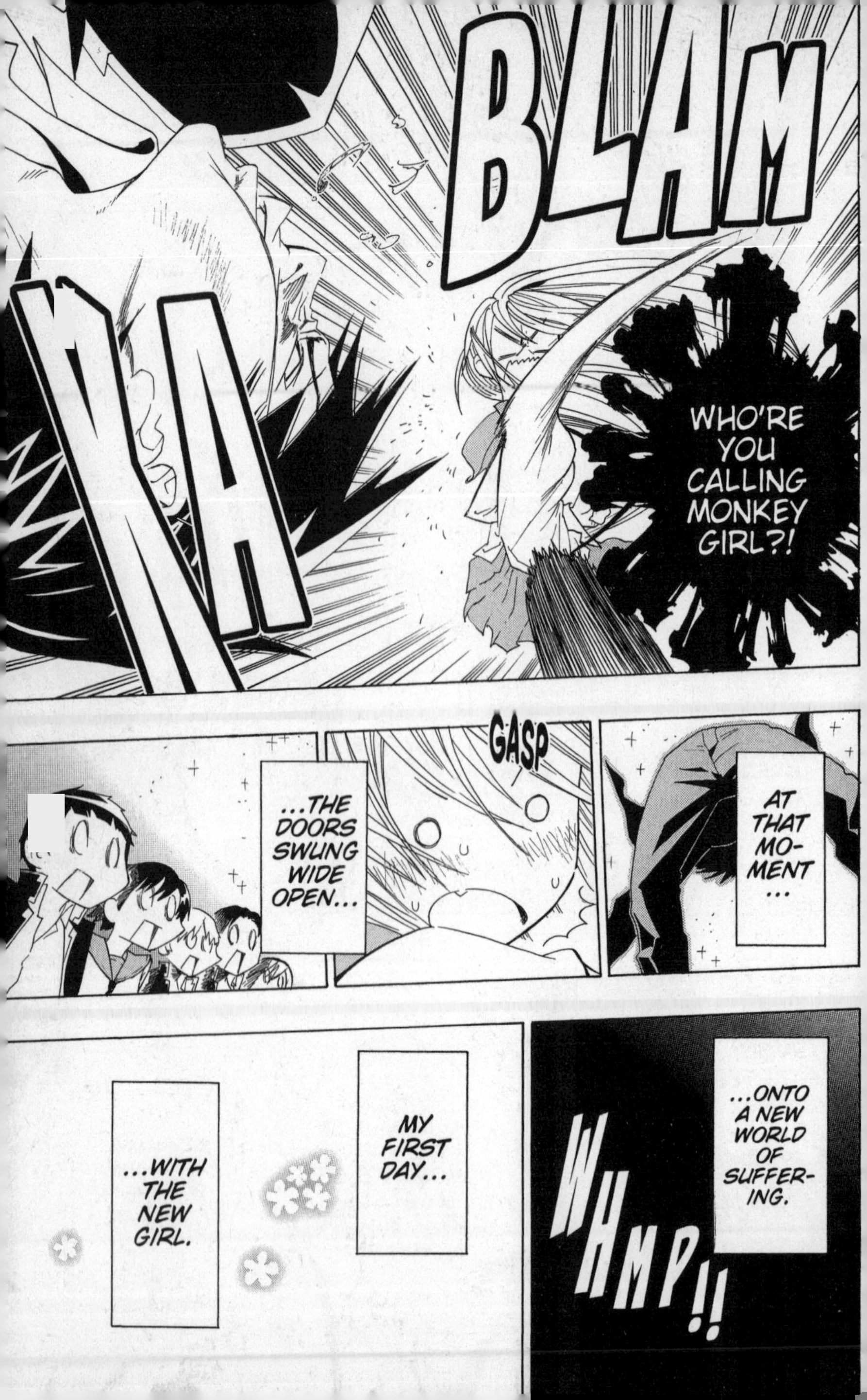
BLAM
WHO'RE YOU CALLING MONKEY GIRL?!
AT THAT MO-MENT...
GASP
...THE DOORS SWUNG WIDE OPEN...
...ONTO A NEW WORLD OF SUFFER-ING.
WHMP!!
MY FIRST DAY...
...WITH THE NEW GIRL.

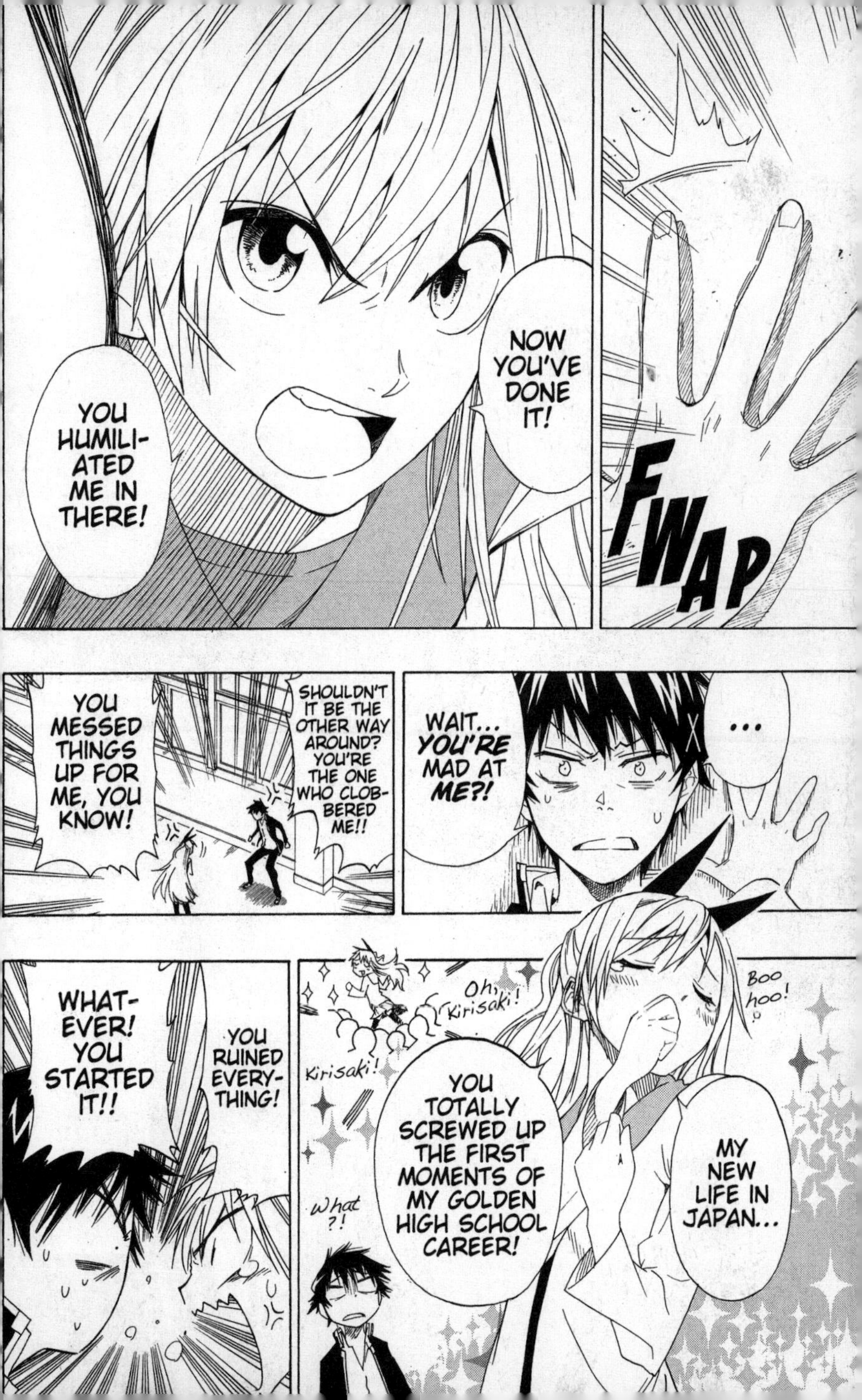
FWAP
NOW YOU'VE DONE IT!
YOU HUMILIATED ME IN THERE!
...
WAIT... *YOU'RE* MAD AT *ME?!*
SHOULDN'T IT BE THE OTHER WAY AROUND? YOU'RE THE ONE WHO CLOBBERED ME!!
YOU MESSED THINGS UP FOR ME, YOU KNOW!
Boo hoo!
MY NEW LIFE IN JAPAN...
YOU TOTALLY SCREWED UP THE FIRST MOMENTS OF MY GOLDEN HIGH SCHOOL CAREER!
Oh, Kirisaki!
Kirisaki!
What?!
YOU RUINED EVERYTHING!
WHATEVER! YOU STARTED IT!!

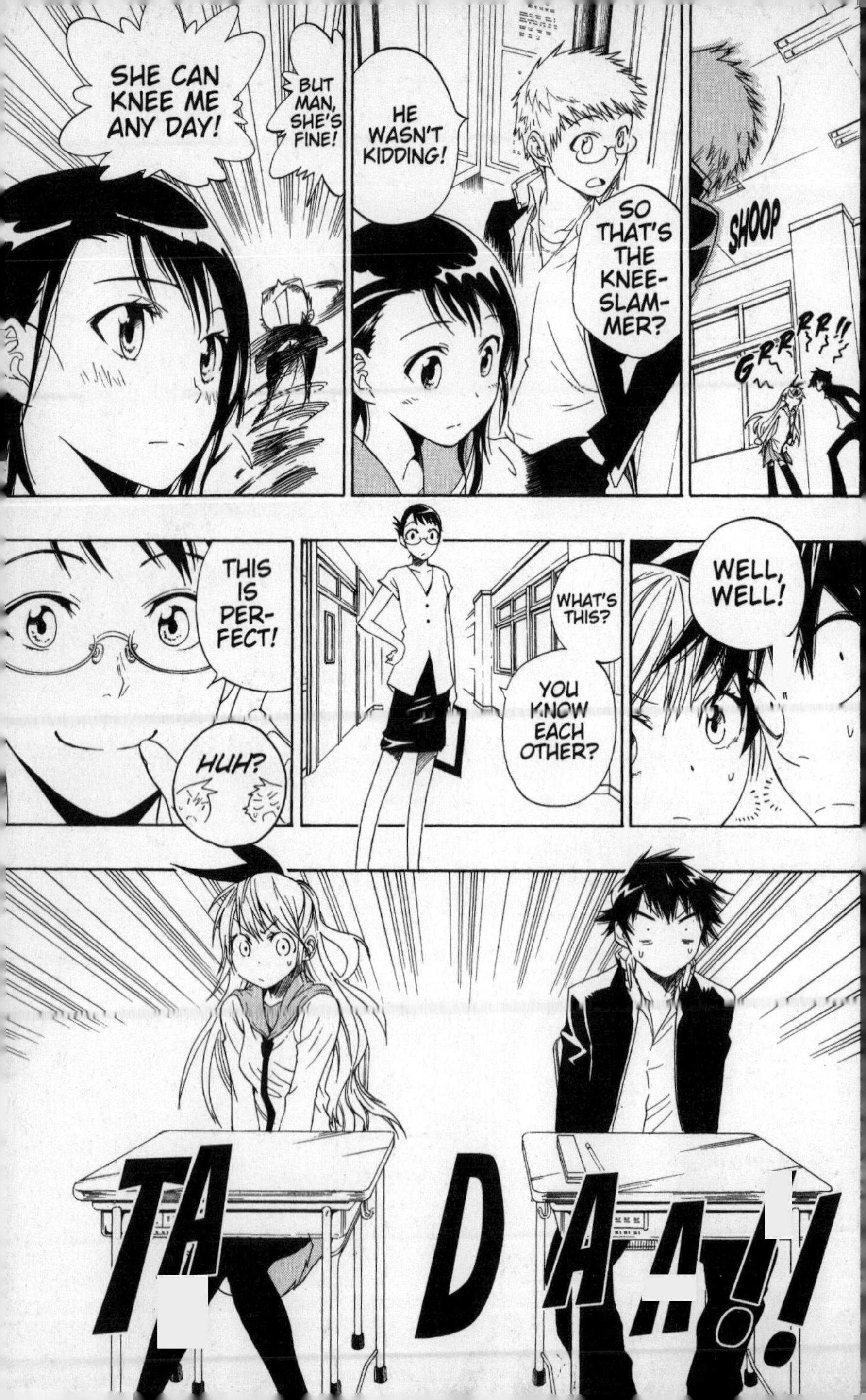
SHOOP
GRRRR!!
SO THAT'S THE KNEE-SLAMMER?
HE WASN'T KIDDING!
BUT MAN, SHE'S FINE!
SHE CAN KNEE ME ANY DAY!
WELL, WELL!
WHAT'S THIS?
YOU KNOW EACH OTHER?
THIS IS PERFECT!
HUH?
TADAA!!

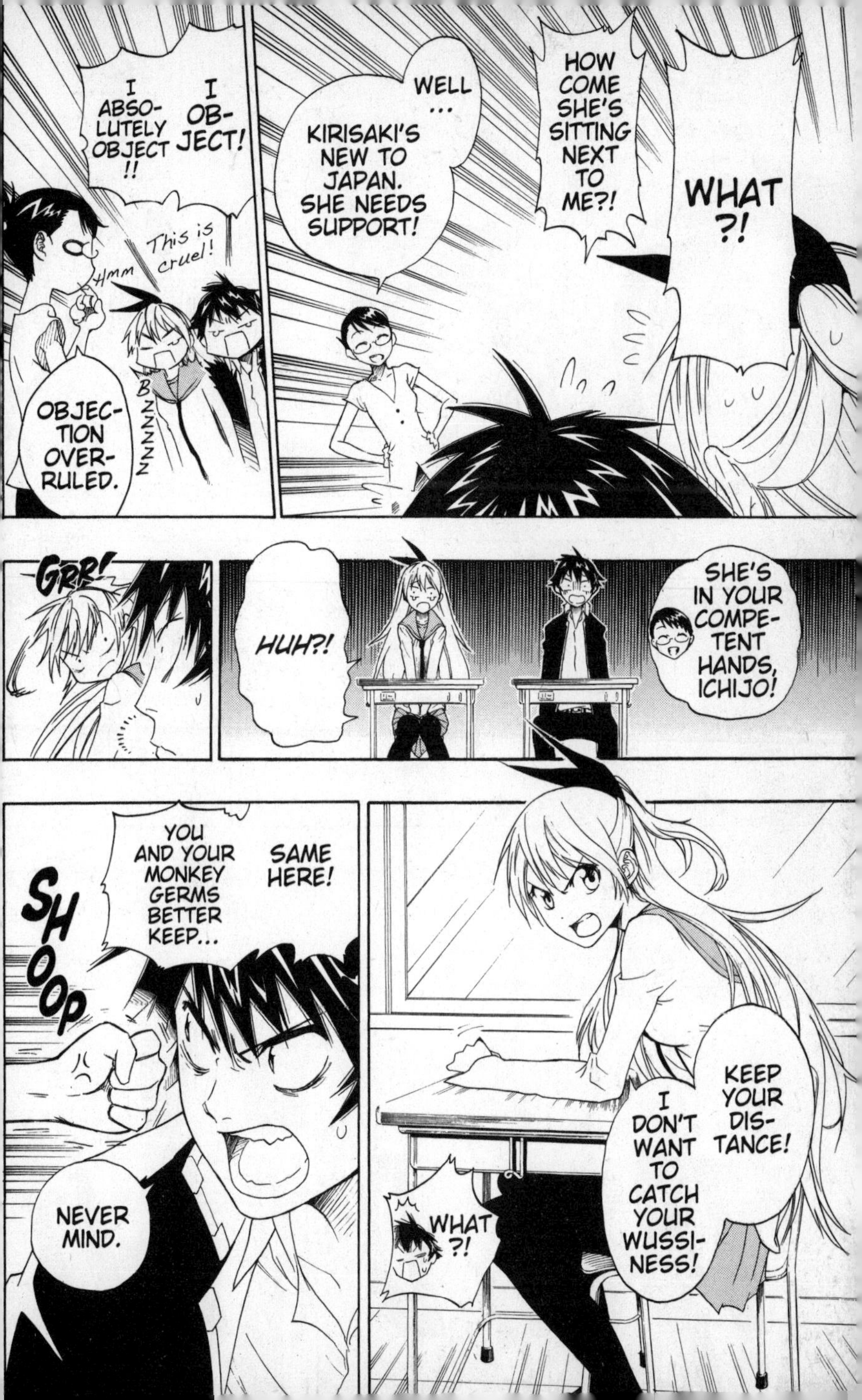
WHAT ?!
HOW COME SHE'S SITTING NEXT TO ME?!
WELL ...
KIRISAKI'S NEW TO JAPAN. SHE NEEDS SUPPORT!
I OBJECT!
I ABSOLUTELY OBJECT !!
This is cruel!
Hmm
BZZZZZ
OBJECTION OVERRULED.
SHE'S IN YOUR COMPETENT HANDS, ICHIJO!
HUH?!
GRR!
KEEP YOUR DISTANCE!
I DON'T WANT TO CATCH YOUR WUSSINESS!
WHAT ?!
SAME HERE!
YOU AND YOUR MONKEY GERMS BETTER KEEP...
SHOOOP
NEVER MIND.

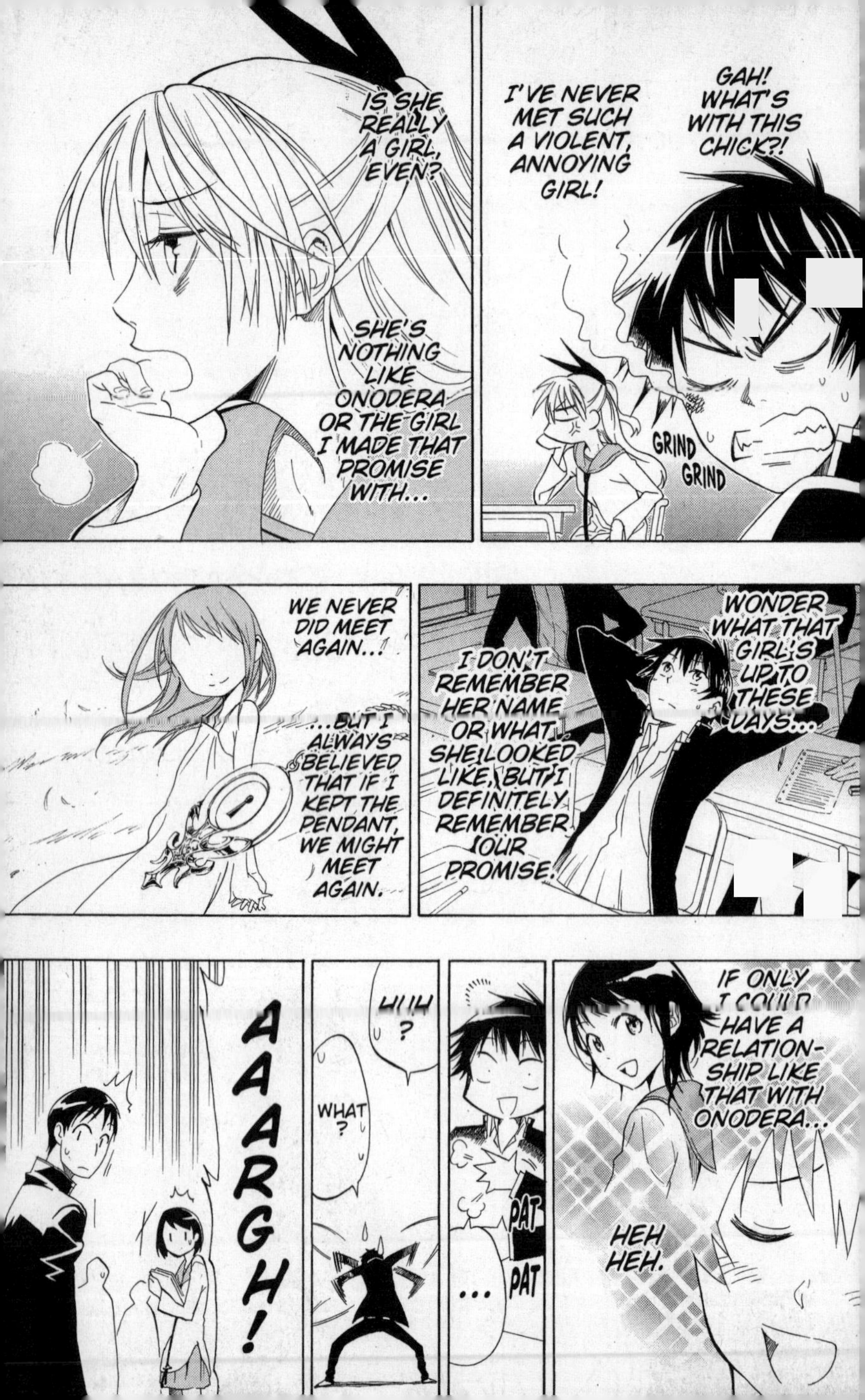
GAH! WHAT'S WITH THIS CHICK?!
I'VE NEVER MET SUCH A VIOLENT, ANNOYING GIRL!
GRIND GRIND
IS SHE REALLY A GIRL, EVEN?
SHE'S NOTHING LIKE ONODERA OR THE GIRL I MADE THAT PROMISE WITH...
WONDER WHAT THAT GIRL'S UP TO THESE DAYS...
I DON'T REMEMBER HER NAME OR WHAT SHE LOOKED LIKE, BUT I DEFINITELY REMEMBER OUR PROMISE.
WE NEVER DID MEET AGAIN...
...BUT I ALWAYS BELIEVED THAT IF I KEPT THE PENDANT, WE MIGHT MEET AGAIN.
IF ONLY I COULD HAVE A RELATION-SHIP LIKE THAT WITH ONODERA...
HEH HEH.
PAT
PAT
...
HUH?
WHAT?
AAARGH!

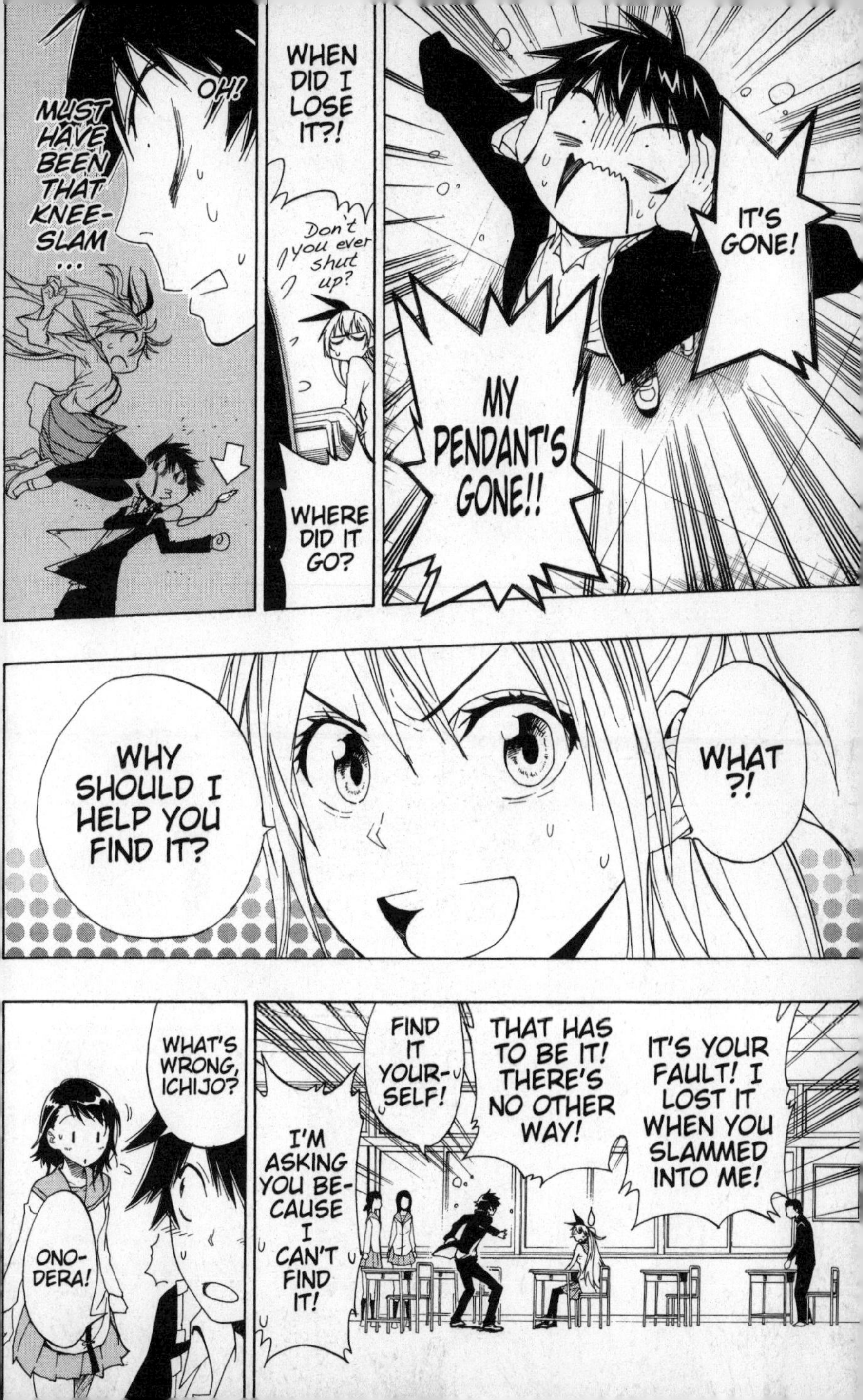

IT'S GONE!
MY PENDANT'S GONE!!
WHEN DID I LOSE IT?!
Don't you ever shut up?
WHERE DID IT GO?
OH!
MUST HAVE BEEN THAT KNEE-SLAM...
WHAT?!
WHY SHOULD I HELP YOU FIND IT?
IT'S YOUR FAULT! I LOST IT WHEN YOU SLAMMED INTO ME!
THAT HAS TO BE IT! THERE'S NO OTHER WAY!
FIND IT YOURSELF!
I'M ASKING YOU BECAUSE I CAN'T FIND IT!
WHAT'S WRONG, ICHIJO?
ONODERA!

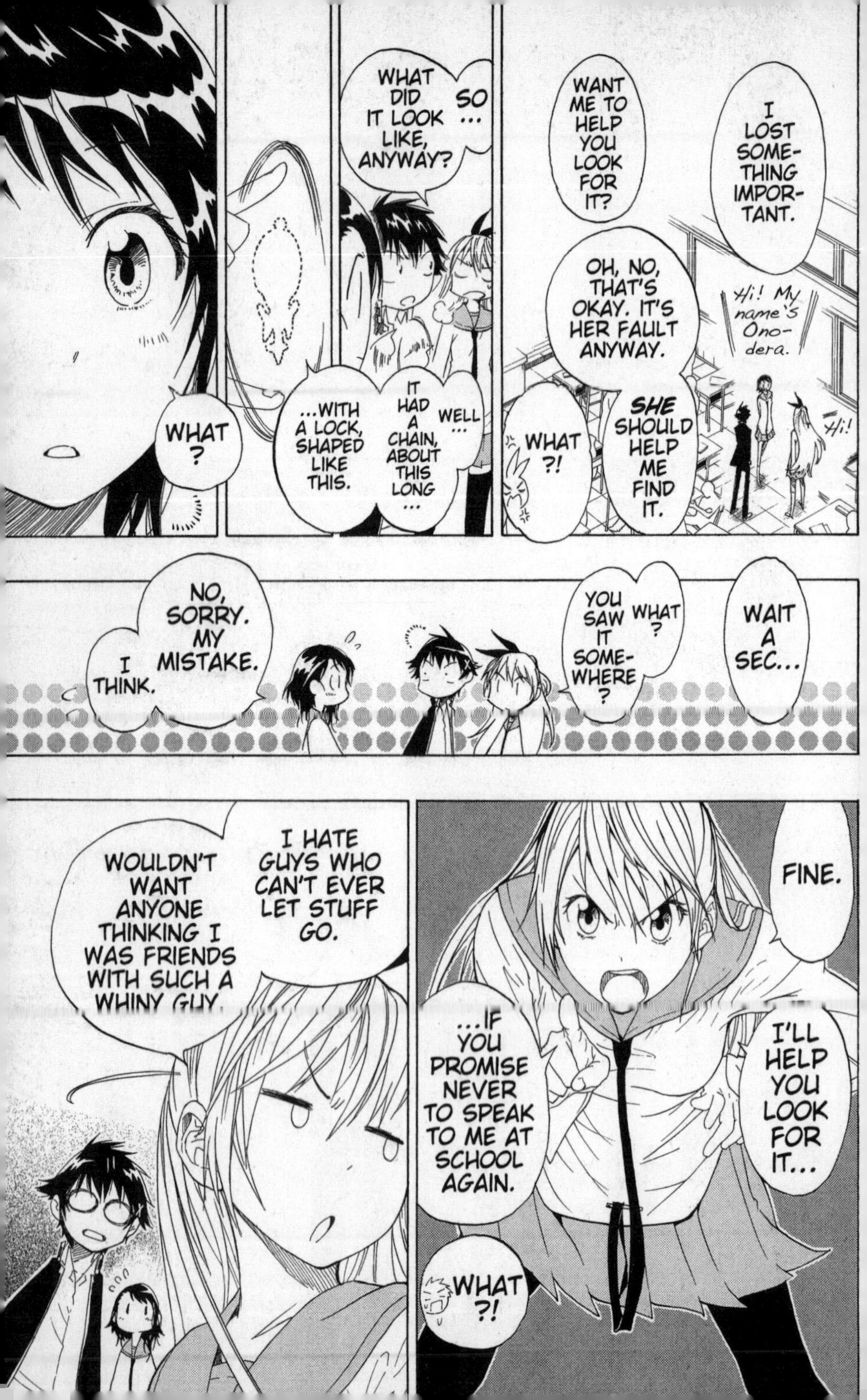
I LOST SOMETHING IMPORTANT.
WANT ME TO HELP YOU LOOK FOR IT?
Hi! My name's Onodera.
Hi!
OH, NO, THAT'S OKAY. IT'S HER FAULT ANYWAY.
SHE SHOULD HELP ME FIND IT.
WHAT?!
SO...
WHAT DID IT LOOK LIKE, ANYWAY?
WELL...
IT HAD A CHAIN, ABOUT THIS LONG...
...WITH A LOCK, SHAPED LIKE THIS.
WHAT?
WAIT A SEC...
WHAT?
YOU SAW IT SOMEWHERE?
NO, SORRY. MY MISTAKE.
I THINK.
FINE.
I'LL HELP YOU LOOK FOR IT...
...IF YOU PROMISE NEVER TO SPEAK TO ME AT SCHOOL AGAIN.
WHAT?!
I HATE GUYS WHO CAN'T EVER LET STUFF GO.
WOULDN'T WANT ANYONE THINKING I WAS FRIENDS WITH SUCH A WHINY GUY.

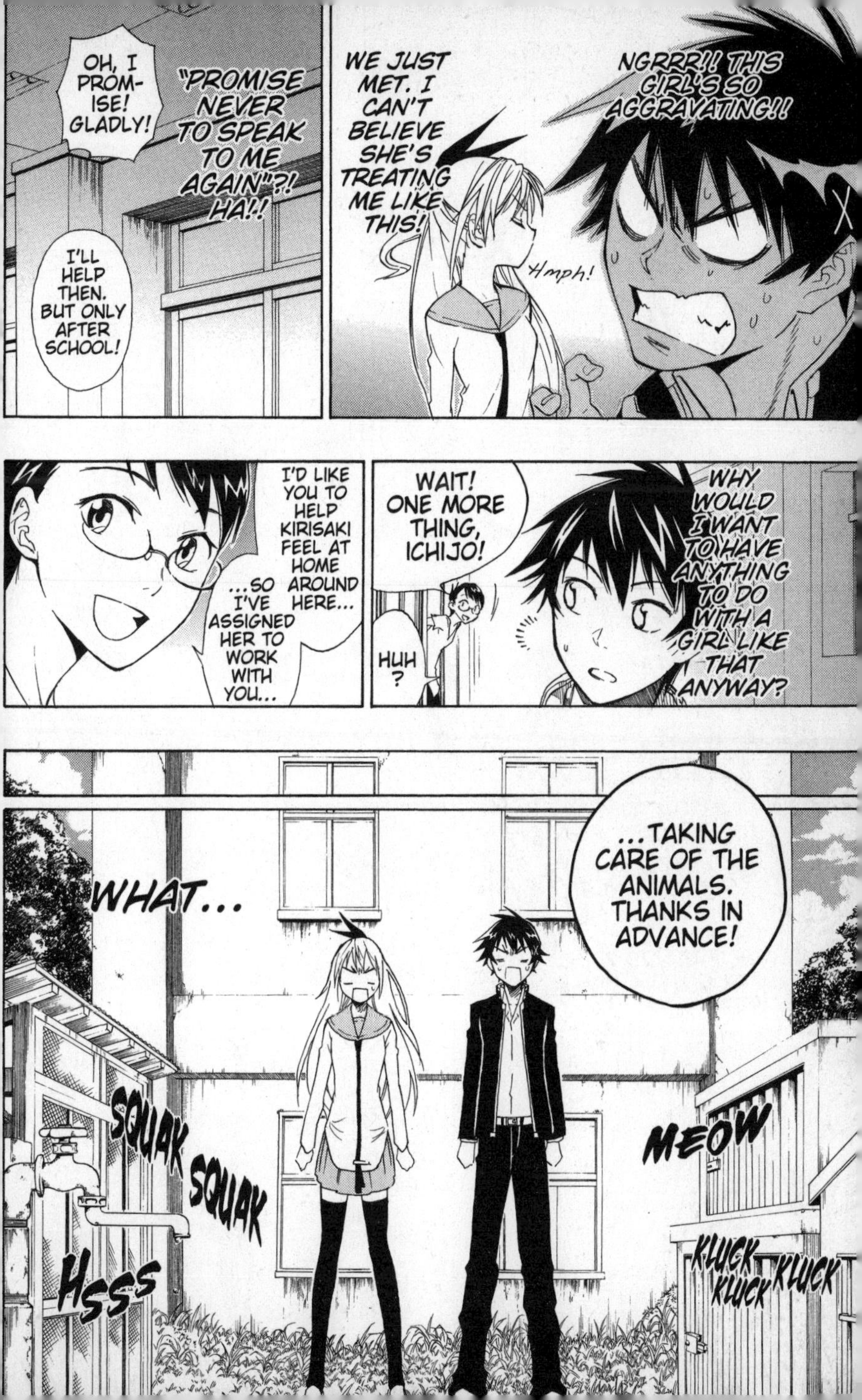
NGRRR!! THIS GIRL'S SO AGGRAVATING!!
Hmph!
WE JUST MET. I CAN'T BELIEVE SHE'S TREATING ME LIKE THIS!
"PROMISE NEVER TO SPEAK TO ME AGAIN"?! HA!!
OH, I PROMISE! GLADLY!
I'LL HELP THEN. BUT ONLY AFTER SCHOOL!
WHY WOULD I WANT TO HAVE ANYTHING TO DO WITH A GIRL LIKE THAT ANYWAY?
WAIT! ONE MORE THING, ICHIJO!
HUH?
I'D LIKE YOU TO HELP KIRISAKI FEEL AT HOME AROUND HERE...
...SO I'VE ASSIGNED HER TO WORK WITH YOU...
...TAKING CARE OF THE ANIMALS. THANKS IN ADVANCE!
WHAT...
MEOW
KLUCK KLUCK KLUCK
SQUAK SQUAK
HSSS

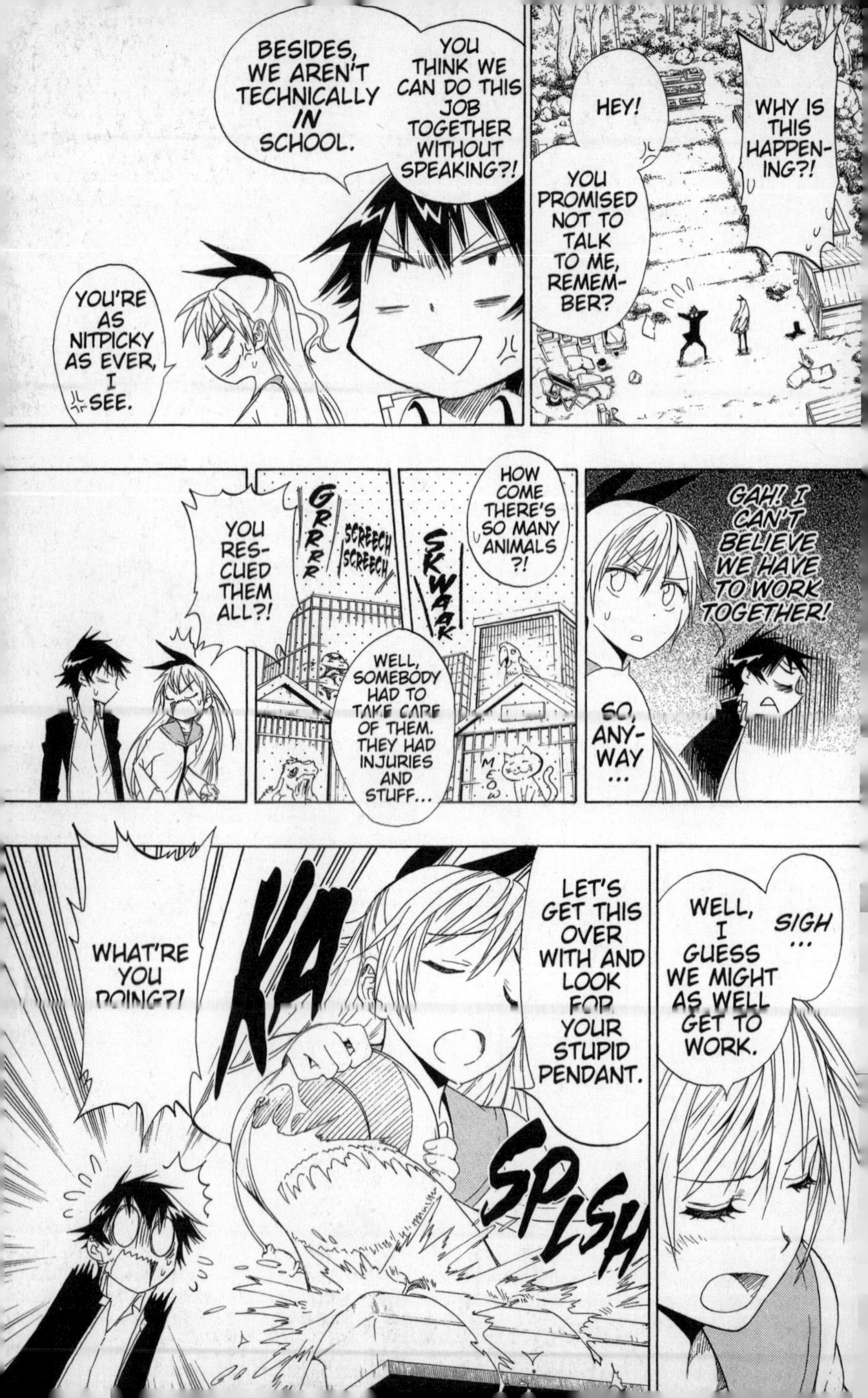
WHY IS THIS HAPPENING?!
HEY!
YOU PROMISED NOT TO TALK TO ME, REMEMBER?
YOU THINK WE CAN DO THIS JOB TOGETHER WITHOUT SPEAKING?!
BESIDES, WE AREN'T TECHNICALLY *IN* SCHOOL.
YOU'RE AS NITPICKY AS EVER, I SEE.
GAH! I CAN'T BELIEVE WE HAVE TO WORK TOGETHER!
SO, ANYWAY...
HOW COME THERE'S SO MANY ANIMALS?!
SKWAAK
MEOW
WELL, SOMEBODY HAD TO TAKE CARE OF THEM. THEY HAD INJURIES AND STUFF...
GRRRR
SCREECH SCREECH
YOU RESCUED THEM ALL?!
WELL, I GUESS WE MIGHT AS WELL GET TO WORK.
SIGH...
LET'S GET THIS OVER WITH AND LOOK FOR YOUR STUPID PENDANT.
SPLISH
KA
WHAT'RE YOU DOING?!

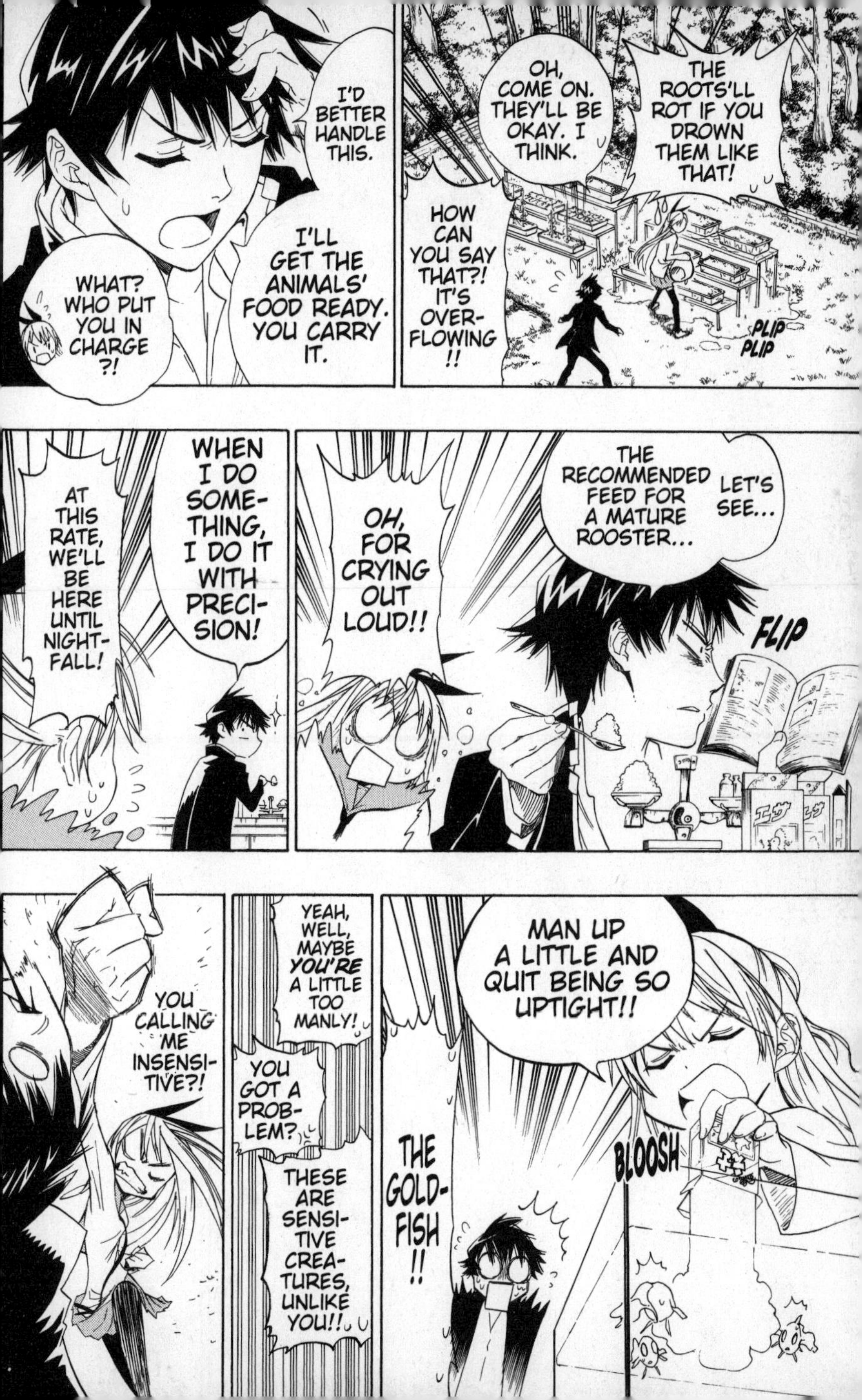
THE ROOTS'LL ROT IF YOU DROWN THEM LIKE THAT!
OH, COME ON. THEY'LL BE OKAY. I THINK.
HOW CAN YOU SAY THAT?! IT'S OVERFLOWING!!
PLIP PLIP
I'D BETTER HANDLE THIS.
I'LL GET THE ANIMALS' FOOD READY. YOU CARRY IT.
WHAT? WHO PUT YOU IN CHARGE?!
LET'S SEE...
THE RECOMMENDED FEED FOR A MATURE ROOSTER...
FLIP
OH, FOR CRYING OUT LOUD!!
WHEN I DO SOMETHING, I DO IT WITH PRECISION!
AT THIS RATE, WE'LL BE HERE UNTIL NIGHTFALL!
MAN UP A LITTLE AND QUIT BEING SO UPTIGHT!!
BLOOSH
THE GOLDFISH!!
YEAH, WELL, MAYBE *YOU'RE* A LITTLE TOO MANLY!
YOU GOT A PROBLEM?
THESE ARE SENSITIVE CREATURES, UNLIKE YOU!!
YOU CALLING ME INSENSITIVE?!

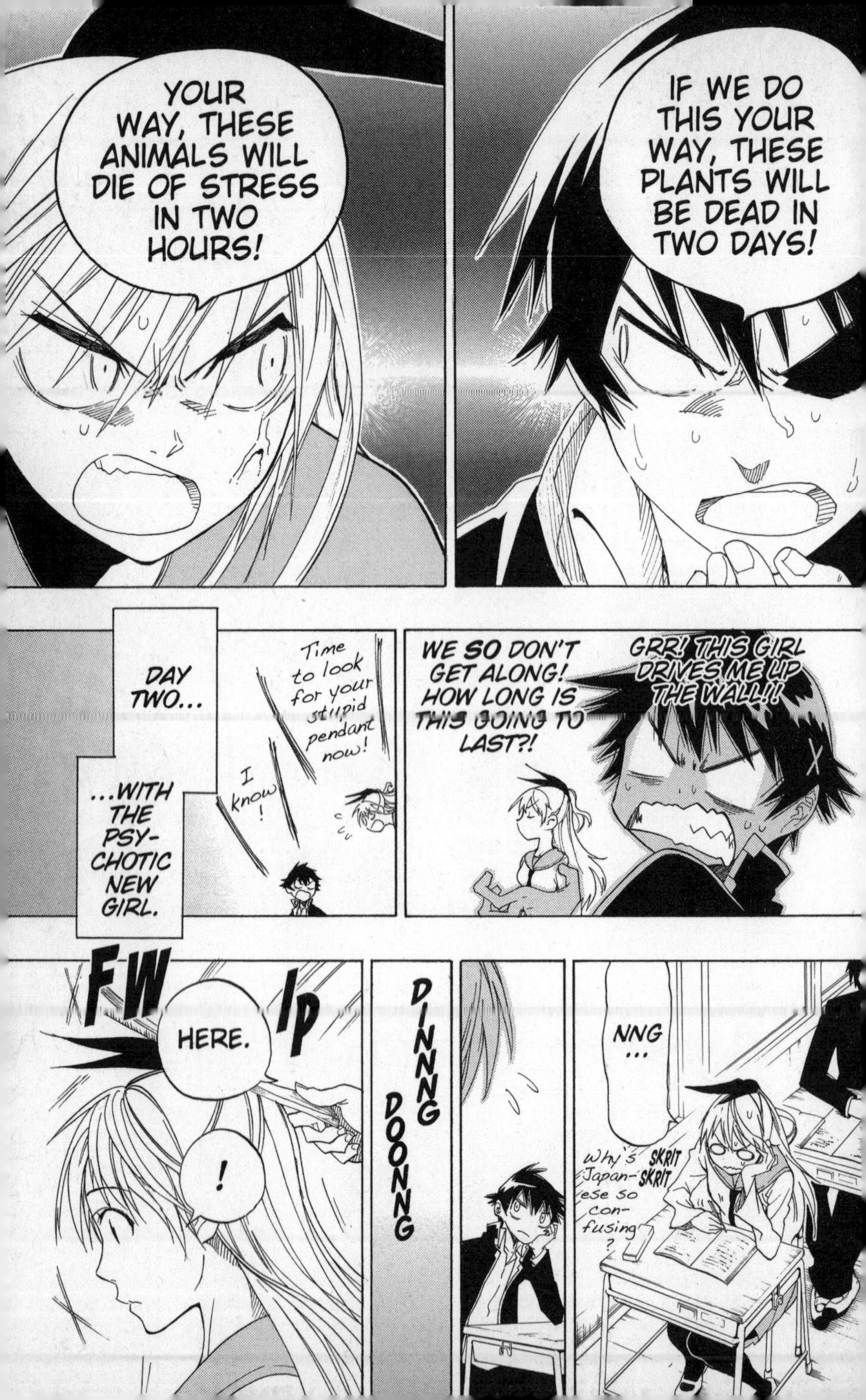
IF WE DO THIS YOUR WAY, THESE PLANTS WILL BE DEAD IN TWO DAYS!
YOUR WAY, THESE ANIMALS WILL DIE OF STRESS IN TWO HOURS!
GRR! THIS GIRL DRIVES ME UP THE WALL!!
WE SO DON'T GET ALONG! HOW LONG IS THIS GOING TO LAST?!
Time to look for your stupid pendant now!
I know!
DAY TWO...
...WITH THE PSY-CHOTIC NEW GIRL.
NNG...
SKRIT SKRIT
Why's Japan-ese so con-fusing?
DINNNG DOOONNG
FWIP
HERE.
!

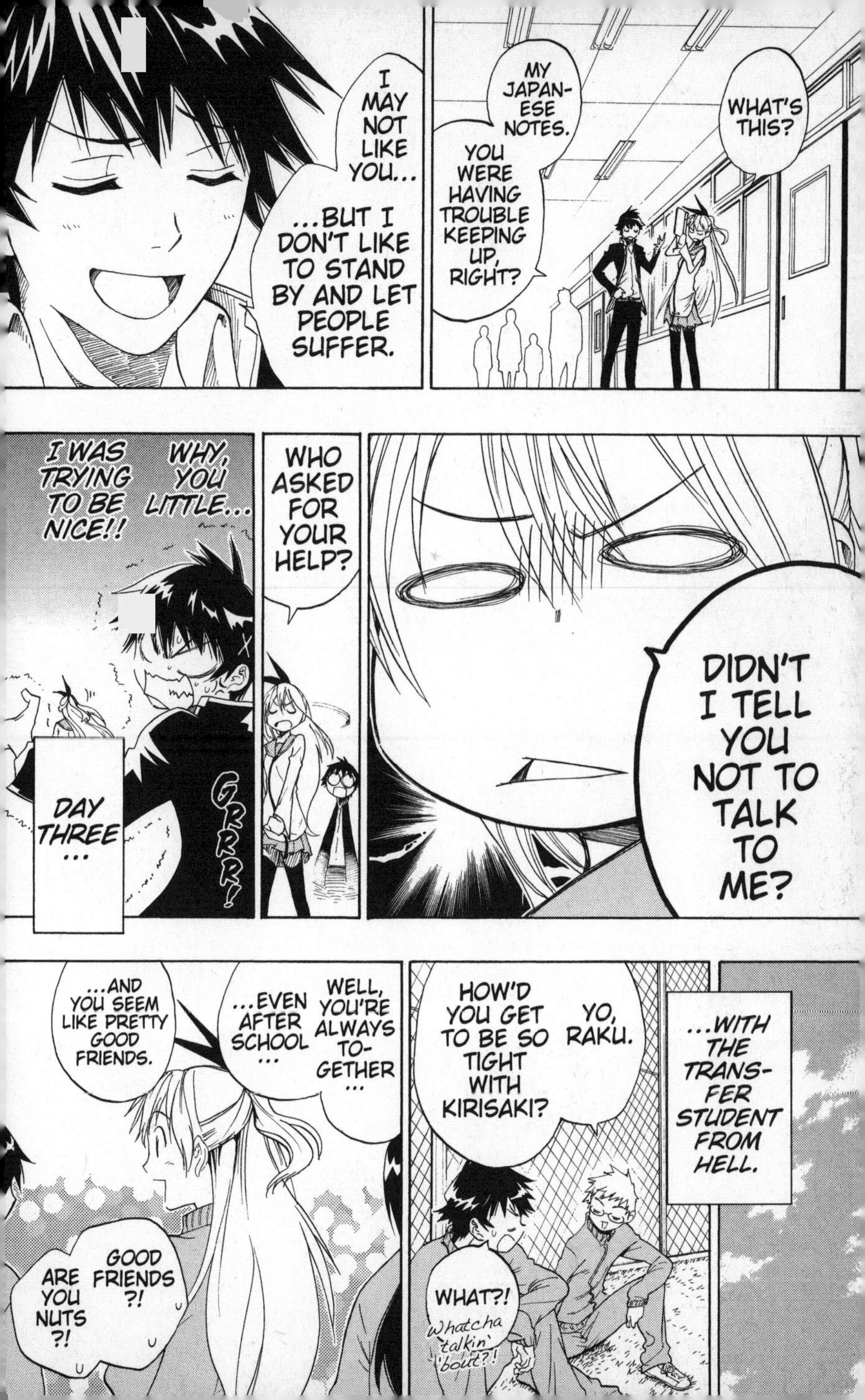
WHAT'S THIS?
MY JAPANESE NOTES.
YOU WERE HAVING TROUBLE KEEPING UP, RIGHT?
I MAY NOT LIKE YOU...
...BUT I DON'T LIKE TO STAND BY AND LET PEOPLE SUFFER.
DIDN'T I TELL YOU NOT TO TALK TO ME?
WHO ASKED FOR YOUR HELP?
WHY, YOU LITTLE...
I WAS TRYING TO BE NICE!!
GRRR!
DAY THREE...
...WITH THE TRANSFER STUDENT FROM HELL.
YO, RAKU.
HOW'D YOU GET TO BE SO TIGHT WITH KIRISAKI?
WHAT?!
Whatcha talkin' 'bout?!
WELL, YOU'RE ALWAYS TOGETHER...
...EVEN AFTER SCHOOL...
...AND YOU SEEM LIKE PRETTY GOOD FRIENDS.
GOOD FRIENDS?!
ARE YOU NUTS?!

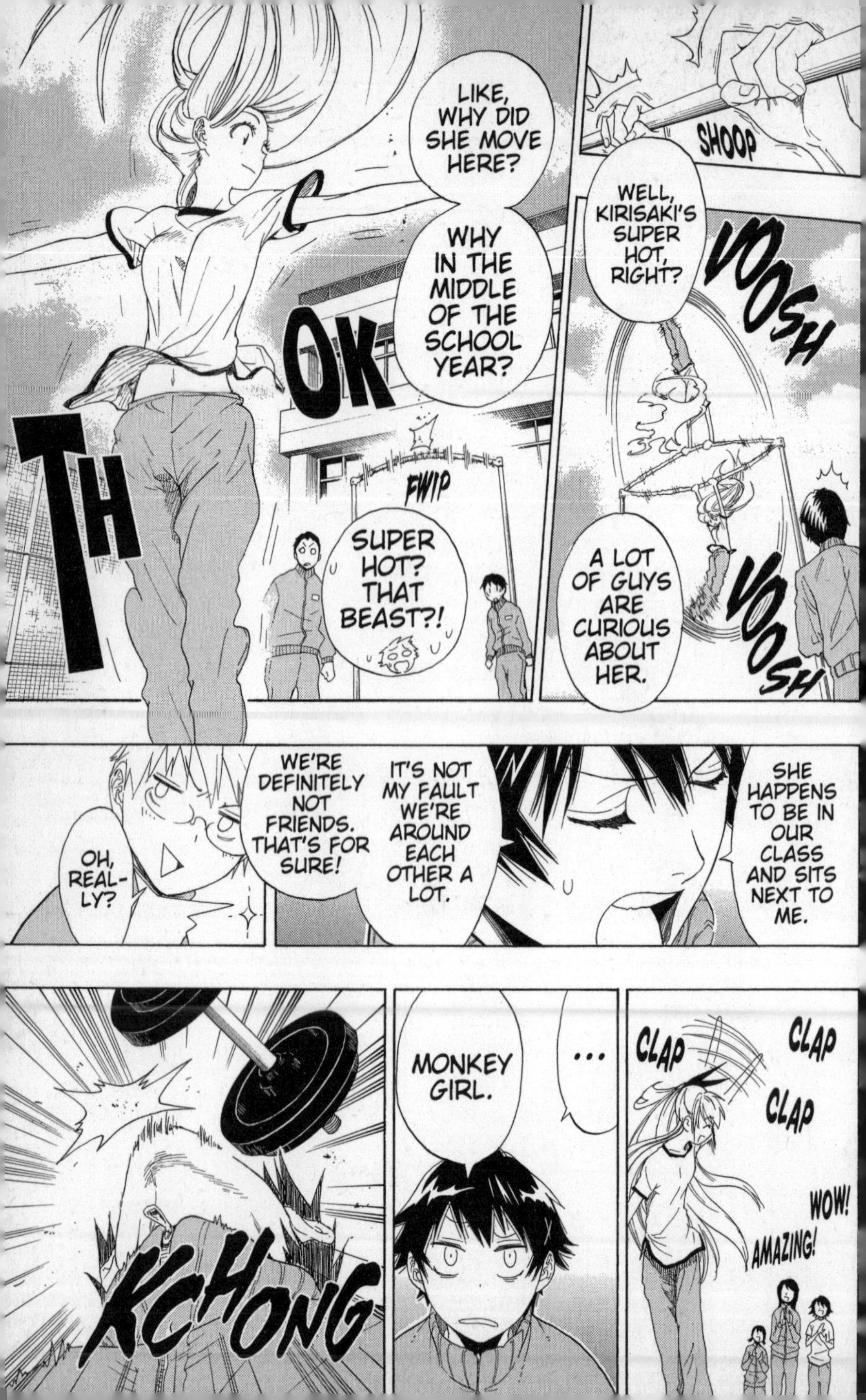
SHOOP
WELL, KIRISAKI'S SUPER HOT, RIGHT?
VOOSH
A LOT OF GUYS ARE CURIOUS ABOUT HER.
VOOSH
LIKE, WHY DID SHE MOVE HERE?
WHY IN THE MIDDLE OF THE SCHOOL YEAR?
THOK
FWIP
SUPER HOT? THAT BEAST?!
SHE HAPPENS TO BE IN OUR CLASS AND SITS NEXT TO ME.
IT'S NOT MY FAULT WE'RE AROUND EACH OTHER A LOT.
WE'RE DEFINITELY NOT FRIENDS. THAT'S FOR SURE!
OH, REAL-LY?
CLAP
CLAP
CLAP
WOW!
AMAZING!
...
MONKEY GIRL.
KCHONG

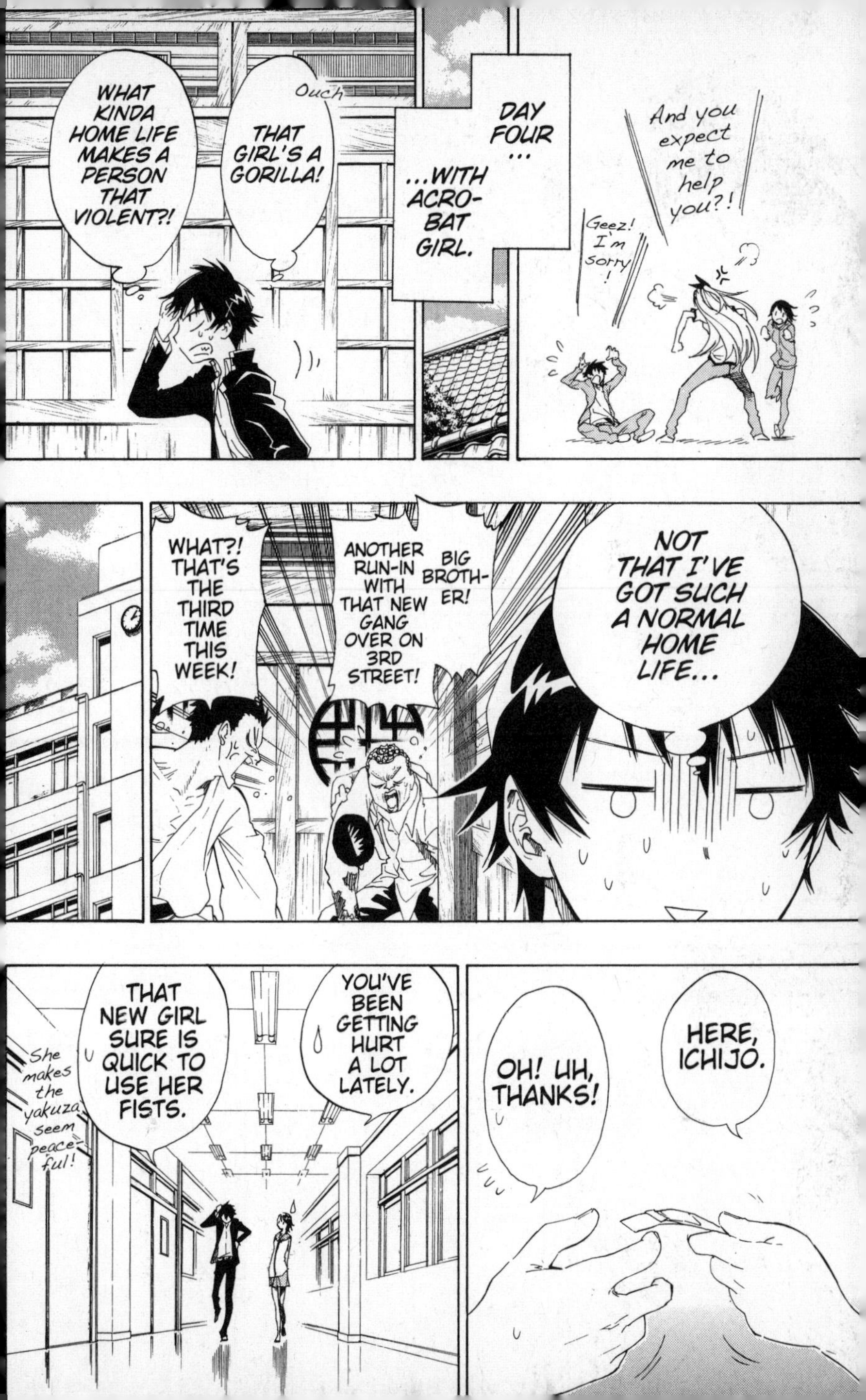
And you expect me to help you?!
Geez! I'm sorry!
DAY FOUR...
...WITH ACRO-BAT GIRL.
Ouch
THAT GIRL'S A GORILLA!
WHAT KINDA HOME LIFE MAKES A PERSON THAT VIOLENT?!
NOT THAT I'VE GOT SUCH A NORMAL HOME LIFE...
BIG BROTHER!
ANOTHER RUN-IN WITH THAT NEW GANG OVER ON 3RD STREET!
WHAT?! THAT'S THE THIRD TIME THIS WEEK!
HERE, ICHIJO.
OH! UH, THANKS!
YOU'VE BEEN GETTING HURT A LOT LATELY.
THAT NEW GIRL SURE IS QUICK TO USE HER FISTS.
She makes the yakuza seem peaceful!

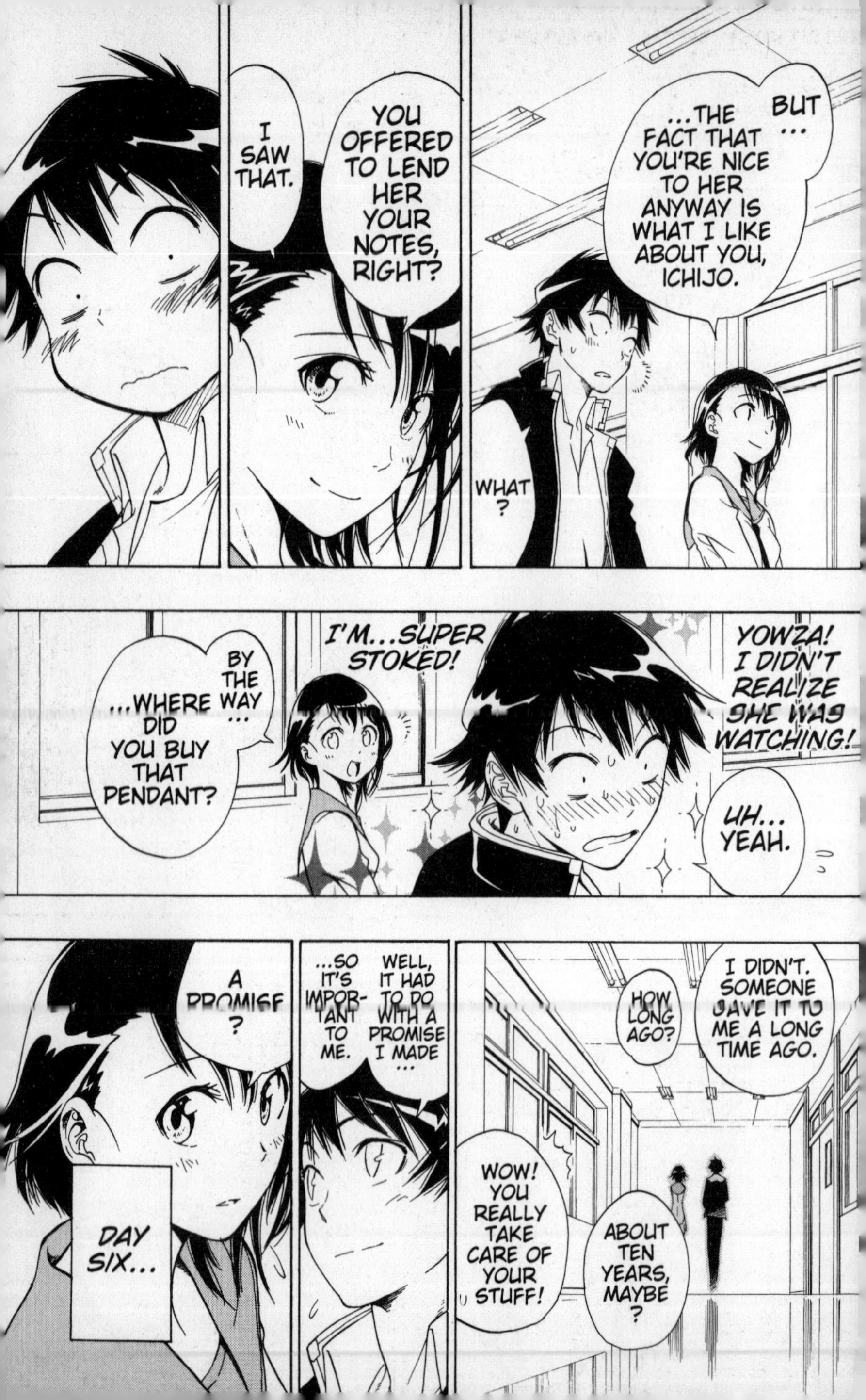
BUT...
...THE FACT THAT YOU'RE NICE TO HER ANYWAY IS WHAT I LIKE ABOUT YOU, ICHIJO.
WHAT?
YOU OFFERED TO LEND HER YOUR NOTES, RIGHT?
I SAW THAT.
YOWZA! I DIDN'T REALIZE SHE WAS WATCHING!
UH... YEAH.
I'M...SUPER STOKED!
BY THE WAY...
...WHERE DID YOU BUY THAT PENDANT?
I DIDN'T. SOMEONE GAVE IT TO ME A LONG TIME AGO.
HOW LONG AGO?
ABOUT TEN YEARS, MAYBE?
WOW! YOU REALLY TAKE CARE OF YOUR STUFF!
WELL, IT HAD TO DO WITH A PROMISE I MADE...
...SO IT'S IMPOR-TANT TO ME.
A PROMISE?
DAY SIX...

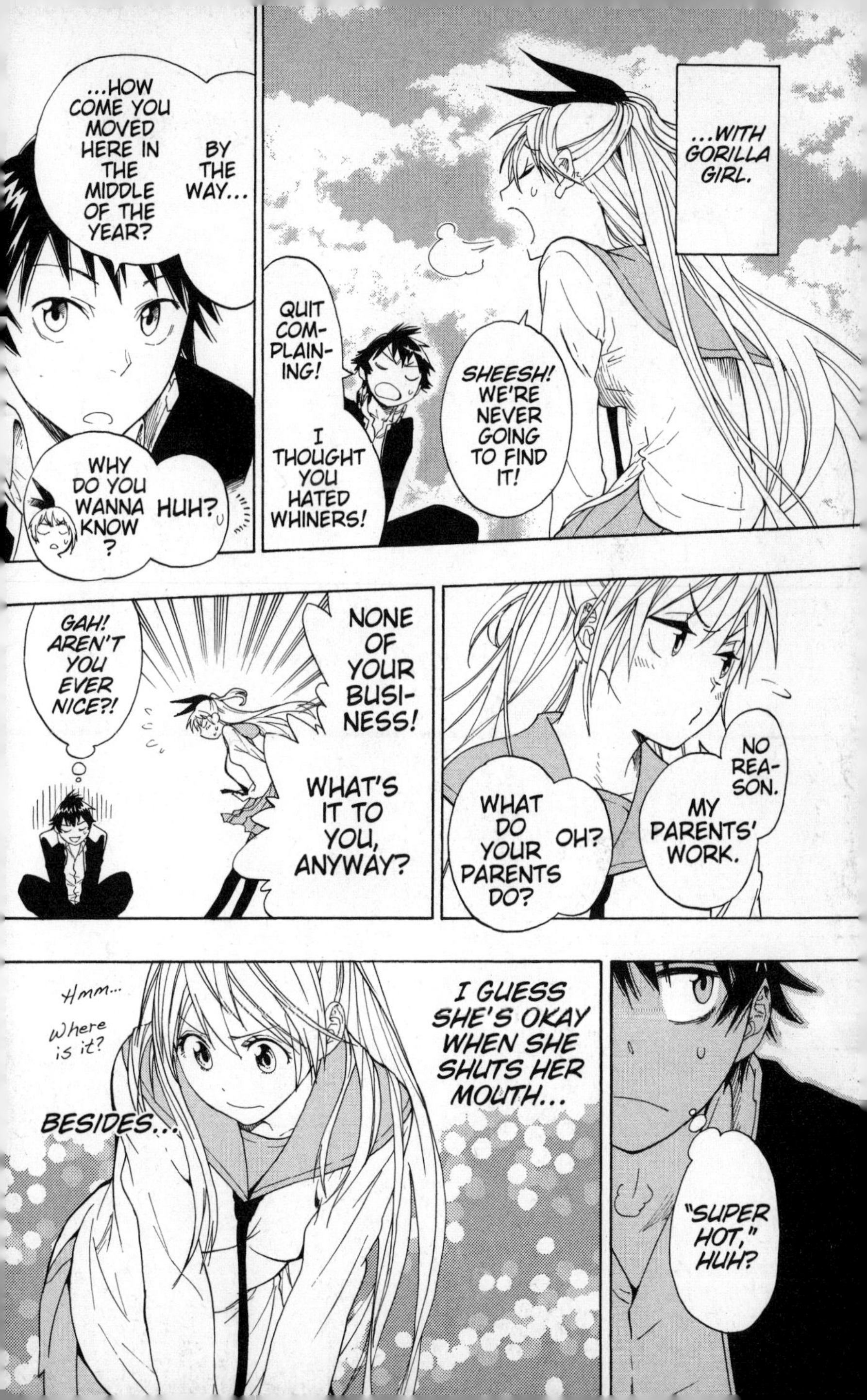

...WITH GORILLA GIRL.
SHEESH! WE'RE NEVER GOING TO FIND IT!
QUIT COM-PLAIN-ING!
I THOUGHT YOU HATED WHINERS!
BY THE WAY...
...HOW COME YOU MOVED HERE IN THE MIDDLE OF THE YEAR?
HUH?
WHY DO YOU WANNA KNOW?
NO REA-SON. MY PARENTS' WORK.
OH?
WHAT DO YOUR PARENTS DO?
NONE OF YOUR BUSI-NESS!
WHAT'S IT TO YOU, ANYWAY?
GAH! AREN'T YOU EVER NICE?!
"SUPER HOT," HUH?
I GUESS SHE'S OKAY WHEN SHE SHUTS HER MOUTH...
Hmm...
Where is it?
BESIDES...

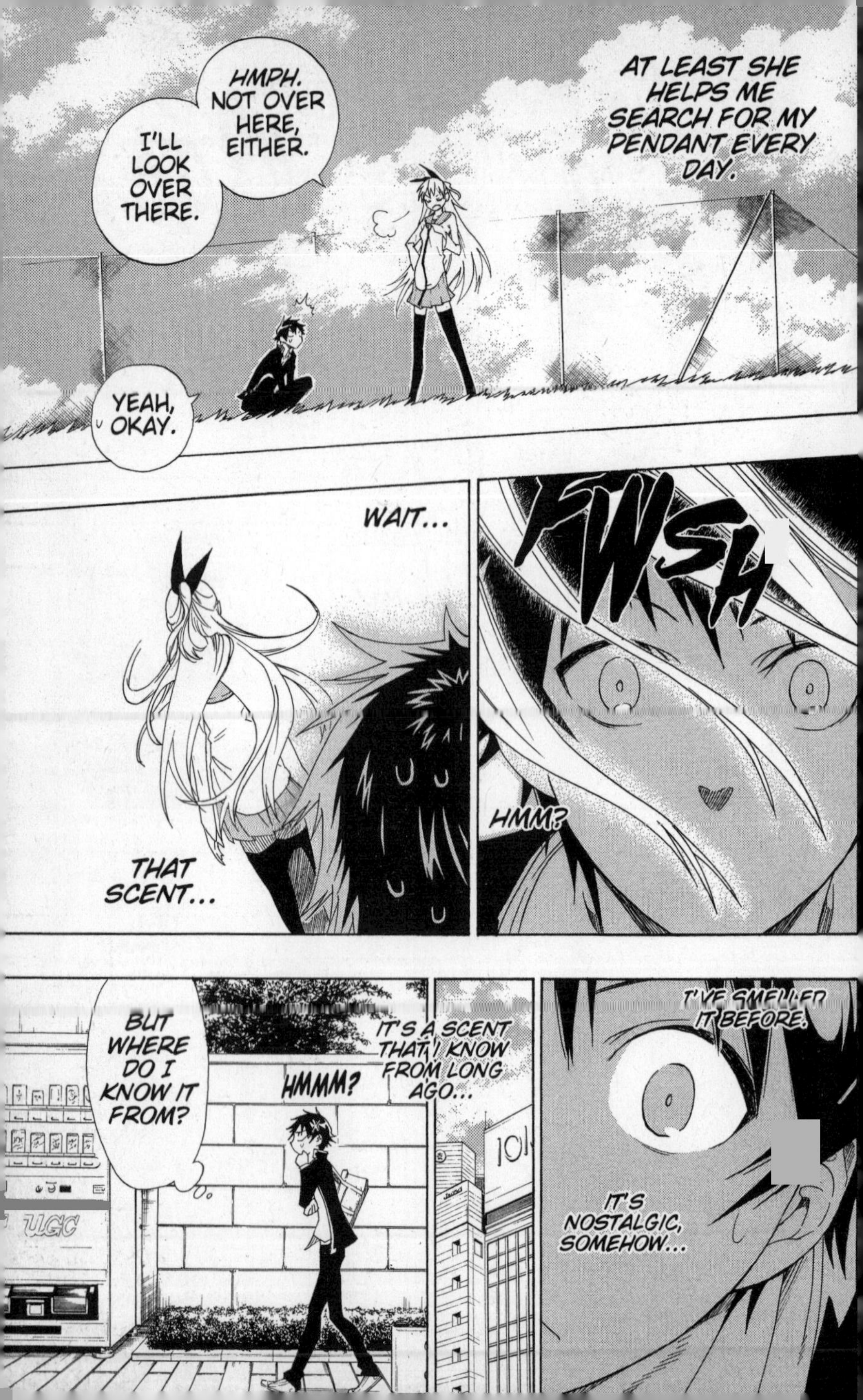
AT LEAST SHE HELPS ME SEARCH FOR MY PENDANT EVERY DAY.
HMPH. NOT OVER HERE, EITHER.
I'LL LOOK OVER THERE.
YEAH, OKAY.
FWSH
HMM?
WAIT...
THAT SCENT...
I'VE SMELLED IT BEFORE.
IT'S NOSTALGIC, SOMEHOW...
IT'S A SCENT THAT I KNOW FROM LONG AGO...
HMMM?
BUT WHERE DO I KNOW IT FROM?
UGC

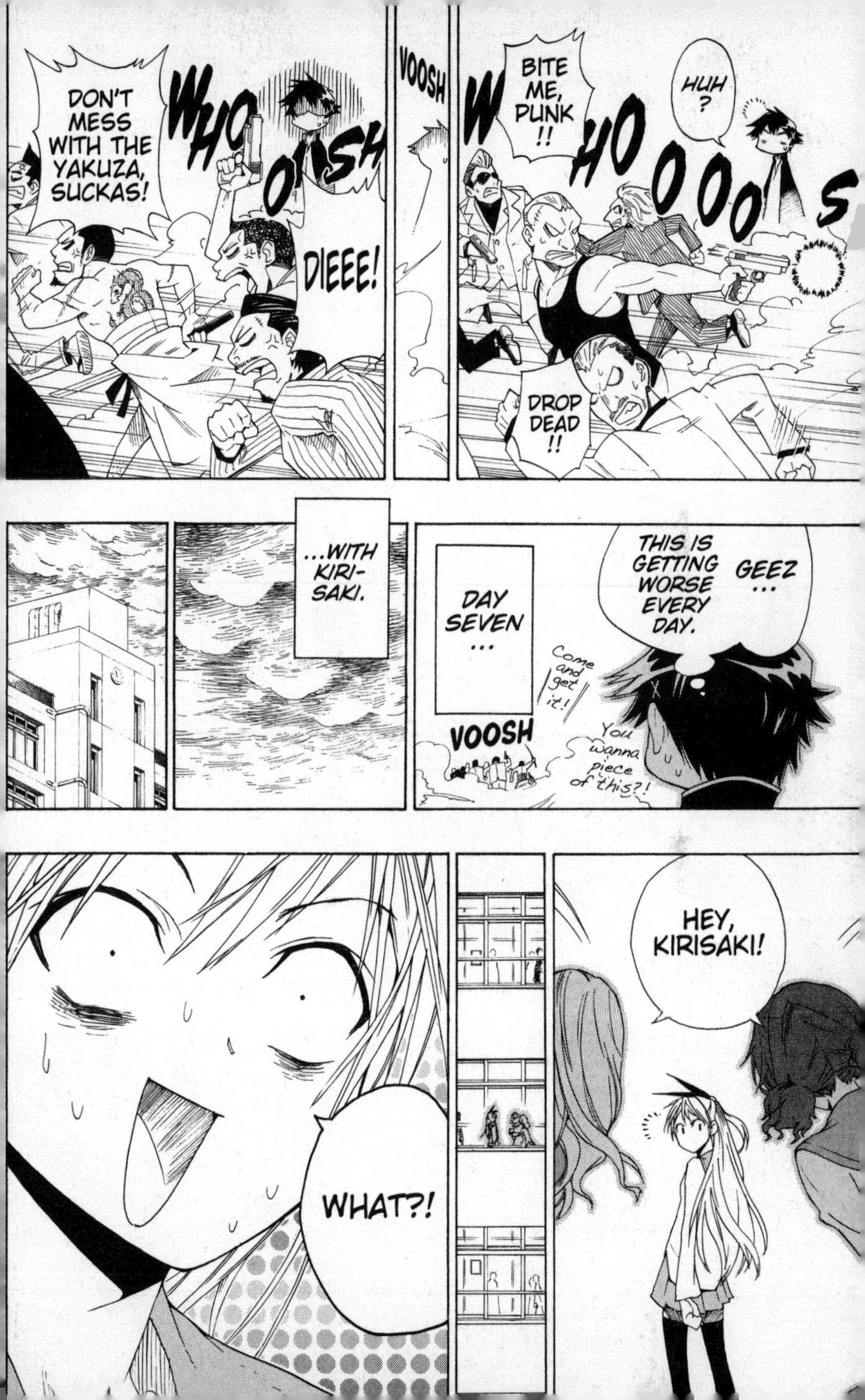
HUH?
BITE ME, PUNK!!
WHOOOOOS
DROP DEAD!!
VOOSH
WHOOSH
DON'T MESS WITH THE YAKUZA, SUCKAS!
DIEEE!
GEEZ...
THIS IS GETTING WORSE EVERY DAY.
Come and get it!
You wanna piece of this?!
DAY SEVEN...
VOOSH
...WITH KIRI-SAKI.
HEY, KIRISAKI!
WHAT?!

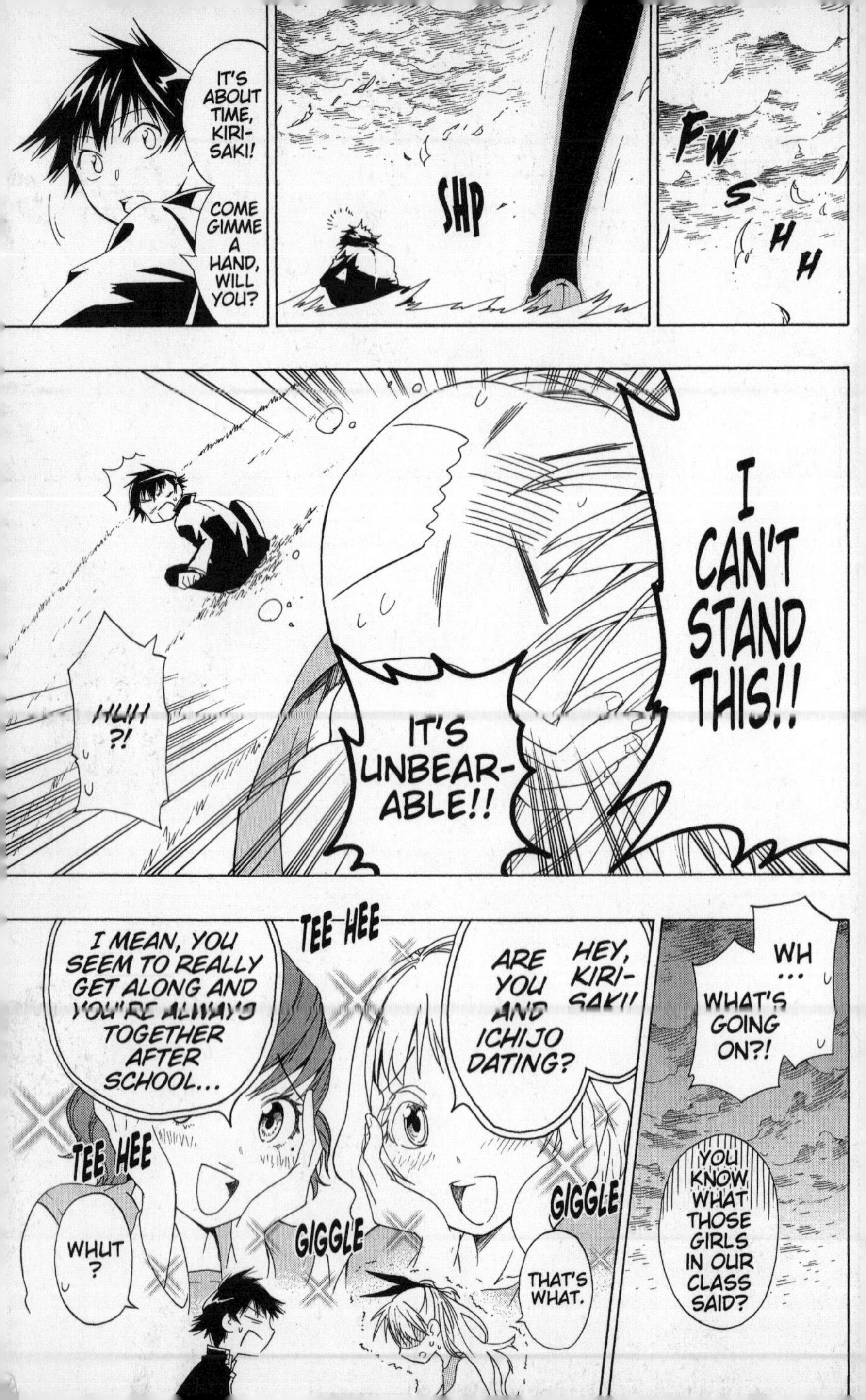
FWSHH
SHP
IT'S ABOUT TIME, KIRI-SAKI!
COME GIMME A HAND, WILL YOU?
I CAN'T STAND THIS!!
IT'S UNBEARABLE!!
HUH?!
WH... WHAT'S GOING ON?!
YOU KNOW WHAT THOSE GIRLS IN OUR CLASS SAID?
HEY, KIRI-SAKI!! ARE YOU AND ICHIJO DATING?
TEE HEE
I MEAN, YOU SEEM TO REALLY GET ALONG AND YOU'RE ALWAYS TOGETHER AFTER SCHOOL...
GIGGLE
GIGGLE
TEE HEE
THAT'S WHAT.
WHUT?

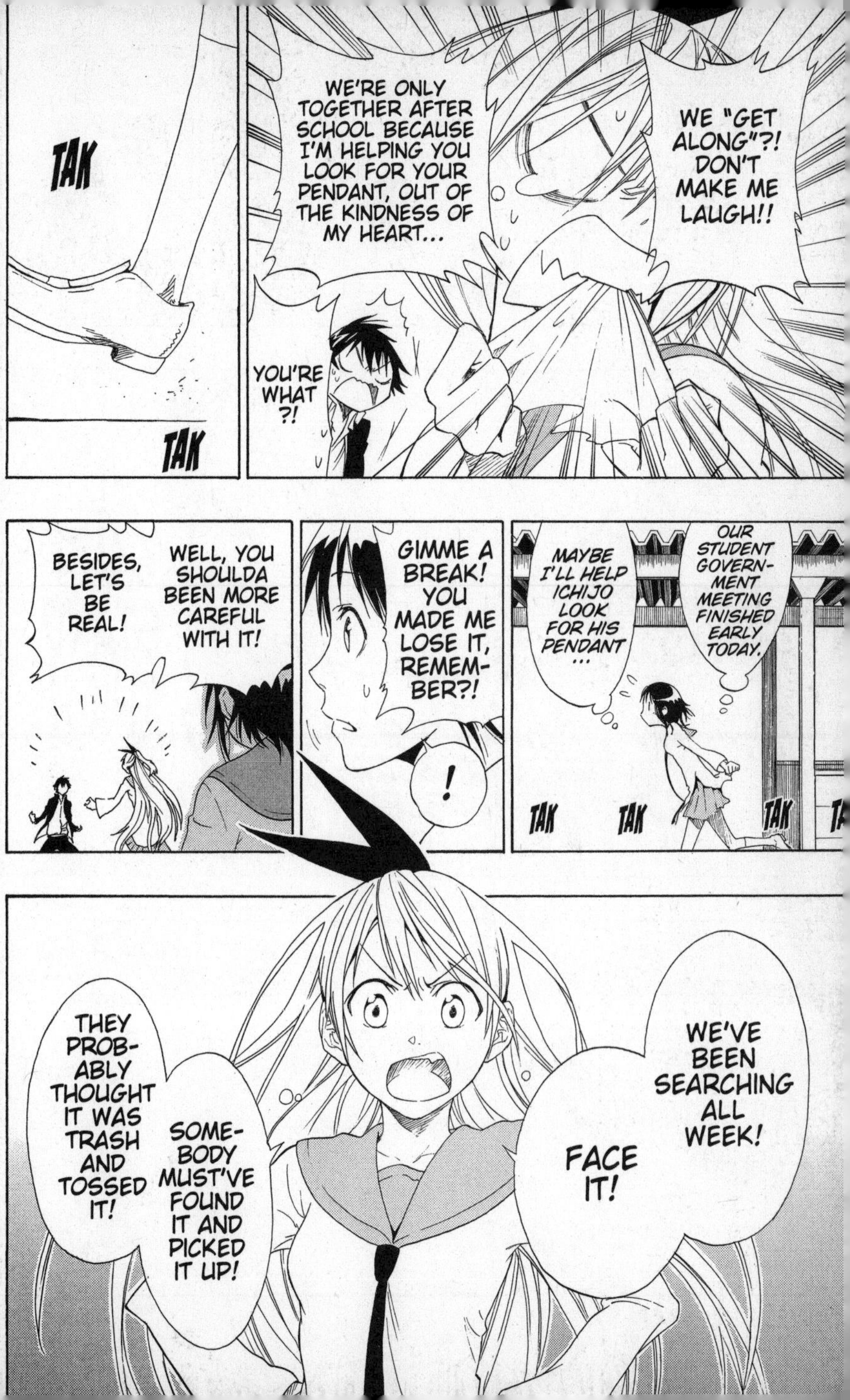
WE "GET ALONG"?! DON'T MAKE ME LAUGH!!
WE'RE ONLY TOGETHER AFTER SCHOOL BECAUSE I'M HELPING YOU LOOK FOR YOUR PENDANT, OUT OF THE KINDNESS OF MY HEART...
YOU'RE WHAT ?!
TAK
TAK
OUR STUDENT GOVERN-MENT MEETING FINISHED EARLY TODAY.
MAYBE I'LL HELP ICHIJO LOOK FOR HIS PENDANT ...
TAK
TAK
TAK
GIMME A BREAK! YOU MADE ME LOSE IT, REMEM-BER?!
!
WELL, YOU SHOULDA BEEN MORE CAREFUL WITH IT!
BESIDES, LET'S BE REAL!
WE'VE BEEN SEARCHING ALL WEEK!
FACE IT!
SOME-BODY MUST'VE FOUND IT AND PICKED IT UP!
THEY PROB-ABLY THOUGHT IT WAS TRASH AND TOSSED IT!

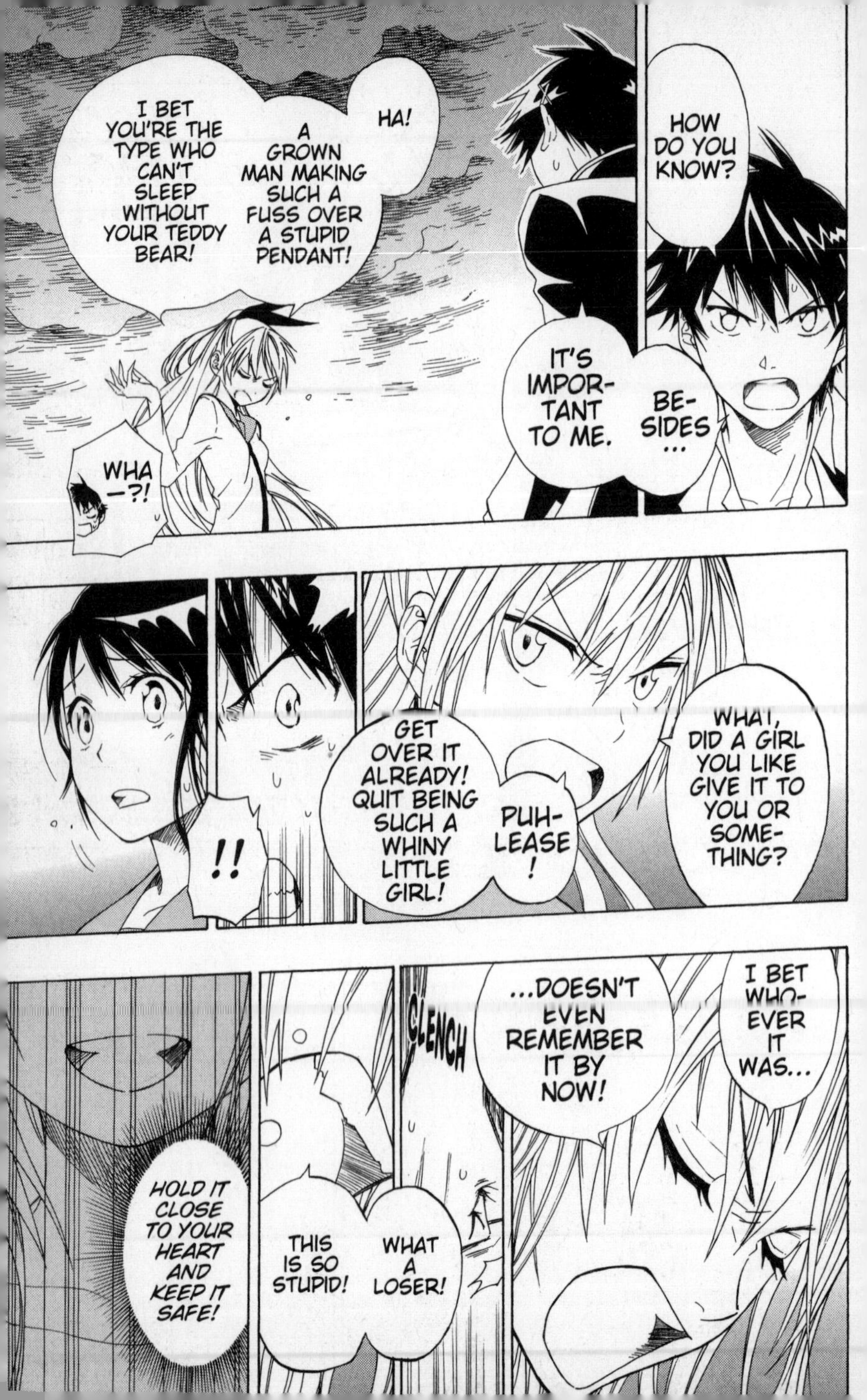
HOW DO YOU KNOW?
IT'S IMPORTANT TO ME.
BESIDES...
HA!
A GROWN MAN MAKING SUCH A FUSS OVER A STUPID PENDANT!
I BET YOU'RE THE TYPE WHO CAN'T SLEEP WITHOUT YOUR TEDDY BEAR!
WHA—?!
WHAT, DID A GIRL YOU LIKE GIVE IT TO YOU OR SOMETHING?
PUH-LEASE!
GET OVER IT ALREADY! QUIT BEING SUCH A WHINY LITTLE GIRL!
!!
I BET WHOEVER IT WAS...
...DOESN'T EVEN REMEMBER IT BY NOW!
CLENCH
WHAT A LOSER!
THIS IS SO STUPID!
HOLD IT CLOSE TO YOUR HEART AND KEEP IT SAFE!

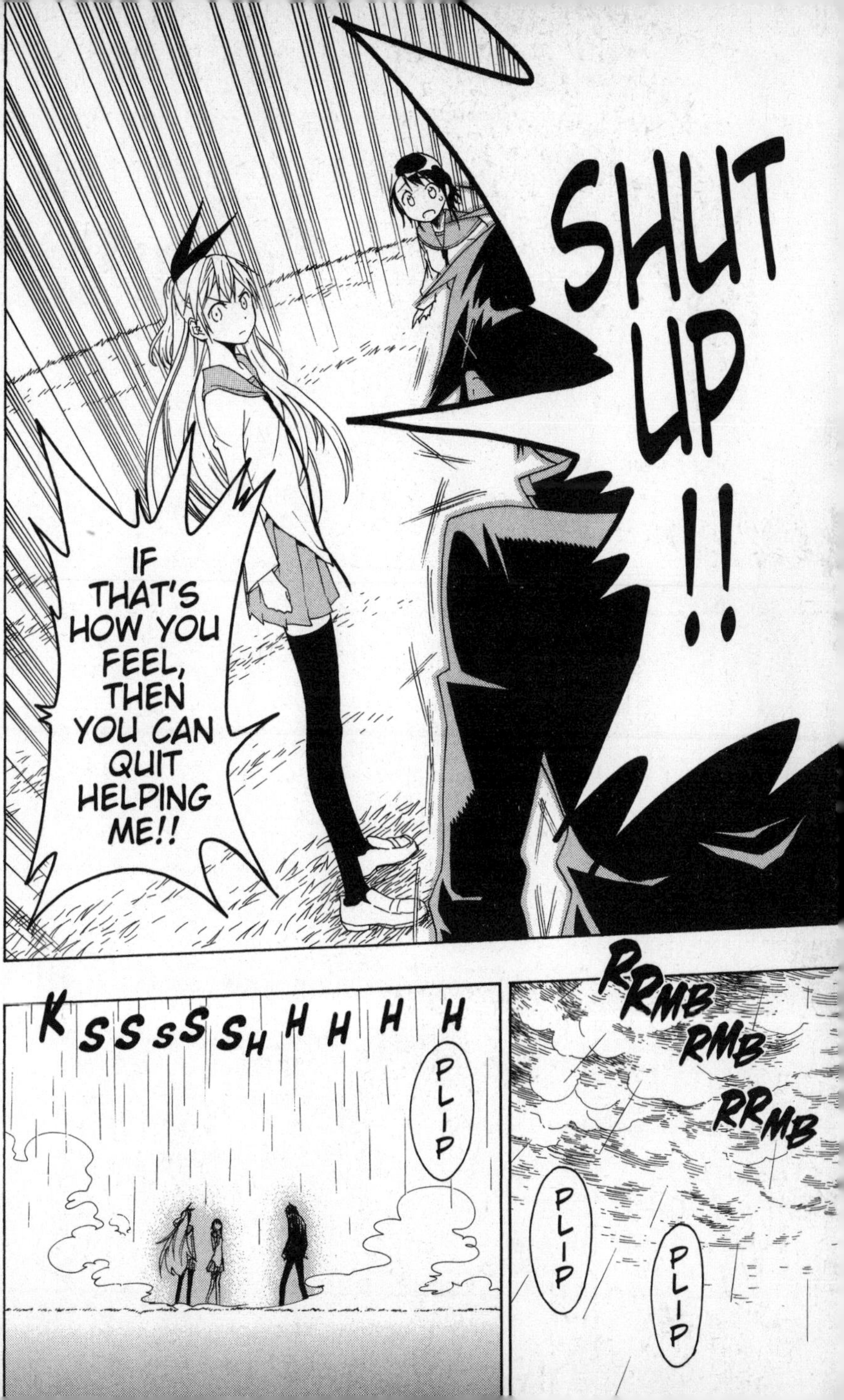
SHUT UP!!
IF THAT'S HOW YOU FEEL, THEN YOU CAN QUIT HELPING ME!!
RRMB RMB RRMB
PLIP
PLIP
KSSSSSH H H H H
PLIP

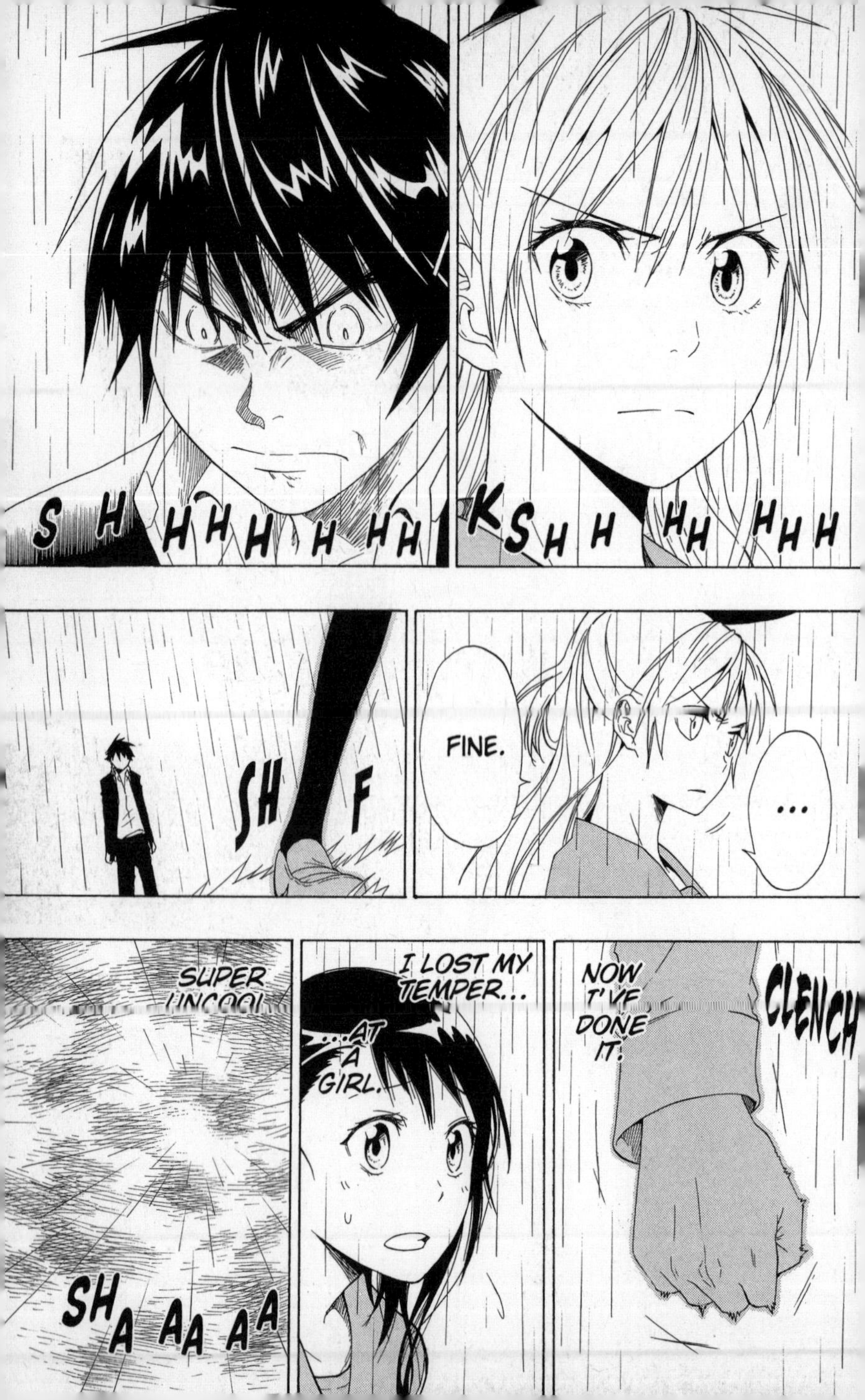
KSHH HH HHH
SHHHHH HHH
...
FINE.
SH F
CLENCH
NOW I'VE DONE IT.
I LOST MY TEMPER...
...AT A GIRL.
SUPER UNCOOL
SHAAAAA

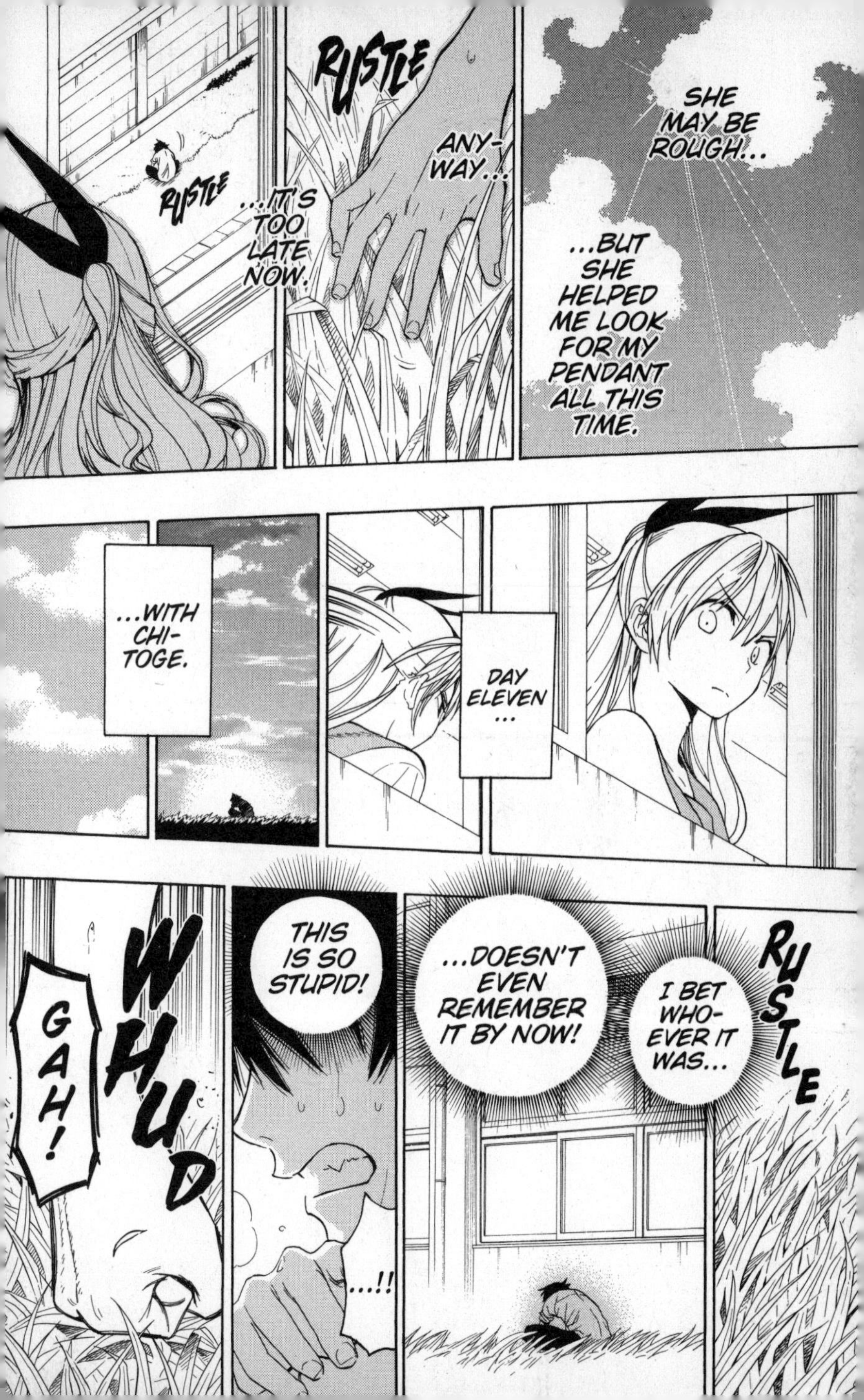
SHE MAY BE ROUGH...
...BUT SHE HELPED ME LOOK FOR MY PENDANT ALL THIS TIME.
RUSTLE
ANY-WAY...
...IT'S TOO LATE NOW.
RUSTLE
DAY ELEVEN ...
...WITH CHI-TOGE.
RUSTLE
I BET WHO-EVER IT WAS...
...DOESN'T EVEN REMEMBER IT BY NOW!
THIS IS SO STUPID!
...!!
WHUD
GAH!

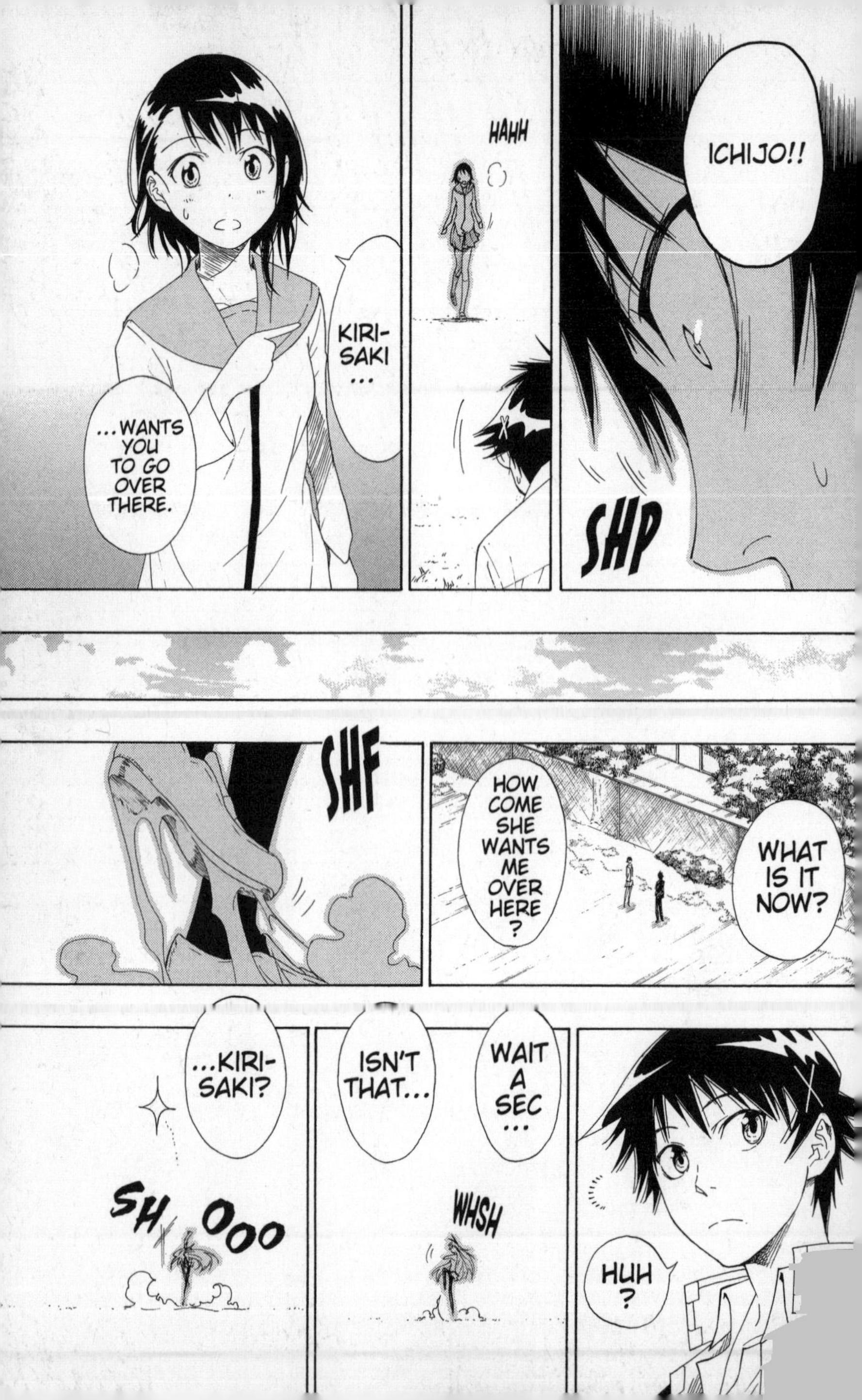
ICHIJO!!
SHP
HAHH
KIRI-SAKI...
...WANTS YOU TO GO OVER THERE.
WHAT IS IT NOW?
HOW COME SHE WANTS ME OVER HERE?
SHF
HUH?
WAIT A SEC...
WHSH
ISN'T THAT...
...KIRI-SAKI?
SH OOO

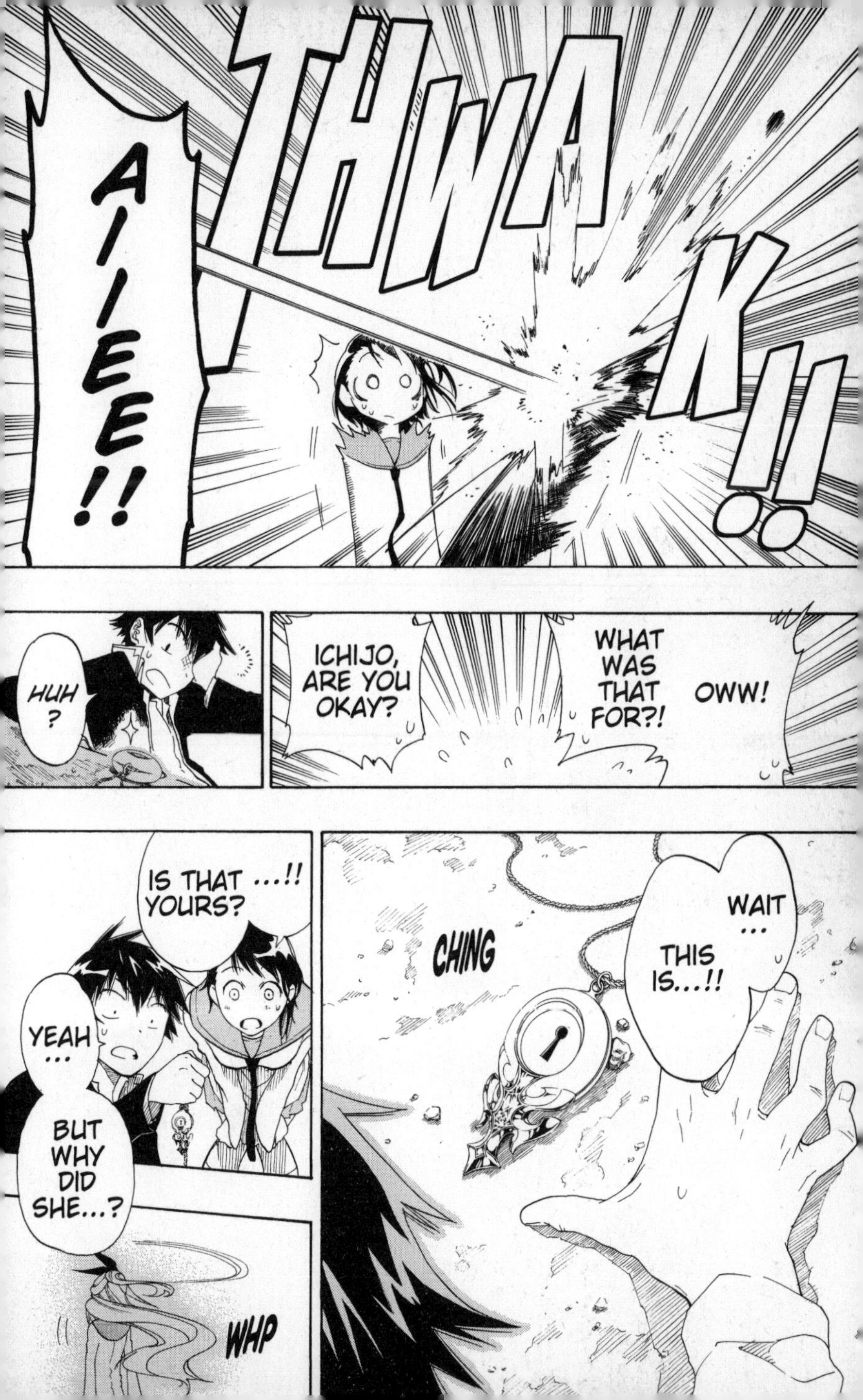

THWAK!!
AIIEE!!
OWW!
WHAT WAS THAT FOR?!
ICHIJO, ARE YOU OKAY?
HUH?
WAIT... THIS IS...!!
CHING
...!!
IS THAT YOURS?
YEAH...
BUT WHY DID SHE...?
WHP

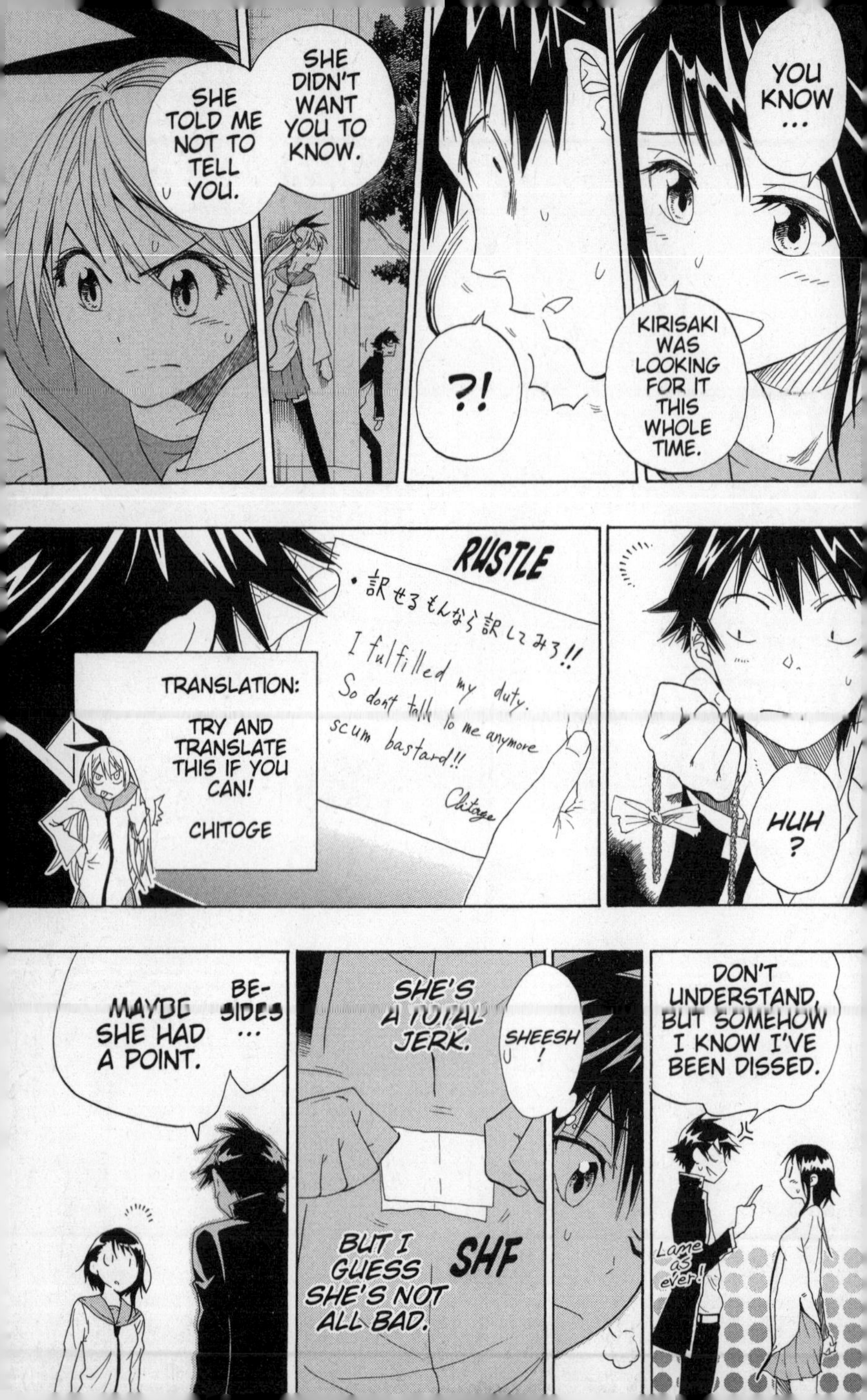
YOU KNOW...
KIRISAKI WAS LOOKING FOR IT THIS WHOLE TIME.
?!
SHE DIDN'T WANT YOU TO KNOW.
SHE TOLD ME NOT TO TELL YOU.
HUH?
RUSTLE
・訳せるもんなら訳してみろ!!
I fulfilled my duty.
So don't talk to me anymore
scum bastard!!
Chitoge
TRANSLATION:
TRY AND TRANSLATE THIS IF YOU CAN!
CHITOGE
DON'T UNDERSTAND, BUT SOMEHOW I KNOW I'VE BEEN DISSED.
Lame as ever!
SHEESH!
SHE'S A TOTAL JERK.
SHF
BUT I GUESS SHE'S NOT ALL BAD.
BE-SIDES...
MAYBE SHE HAD A POINT.

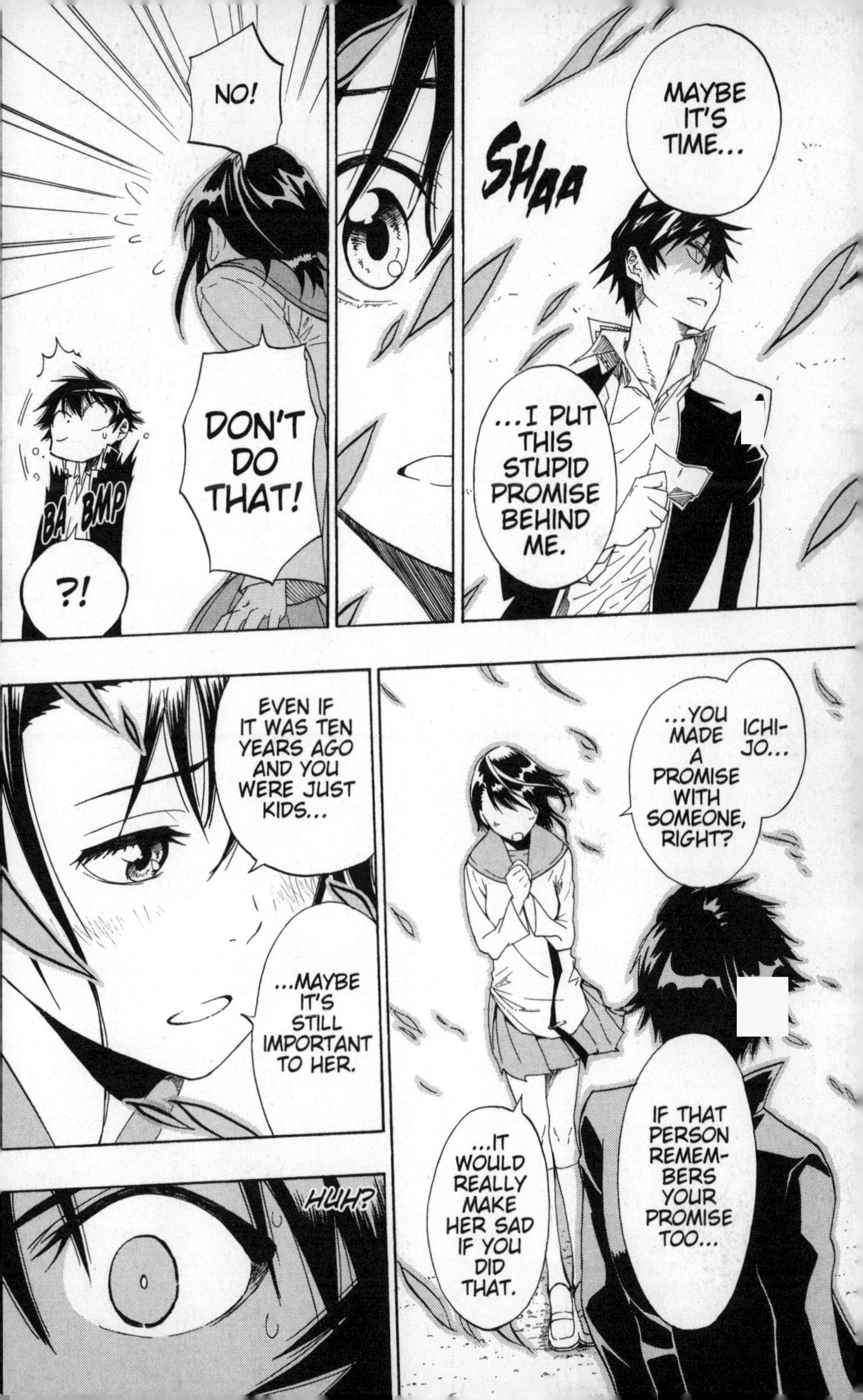
MAYBE IT'S TIME...
SHAA
...I PUT THIS STUPID PROMISE BEHIND ME.
NO!
DON'T DO THAT!
BA BMP
?!
ICHI-JO...
...YOU MADE A PROMISE WITH SOMEONE, RIGHT?
IF THAT PERSON REMEM-BERS YOUR PROMISE TOO...
...IT WOULD REALLY MAKE HER SAD IF YOU DID THAT.
EVEN IF IT WAS TEN YEARS AGO AND YOU WERE JUST KIDS...
...MAYBE IT'S STILL IMPORTANT TO HER.
HUH?

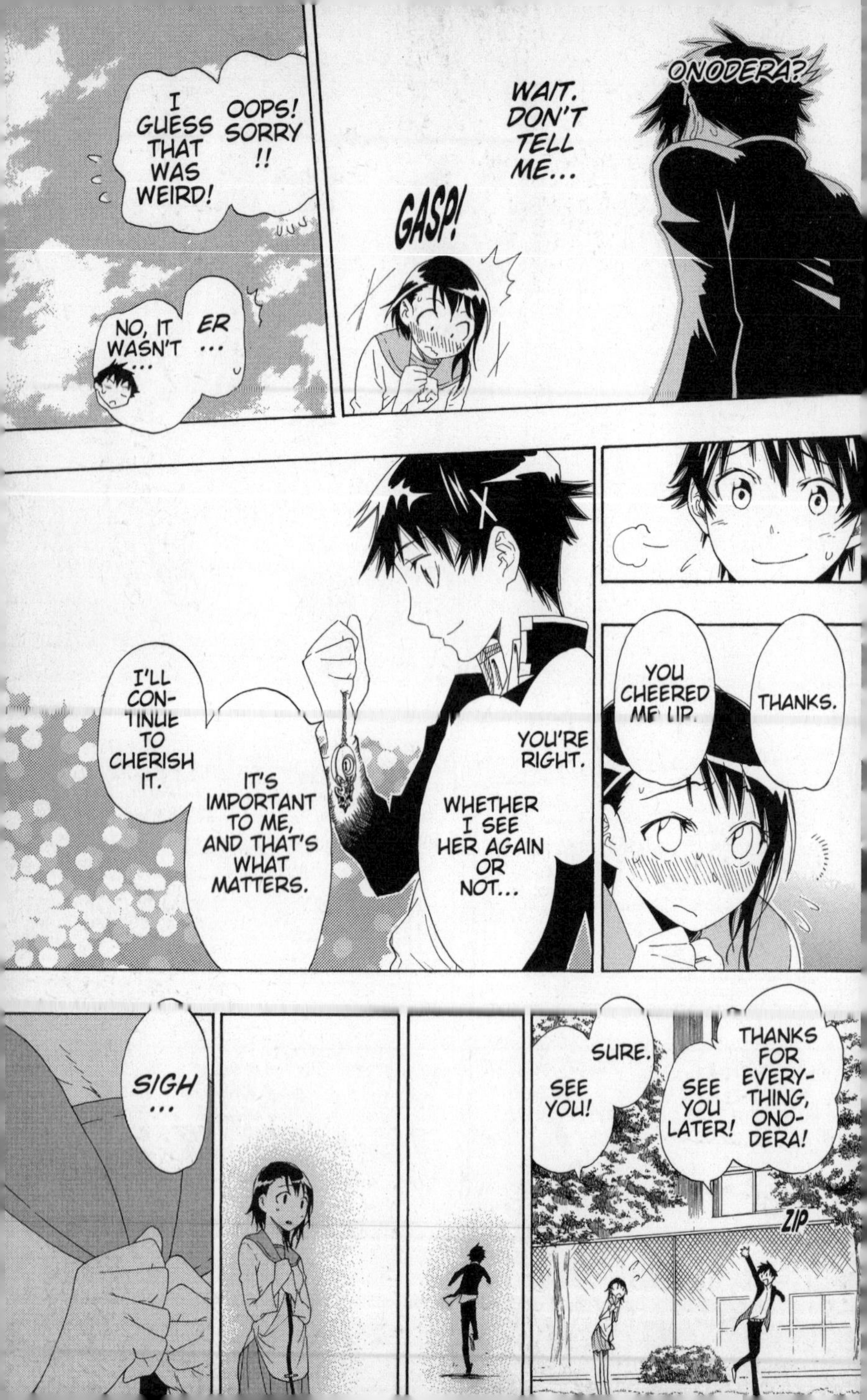
ONODERA?
WAIT. DON'T TELL ME...
GASP!
OOPS! SORRY!!
I GUESS THAT WAS WEIRD!
ER...
NO, IT WASN'T...
THANKS.
YOU CHEERED ME UP.
YOU'RE RIGHT.
WHETHER I SEE HER AGAIN OR NOT...
IT'S IMPORTANT TO ME, AND THAT'S WHAT MATTERS.
I'LL CONTINUE TO CHERISH IT.
THANKS FOR EVERYTHING, ONODERA!
SEE YOU LATER!
SURE.
SEE YOU!
ZIP
SIGH...

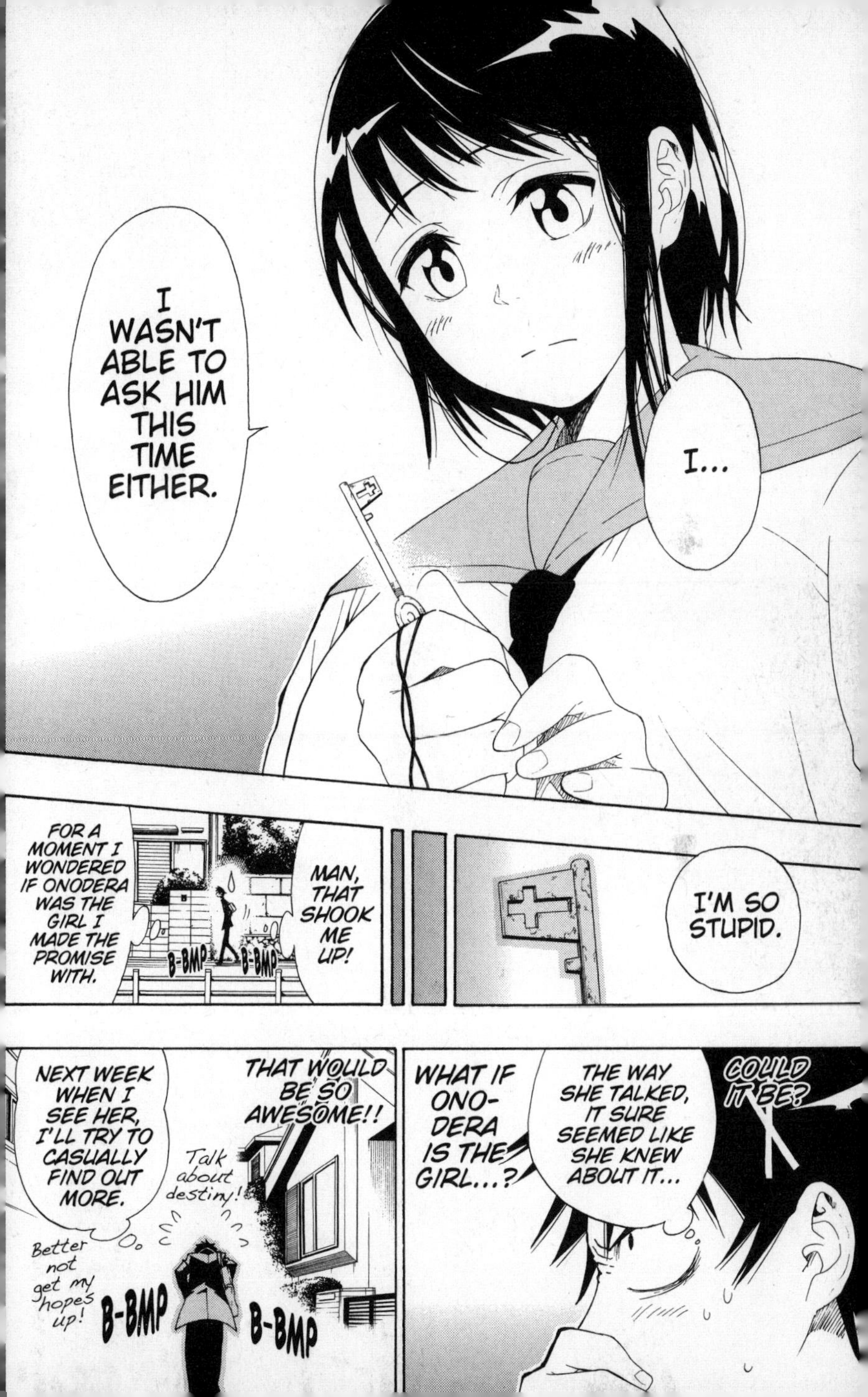
I...
I WASN'T ABLE TO ASK HIM THIS TIME EITHER.
I'M SO STUPID.
MAN, THAT SHOOK ME UP!
FOR A MOMENT I WONDERED IF ONODERA WAS THE GIRL I MADE THE PROMISE WITH.
B-BMP
B-BMP
COULD IT BE?
THE WAY SHE TALKED, IT SURE SEEMED LIKE SHE KNEW ABOUT IT...
WHAT IF ONODERA IS THE GIRL...?
THAT WOULD BE SO AWESOME!!
Talk about destiny!
NEXT WEEK WHEN I SEE HER, I'LL TRY TO CASUALLY FIND OUT MORE.
Better not get my hopes up!
B-BMP
B-BMP

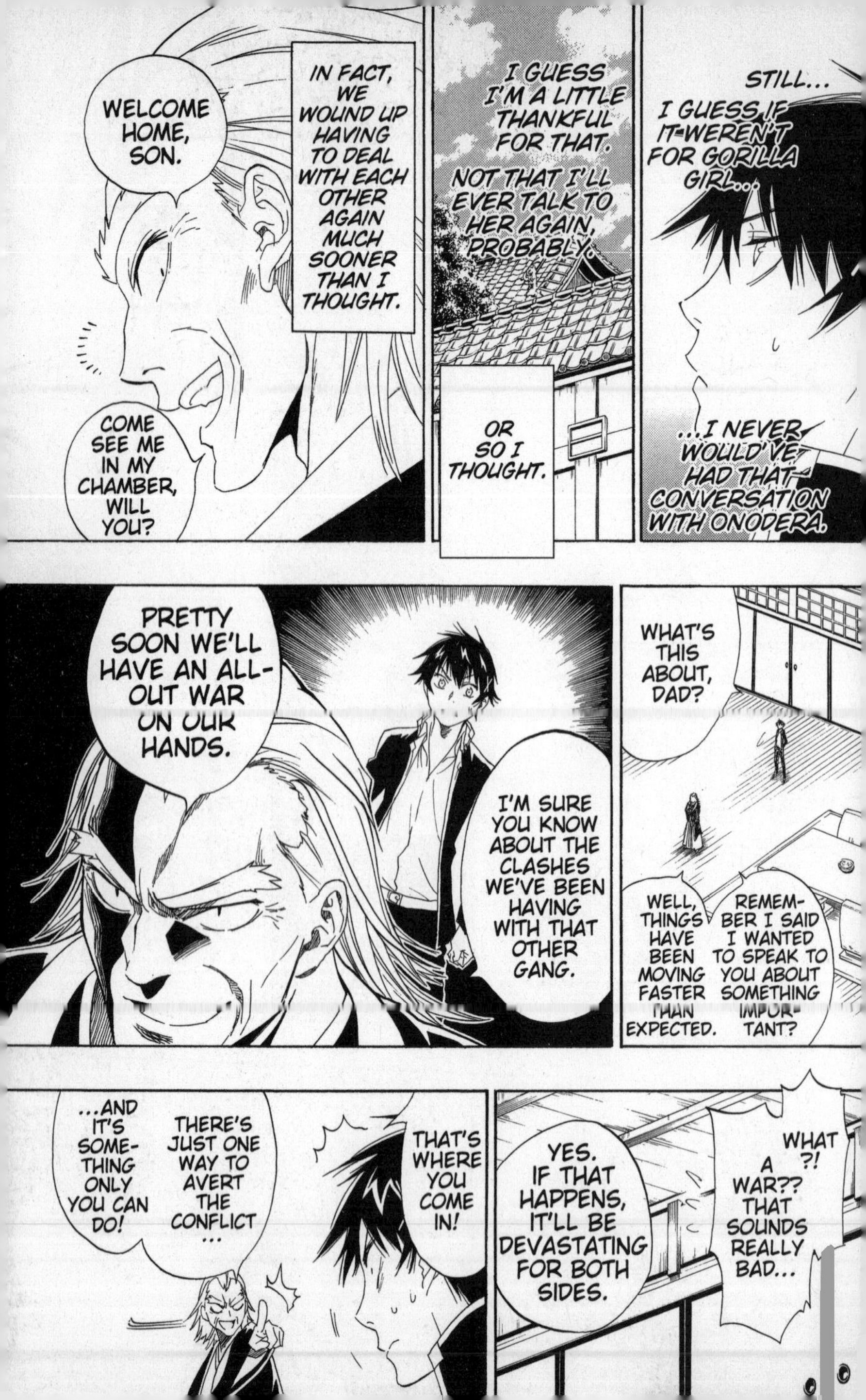
STILL... I GUESS IF IT WEREN'T FOR GORILLA GIRL...
...I NEVER WOULD'VE HAD THAT CONVERSATION WITH ONODERA.
I GUESS I'M A LITTLE THANKFUL FOR THAT.
NOT THAT I'LL EVER TALK TO HER AGAIN, PROBABLY.
OR SO I THOUGHT.
IN FACT, WE WOUND UP HAVING TO DEAL WITH EACH OTHER AGAIN MUCH SOONER THAN I THOUGHT.
WELCOME HOME, SON.
COME SEE ME IN MY CHAMBER, WILL YOU?
WHAT'S THIS ABOUT, DAD?
REMEMBER I SAID I WANTED TO SPEAK TO YOU ABOUT SOMETHING IMPORTANT?
WELL, THINGS HAVE BEEN MOVING FASTER THAN EXPECTED.
I'M SURE YOU KNOW ABOUT THE CLASHES WE'VE BEEN HAVING WITH THAT OTHER GANG.
PRETTY SOON WE'LL HAVE AN ALL-OUT WAR ON OUR HANDS.
WHAT?! A WAR?? THAT SOUNDS REALLY BAD...
YES. IF THAT HAPPENS, IT'LL BE DEVASTATING FOR BOTH SIDES.
THERE'S JUST ONE WAY TO AVERT THE CONFLICT...
...AND IT'S SOMETHING ONLY YOU CAN DO!
THAT'S WHERE YOU COME IN!

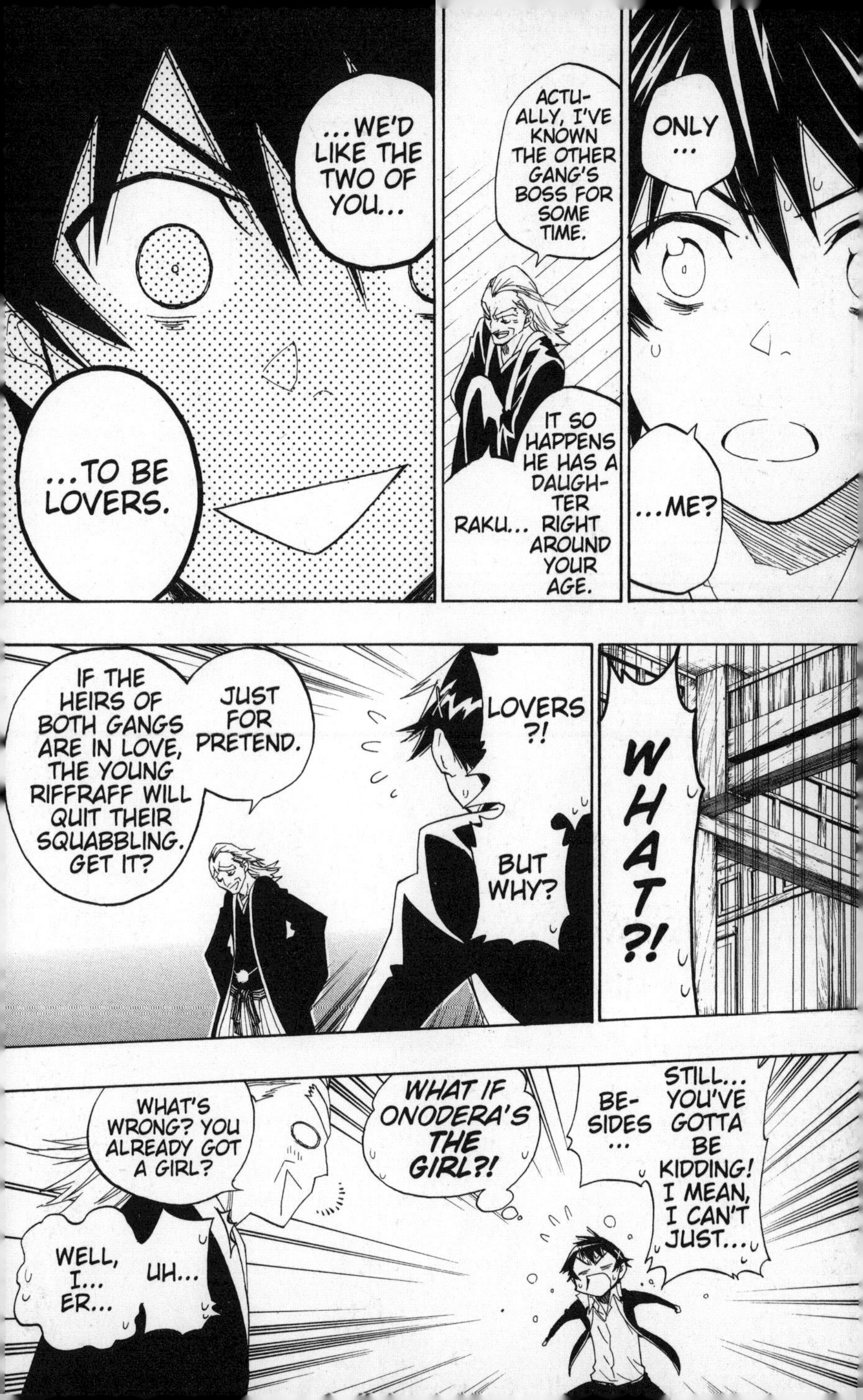
ONLY...
...ME?
ACTUALLY, I'VE KNOWN THE OTHER GANG'S BOSS FOR SOME TIME.
IT SO HAPPENS HE HAS A DAUGHTER RIGHT AROUND YOUR AGE.
RAKU...
...WE'D LIKE THE TWO OF YOU...
...TO BE LOVERS.
WHAT?!
LOVERS?!
BUT WHY?
JUST FOR PRETEND.
IF THE HEIRS OF BOTH GANGS ARE IN LOVE, THE YOUNG RIFFRAFF WILL QUIT THEIR SQUABBLING. GET IT?
STILL... YOU'VE GOTTA BE KIDDING! I MEAN, I CAN'T JUST...
BESIDES...
WHAT IF ONODERA'S THE GIRL?!
WHAT'S WRONG? YOU ALREADY GOT A GIRL?
UH...
WELL, I... ER...

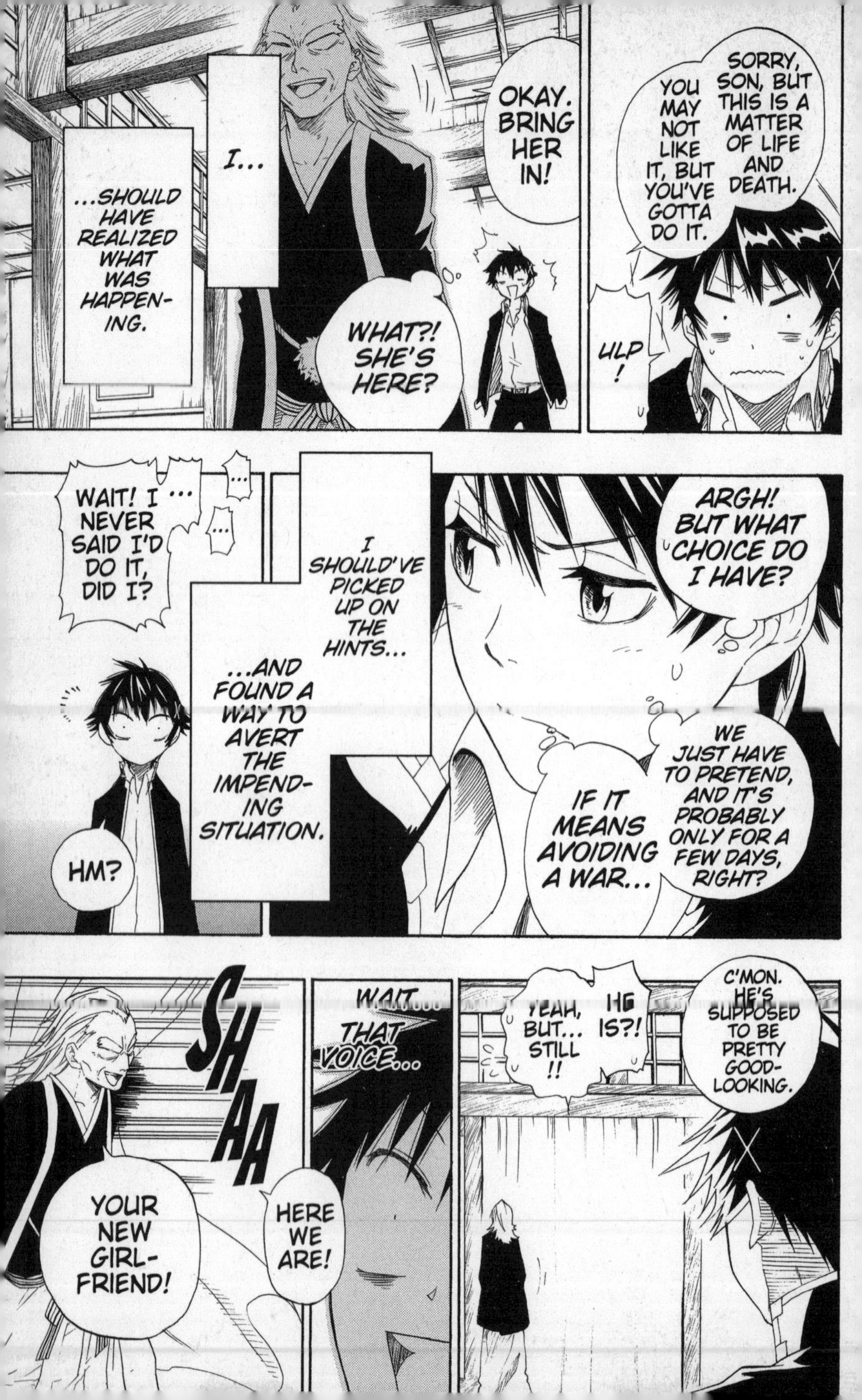
SORRY, SON, BUT THIS IS A MATTER OF LIFE AND DEATH.
YOU MAY NOT LIKE IT, BUT YOU'VE GOTTA DO IT.
ULP!
OKAY. BRING HER IN!
WHAT?! SHE'S HERE?
I...
...SHOULD HAVE REALIZED WHAT WAS HAPPEN-ING.
ARGH! BUT WHAT CHOICE DO I HAVE?
WE JUST HAVE TO PRETEND, AND IT'S PROBABLY ONLY FOR A FEW DAYS, RIGHT?
IF IT MEANS AVOIDING A WAR...
I SHOULD'VE PICKED UP ON THE HINTS...
...AND FOUND A WAY TO AVERT THE IMPEND-ING SITUATION.
...
...
WAIT! I NEVER SAID I'D DO IT, DID I?
...
HM?
C'MON. HE'S SUPPOSED TO BE PRETTY GOOD-LOOKING.
HE IS?!
YEAH, BUT... STILL!!
WAIT...
THAT VOICE...
HERE WE ARE!
SHAA
YOUR NEW GIRL-FRIEND!

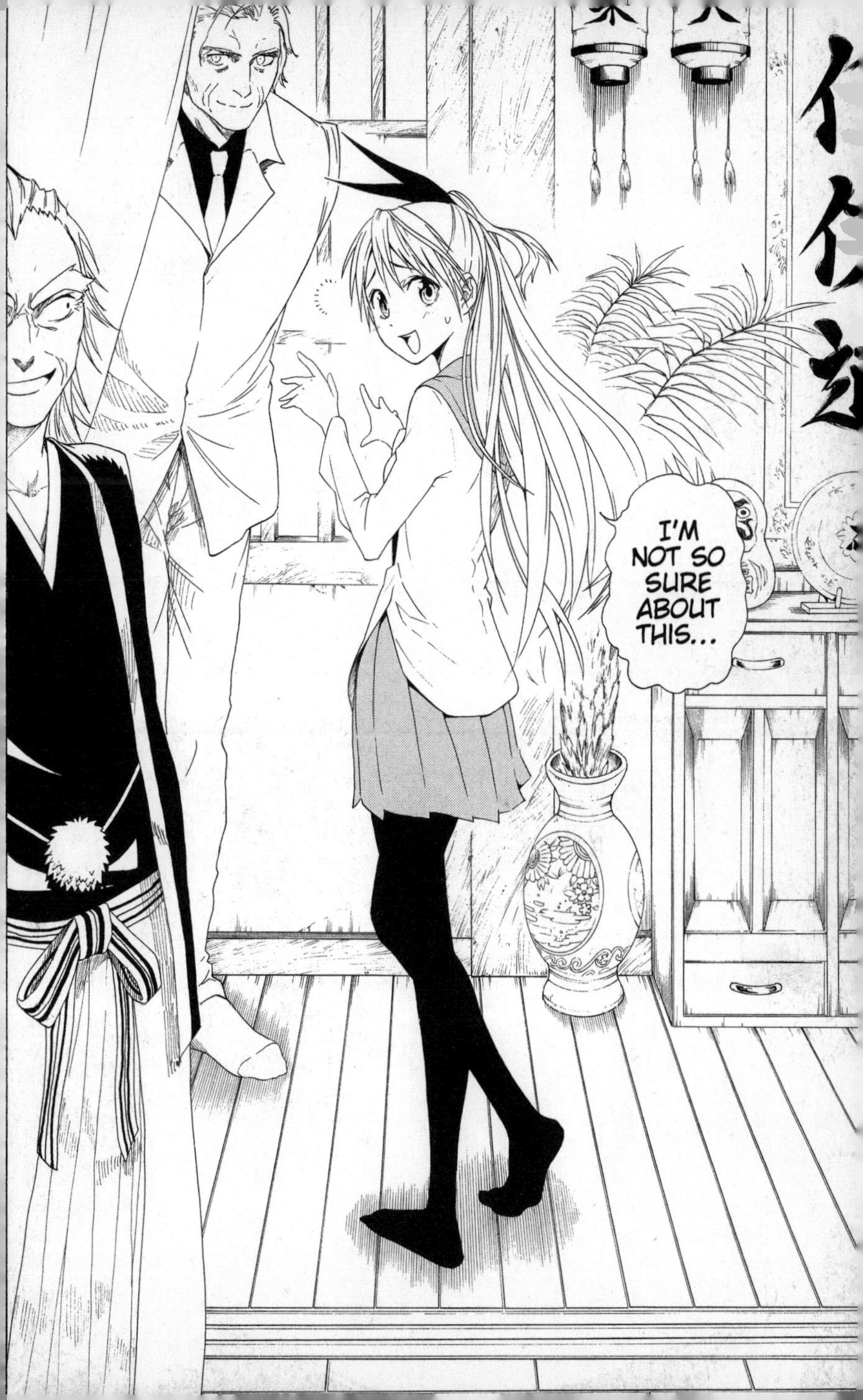
I'M NOT SO SURE ABOUT THIS...

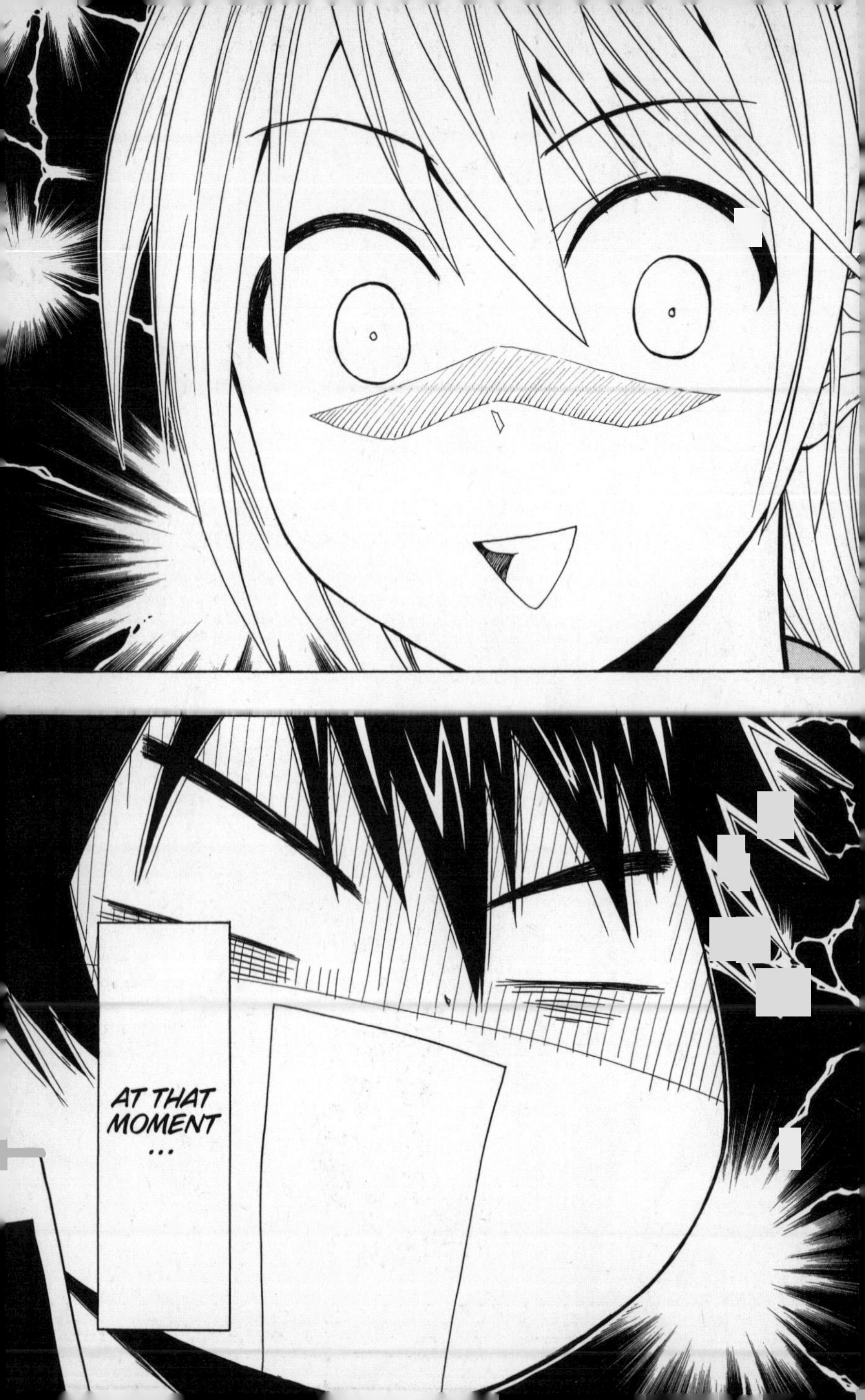
AT THAT MOMENT ...

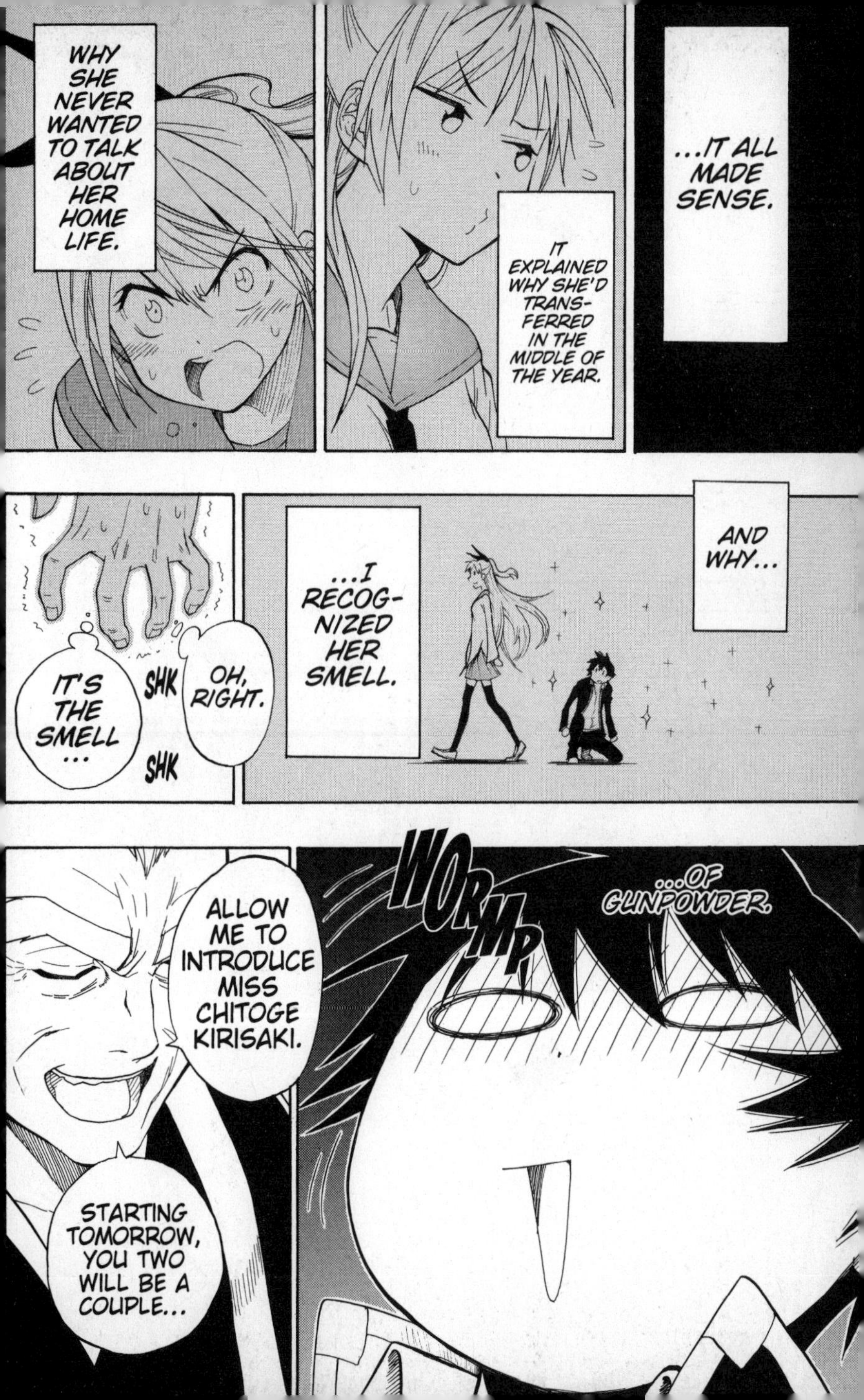
...IT ALL MADE SENSE.
IT EXPLAINED WHY SHE'D TRANSFERRED IN THE MIDDLE OF THE YEAR.
WHY SHE NEVER WANTED TO TALK ABOUT HER HOME LIFE.
AND WHY...
...I RECOGNIZED HER SMELL.
OH, RIGHT.
SHK
IT'S THE SMELL...
SHK
WORMP
...OF GUNPOWDER.
ALLOW ME TO INTRODUCE MISS CHITOGE KIRISAKI.
STARTING TOMORROW, YOU TWO WILL BE A COUPLE...

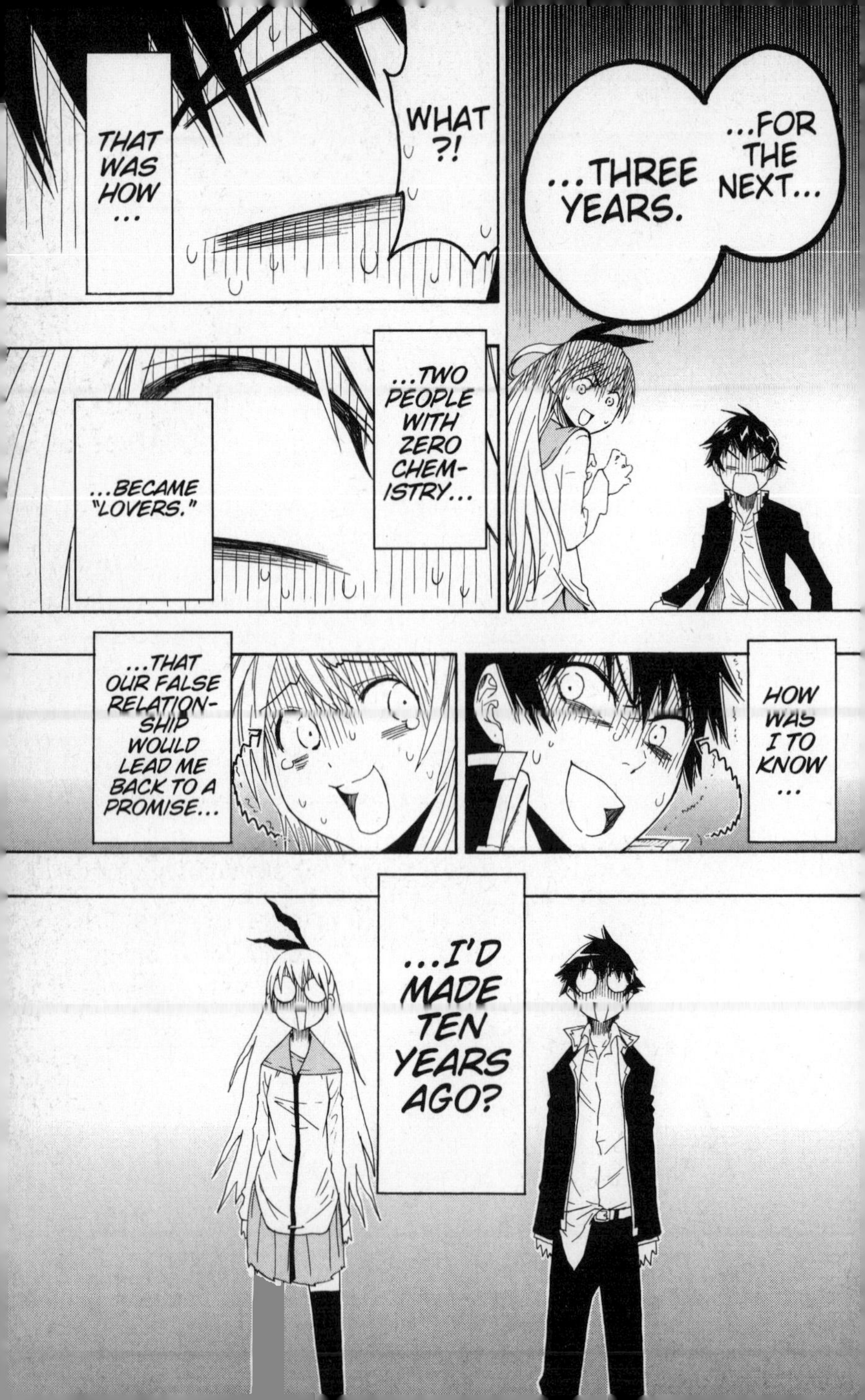
...FOR THE NEXT... ...THREE YEARS.
WHAT?!
THAT WAS HOW...
...TWO PEOPLE WITH ZERO CHEMISTRY...
...BECAME "LOVERS."
HOW WAS I TO KNOW...
...THAT OUR FALSE RELATIONSHIP WOULD LEAD ME BACK TO A PROMISE...
...I'D MADE TEN YEARS AGO?

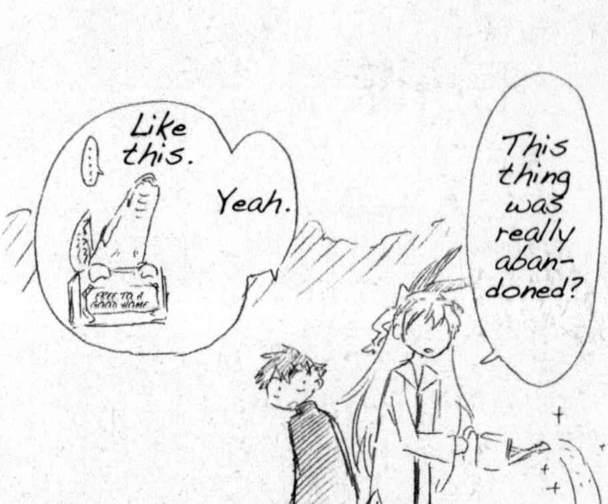
This thing was really aban-doned?
Like this.
FREE TO A GOOD HOME
Yeah.

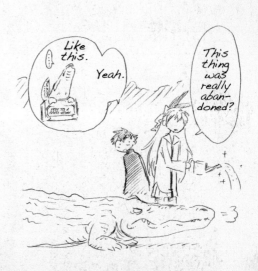

Chapter 2: Questions

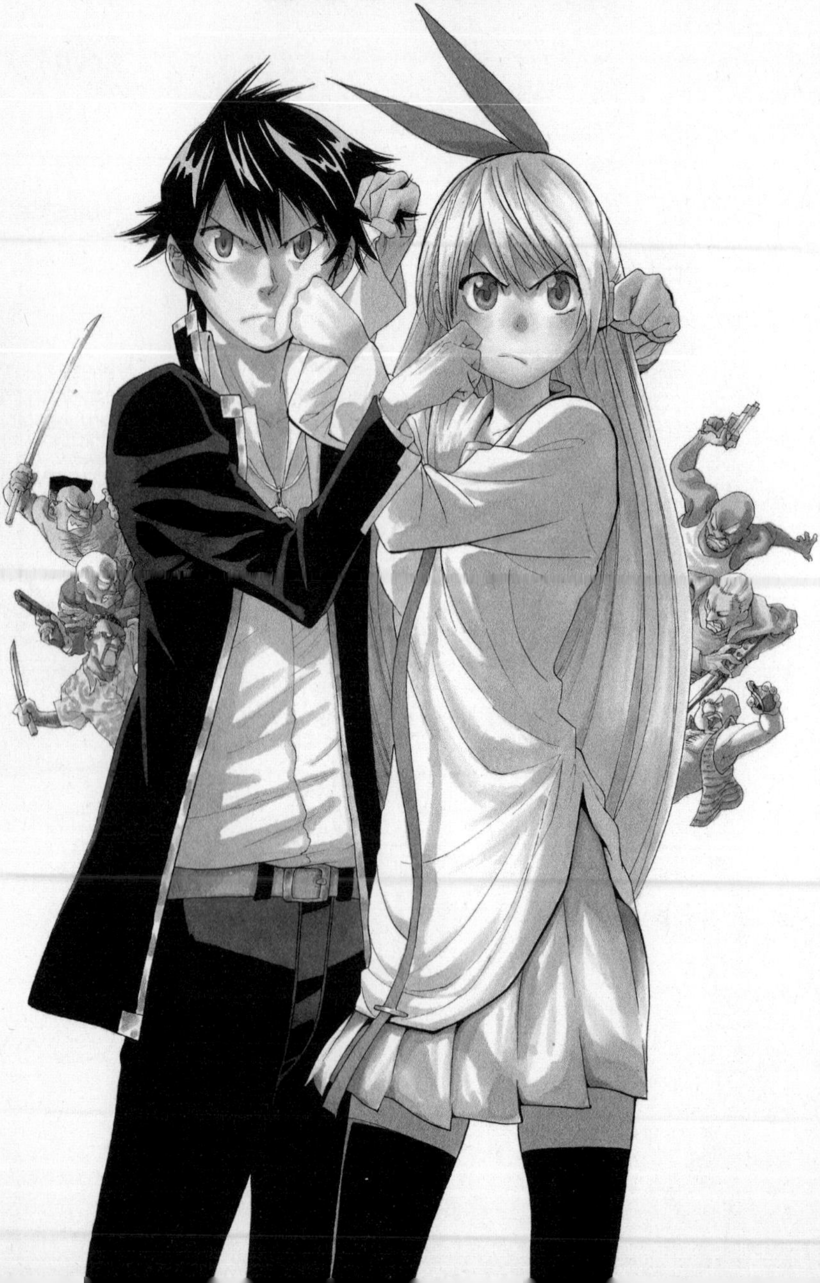

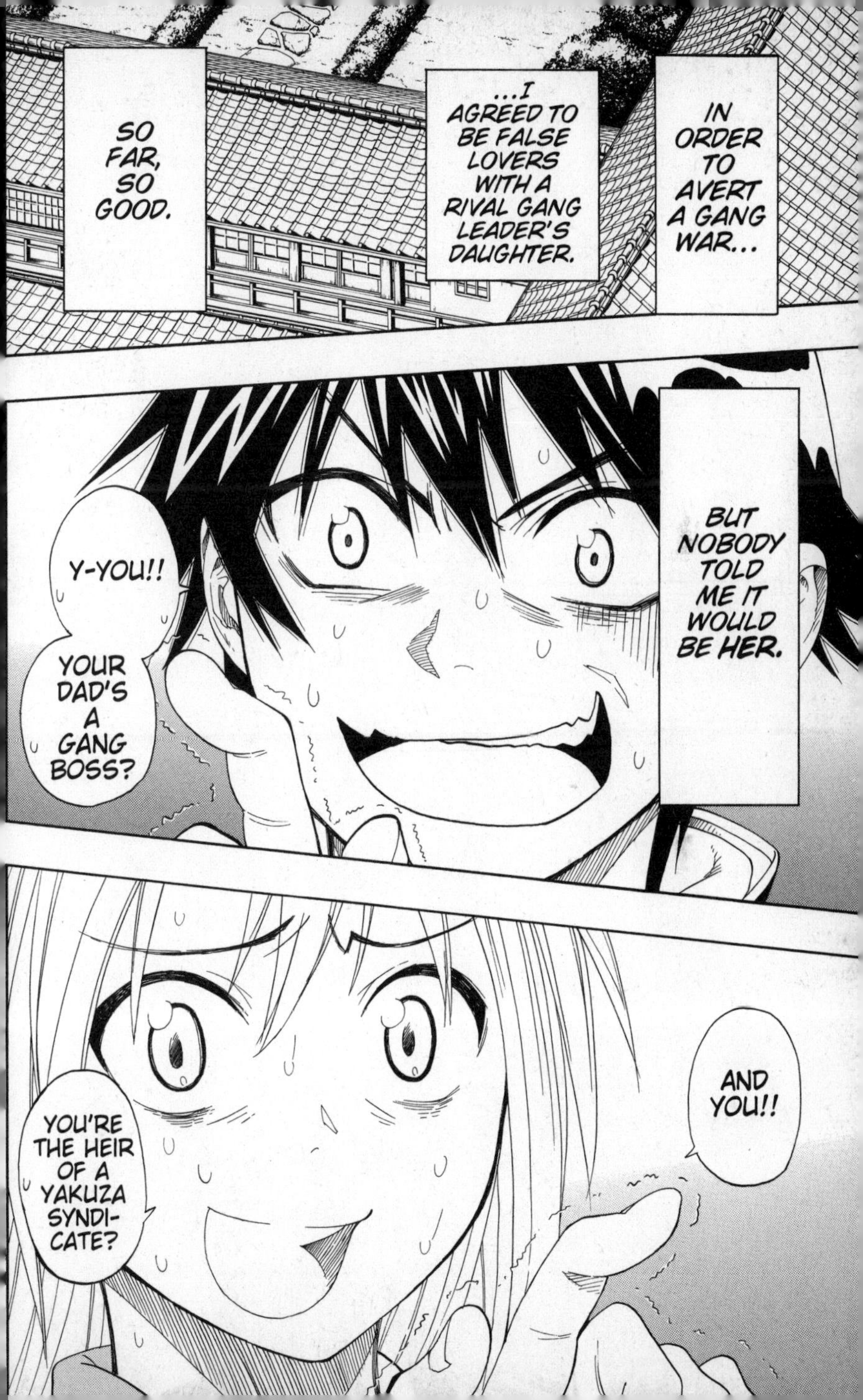
IN ORDER TO AVERT A GANG WAR...
...I AGREED TO BE FALSE LOVERS WITH A RIVAL GANG LEADER'S DAUGHTER.
SO FAR, SO GOOD.
BUT NOBODY TOLD ME IT WOULD BE HER.
Y-YOU!!
YOUR DAD'S A GANG BOSS?
AND YOU!!
YOU'RE THE HEIR OF A YAKUZA SYNDI-CATE?

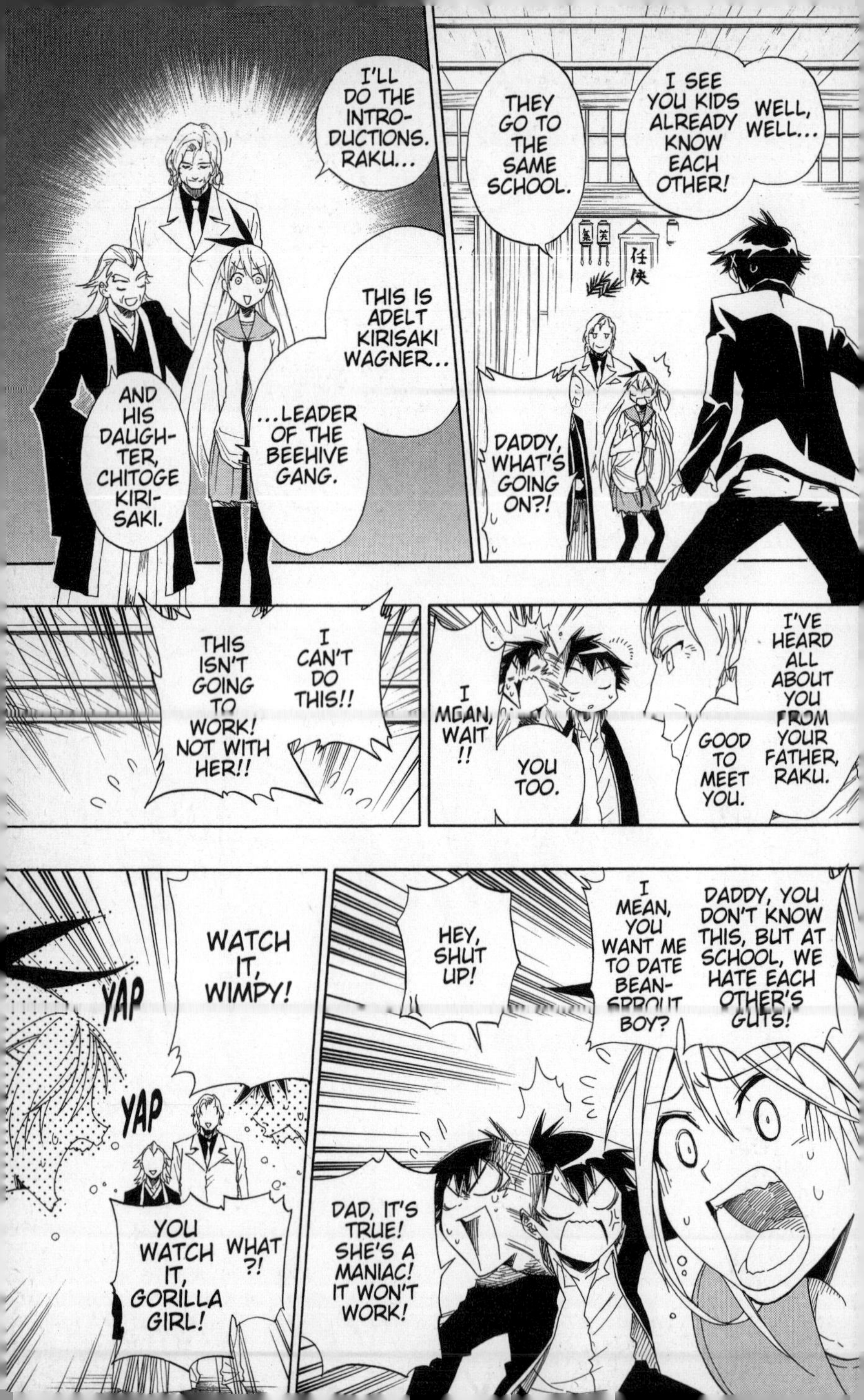
WELL, WELL...
I SEE YOU KIDS ALREADY KNOW EACH OTHER!
THEY GO TO THE SAME SCHOOL.
DADDY, WHAT'S GOING ON?!
I'LL DO THE INTRODUCTIONS. RAKU...
THIS IS ADELT KIRISAKI WAGNER...
...LEADER OF THE BEEHIVE GANG.
AND HIS DAUGHTER, CHITOGE KIRISAKI.
I'VE HEARD ALL ABOUT YOU FROM YOUR FATHER, RAKU.
GOOD TO MEET YOU.
YOU TOO.
I MEAN, WAIT!!
I CAN'T DO THIS!!
THIS ISN'T GOING TO WORK! NOT WITH HER!!
DADDY, YOU DON'T KNOW THIS, BUT AT SCHOOL, WE HATE EACH OTHER'S GUTS!
I MEAN, YOU WANT ME TO DATE BEAN-SPROUT BOY?
HEY, SHUT UP!
DAD, IT'S TRUE! SHE'S A MANIAC! IT WON'T WORK!
WATCH IT, WIMPY!
YAP
YAP
WHAT?!
YOU WATCH IT, GORILLA GIRL!

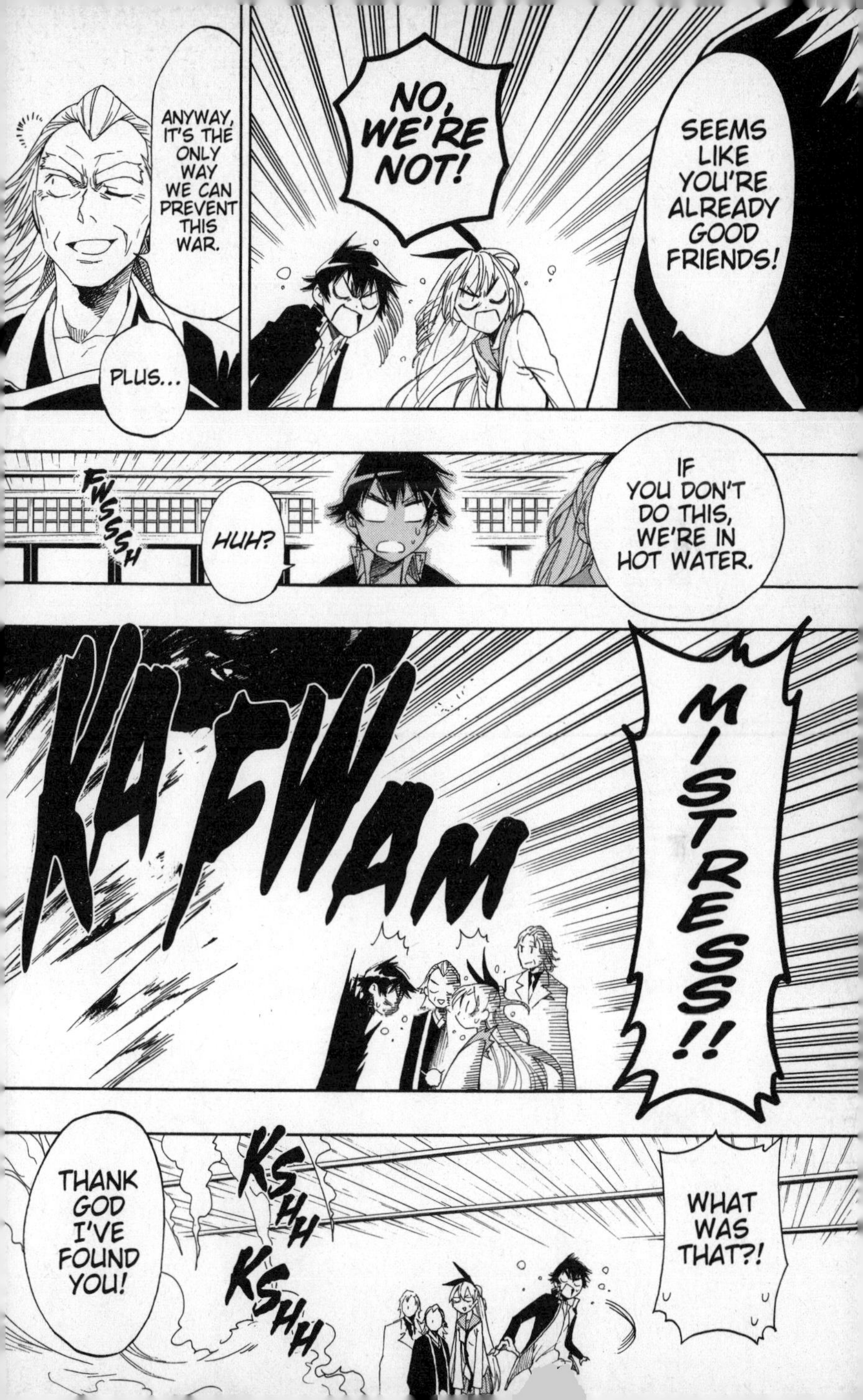
SEEMS LIKE YOU'RE ALREADY GOOD FRIENDS!
NO, WE'RE NOT!
ANYWAY, IT'S THE ONLY WAY WE CAN PREVENT THIS WAR.
PLUS...
IF YOU DON'T DO THIS, WE'RE IN HOT WATER.
HUH?
FWSSSH
MISTRESS!!
KAFWAM
WHAT WAS THAT?!
KSHH
KSHH
THANK GOD I'VE FOUND YOU!

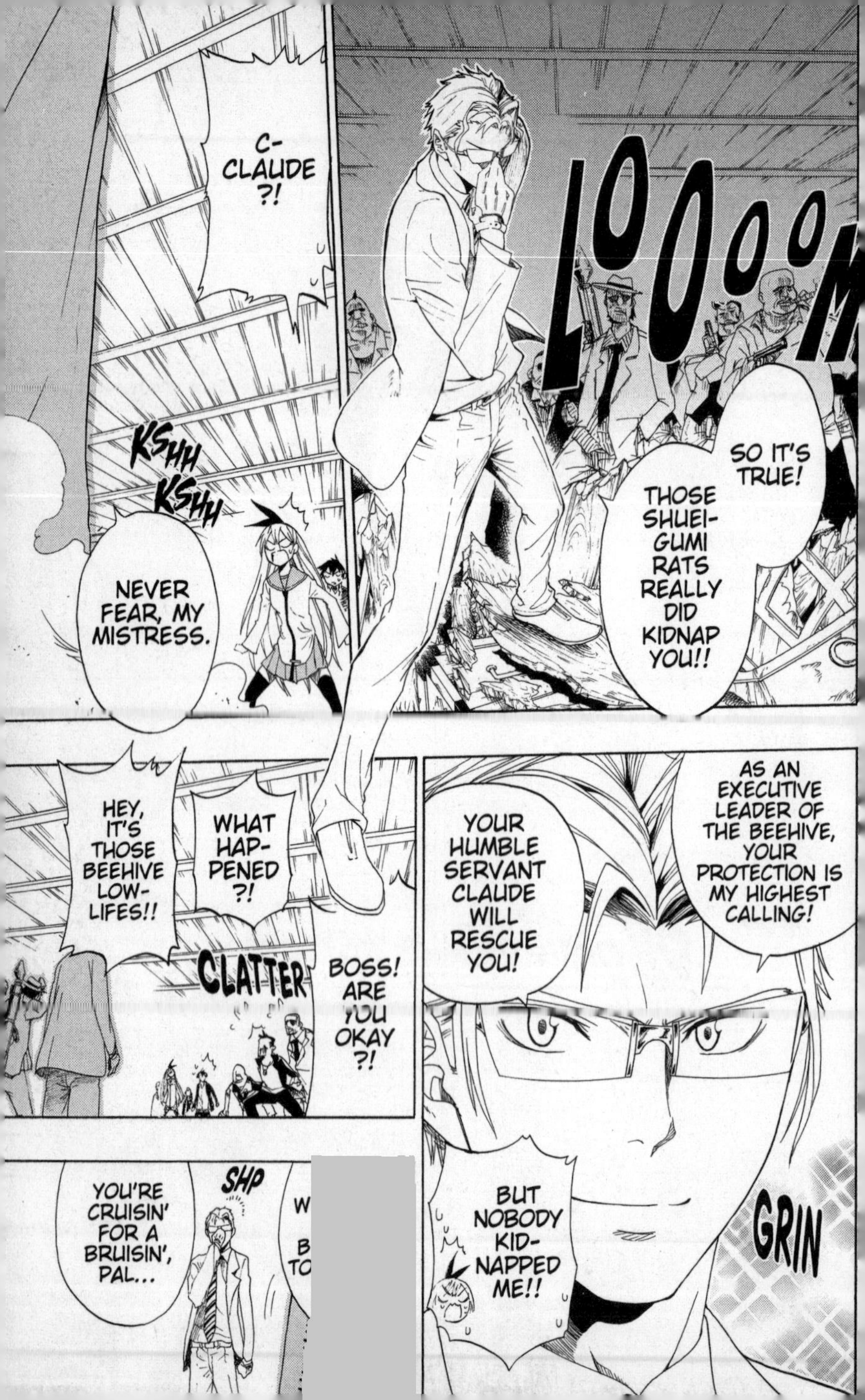
LOOOOM
SO IT'S TRUE!
THOSE SHUEI-GUMI RATS REALLY DID KIDNAP YOU!!
C-CLAUDE?!
KSHH KSHH
NEVER FEAR, MY MISTRESS.
AS AN EXECUTIVE LEADER OF THE BEEHIVE, YOUR PROTECTION IS MY HIGHEST CALLING!
YOUR HUMBLE SERVANT CLAUDE WILL RESCUE YOU!
WHAT HAP-PENED?!
HEY, IT'S THOSE BEEHIVE LOW-LIFES!!
BOSS! ARE YOU OKAY?!
CLATTER
GRIN
BUT NOBODY KID-NAPPED ME!!
SHP
YOU'RE CRUISIN' FOR A BRUISIN', PAL...

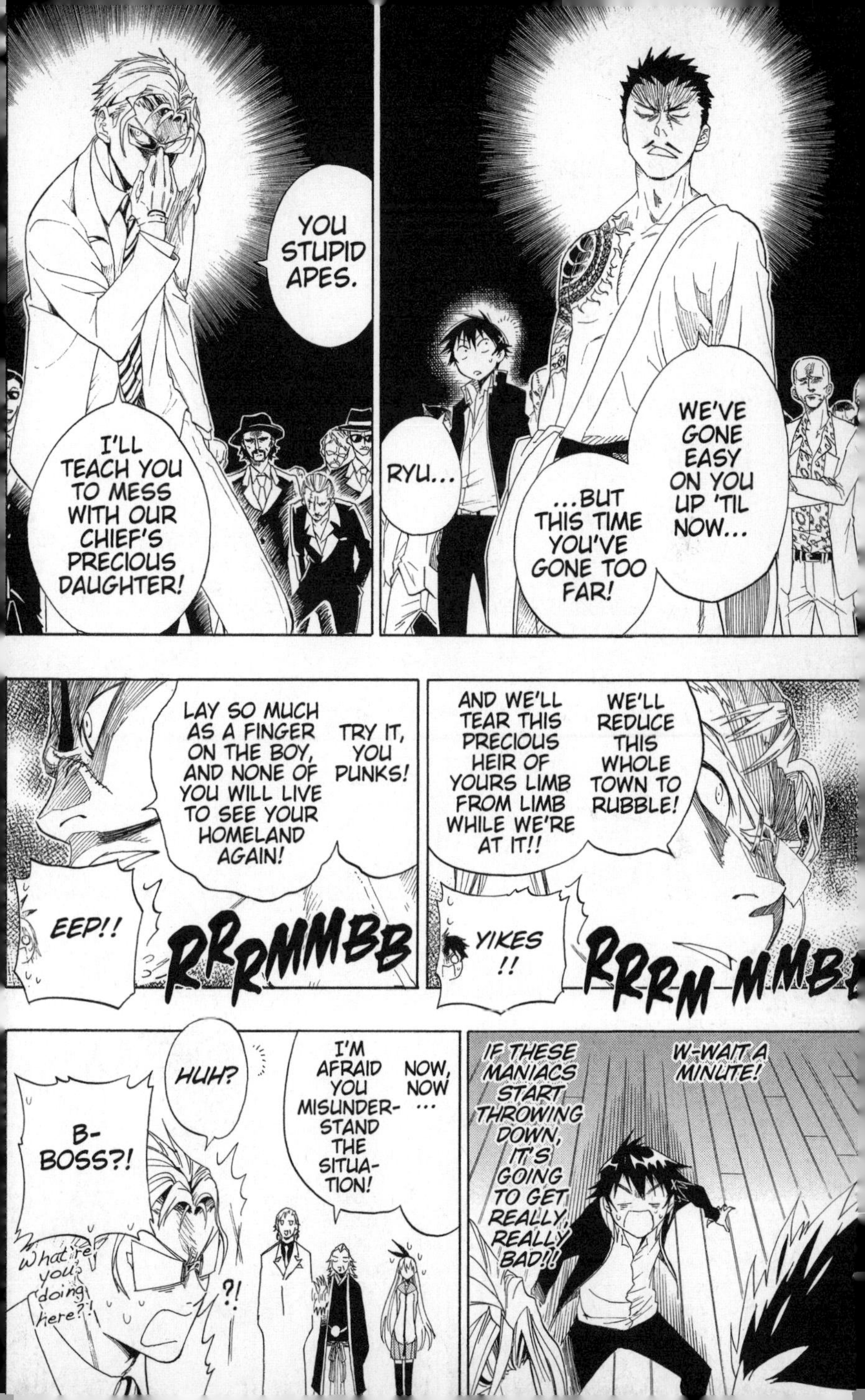
WE'VE GONE EASY ON YOU UP 'TIL NOW...
...BUT THIS TIME YOU'VE GONE TOO FAR!
RYU...
YOU STUPID APES.
I'LL TEACH YOU TO MESS WITH OUR CHIEF'S PRECIOUS DAUGHTER!
WE'LL REDUCE THIS WHOLE TOWN TO RUBBLE!
AND WE'LL TEAR THIS PRECIOUS HEIR OF YOURS LIMB FROM LIMB WHILE WE'RE AT IT!!
YIKES !!
RRRM MMB
TRY IT, YOU PUNKS!
LAY SO MUCH AS A FINGER ON THE BOY, AND NONE OF YOU WILL LIVE TO SEE YOUR HOMELAND AGAIN!
EEP!!
RRRMMBB
W-WAIT A MINUTE!
IF THESE MANIACS START THROWING DOWN, IT'S GOING TO GET REALLY, REALLY BAD!!
NOW, NOW...
I'M AFRAID YOU MISUNDERSTAND THE SITUATION!
HUH?
B-BOSS?!
What're you doing here?!
?!

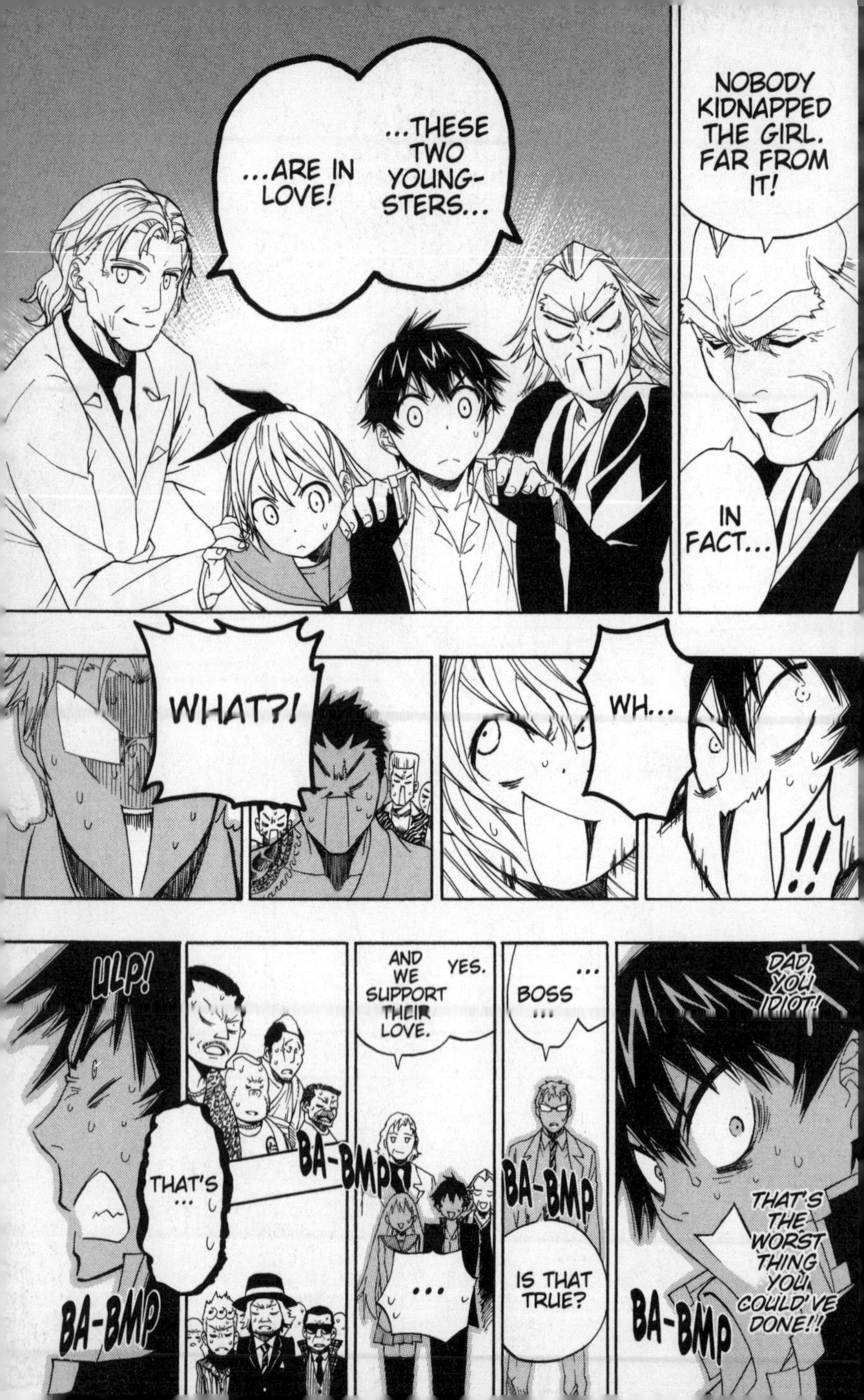
NOBODY KIDNAPPED THE GIRL. FAR FROM IT!
IN FACT...
...THESE TWO YOUNGSTERS...
...ARE IN LOVE!
WH...
!!
WHAT?!
DAD, YOU IDIOT!
THAT'S THE WORST THING YOU COULD'VE DONE!!
BA-BMP
...
BOSS...
IS THAT TRUE?
BA-BMP
YES.
AND WE SUPPORT THEIR LOVE.
...
BA-BMP
THAT'S...
ULP!
BA-BMP

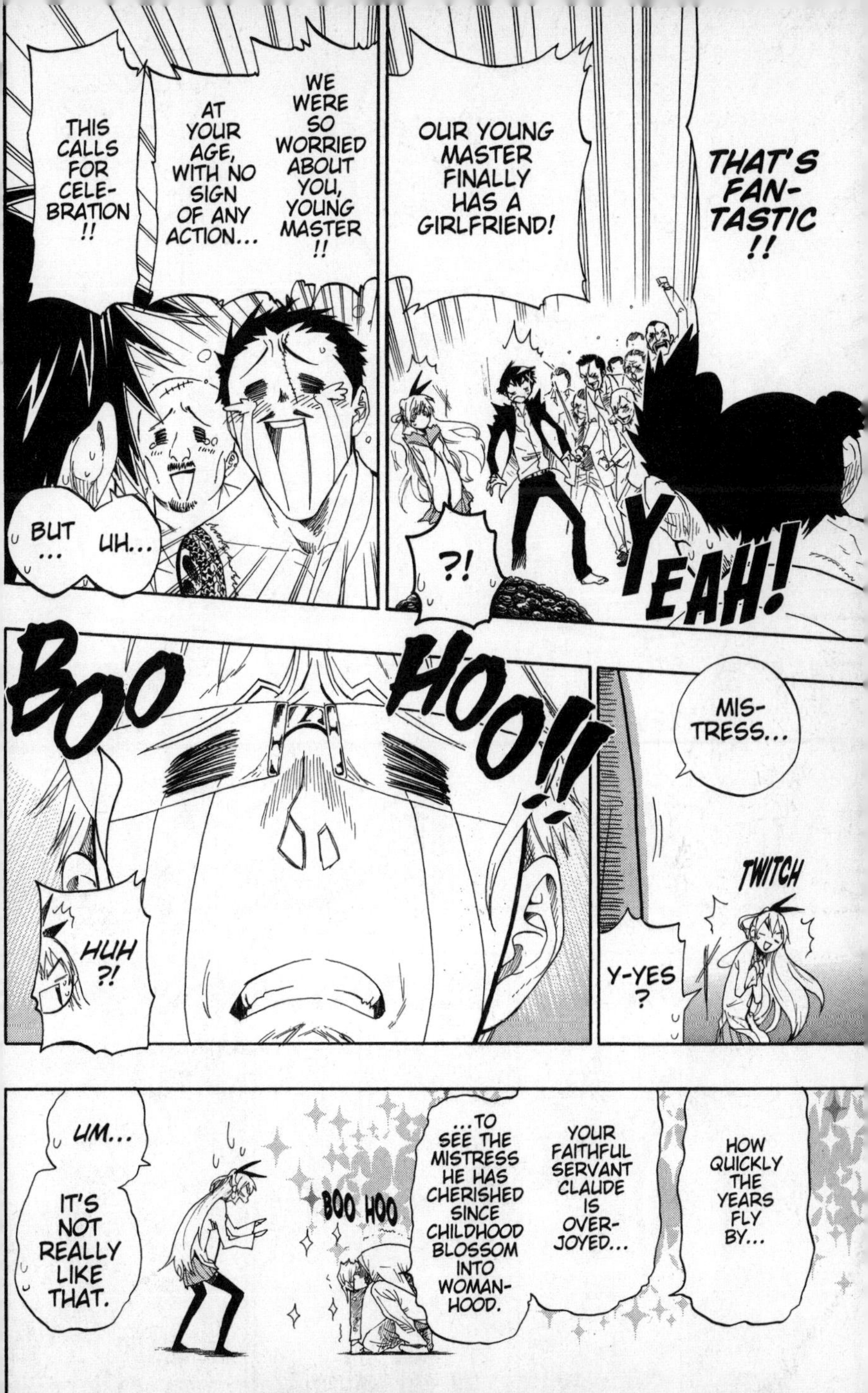
THAT'S FAN-TASTIC!!
OUR YOUNG MASTER FINALLY HAS A GIRLFRIEND!
YEAH!
?!
WE WERE SO WORRIED ABOUT YOU, YOUNG MASTER!!
AT YOUR AGE, WITH NO SIGN OF ANY ACTION...
THIS CALLS FOR CELE-BRATION!!
UH...
BUT...
MIS-TRESS...
TWITCH
Y-YES?
BOO HOO!!
HUH?!
HOW QUICKLY THE YEARS FLY BY...
YOUR FAITHFUL SERVANT CLAUDE IS OVER-JOYED...
...TO SEE THE MISTRESS HE HAS CHERISHED SINCE CHILDHOOD BLOSSOM INTO WOMAN-HOOD.
BOO HOO
UM...
IT'S NOT REALLY LIKE THAT.

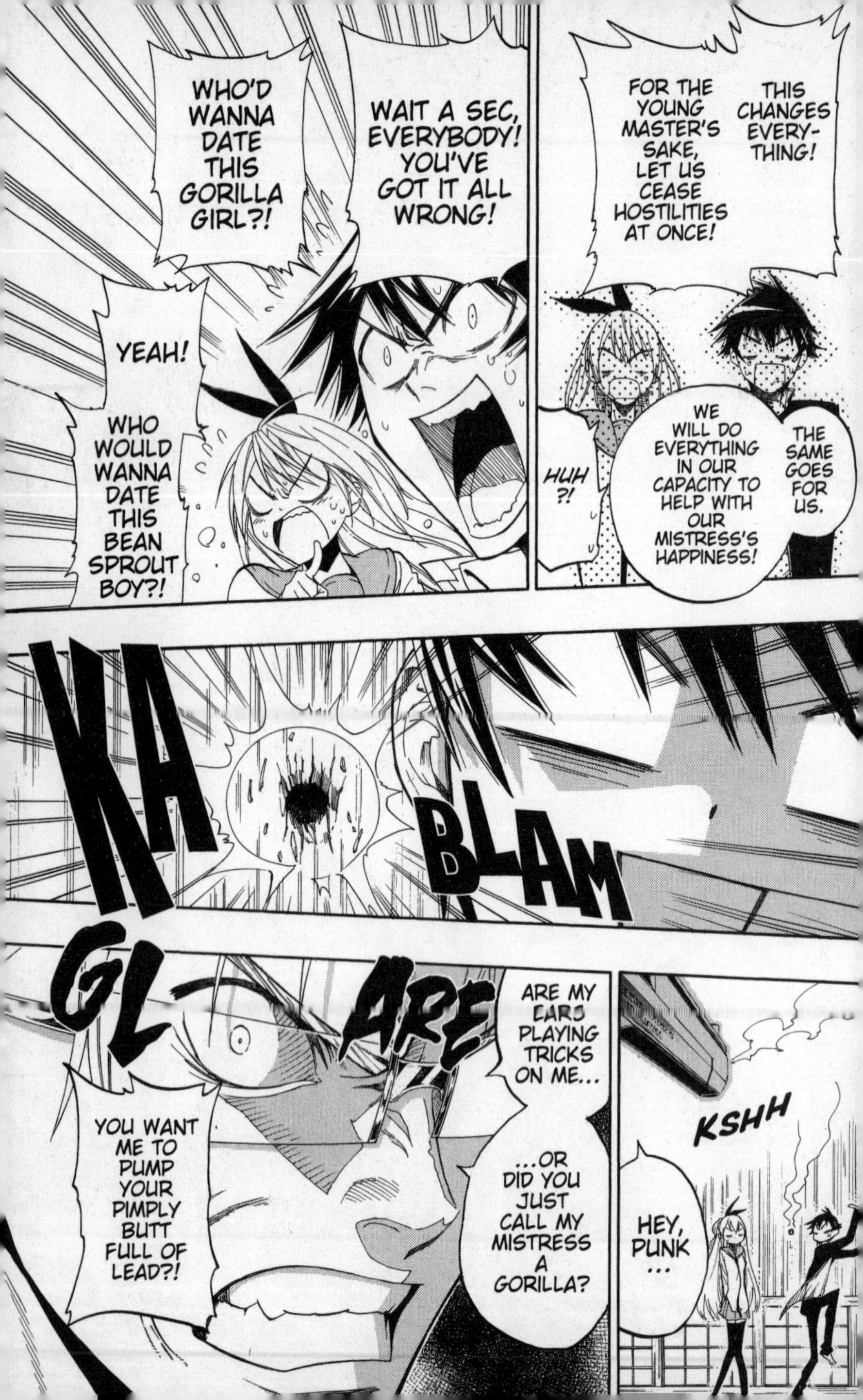
THIS CHANGES EVERY-THING!
FOR THE YOUNG MASTER'S SAKE, LET US CEASE HOSTILITIES AT ONCE!
THE SAME GOES FOR US.
WE WILL DO EVERYTHING IN OUR CAPACITY TO HELP WITH OUR MISTRESS'S HAPPINESS!
HUH?!
WAIT A SEC, EVERYBODY! YOU'VE GOT IT ALL WRONG!
WHO'D WANNA DATE THIS GORILLA GIRL?!
YEAH!
WHO WOULD WANNA DATE THIS BEAN SPROUT BOY?!
KA BLAM
KSHH
HEY, PUNK...
ARE MY EARS PLAYING TRICKS ON ME...
...OR DID YOU JUST CALL MY MISTRESS A GORILLA?
GLARE
YOU WANT ME TO PUMP YOUR PIMPLY BUTT FULL OF LEAD?!

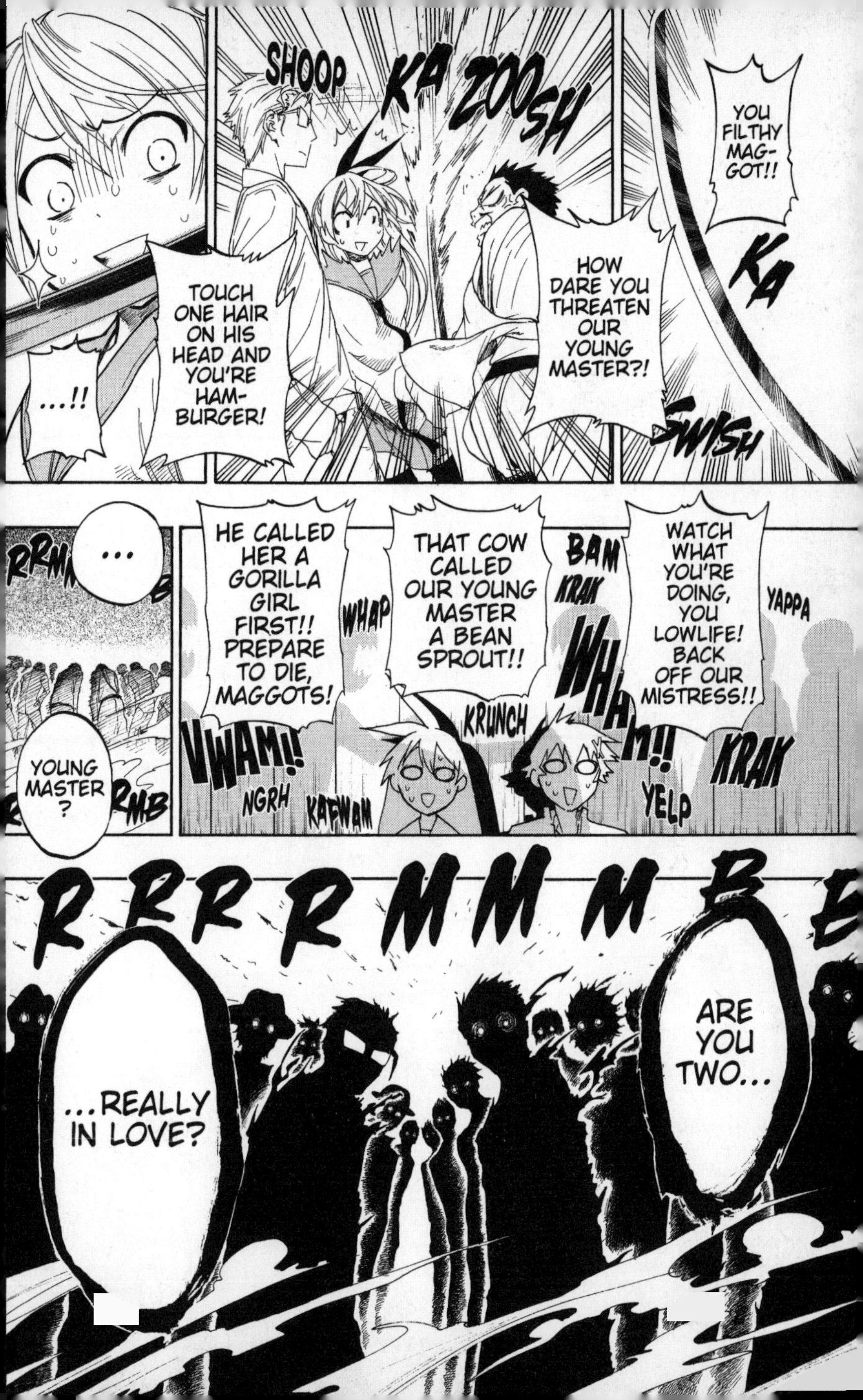
YOU FILTHY MAG-GOT!!
KA
SWISH
KA ZOOSH
SHOOP
HOW DARE YOU THREATEN OUR YOUNG MASTER?!
TOUCH ONE HAIR ON HIS HEAD AND YOU'RE HAM-BURGER!
...!!
WATCH WHAT YOU'RE DOING, YOU LOWLIFE! BACK OFF OUR MISTRESS!!
YAPPA
BAM
KRAK
THAT COW CALLED OUR YOUNG MASTER A BEAN SPROUT!!
WHAP
HE CALLED HER A GORILLA GIRL FIRST!! PREPARE TO DIE, MAGGOTS!
WHAM!!
KRAK
YELP
KRUNCH
VWAM!!
NGRH
KAPWAM
...
YOUNG MASTER?
RMB
RRRRMMMMB
ARE YOU TWO...
...REALLY IN LOVE?

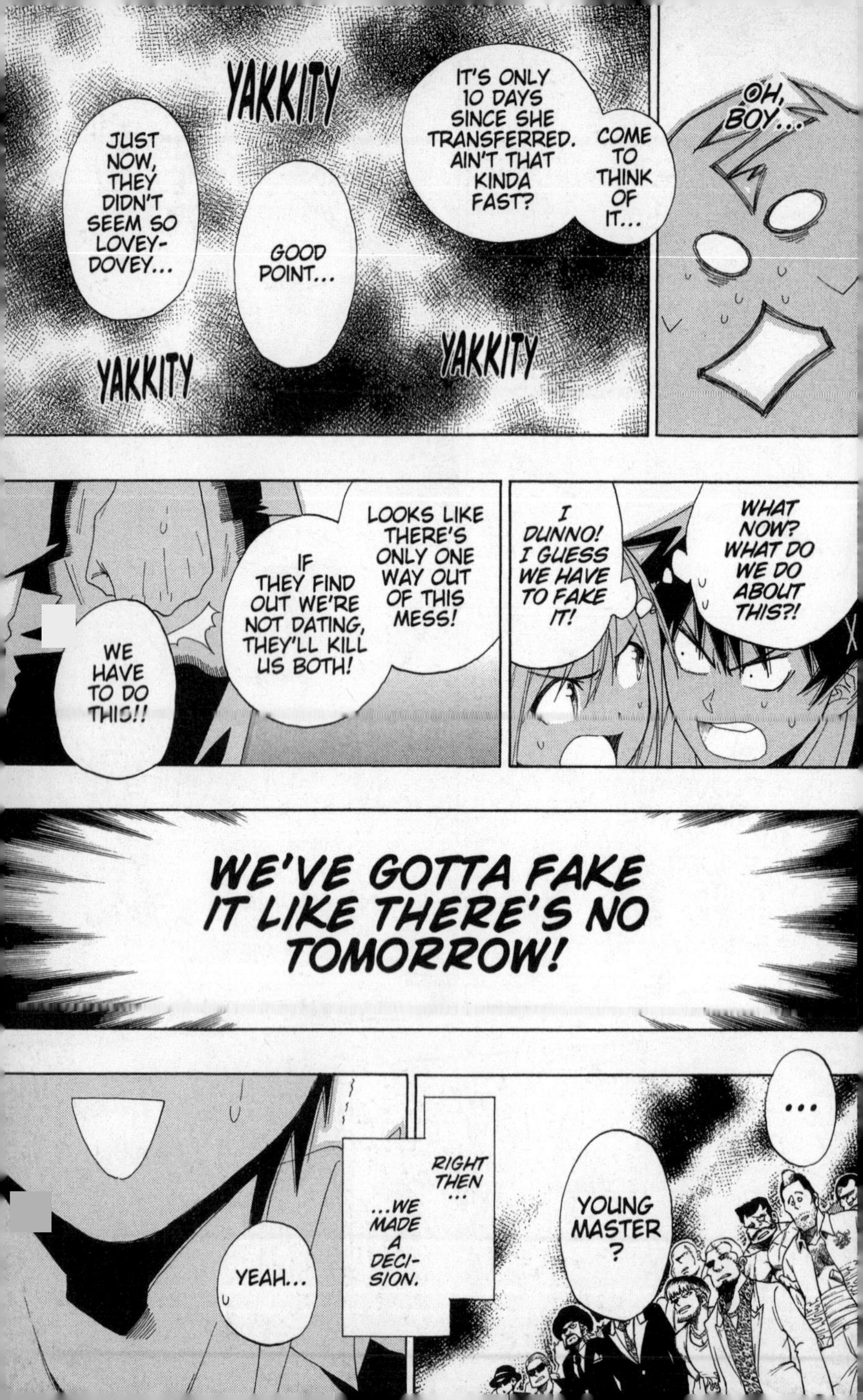
OH, BOY...
COME TO THINK OF IT...
IT'S ONLY 10 DAYS SINCE SHE TRANSFERRED. AIN'T THAT KINDA FAST?
YAKKITY
GOOD POINT...
JUST NOW, THEY DIDN'T SEEM SO LOVEY-DOVEY...
YAKKITY
YAKKITY
WHAT NOW? WHAT DO WE DO ABOUT THIS?!
I DUNNO! I GUESS WE HAVE TO FAKE IT!
LOOKS LIKE THERE'S ONLY ONE WAY OUT OF THIS MESS!
IF THEY FIND OUT WE'RE NOT DATING, THEY'LL KILL US BOTH!
WE HAVE TO DO THIS!!
WE'VE GOTTA FAKE IT LIKE THERE'S NO TOMORROW!
...
YOUNG MASTER?
RIGHT THEN...
...WE MADE A DECISION.
YEAH...

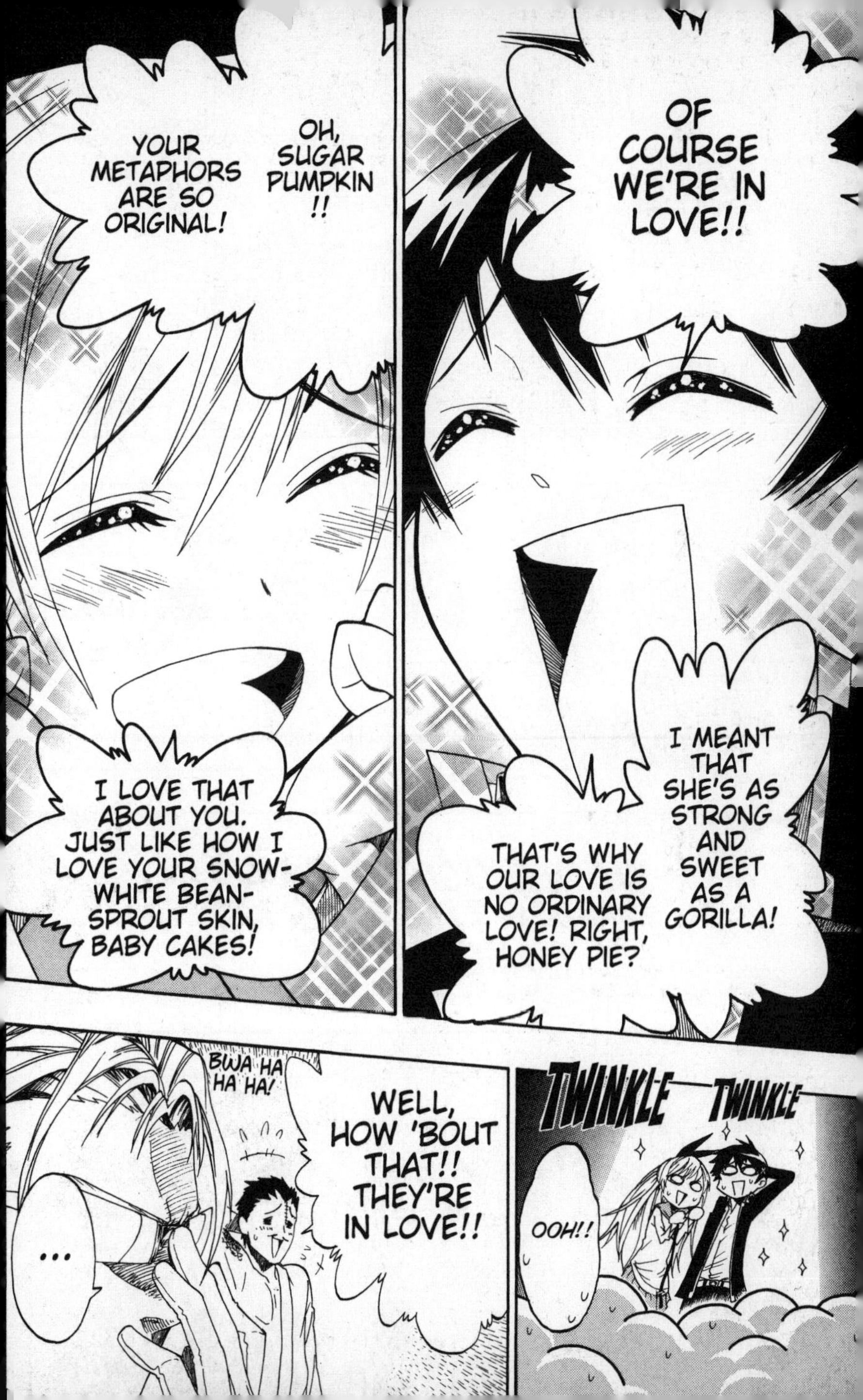
OF COURSE WE'RE IN LOVE!!
I MEANT THAT SHE'S AS STRONG AND SWEET AS A GORILLA!
THAT'S WHY OUR LOVE IS NO ORDINARY LOVE! RIGHT, HONEY PIE?
OH, SUGAR PUMPKIN!!
YOUR METAPHORS ARE SO ORIGINAL!
I LOVE THAT ABOUT YOU. JUST LIKE HOW I LOVE YOUR SNOW-WHITE BEAN-SPROUT SKIN, BABY CAKES!
TWINKLE TWINKLE
OOH!!
BWA HA HA HA!
WELL, HOW 'BOUT THAT!! THEY'RE IN LOVE!!
...

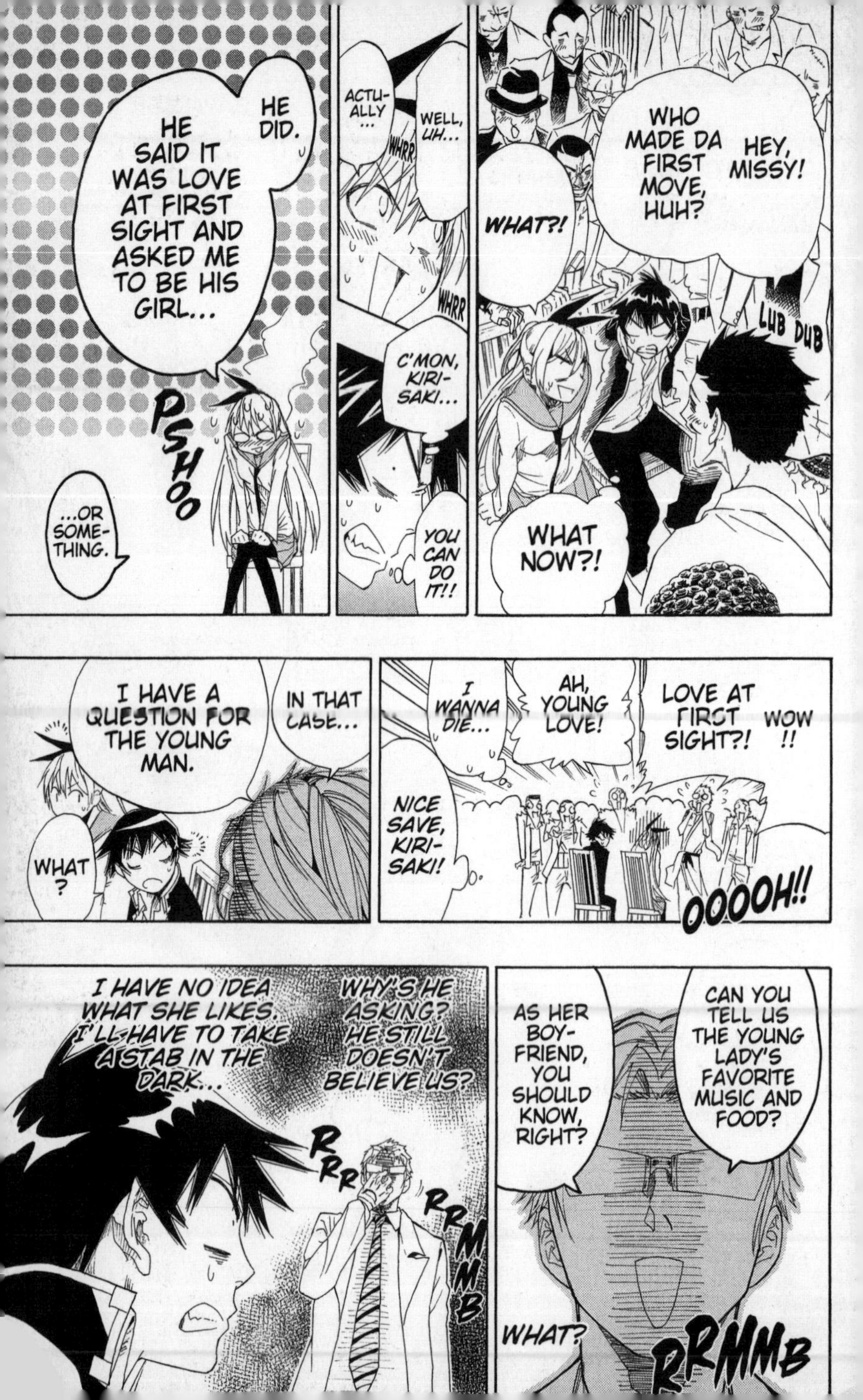
HEY, MISSY!
WHO MADE DA FIRST MOVE, HUH?
WHAT?!
LUB DUB
WHAT NOW?!
WELL, UH...
ACTU-ALLY...
WHRR
WHRR
C'MON, KIRI-SAKI...
YOU CAN DO IT!!
HE DID.
HE SAID IT WAS LOVE AT FIRST SIGHT AND ASKED ME TO BE HIS GIRL...
PSHOO
...OR SOME-THING.
WOW!!
LOVE AT FIRST SIGHT?!
AH, YOUNG LOVE!
I WANNA DIE...
NICE SAVE, KIRI-SAKI!
OOOOH!!
IN THAT CASE...
I HAVE A QUESTION FOR THE YOUNG MAN.
WHAT?
CAN YOU TELL US THE YOUNG LADY'S FAVORITE MUSIC AND FOOD?
AS HER BOY-FRIEND, YOU SHOULD KNOW, RIGHT?
WHAT?
RRMMB
WHY'S HE ASKING? HE STILL DOESN'T BELIEVE US?
RRR
RRMMB
I HAVE NO IDEA WHAT SHE LIKES. I'LL HAVE TO TAKE A STAB IN THE DARK...

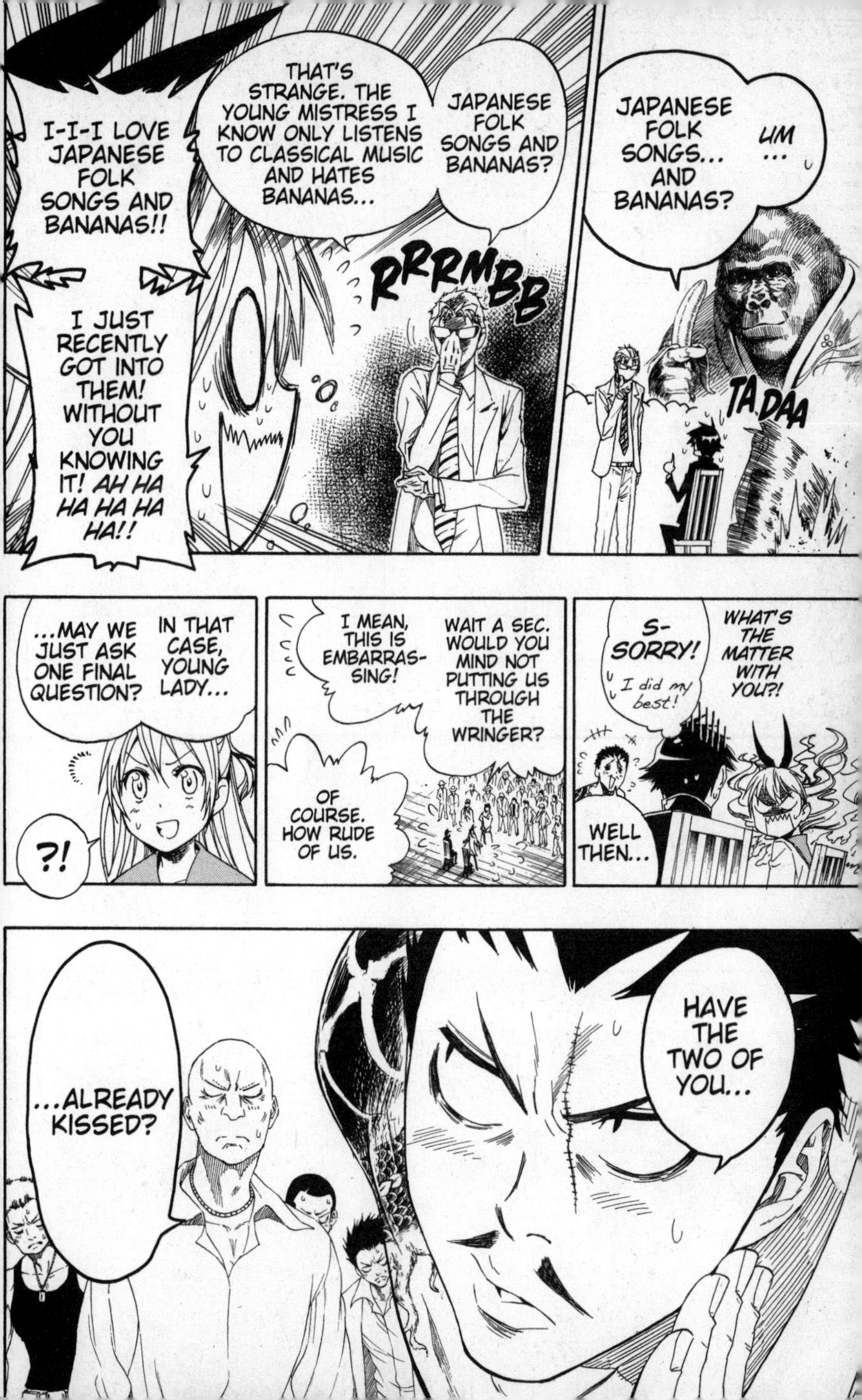
JAPANESE FOLK SONGS... AND BANANAS?
UM...
TA DAA
JAPANESE FOLK SONGS AND BANANAS?
THAT'S STRANGE. THE YOUNG MISTRESS I KNOW ONLY LISTENS TO CLASSICAL MUSIC AND HATES BANANAS...
RRRMBB
I-I-I LOVE JAPANESE FOLK SONGS AND BANANAS!!
I JUST RECENTLY GOT INTO THEM! WITHOUT YOU KNOWING IT! AH HA HA HA HA HA!!
WHAT'S THE MATTER WITH YOU?!
S-SORRY!
I did my best!
WELL THEN...
WAIT A SEC. WOULD YOU MIND NOT PUTTING US THROUGH THE WRINGER?
I MEAN, THIS IS EMBARRASSING!
OF COURSE. HOW RUDE OF US.
IN THAT CASE, YOUNG LADY...
...MAY WE JUST ASK ONE FINAL QUESTION?
?!
HAVE THE TWO OF YOU...
...ALREADY KISSED?

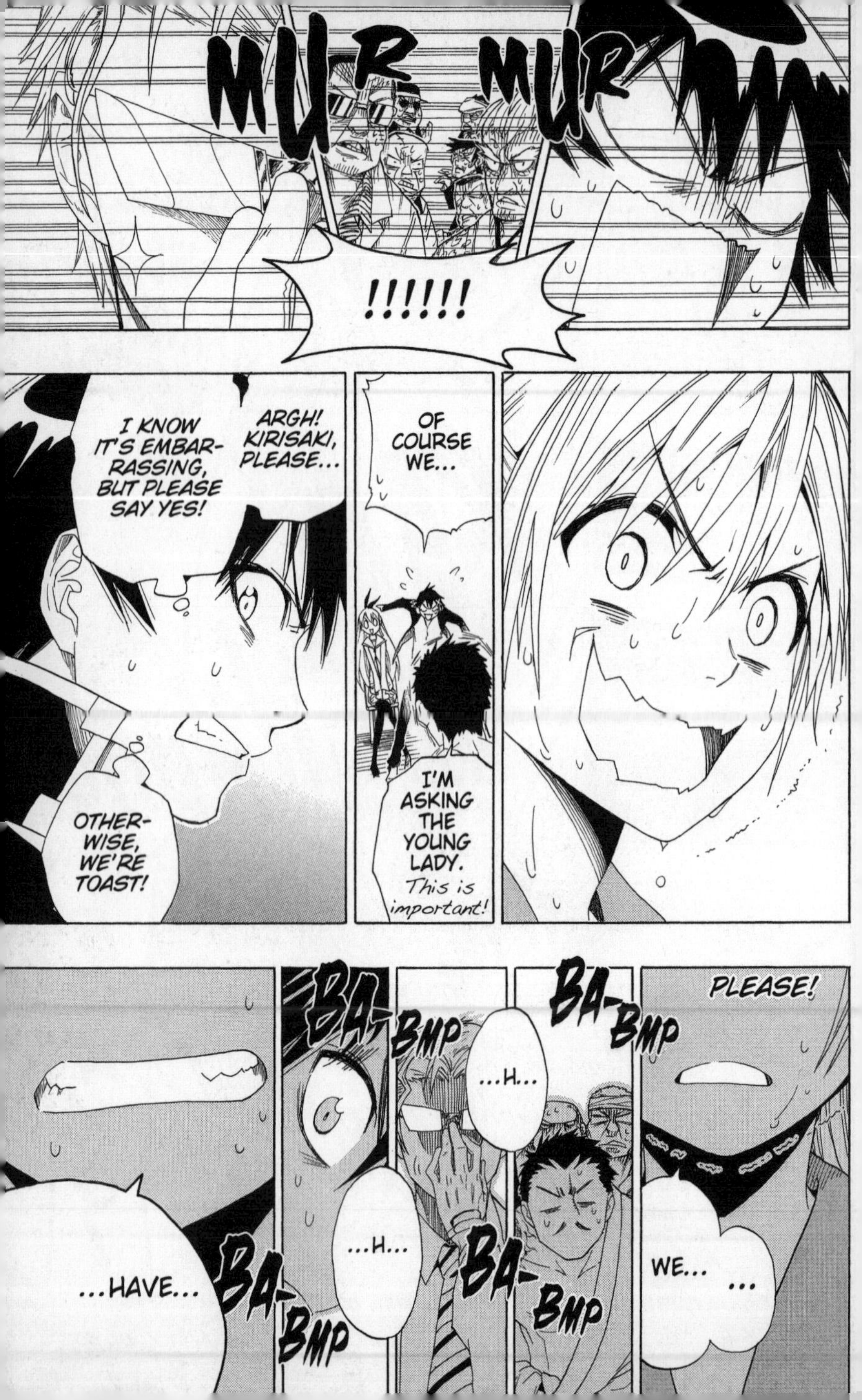
MUR MUR
!!!!!!
OF COURSE WE...
I'M ASKING THE YOUNG LADY. This is important!
ARGH! KIRISAKI, PLEASE...
I KNOW IT'S EMBARRASSING, BUT PLEASE SAY YES!
OTHERWISE, WE'RE TOAST!
PLEASE!
WE... ...
BA-BMP
...H...
BA-BMP
...H...
BA-BMP
BA-BMP
...HAVE...
BA-BMP

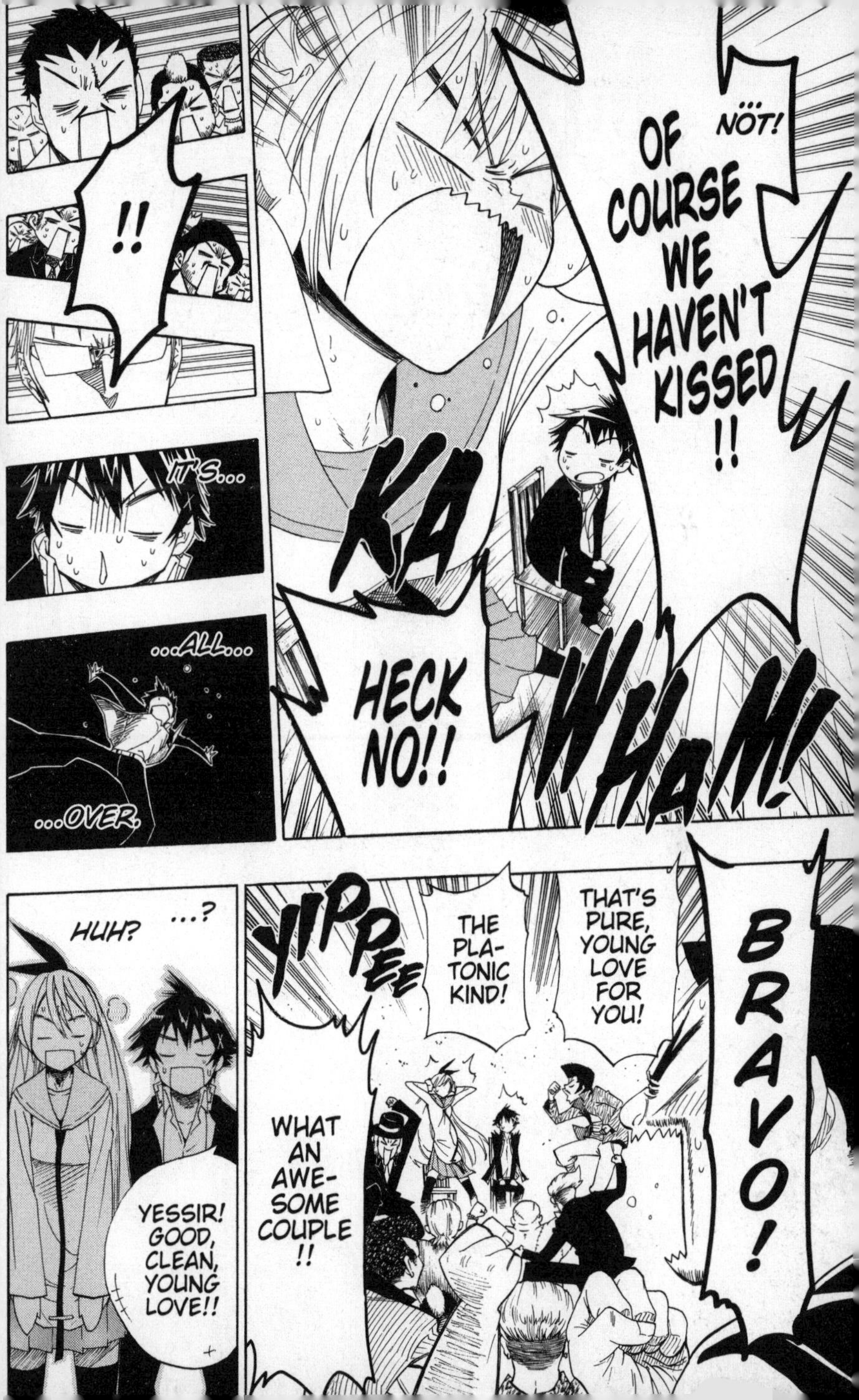

OF COURSE WE HAVEN'T KISSED!!
...NOT!
KA
HECK NO!!
WHAM!
!!
IT'S...
...ALL...
...OVER.
BRAVO!
THAT'S PURE, YOUNG LOVE FOR YOU!
THE PLA-TONIC KIND!
YIPPEE
WHAT AN AWE-SOME COUPLE!!
YESSIR! GOOD, CLEAN, YOUNG LOVE!!
...?
HUH?

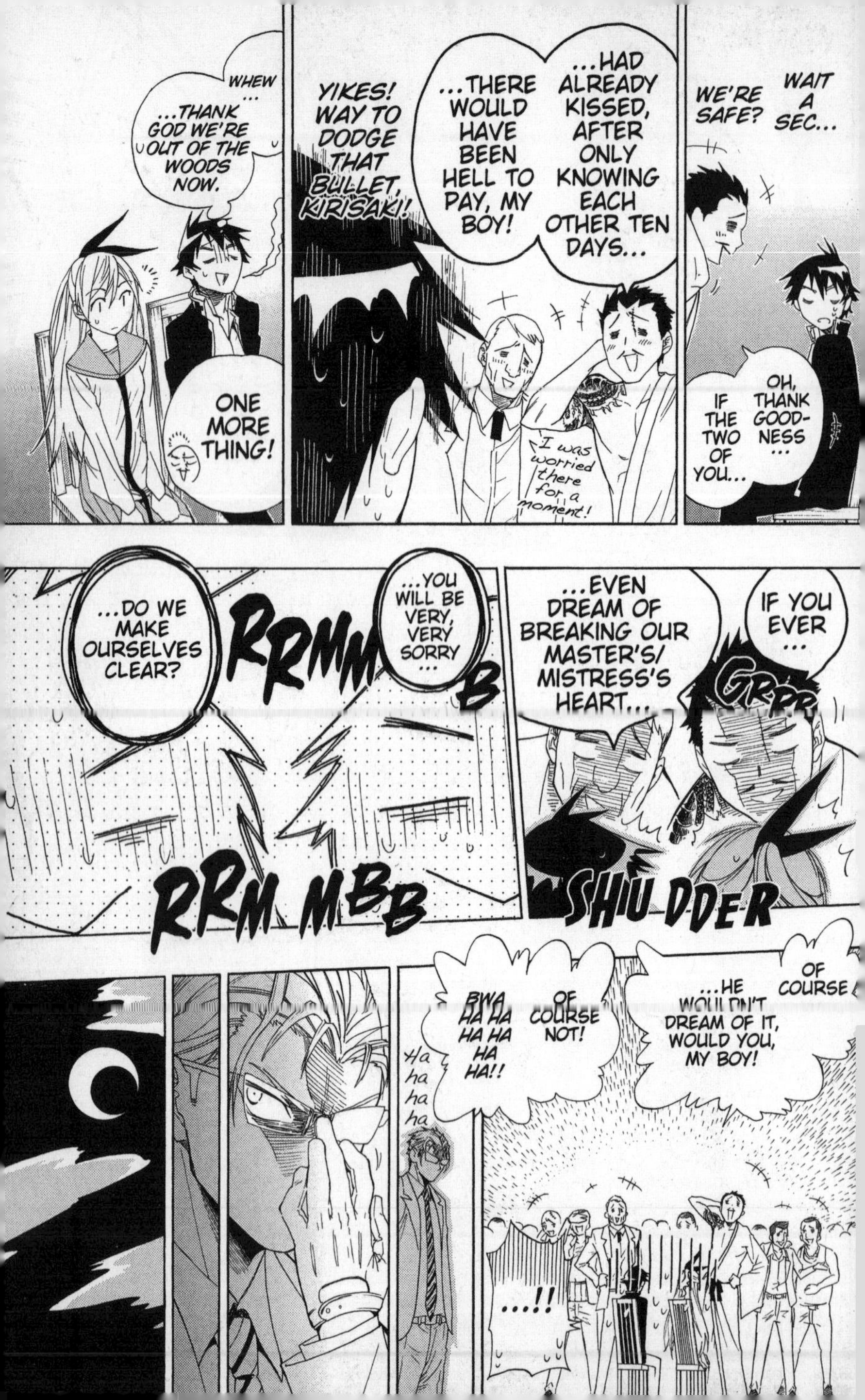
WAIT A SEC...
WE'RE SAFE?
OH, THANK GOODNESS...
IF THE TWO OF YOU...
...HAD ALREADY KISSED, AFTER ONLY KNOWING EACH OTHER TEN DAYS...
...THERE WOULD HAVE BEEN HELL TO PAY, MY BOY!
YIKES! WAY TO DODGE THAT BULLET, KIRISAKI!
I was worried there for a moment!
WHEW... ...THANK GOD WE'RE OUT OF THE WOODS NOW.
ONE MORE THING!
IF YOU EVER...
...EVEN DREAM OF BREAKING OUR MASTER'S/MISTRESS'S HEART...
GRRR
SHIUDDER
...YOU WILL BE VERY, VERY SORRY...
RRMMB
...DO WE MAKE OURSELVES CLEAR?
RRMMBB
OF COURSE
...HE WOULDN'T DREAM OF IT, WOULD YOU, MY BOY!
OF COURSE NOT!
BWA HA HA HA HA HA HA!!
...!!
Ha ha ha ha

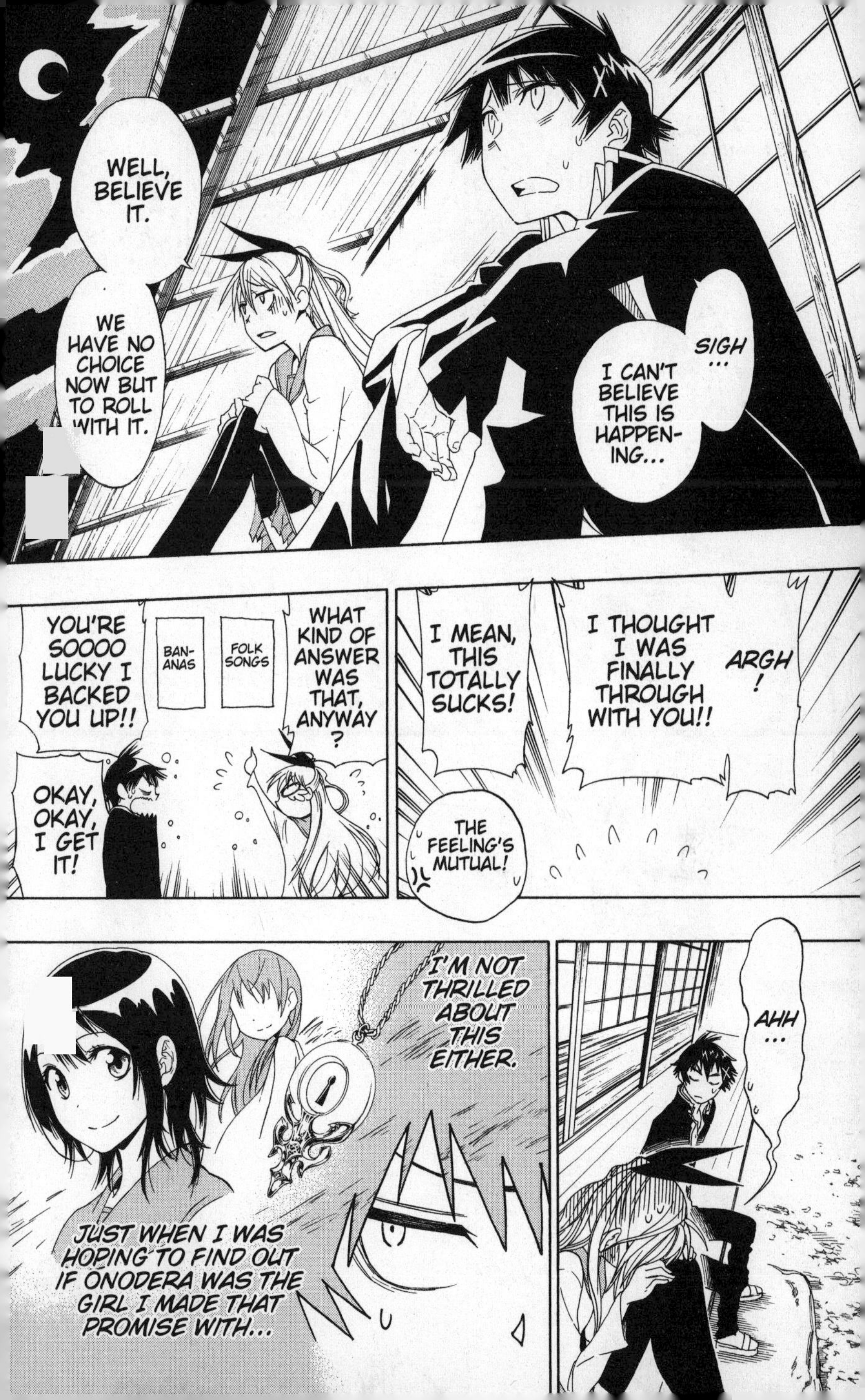
SIGH...
I CAN'T BELIEVE THIS IS HAPPENING...
WELL, BELIEVE IT.
WE HAVE NO CHOICE NOW BUT TO ROLL WITH IT.
ARGH!
I THOUGHT I WAS FINALLY THROUGH WITH YOU!!
I MEAN, THIS TOTALLY SUCKS!
THE FEELING'S MUTUAL!
WHAT KIND OF ANSWER WAS THAT, ANYWAY?
FOLK SONGS
BANANAS
YOU'RE SOOOO LUCKY I BACKED YOU UP!!
OKAY, OKAY, I GET IT!
AHH...
I'M NOT THRILLED ABOUT THIS EITHER.
JUST WHEN I WAS HOPING TO FIND OUT IF ONODERA WAS THE GIRL I MADE THAT PROMISE WITH...

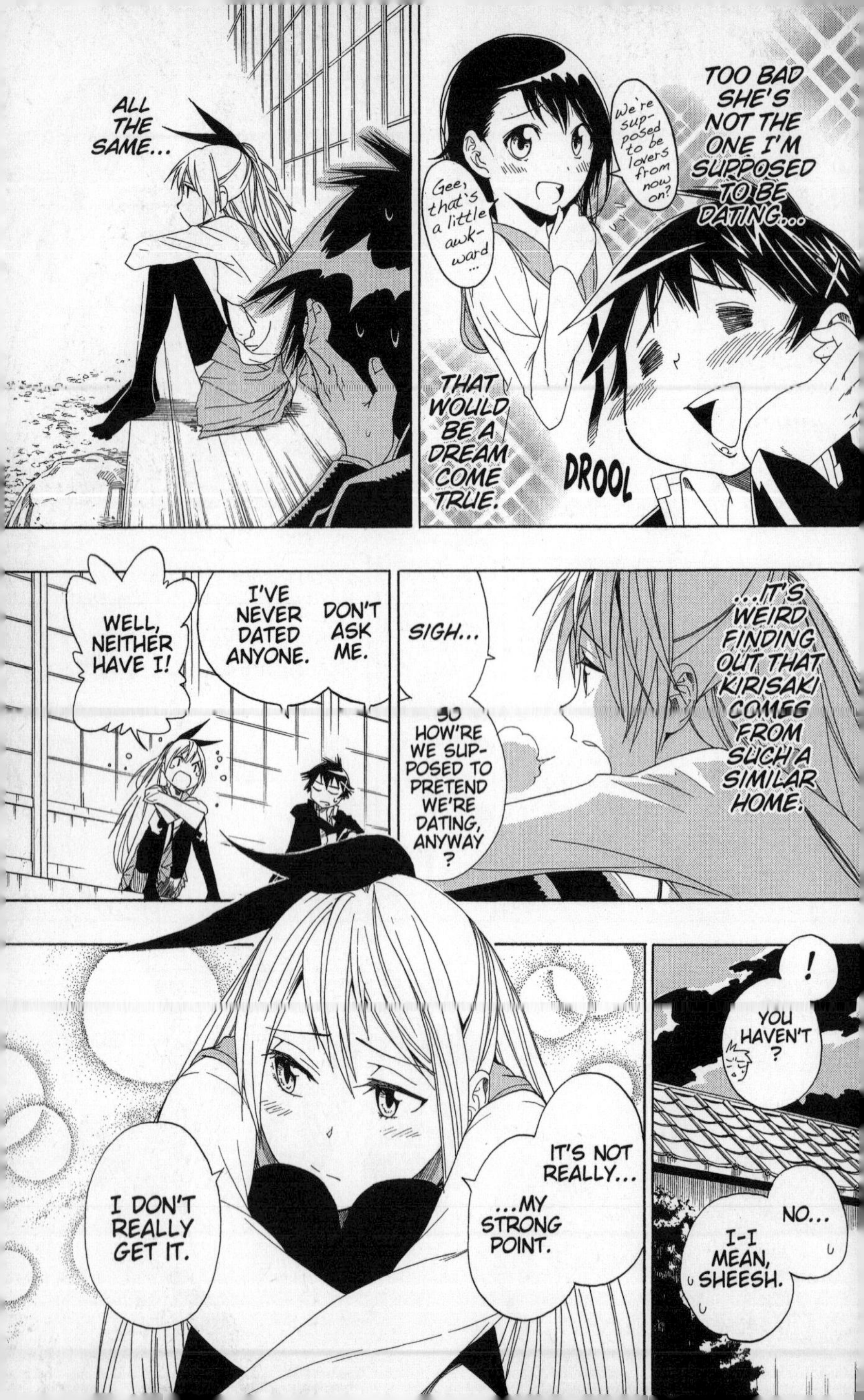
TOO BAD SHE'S NOT THE ONE I'M SUPPOSED TO BE DATING...
We're supposed to be lovers from now on?
Gee, that's a little awkward...
THAT WOULD BE A DREAM COME TRUE.
DROOL
ALL THE SAME...
...IT'S WEIRD FINDING OUT THAT KIRISAKI COMES FROM SUCH A SIMILAR HOME.
SIGH...
SO HOW'RE WE SUPPOSED TO PRETEND WE'RE DATING, ANYWAY?
DON'T ASK ME.
I'VE NEVER DATED ANYONE.
WELL, NEITHER HAVE I!
!
YOU HAVEN'T?
NO...
I-I MEAN, SHEESH.
IT'S NOT REALLY...
...MY STRONG POINT.
I DON'T REALLY GET IT.

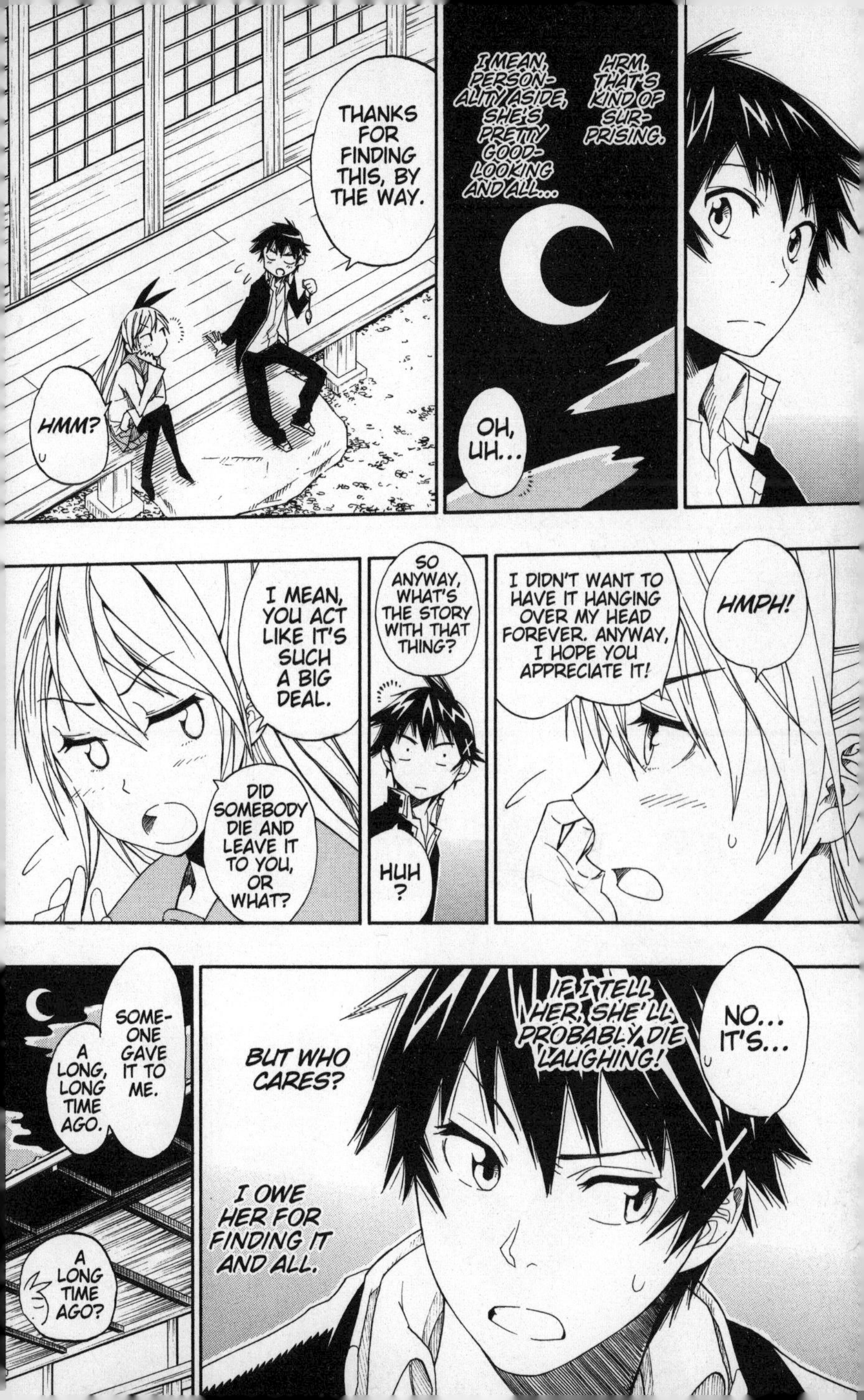
HRM. THAT'S KIND OF SURPRISING.
I MEAN, PERSONALITY ASIDE, SHE'S PRETTY GOOD-LOOKING AND ALL...
OH, UH...
THANKS FOR FINDING THIS, BY THE WAY.
HMM?
HMPH!
I DIDN'T WANT TO HAVE IT HANGING OVER MY HEAD FOREVER. ANYWAY, I HOPE YOU APPRECIATE IT!
SO ANYWAY, WHAT'S THE STORY WITH THAT THING?
HUH?
I MEAN, YOU ACT LIKE IT'S SUCH A BIG DEAL.
DID SOMEBODY DIE AND LEAVE IT TO YOU, OR WHAT?
NO... IT'S...
IF I TELL HER, SHE'LL PROBABLY DIE LAUGHING!
BUT WHO CARES?
I OWE HER FOR FINDING IT AND ALL.
SOME-ONE GAVE IT TO ME.
A LONG, LONG TIME AGO.
A LONG TIME AGO?

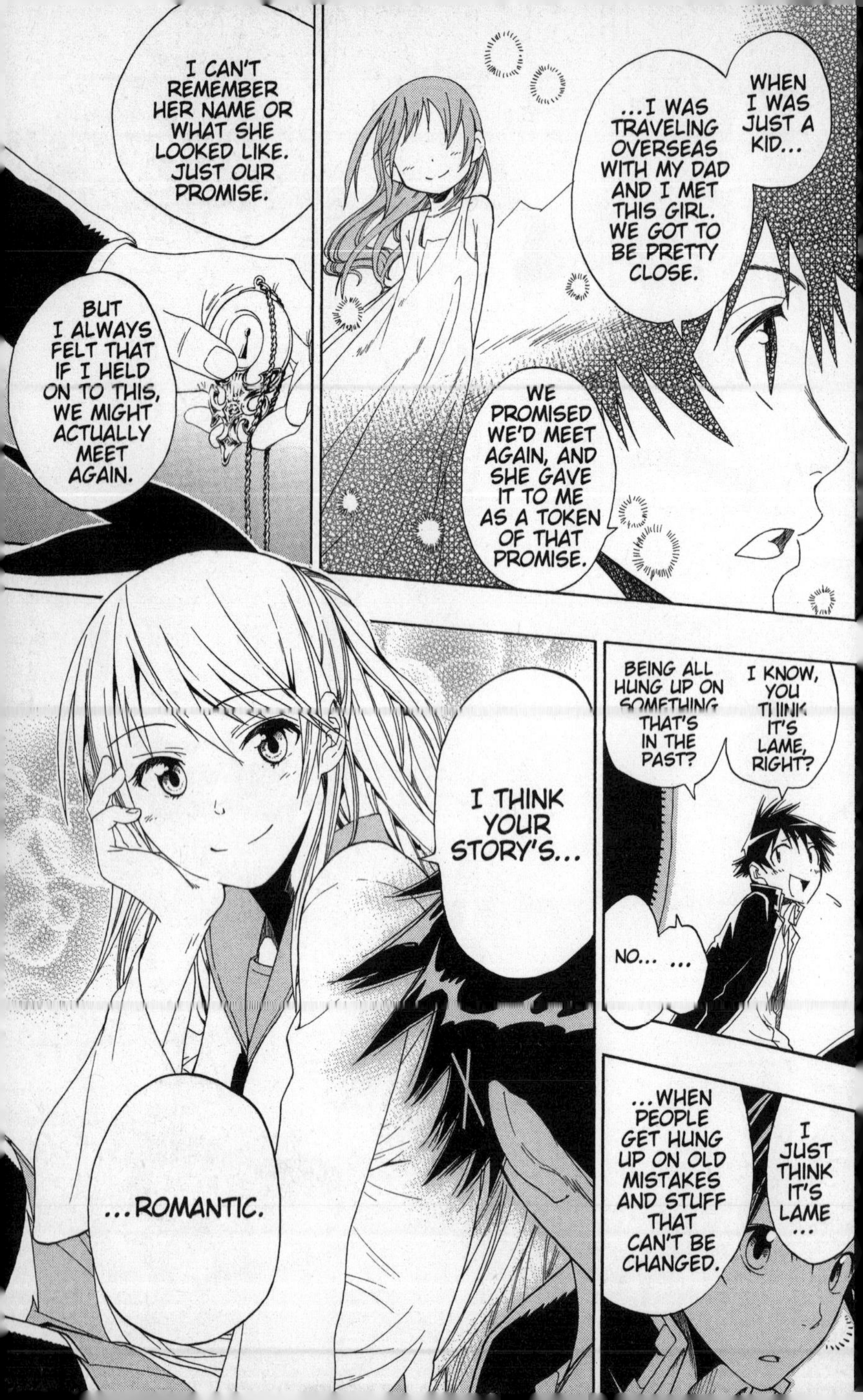
WHEN I WAS JUST A KID...
...I WAS TRAVELING OVERSEAS WITH MY DAD AND I MET THIS GIRL. WE GOT TO BE PRETTY CLOSE.
WE PROMISED WE'D MEET AGAIN, AND SHE GAVE IT TO ME AS A TOKEN OF THAT PROMISE.
I CAN'T REMEMBER HER NAME OR WHAT SHE LOOKED LIKE. JUST OUR PROMISE.
BUT I ALWAYS FELT THAT IF I HELD ON TO THIS, WE MIGHT ACTUALLY MEET AGAIN.
I KNOW, YOU THINK IT'S LAME, RIGHT?
BEING ALL HUNG UP ON SOMETHING THAT'S IN THE PAST?
NO... ...
I JUST THINK IT'S LAME...
...WHEN PEOPLE GET HUNG UP ON OLD MISTAKES AND STUFF THAT CAN'T BE CHANGED.
I THINK YOUR STORY'S...
...ROMANTIC.

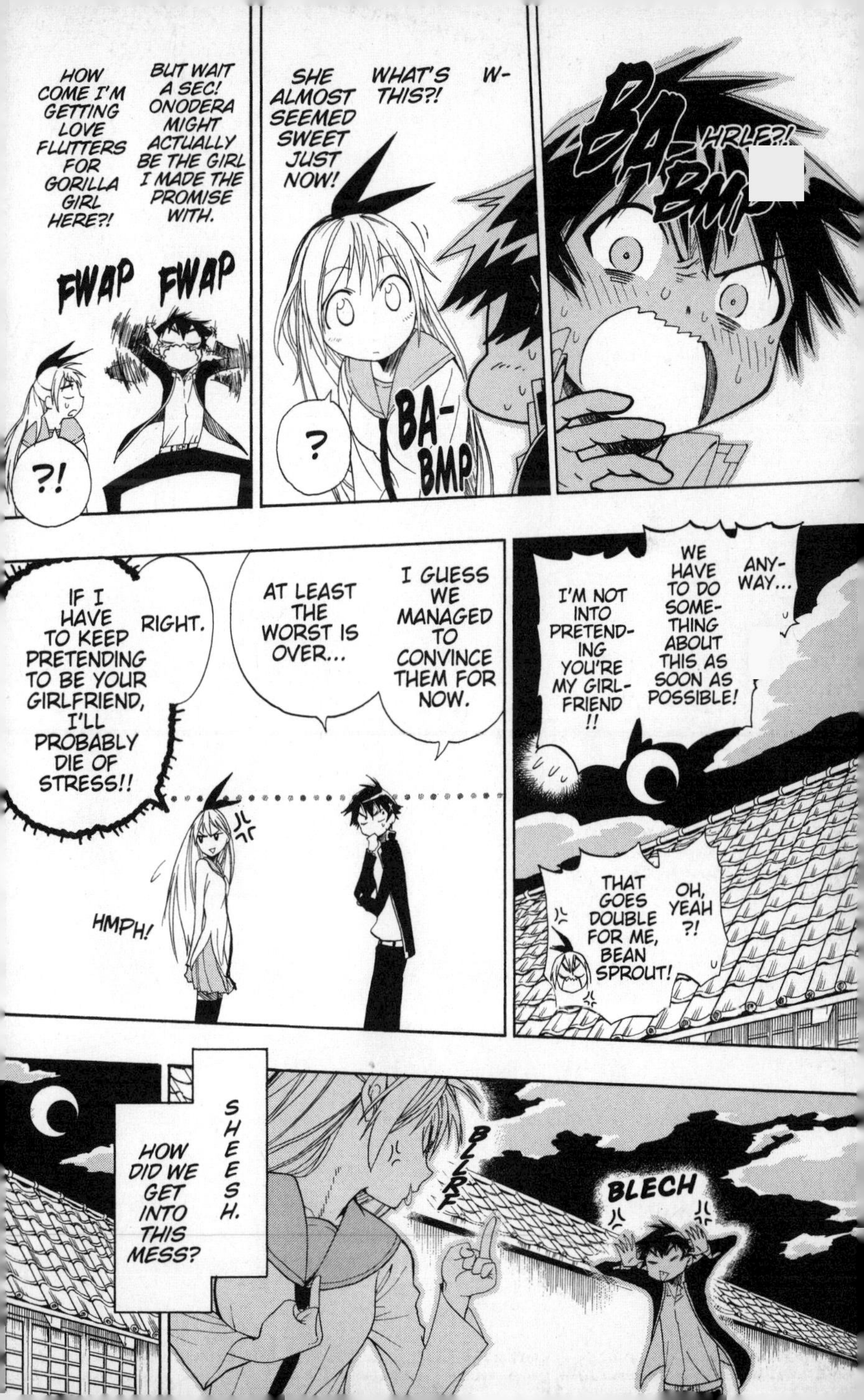
W-
BA-BMP
HRLF?!
WHAT'S THIS?!
SHE ALMOST SEEMED SWEET JUST NOW!
?
BA-BMP
BUT WAIT A SEC! ONODERA MIGHT ACTUALLY BE THE GIRL I MADE THE PROMISE WITH.
HOW COME I'M GETTING LOVE FLUTTERS FOR GORILLA GIRL HERE?!
FWAP FWAP
?!
ANY-WAY...
WE HAVE TO DO SOME-THING ABOUT THIS AS SOON AS POSSIBLE!
I'M NOT INTO PRETEND-ING YOU'RE MY GIRL-FRIEND!!
OH, YEAH?!
THAT GOES DOUBLE FOR ME, BEAN SPROUT!
I GUESS WE MANAGED TO CONVINCE THEM FOR NOW.
AT LEAST THE WORST IS OVER...
RIGHT.
IF I HAVE TO KEEP PRETENDING TO BE YOUR GIRLFRIEND, I'LL PROBABLY DIE OF STRESS!!
HMPH!
SHEESH.
HOW DID WE GET INTO THIS MESS?
BLLRF
BLECH

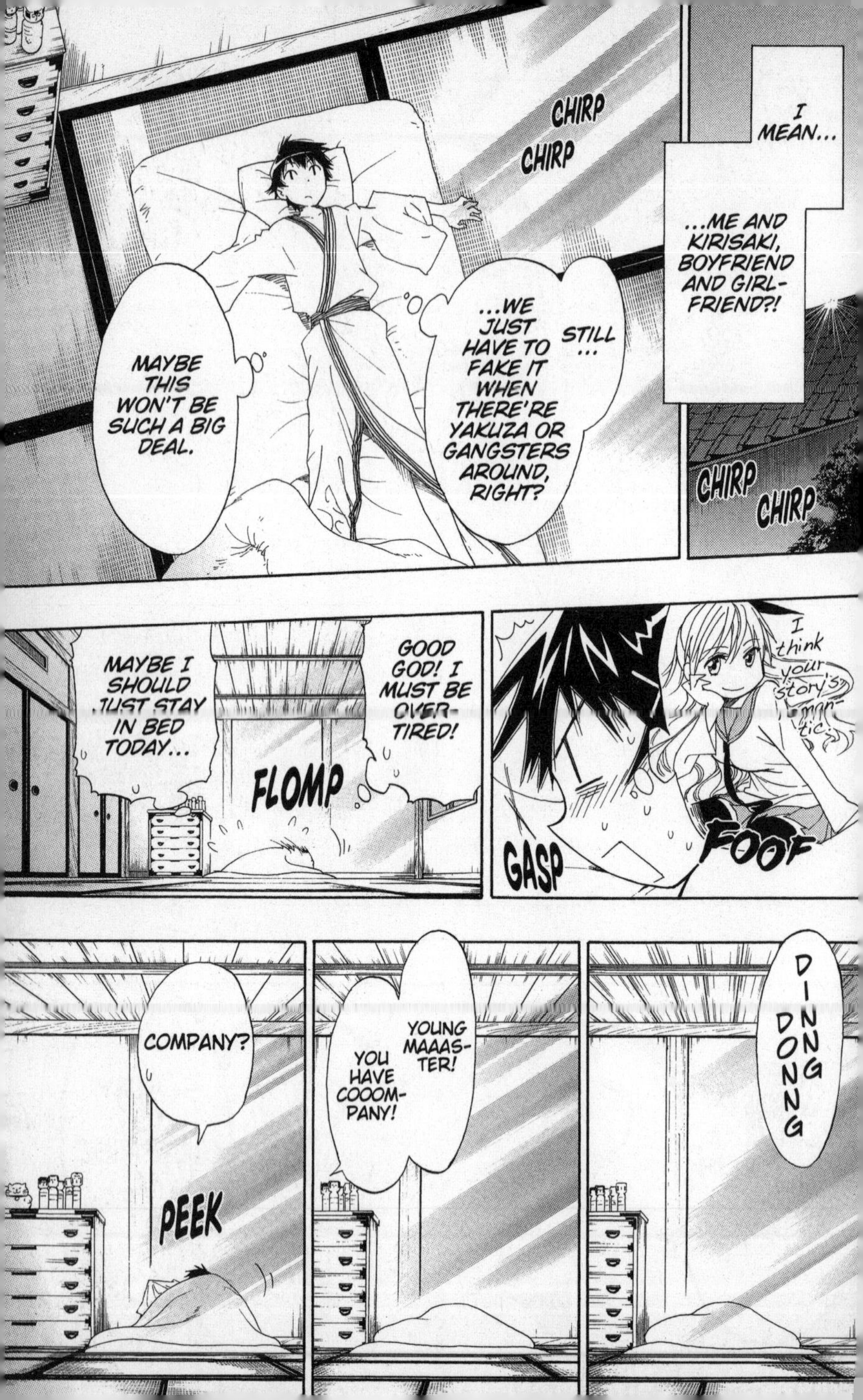
I MEAN...
...ME AND KIRISAKI, BOYFRIEND AND GIRL-FRIEND?!
CHIRP
CHIRP
CHIRP
CHIRP
STILL...
...WE JUST HAVE TO FAKE IT WHEN THERE'RE YAKUZA OR GANGSTERS AROUND, RIGHT?
MAYBE THIS WON'T BE SUCH A BIG DEAL.
I think your story's ro-man-tic.
FOOF
GASP
GOOD GOD! I MUST BE OVER-TIRED!
MAYBE I SHOULD JUST STAY IN BED TODAY...
FLOMP
DINNG DONNG
YOUNG MAAAS-TER!
YOU HAVE COOOM-PANY!
COMPANY?
PEEK

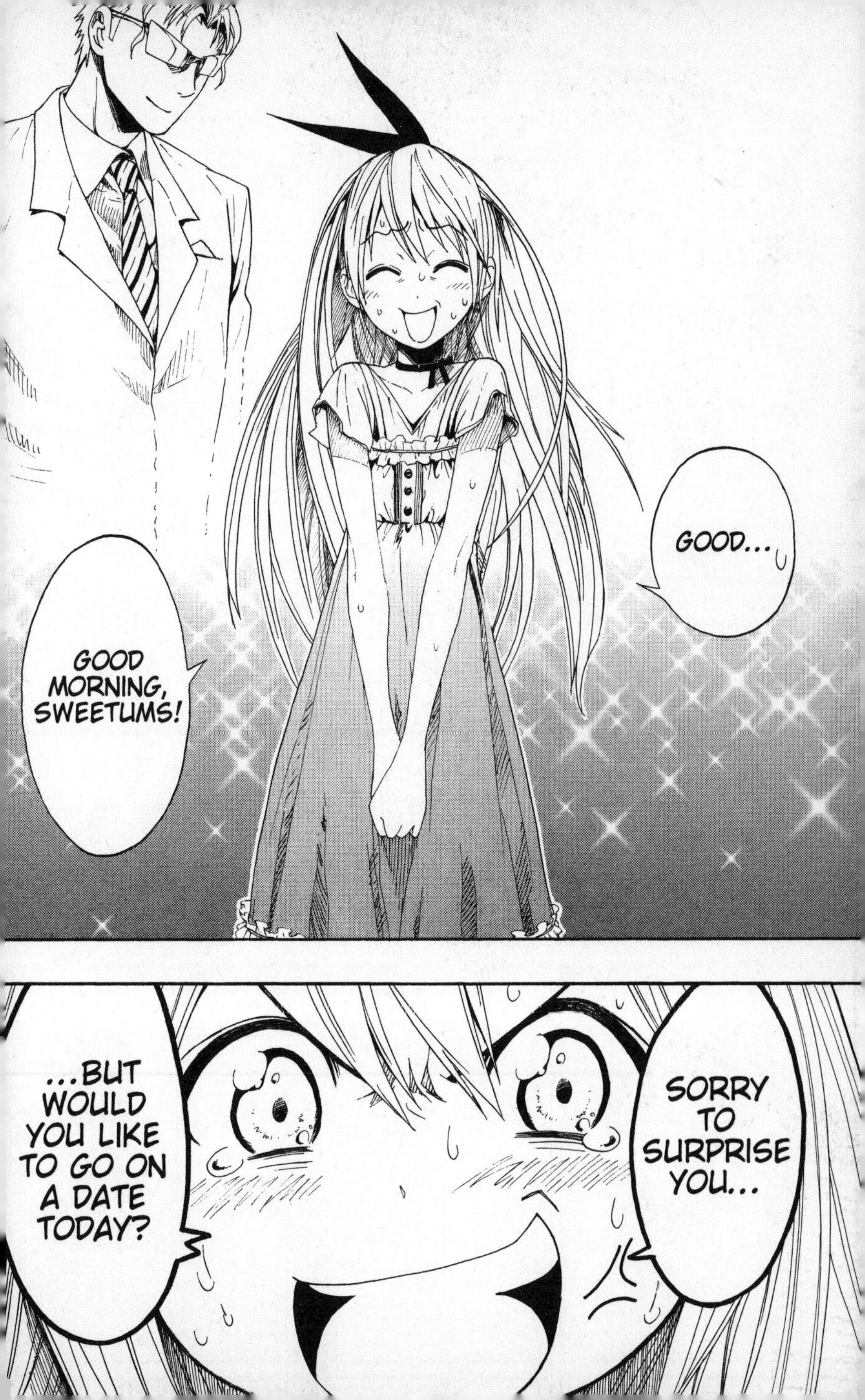
GOOD...
GOOD MORNING, SWEETUMS!
SORRY TO SURPRISE YOU...
...BUT WOULD YOU LIKE TO GO ON A DATE TODAY?

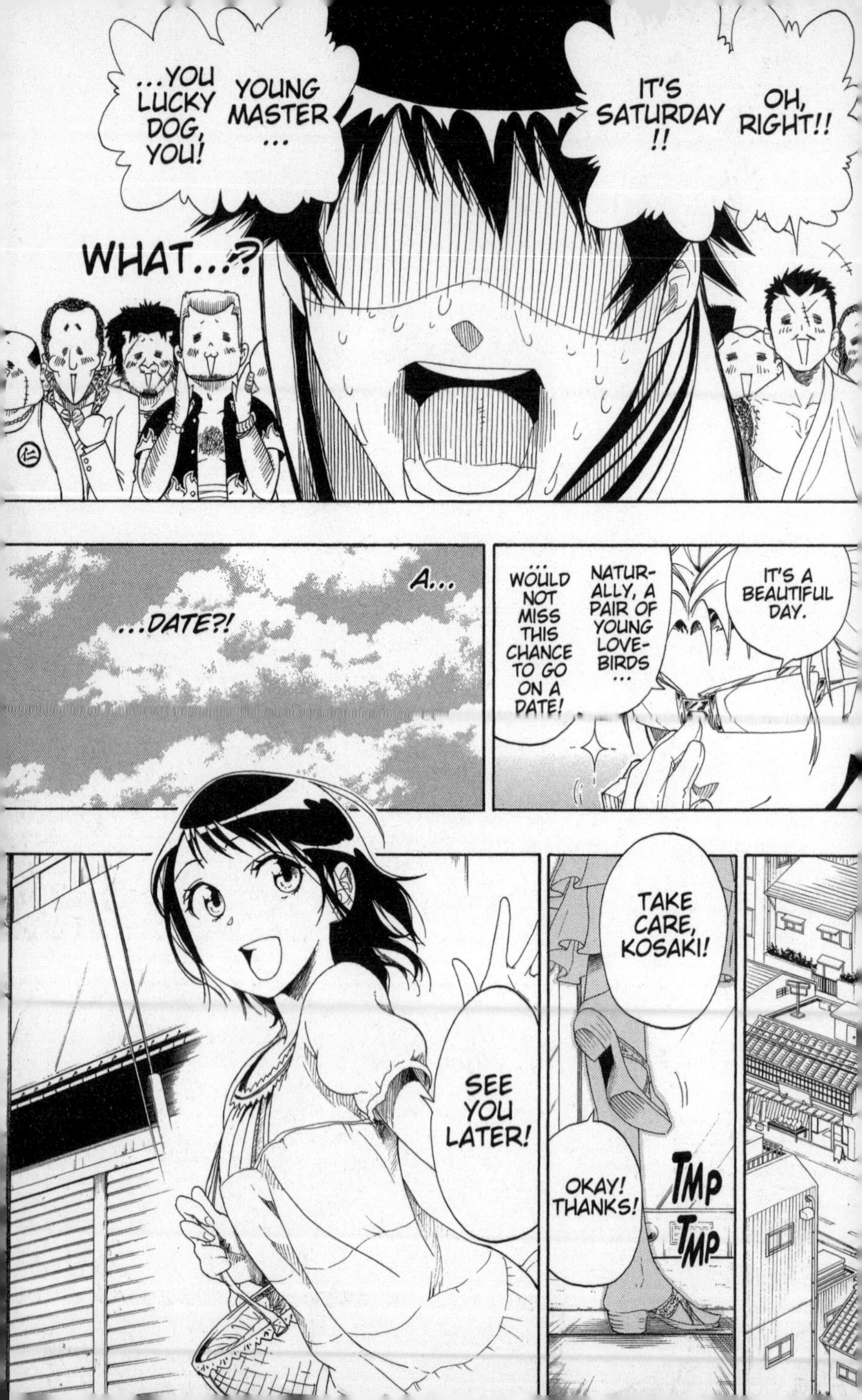
OH, RIGHT!!
IT'S SATURDAY !!
YOUNG MASTER ...
...YOU LUCKY DOG, YOU!
WHAT...?
IT'S A BEAUTIFUL DAY.
NATURALLY, A PAIR OF YOUNG LOVEBIRDS ...
...WOULD NOT MISS THIS CHANCE TO GO ON A DATE!
A...
...DATE?!
TAKE CARE, KOSAKI!
OKAY! THANKS!
TMP
TMP
SEE YOU LATER!

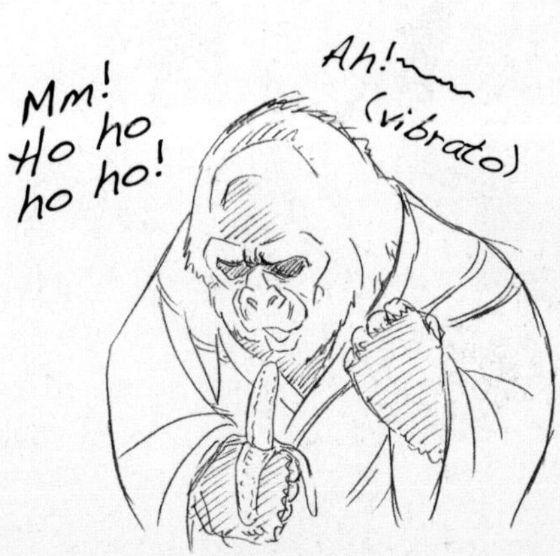
Mm! Ho ho ho ho!
Ah!~~ (vibrato)

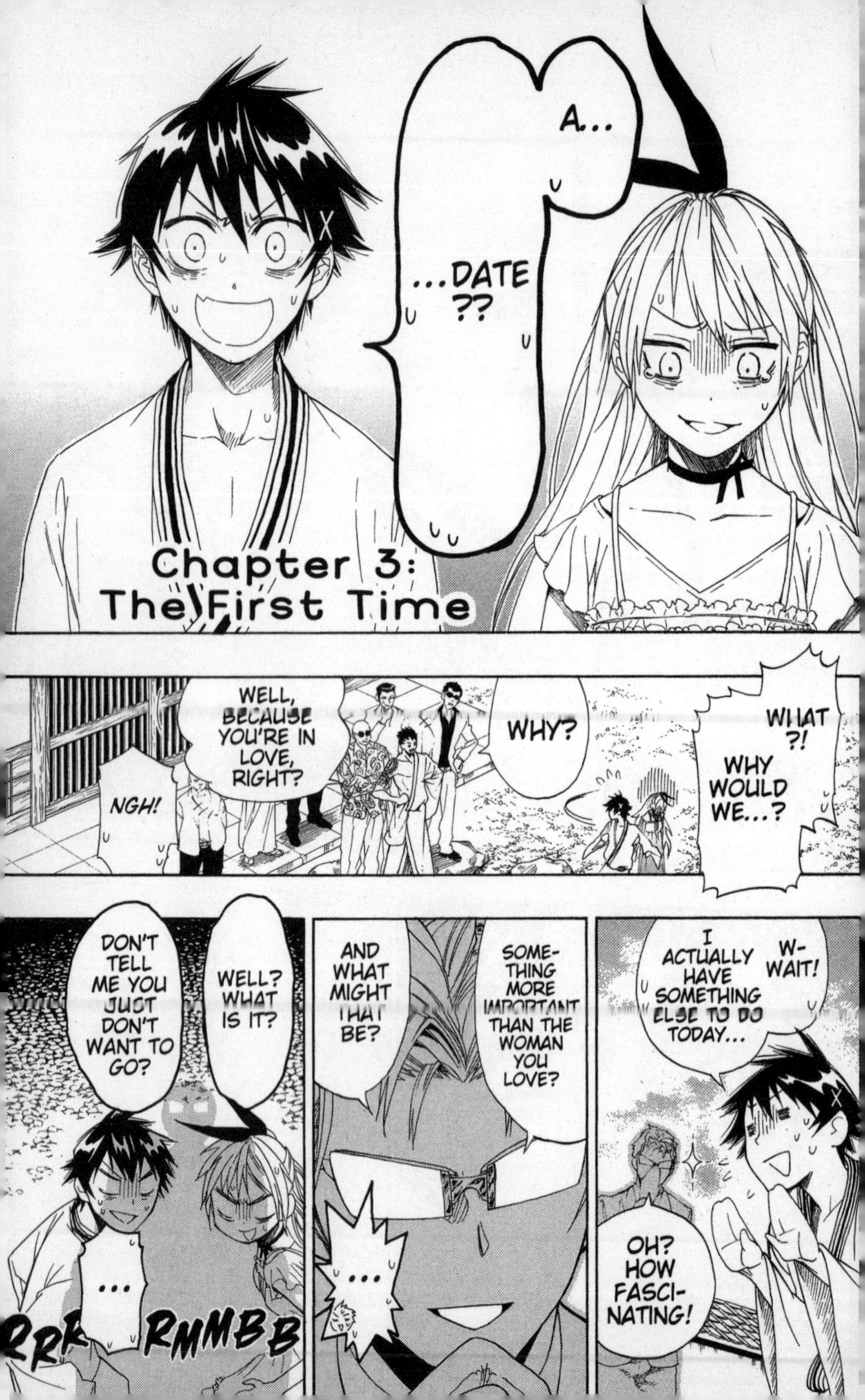
A...
...DATE ??
Chapter 3: The First Time
WHAT?!
WHY WOULD WE...?
WHY?
WELL, BECAUSE YOU'RE IN LOVE, RIGHT?
NGH!
W-WAIT!
I ACTUALLY HAVE SOMETHING ELSE TO DO TODAY...
OH? HOW FASCINATING!
SOMETHING MORE IMPORTANT THAN THE WOMAN YOU LOVE?
AND WHAT MIGHT THAT BE?
...
WELL? WHAT IS IT?
DON'T TELL ME YOU JUST DON'T WANT TO GO?
...
RRR RMMBB

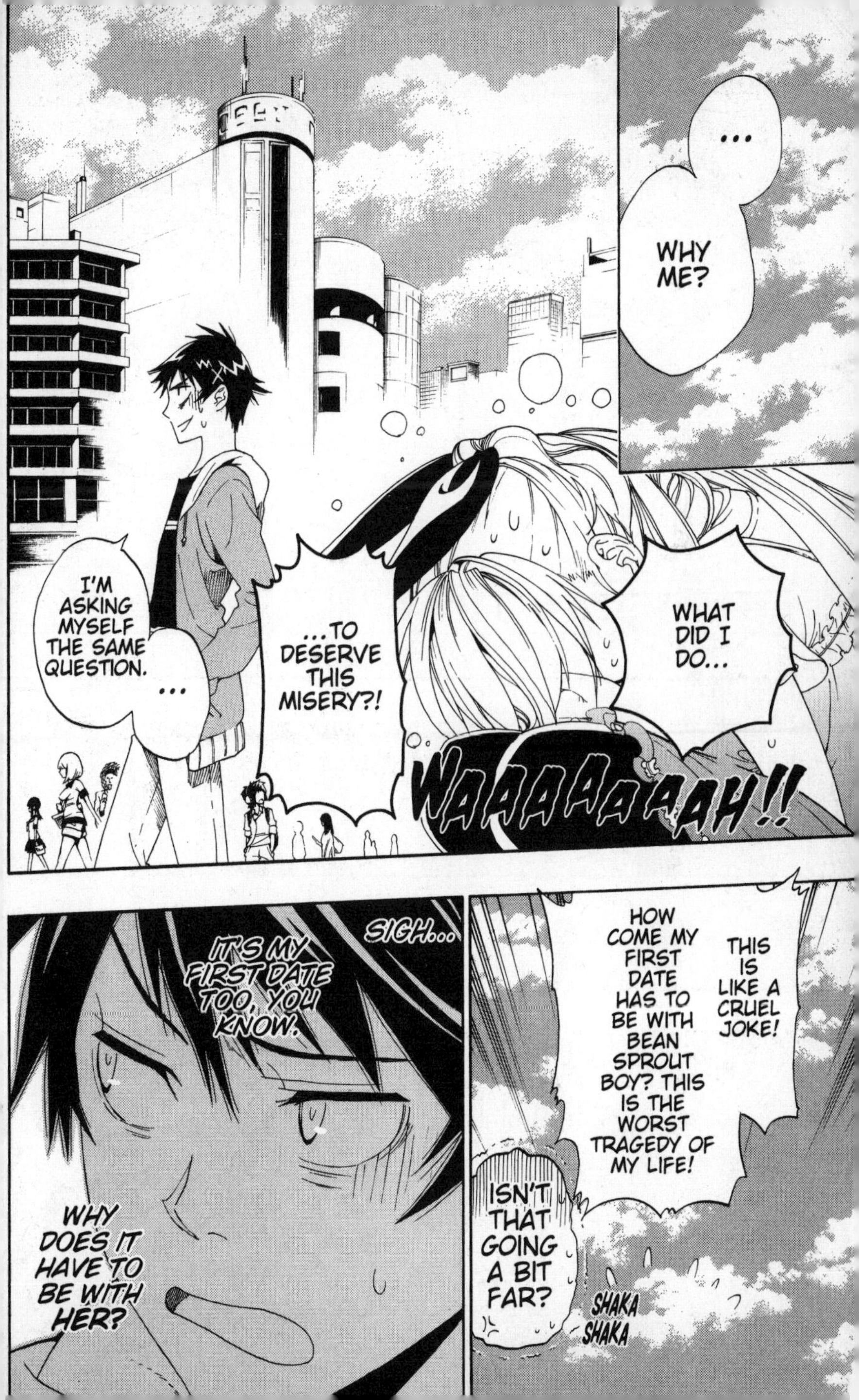
...
WHY ME?
WHAT DID I DO...
...TO DESERVE THIS MISERY?!
WAAAAAAAAH!!
I'M ASKING MYSELF THE SAME QUESTION.
...
THIS IS LIKE A CRUEL JOKE!
HOW COME MY FIRST DATE HAS TO BE WITH BEAN SPROUT BOY? THIS IS THE WORST TRAGEDY OF MY LIFE!
ISN'T THAT GOING A BIT FAR?
SHAKA SHAKA
SIGH...
IT'S MY FIRST DATE TOO, YOU KNOW.
WHY DOES IT HAVE TO BE WITH HER?

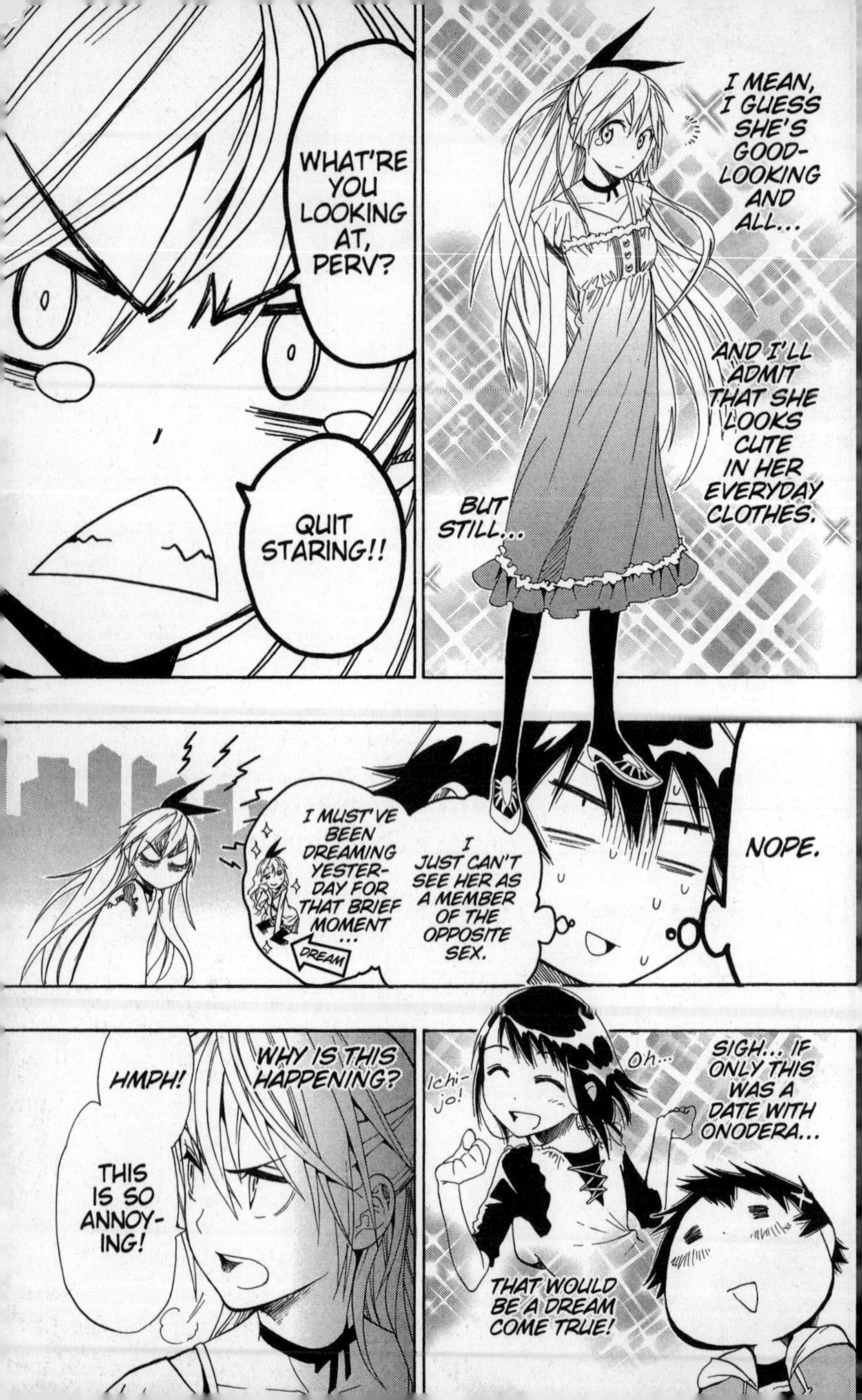
I MEAN, I GUESS SHE'S GOOD-LOOKING AND ALL...
AND I'LL ADMIT THAT SHE LOOKS CUTE IN HER EVERYDAY CLOTHES.
BUT STILL...
WHAT'RE YOU LOOKING AT, PERV?
QUIT STARING!!
NOPE.
I JUST CAN'T SEE HER AS A MEMBER OF THE OPPOSITE SEX.
I MUST'VE BEEN DREAMING YESTERDAY FOR THAT BRIEF MOMENT...
DREAM
SIGH... IF ONLY THIS WAS A DATE WITH ONODERA...
Oh...
Ichi-jo!
THAT WOULD BE A DREAM COME TRUE!
WHY IS THIS HAPPENING?
HMPH!
THIS IS SO ANNOYING!

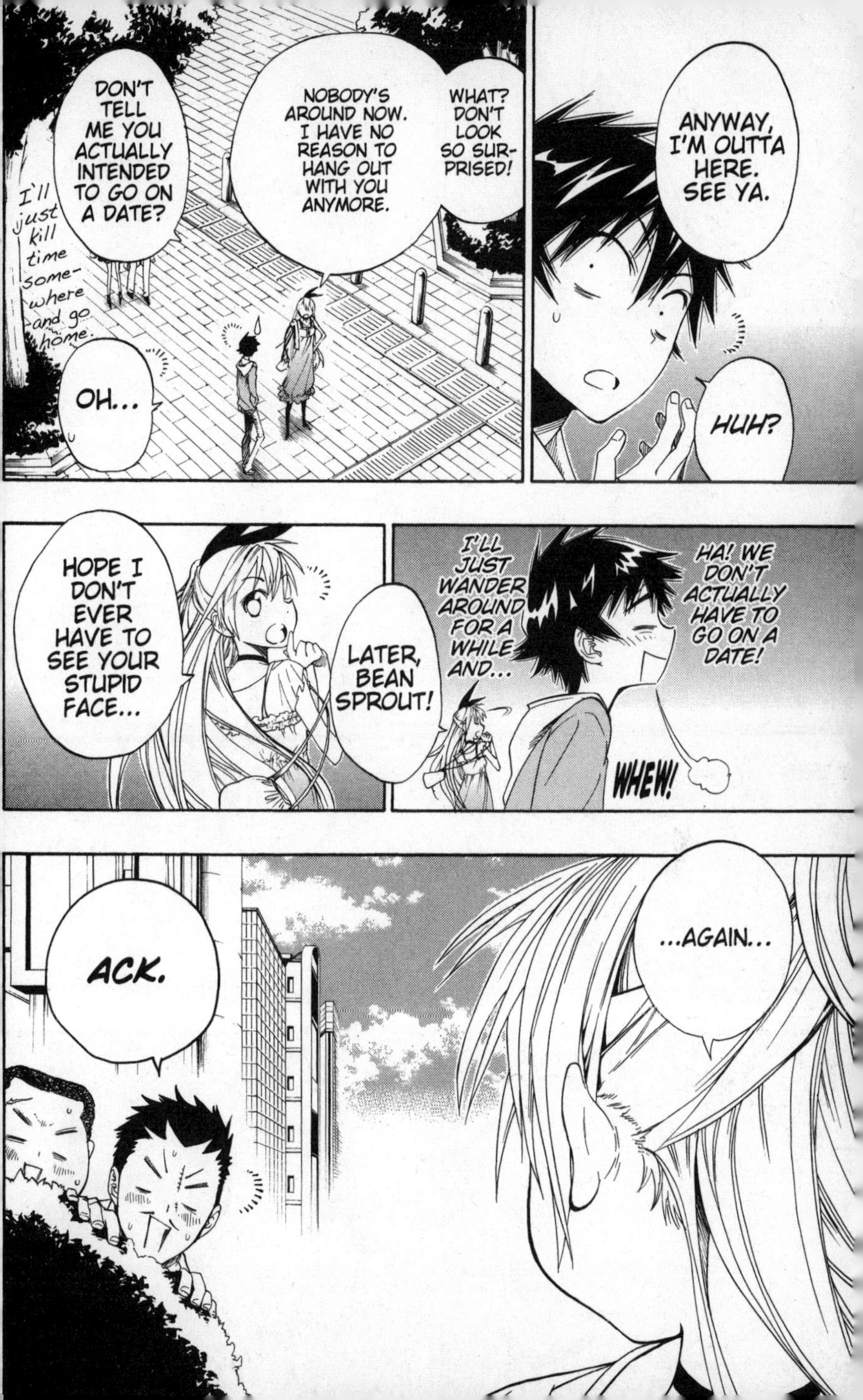
ANYWAY, I'M OUTTA HERE. SEE YA.
HUH?
WHAT? DON'T LOOK SO SURPRISED!
NOBODY'S AROUND NOW. I HAVE NO REASON TO HANG OUT WITH YOU ANYMORE.
DON'T TELL ME YOU ACTUALLY INTENDED TO GO ON A DATE?
I'll just kill time somewhere and go home.
OH...
HA! WE DON'T ACTUALLY HAVE TO GO ON A DATE!
I'LL JUST WANDER AROUND FOR A WHILE AND...
LATER, BEAN SPROUT!
WHEW!
HOPE I DON'T EVER HAVE TO SEE YOUR STUPID FACE...
...AGAIN...
ACK.

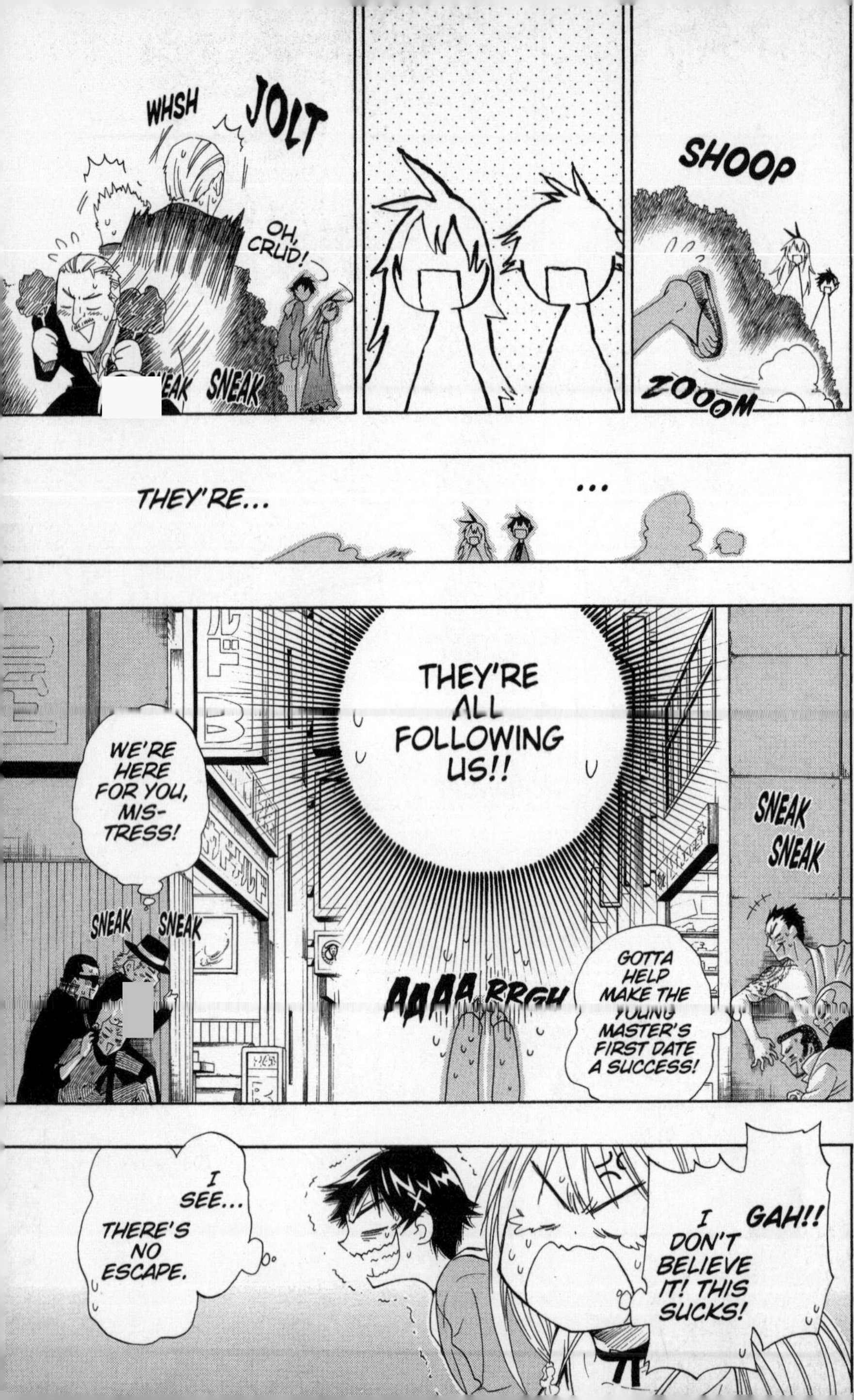
SHOOP
ZOOOM
JOLT
WHSH
OH, CRUD!
SNEAK
...
THEY'RE...
SNEAK SNEAK
GOTTA HELP MAKE THE YOUNG MASTER'S FIRST DATE A SUCCESS!
THEY'RE ALL FOLLOWING US!!
AAAARRGH
WE'RE HERE FOR YOU, MIS-TRESS!
SNEAK SNEAK
GAH!!
I DON'T BELIEVE IT! THIS SUCKS!
I SEE... THERE'S NO ESCAPE.

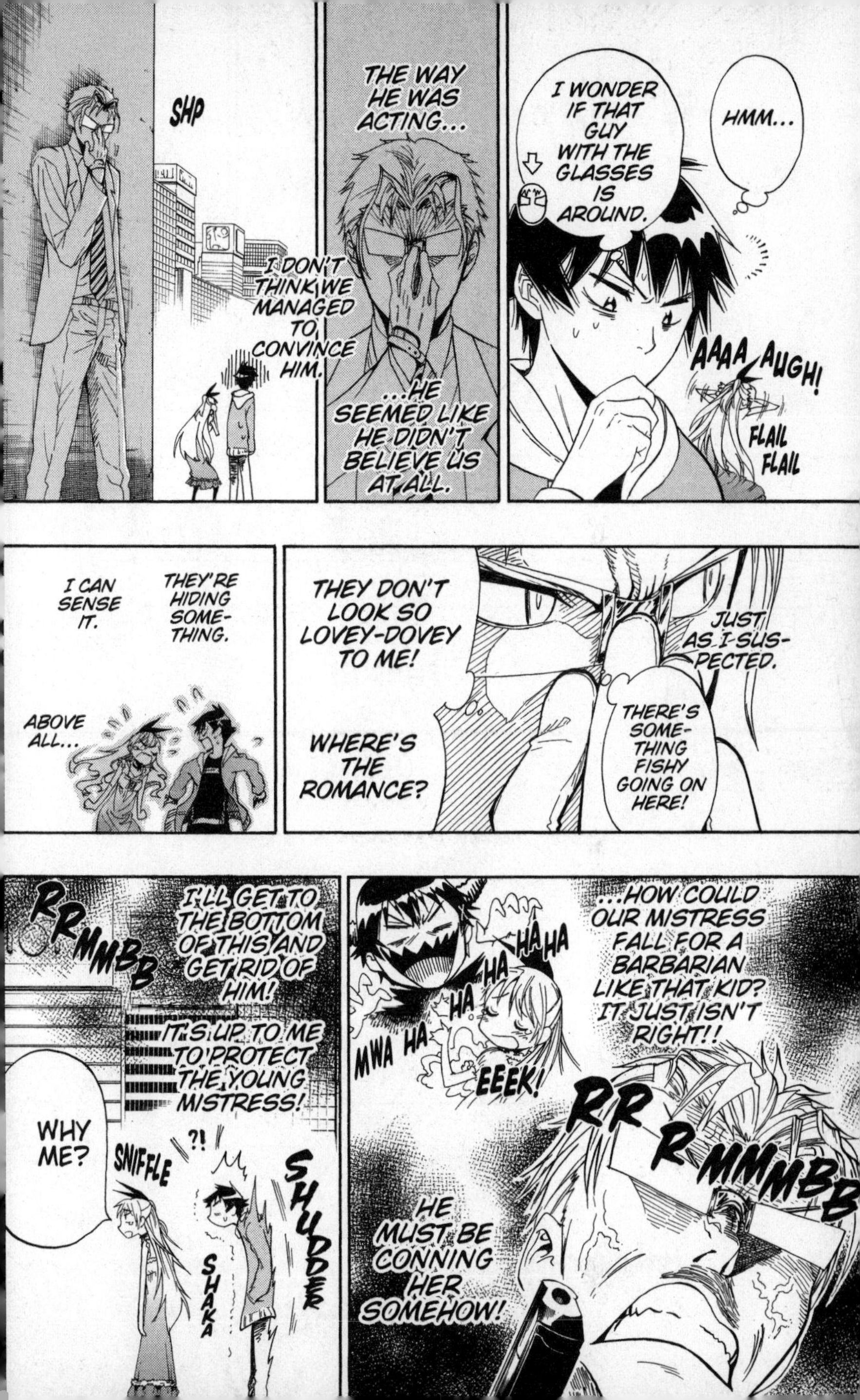
HMM...
I WONDER IF THAT GUY WITH THE GLASSES IS AROUND.
AAAA AUGH!
FLAIL FLAIL
THE WAY HE WAS ACTING...
...HE SEEMED LIKE HE DIDN'T BELIEVE US AT ALL.
I DON'T THINK WE MANAGED TO CONVINCE HIM.
SHP
JUST AS I SUS-PECTED.
THERE'S SOME-THING FISHY GOING ON HERE!
THEY DON'T LOOK SO LOVEY-DOVEY TO ME!
WHERE'S THE ROMANCE?
THEY'RE HIDING SOME-THING.
I CAN SENSE IT.
ABOVE ALL...
...HOW COULD OUR MISTRESS FALL FOR A BARBARIAN LIKE THAT KID? IT JUST ISN'T RIGHT!!
HA HA HA HA
MWA HA
EEEK!
RRRMMMBB
HE MUST BE CONNING HER SOMEHOW!
I'LL GET TO THE BOTTOM OF THIS AND GET RID OF HIM!
RRMMBB
IT'S UP TO ME TO PROTECT THE YOUNG MISTRESS!
SHUDDER
?!
SHAKA
SNIFFLE
WHY ME?

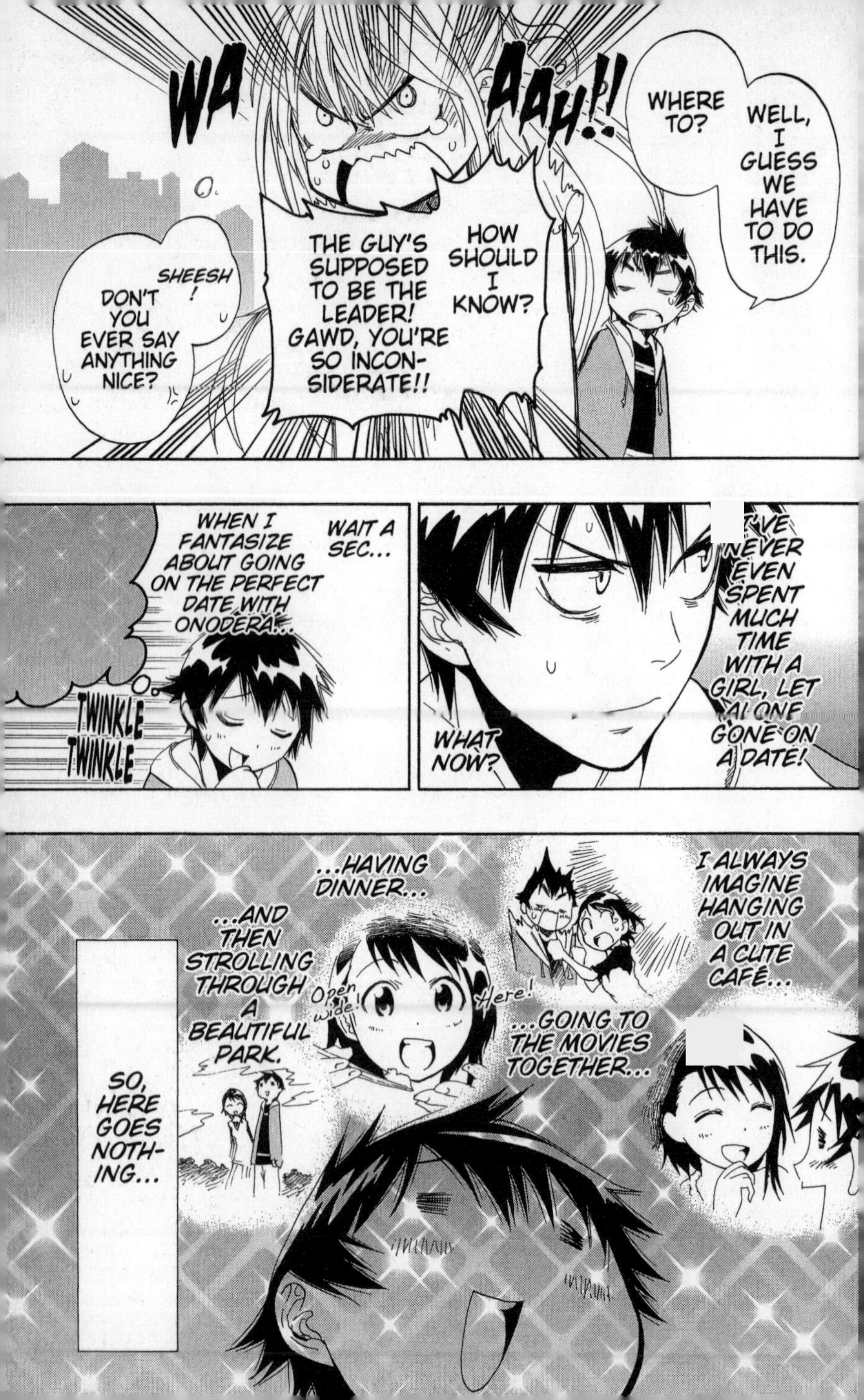
WELL, I GUESS WE HAVE TO DO THIS.
WHERE TO?
HOW SHOULD I KNOW?
THE GUY'S SUPPOSED TO BE THE LEADER! GAWD, YOU'RE SO INCON-SIDERATE!!
WAAAH!!
DON'T YOU EVER SAY ANYTHING NICE?
SHEESH!
'VE NEVER EVEN SPENT MUCH TIME WITH A GIRL, LET ALONE GONE ON A DATE!
WHAT NOW?
WAIT A SEC...
WHEN I FANTASIZE ABOUT GOING ON THE PERFECT DATE WITH ONODERA...
TWINKLE TWINKLE
I ALWAYS IMAGINE HANGING OUT IN A CUTE CAFÉ...
...GOING TO THE MOVIES TOGETHER...
...HAVING DINNER...
Here!
Open wide!
...AND THEN STROLLING THROUGH A BEAUTIFUL PARK.
SO, HERE GOES NOTHING...

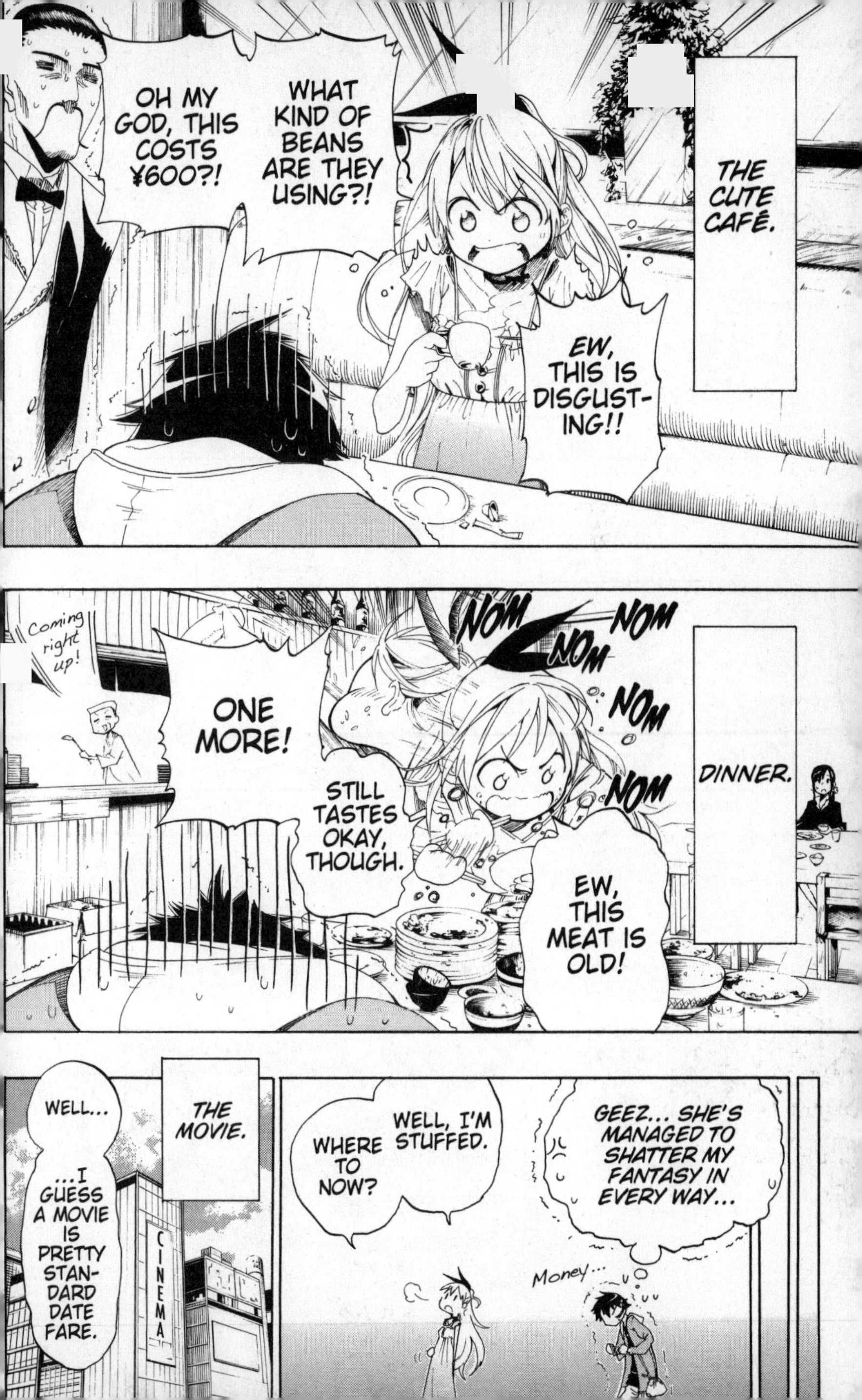
THE CUTE CAFÉ.
EW, THIS IS DISGUSTING!!
WHAT KIND OF BEANS ARE THEY USING?!
OH MY GOD, THIS COSTS ¥600?!
DINNER.
NOM NOM NOM NOM NOM
EW, THIS MEAT IS OLD!
STILL TASTES OKAY, THOUGH.
ONE MORE!
Coming right up!
GEEZ... SHE'S MANAGED TO SHATTER MY FANTASY IN EVERY WAY...
WELL, I'M STUFFED.
WHERE TO NOW?
Money...
THE MOVIE.
WELL...
...I GUESS A MOVIE IS PRETTY STANDARD DATE FARE.
CINEMA

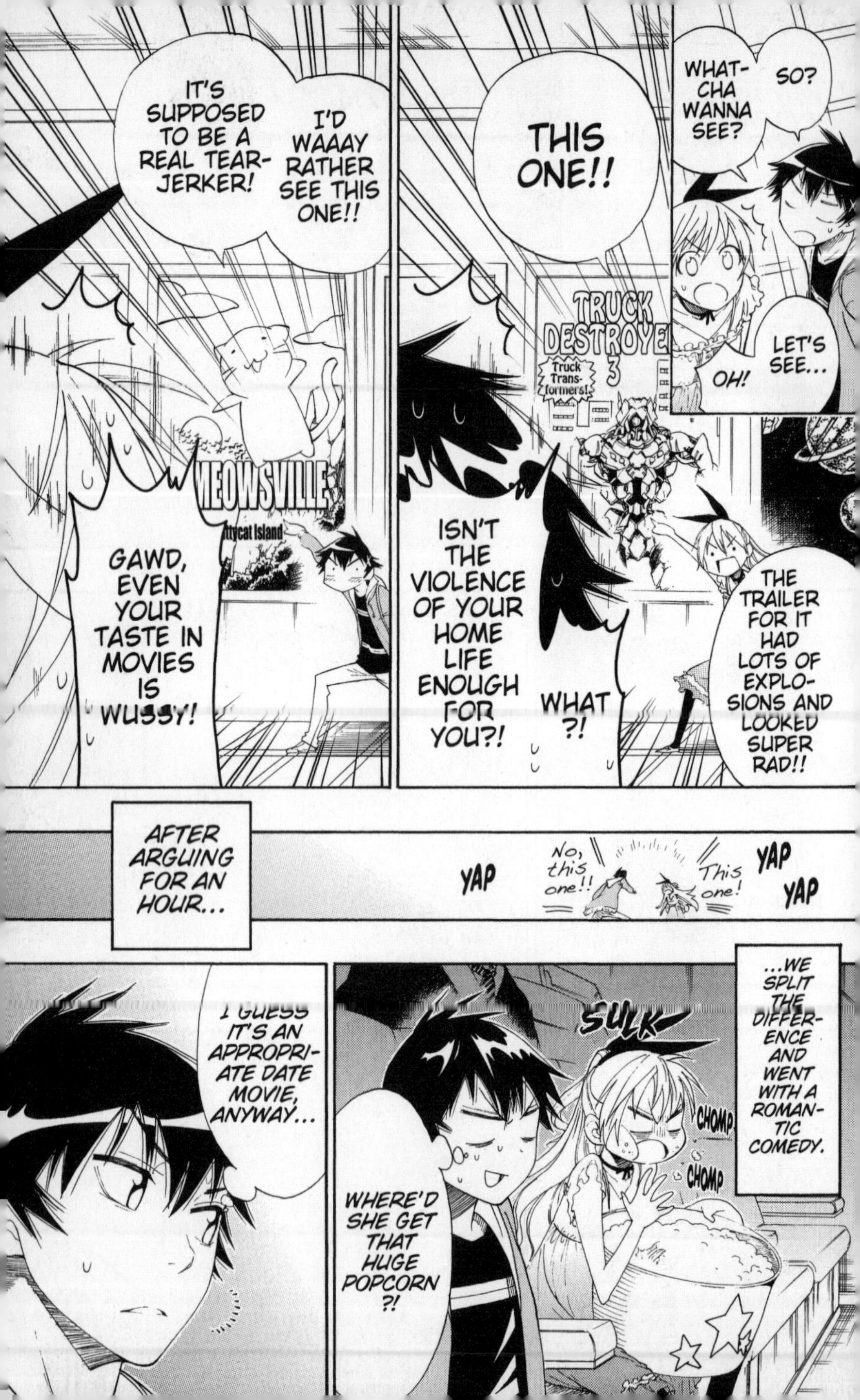
SO?
WHAT-CHA WANNA SEE?
LET'S SEE...
OH!
THIS ONE!!
TRUCK DESTROYE
3
Truck Trans-formers!
THE TRAILER FOR IT HAD LOTS OF EXPLO-SIONS AND LOOKED SUPER RAD!!
WHAT?!
ISN'T THE VIOLENCE OF YOUR HOME LIFE ENOUGH FOR YOU?!
I'D WAAAY RATHER SEE THIS ONE!!
IT'S SUPPOSED TO BE A REAL TEAR-JERKER!
MEOWSVILLE
ttycat Island
GAWD, EVEN YOUR TASTE IN MOVIES IS WUSSY!
YAP
YAP
This one!
No, this one!!
YAP
AFTER ARGUING FOR AN HOUR...
...WE SPLIT THE DIFFER-ENCE AND WENT WITH A ROMAN-TIC COMEDY.
SULK
CHOMP
CHOMP
WHERE'D SHE GET THAT HUGE POPCORN?!
I GUESS IT'S AN APPROPRI-ATE DATE MOVIE, ANYWAY...

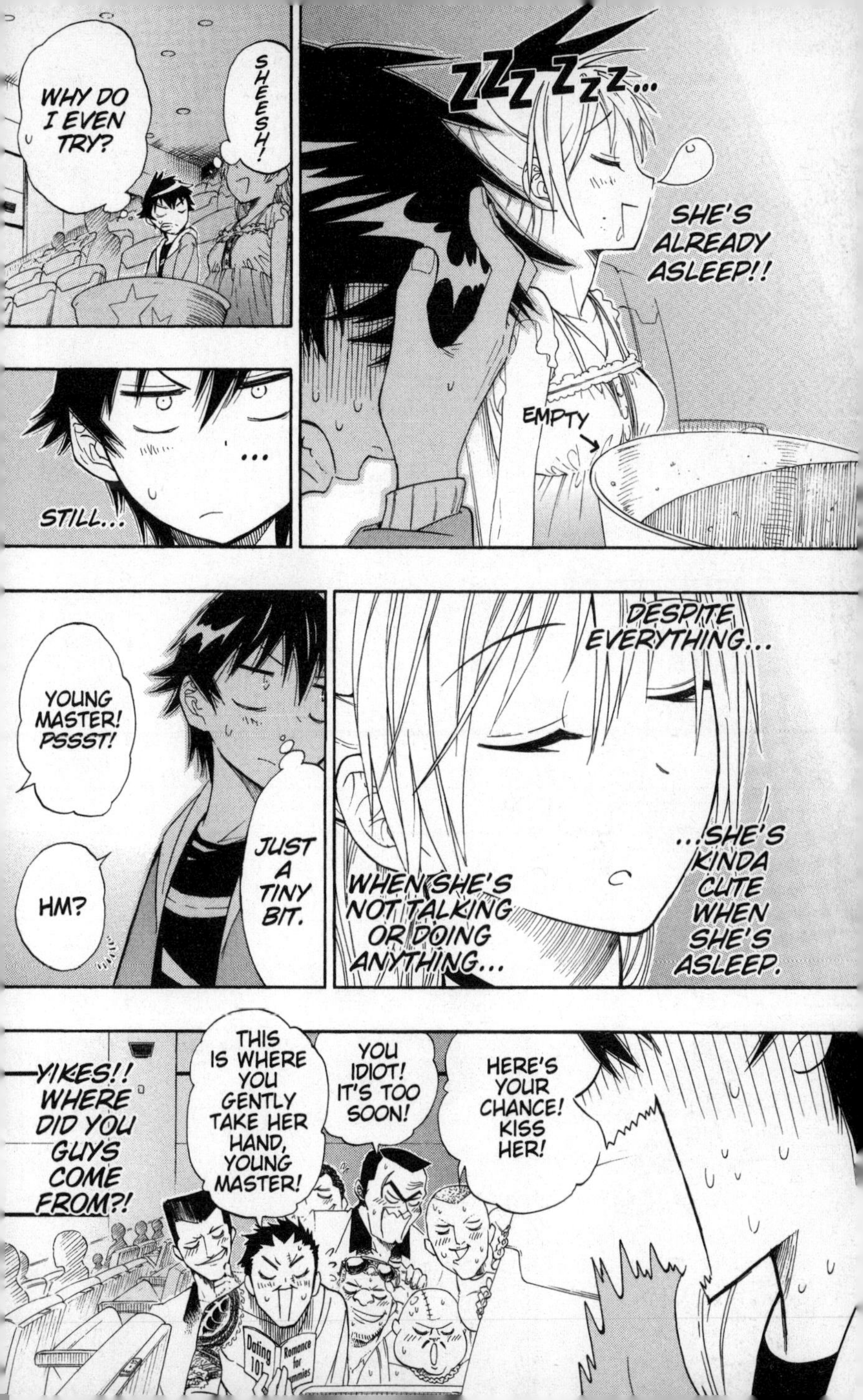
ZZZZZZ...
SHE'S ALREADY ASLEEP!!
EMPTY
SHEESH!
WHY DO I EVEN TRY?
...
STILL...
DESPITE EVERYTHING...
...SHE'S KINDA CUTE WHEN SHE'S ASLEEP.
WHEN SHE'S NOT TALKING OR DOING ANYTHING...
JUST A TINY BIT.
YOUNG MASTER! PSSST!
HM?
HERE'S YOUR CHANCE! KISS HER!
YOU IDIOT! IT'S TOO SOON!
THIS IS WHERE YOU GENTLY TAKE HER HAND, YOUNG MASTER!
YIKES!! WHERE DID YOU GUYS COME FROM?!
Dating 101
Romance for

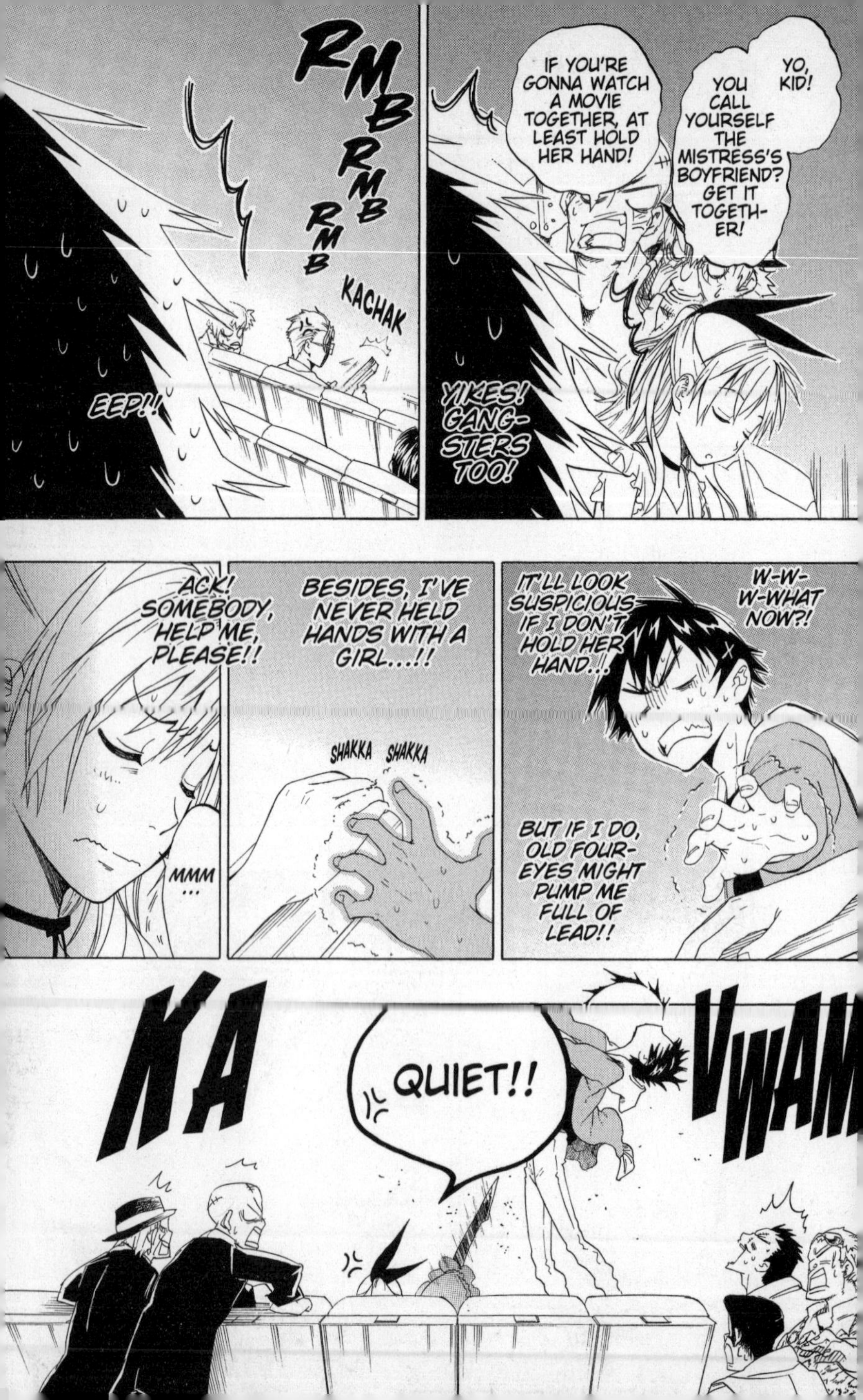
YO, KID!
YOU CALL YOURSELF THE MISTRESS'S BOYFRIEND? GET IT TOGETH-ER!
IF YOU'RE GONNA WATCH A MOVIE TOGETHER, AT LEAST HOLD HER HAND!
YIKES! GANG-STERS TOO!
RMB RMB RMB
KACHAK
EEP!!
W-W-W-WHAT NOW?!
IT'LL LOOK SUSPICIOUS IF I DON'T HOLD HER HAND..!
BUT IF I DO, OLD FOUR-EYES MIGHT PUMP ME FULL OF LEAD!!
BESIDES, I'VE NEVER HELD HANDS WITH A GIRL...!!
SHAKKA SHAKKA
ACK! SOMEBODY, HELP ME, PLEASE!!
MMM...
KA VWAM
QUIET!!

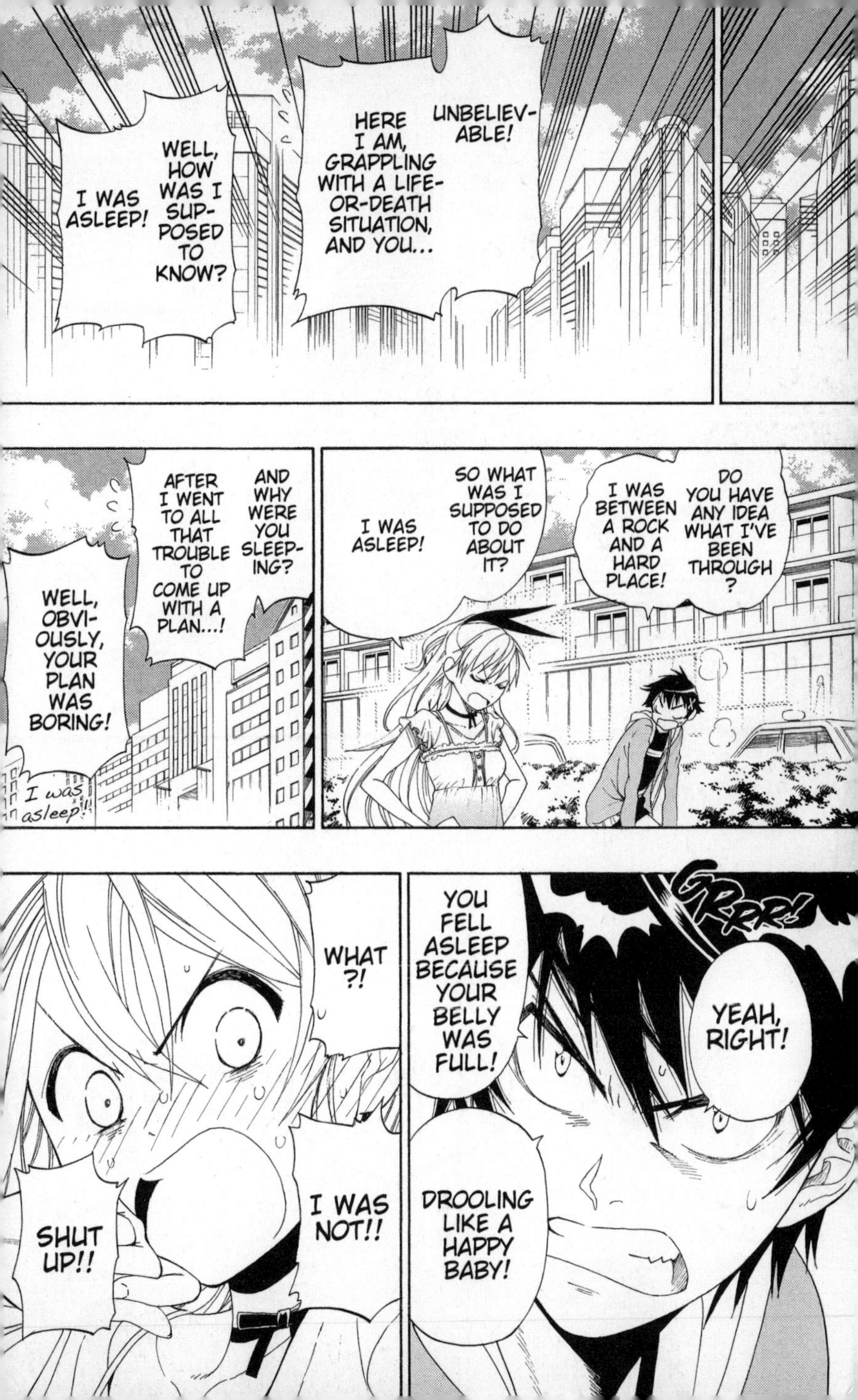
UNBELIEVABLE!
HERE I AM, GRAPPLING WITH A LIFE-OR-DEATH SITUATION, AND YOU...
WELL, HOW WAS I SUPPOSED TO KNOW?
I WAS ASLEEP!
DO YOU HAVE ANY IDEA WHAT I'VE BEEN THROUGH?
I WAS BETWEEN A ROCK AND A HARD PLACE!
SO WHAT WAS I SUPPOSED TO DO ABOUT IT?
I WAS ASLEEP!
AND WHY WERE YOU SLEEPING?
AFTER I WENT TO ALL THAT TROUBLE TO COME UP WITH A PLAN...!
WELL, OBVIOUSLY, YOUR PLAN WAS BORING!
I was asleep!!
GRRR!
YEAH, RIGHT!
YOU FELL ASLEEP BECAUSE YOUR BELLY WAS FULL!
DROOLING LIKE A HAPPY BABY!
WHAT?!
I WAS NOT!!
SHUT UP!!

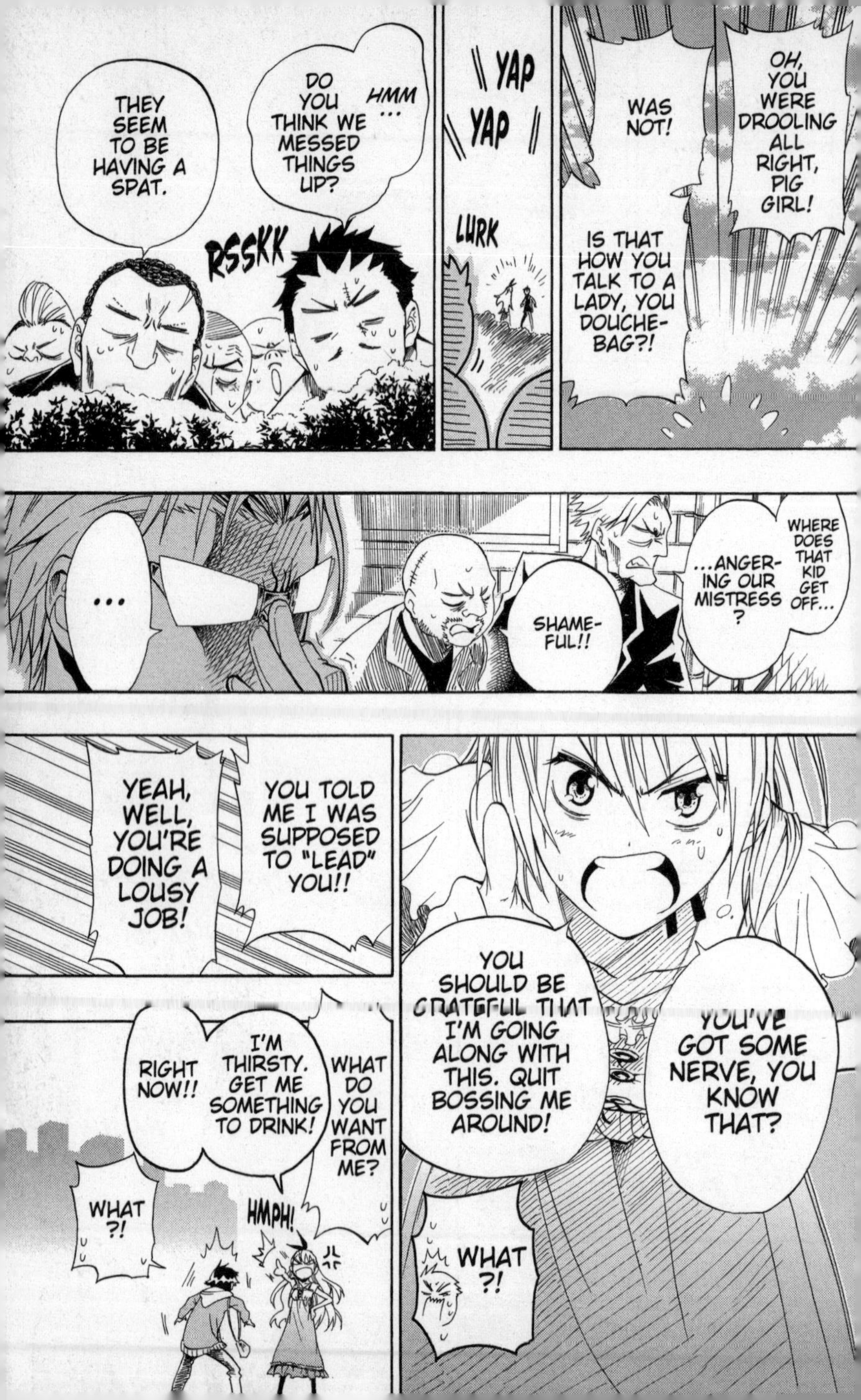
OH, YOU WERE DROOLING ALL RIGHT, PIG GIRL!
WAS NOT!
IS THAT HOW YOU TALK TO A LADY, YOU DOUCHE-BAG?!
YAP
YAP
LURK
HMM...
DO YOU THINK WE MESSED THINGS UP?
THEY SEEM TO BE HAVING A SPAT.
RSSKK
WHERE DOES THAT KID GET OFF...
...ANGER-ING OUR MISTRESS?
SHAME-FUL!!
...
YOU'VE GOT SOME NERVE, YOU KNOW THAT?
YOU SHOULD BE GRATEFUL THAT I'M GOING ALONG WITH THIS. QUIT BOSSING ME AROUND!
WHAT?!
YOU TOLD ME I WAS SUPPOSED TO "LEAD" YOU!!
YEAH, WELL, YOU'RE DOING A LOUSY JOB!
WHAT DO YOU WANT FROM ME?
I'M THIRSTY. GET ME SOMETHING TO DRINK!
RIGHT NOW!!
HMPH!
WHAT?!

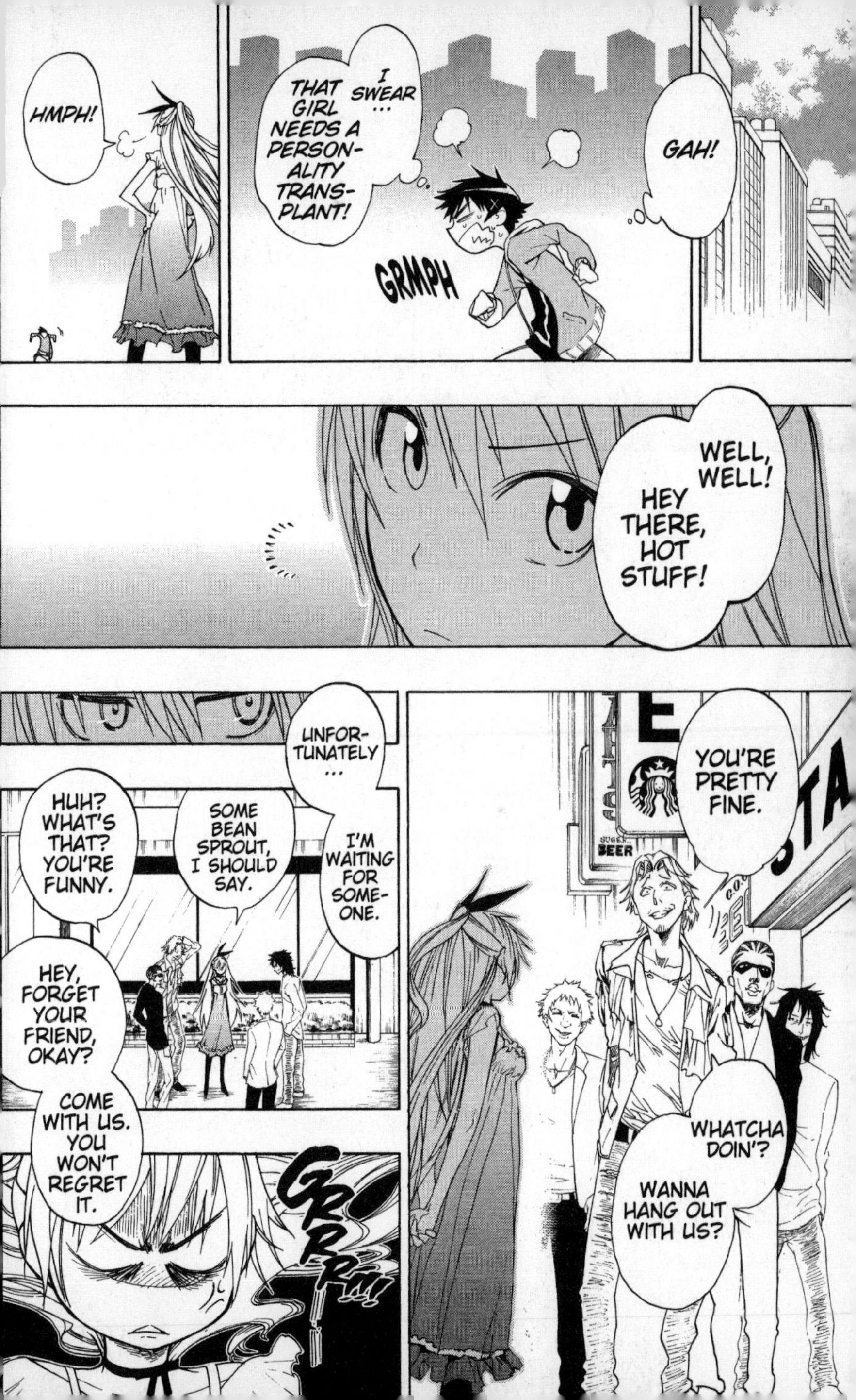
GAH!
I SWEAR... THAT GIRL NEEDS A PERSONALITY TRANSPLANT!
GRMPH
HMPH!
WELL, WELL! HEY THERE, HOT STUFF!
YOU'RE PRETTY FINE.
WHATCHA DOIN'?
WANNA HANG OUT WITH US?
BEER
UNFORTUNATELY...
I'M WAITING FOR SOMEONE.
SOME BEAN SPROUT, I SHOULD SAY.
HUH? WHAT'S THAT? YOU'RE FUNNY.
HEY, FORGET YOUR FRIEND, OKAY?
COME WITH US. YOU WON'T REGRET IT.
GRRR!!

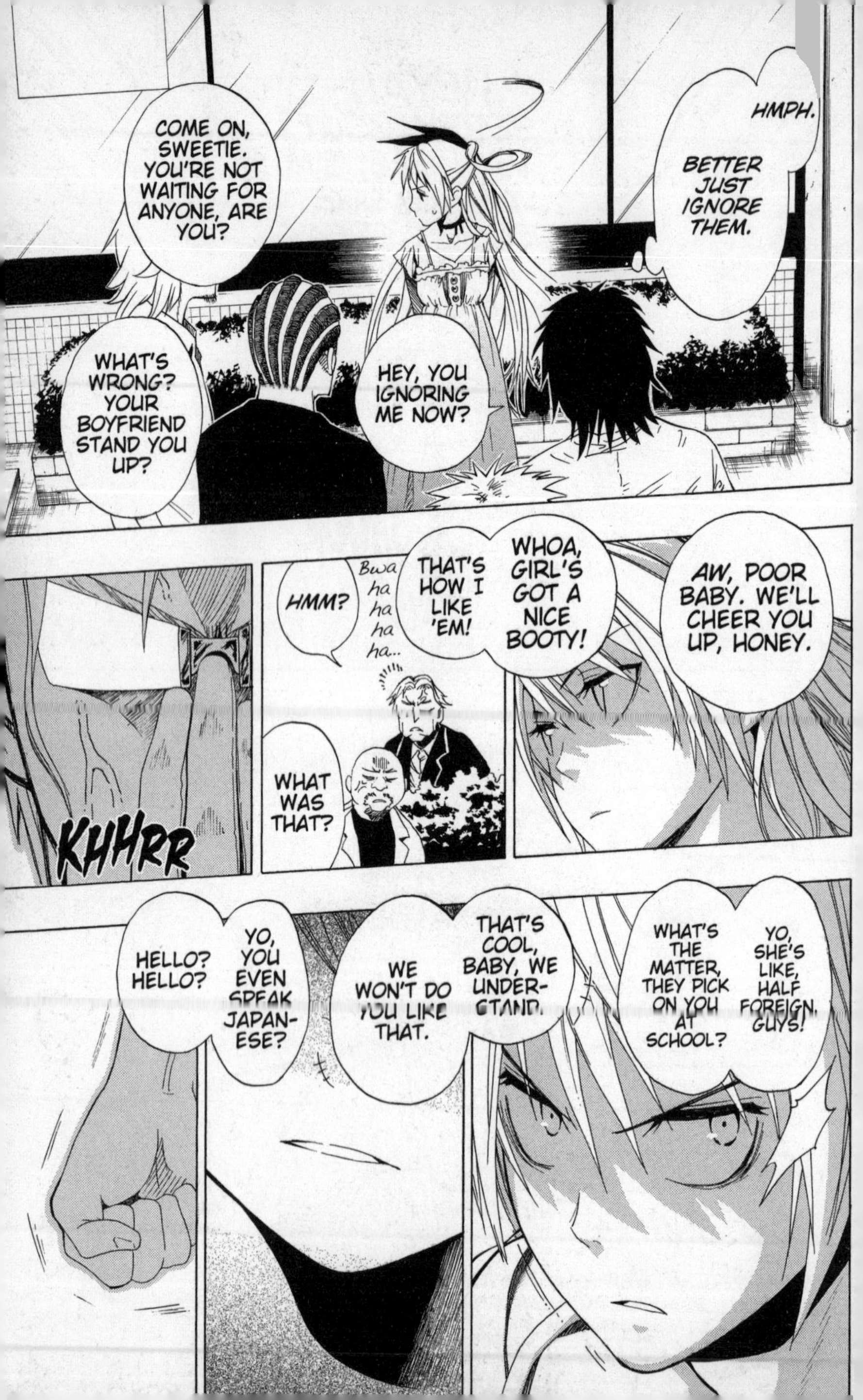
HMPH.
BETTER JUST IGNORE THEM.
COME ON, SWEETIE. YOU'RE NOT WAITING FOR ANYONE, ARE YOU?
HEY, YOU IGNORING ME NOW?
WHAT'S WRONG? YOUR BOYFRIEND STAND YOU UP?
AW, POOR BABY. WE'LL CHEER YOU UP, HONEY.
WHOA, GIRL'S GOT A NICE BOOTY!
THAT'S HOW I LIKE 'EM!
Bwa ha ha ha ha...
HMM?
WHAT WAS THAT?
KHHRR
YO, SHE'S LIKE, HALF FOREIGN, GUYS!
WHAT'S THE MATTER, THEY PICK ON YOU AT SCHOOL?
THAT'S COOL, BABY, WE UNDER-STAND.
WE WON'T DO YOU LIKE THAT.
YO, YOU EVEN SPEAK JAPAN-ESE?
HELLO? HELLO?

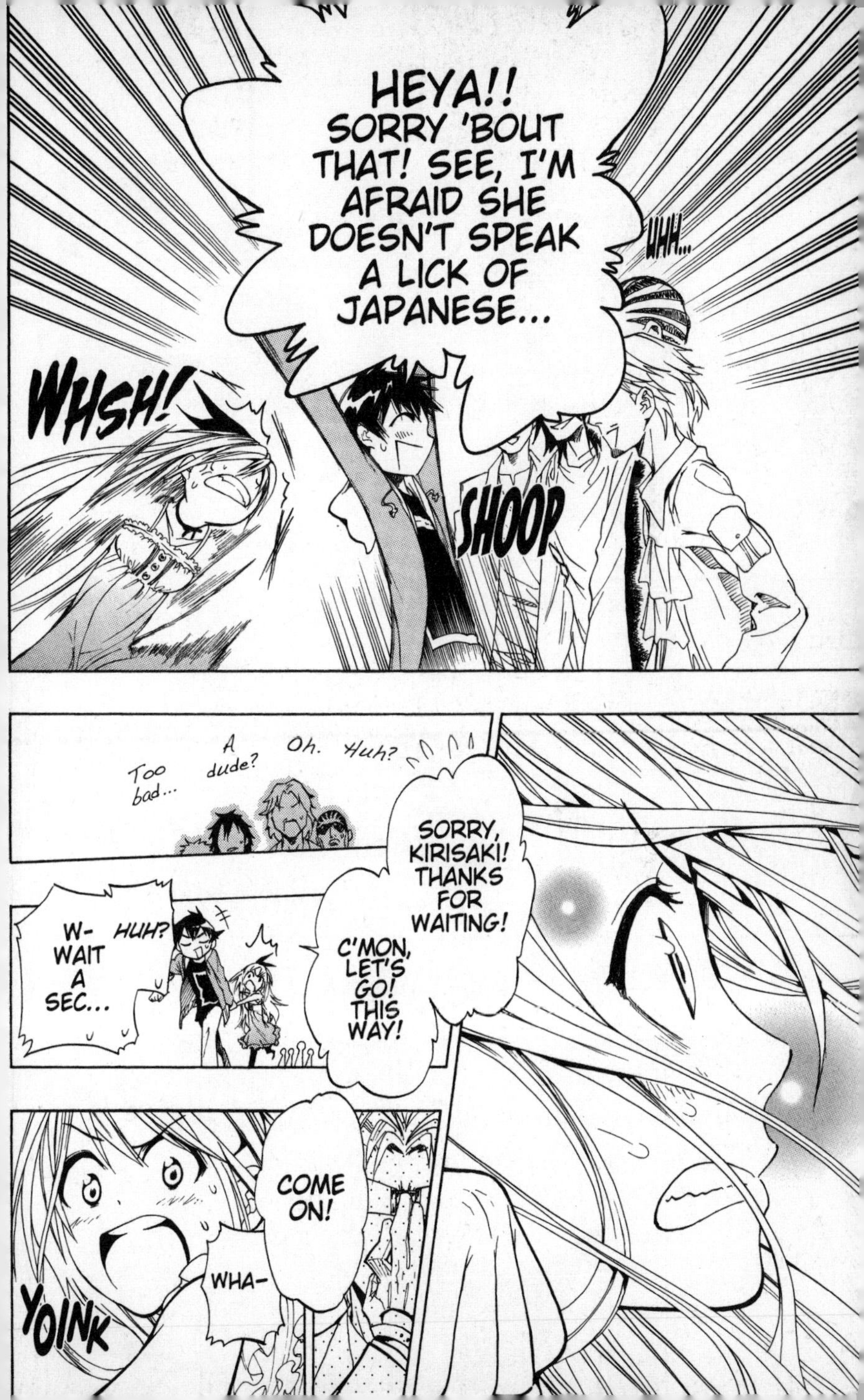

HEYA!! SORRY 'BOUT THAT! SEE, I'M AFRAID SHE DOESN'T SPEAK A LICK OF JAPANESE...
UHH...
WHSH!
SHOOP
Huh?
Oh.
A dude?
Too bad...
SORRY, KIRISAKI! THANKS FOR WAITING!
C'MON, LET'S GO! THIS WAY!
HUH?
W- WAIT A SEC...
COME ON!
WHA-
YOINK

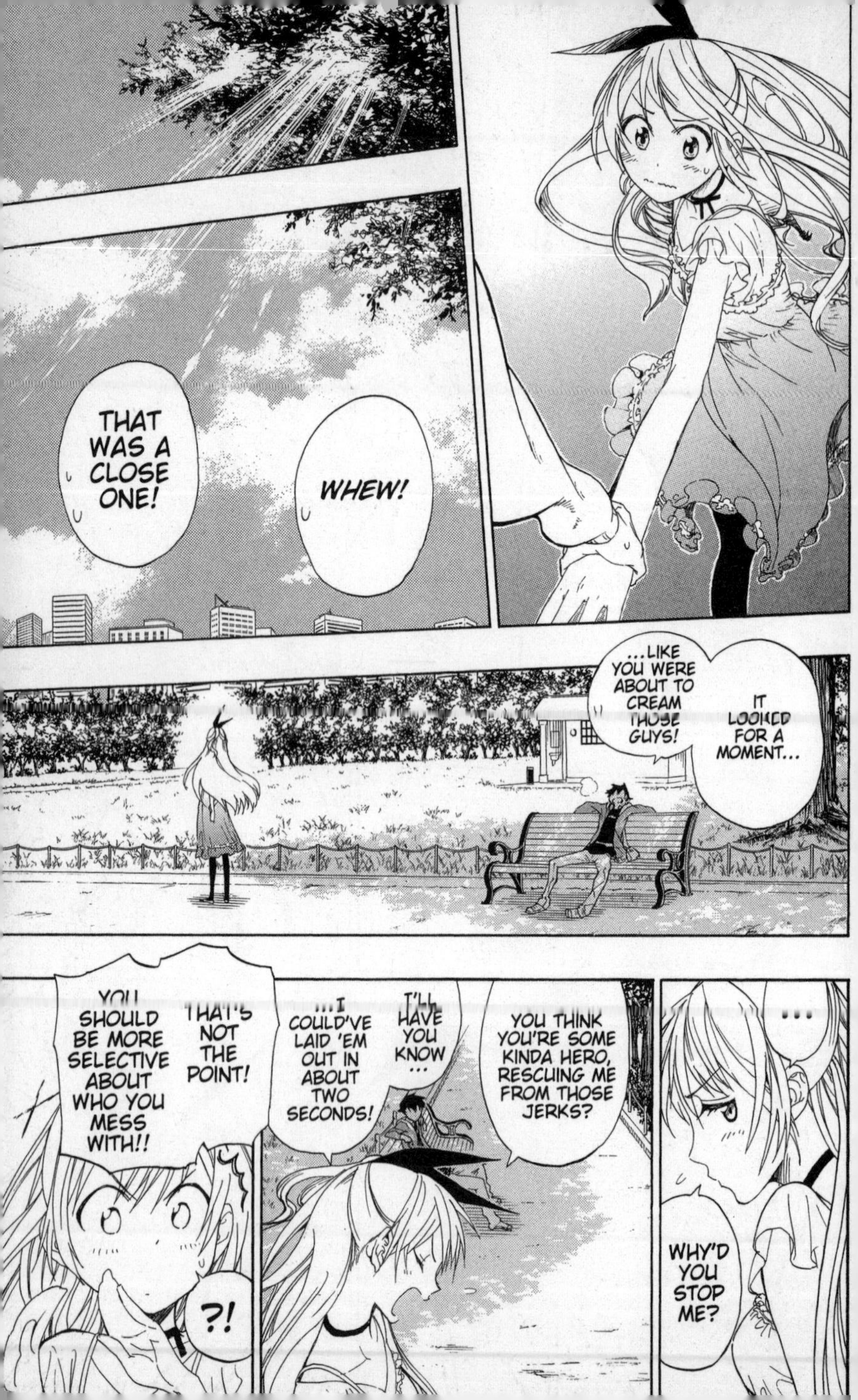
WHEW!
THAT WAS A CLOSE ONE!
IT LOOKED FOR A MOMENT...
...LIKE YOU WERE ABOUT TO CREAM THOSE GUYS!
...
WHY'D YOU STOP ME?
YOU THINK YOU'RE SOME KINDA HERO, RESCUING ME FROM THOSE JERKS?
I'LL HAVE YOU KNOW...
...I COULD'VE LAID 'EM OUT IN ABOUT TWO SECONDS!
THAT'S NOT THE POINT!
YOU SHOULD BE MORE SELECTIVE ABOUT WHO YOU MESS WITH!!
?!

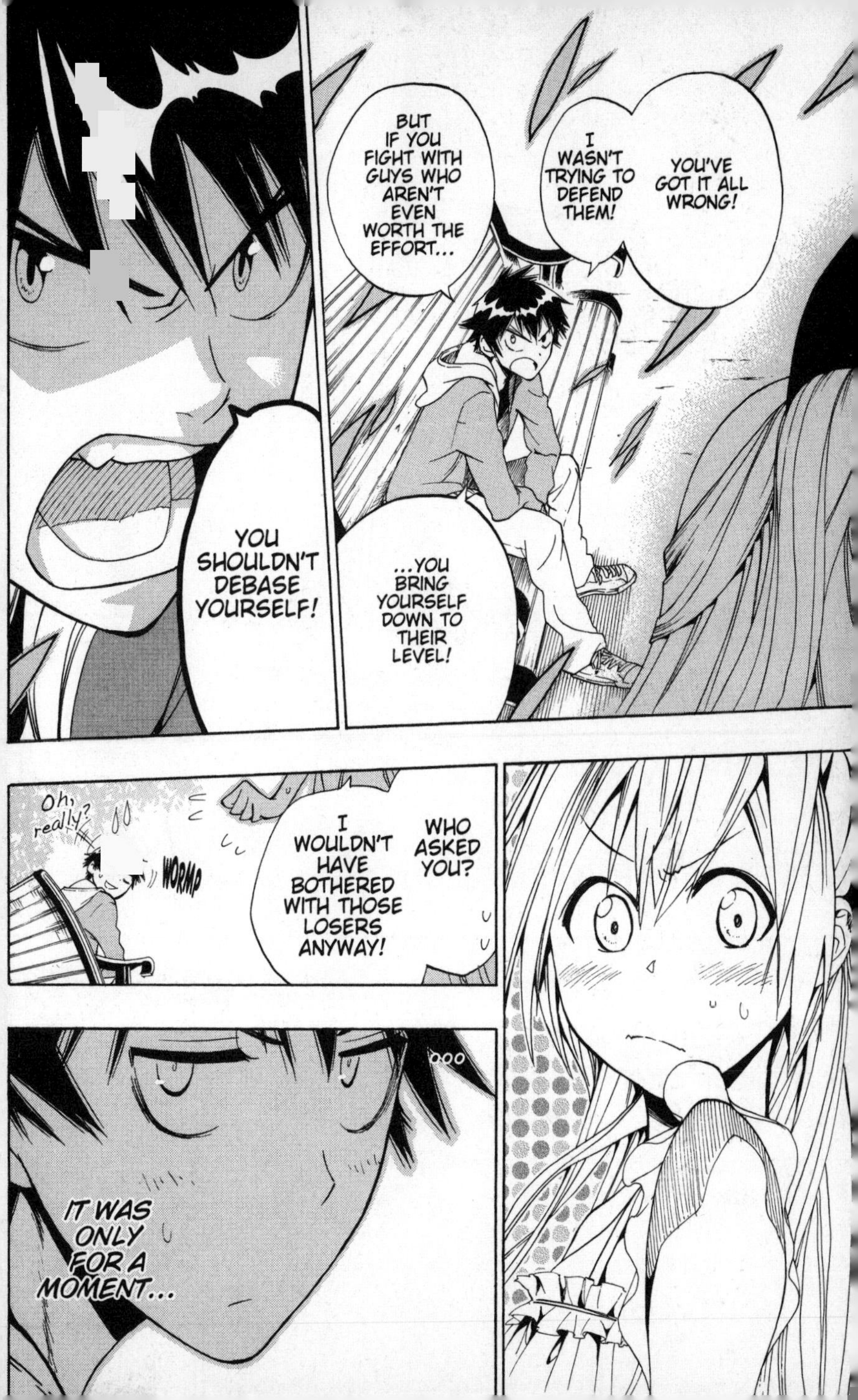
YOU'VE GOT IT ALL WRONG!
I WASN'T TRYING TO DEFEND THEM!
BUT IF YOU FIGHT WITH GUYS WHO AREN'T EVEN WORTH THE EFFORT...
...YOU BRING YOURSELF DOWN TO THEIR LEVEL!
YOU SHOULDN'T DEBASE YOURSELF!
WHO ASKED YOU?
I WOULDN'T HAVE BOTHERED WITH THOSE LOSERS ANYWAY!
WORMP
Oh, really?
IT WAS ONLY FOR A MOMENT...

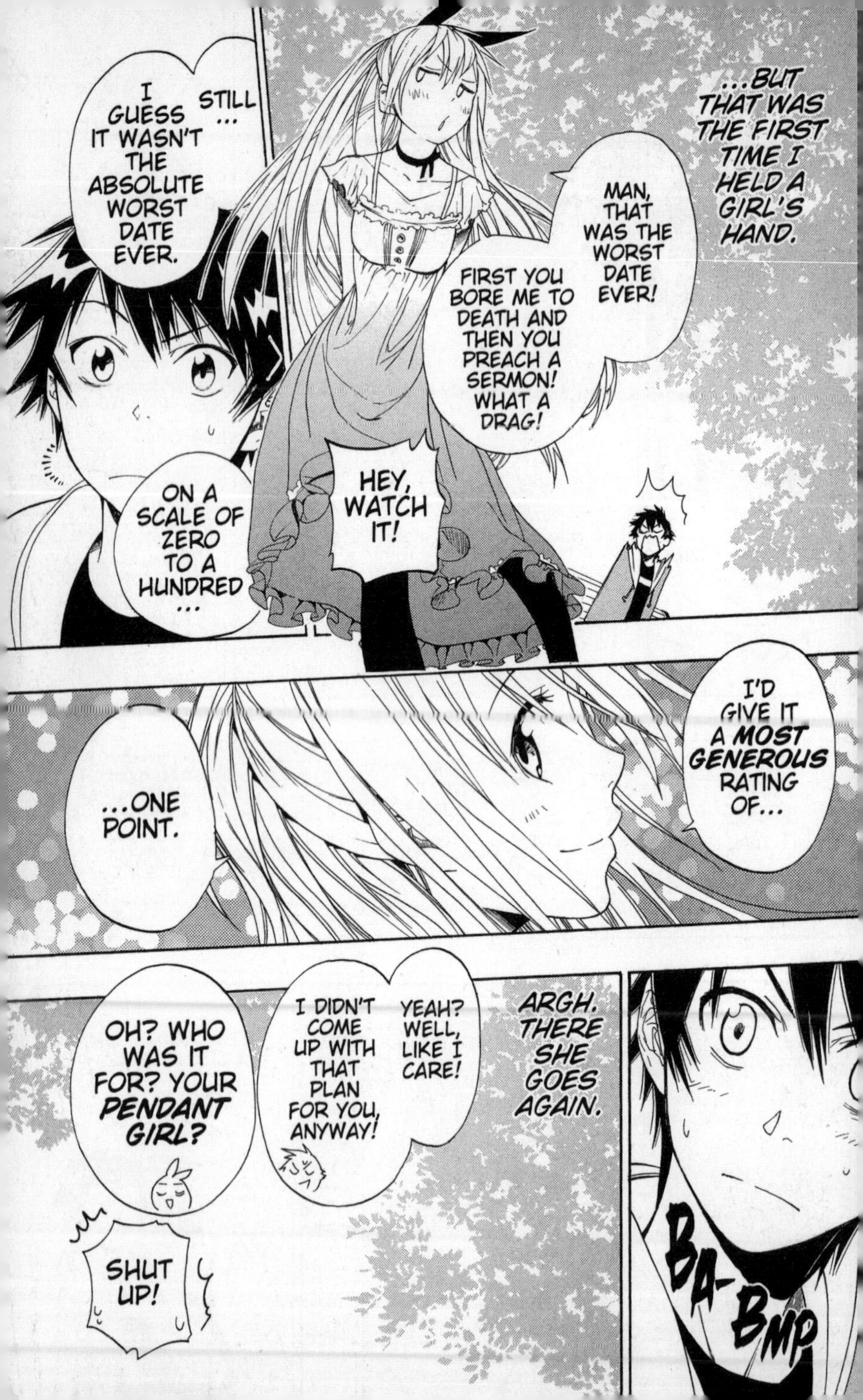
...BUT THAT WAS THE FIRST TIME I HELD A GIRL'S HAND.
MAN, THAT WAS THE WORST DATE EVER!
FIRST YOU BORE ME TO DEATH AND THEN YOU PREACH A SERMON! WHAT A DRAG!
HEY, WATCH IT!
STILL...
I GUESS IT WASN'T THE ABSOLUTE WORST DATE EVER.
ON A SCALE OF ZERO TO A HUNDRED...
I'D GIVE IT A MOST GENEROUS RATING OF...
...ONE POINT.
BA-BMP
ARGH. THERE SHE GOES AGAIN.
YEAH? WELL, LIKE I CARE!
I DIDN'T COME UP WITH THAT PLAN FOR YOU, ANYWAY!
OH? WHO WAS IT FOR? YOUR PENDANT GIRL?
SHUT UP!

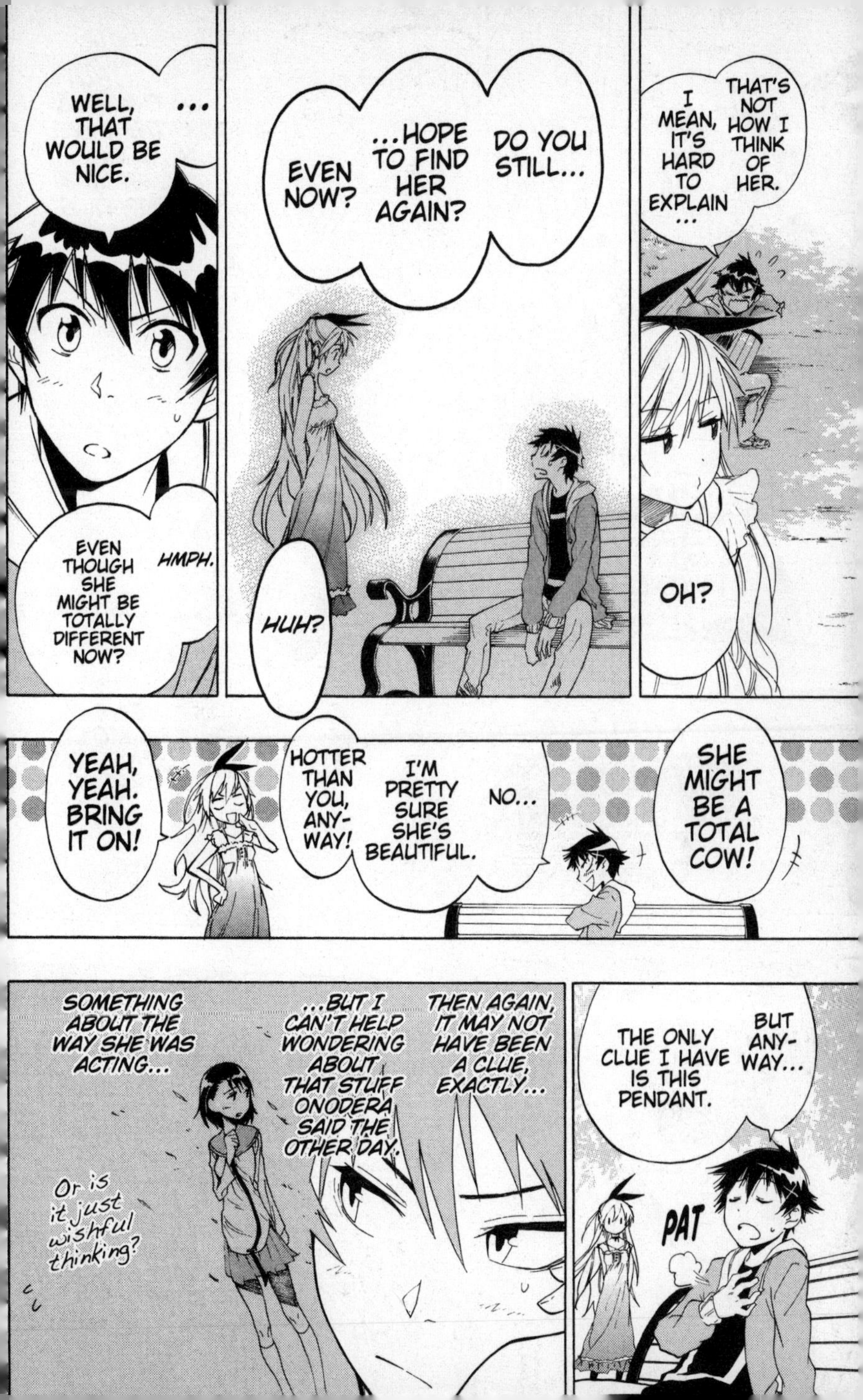
THAT'S NOT HOW I THINK OF HER.
I MEAN, IT'S HARD TO EXPLAIN...
OH?
DO YOU STILL...
...HOPE TO FIND HER AGAIN?
EVEN NOW?
HUH?
...
WELL, THAT WOULD BE NICE.
HMPH.
EVEN THOUGH SHE MIGHT BE TOTALLY DIFFERENT NOW?
SHE MIGHT BE A TOTAL COW!
NO...
I'M PRETTY SURE SHE'S BEAUTIFUL.
HOTTER THAN YOU, ANY-WAY!
YEAH, YEAH. BRING IT ON!
BUT ANY-WAY...
THE ONLY CLUE I HAVE IS THIS PENDANT.
PAT
THEN AGAIN, IT MAY NOT HAVE BEEN A CLUE, EXACTLY...
...BUT I CAN'T HELP WONDERING ABOUT THAT STUFF ONODERA SAID THE OTHER DAY.
SOMETHING ABOUT THE WAY SHE WAS ACTING...
Or is it just wishful thinking?

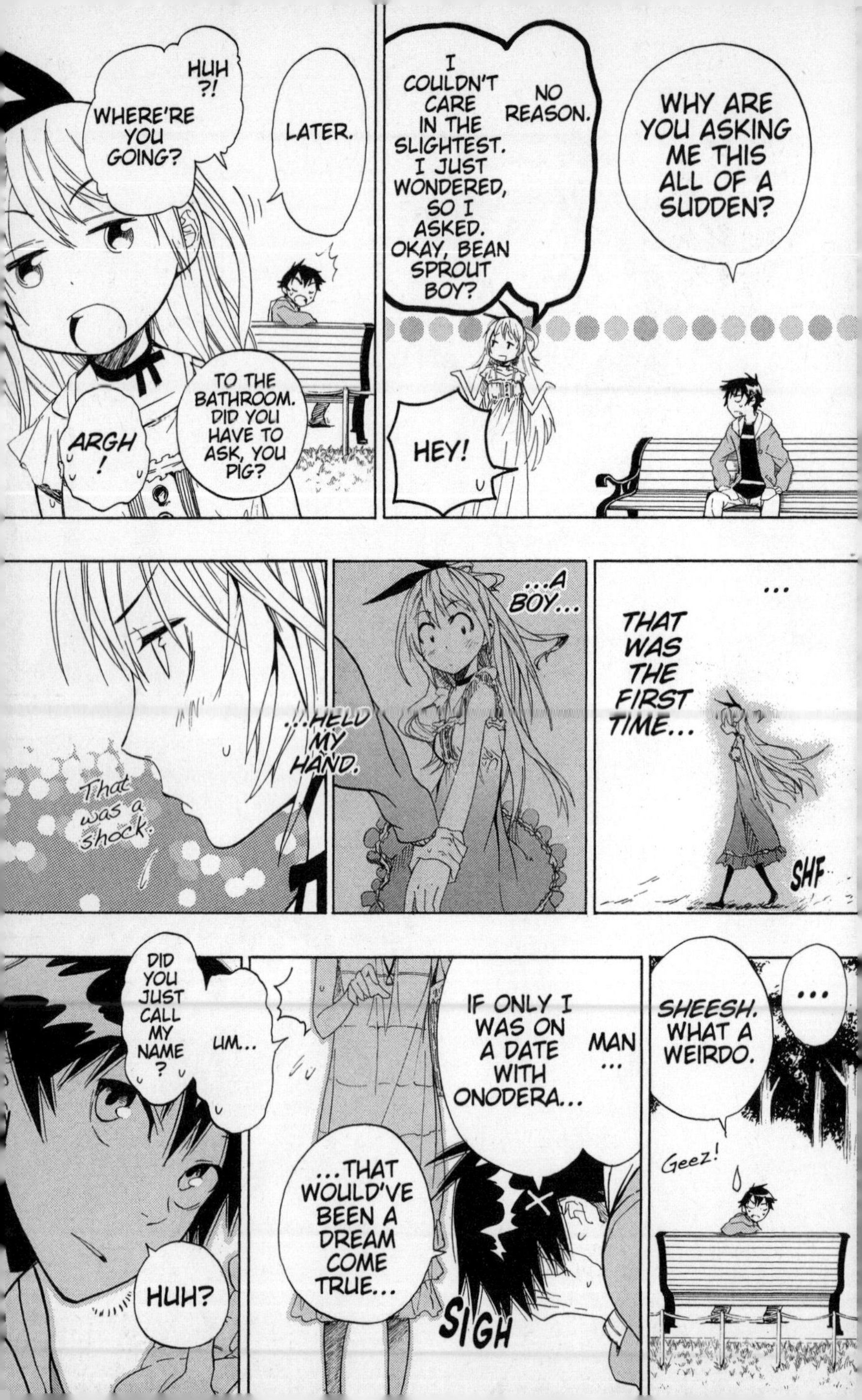
WHY ARE YOU ASKING ME THIS ALL OF A SUDDEN?
NO REASON.
I COULDN'T CARE IN THE SLIGHTEST. I JUST WONDERED, SO I ASKED. OKAY, BEAN SPROUT BOY?
HEY!
LATER.
HUH ?!
WHERE'RE YOU GOING?
TO THE BATHROOM. DID YOU HAVE TO ASK, YOU PIG?
ARGH !
...
THAT WAS THE FIRST TIME...
SHF
...A BOY...
...HELD MY HAND.
That was a shock.
...
SHEESH. WHAT A WEIRDO.
Geez!
MAN ...
IF ONLY I WAS ON A DATE WITH ONODERA...
...THAT WOULD'VE BEEN A DREAM COME TRUE...
SIGH
UM...
DID YOU JUST CALL MY NAME ?
HUH?

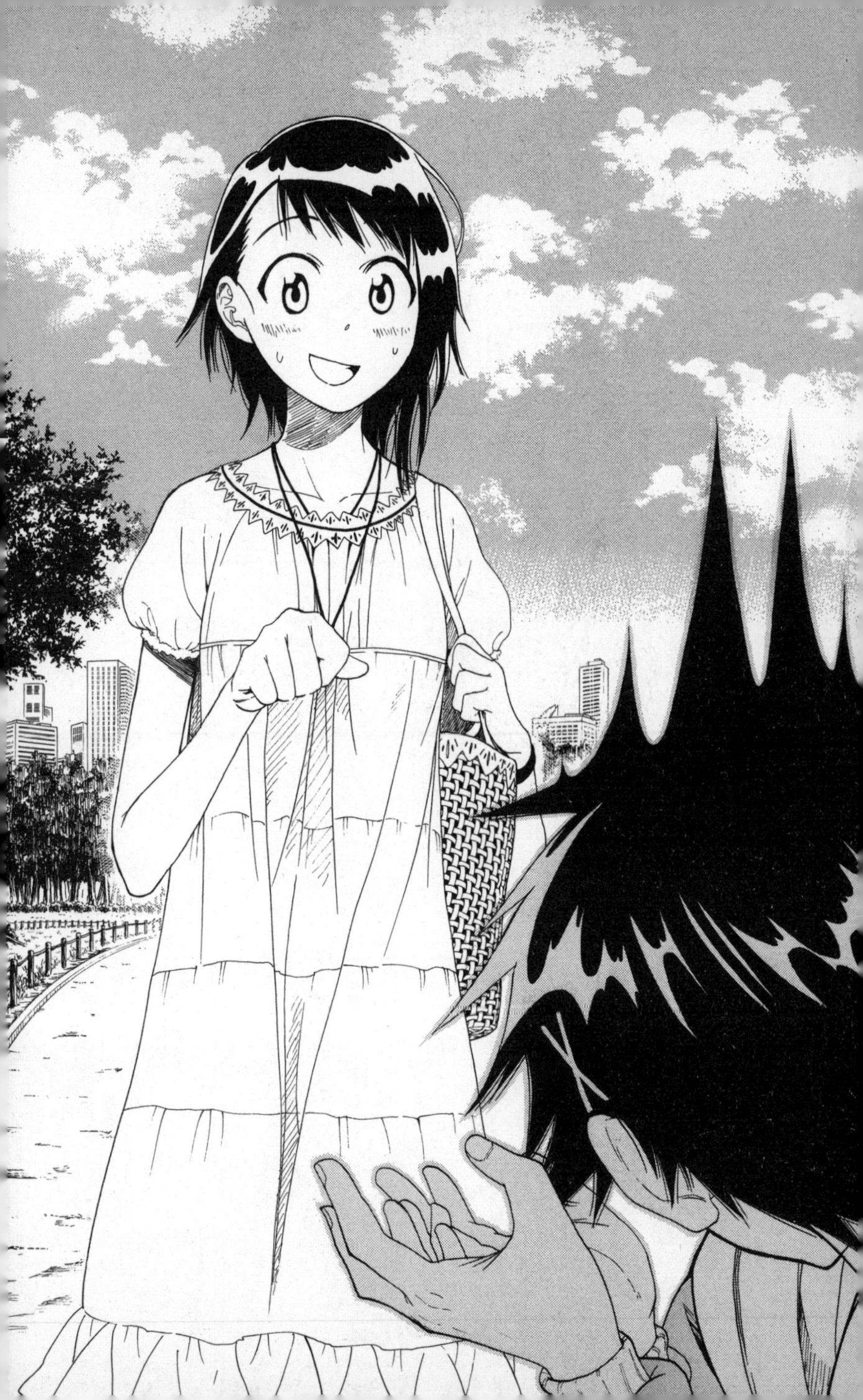

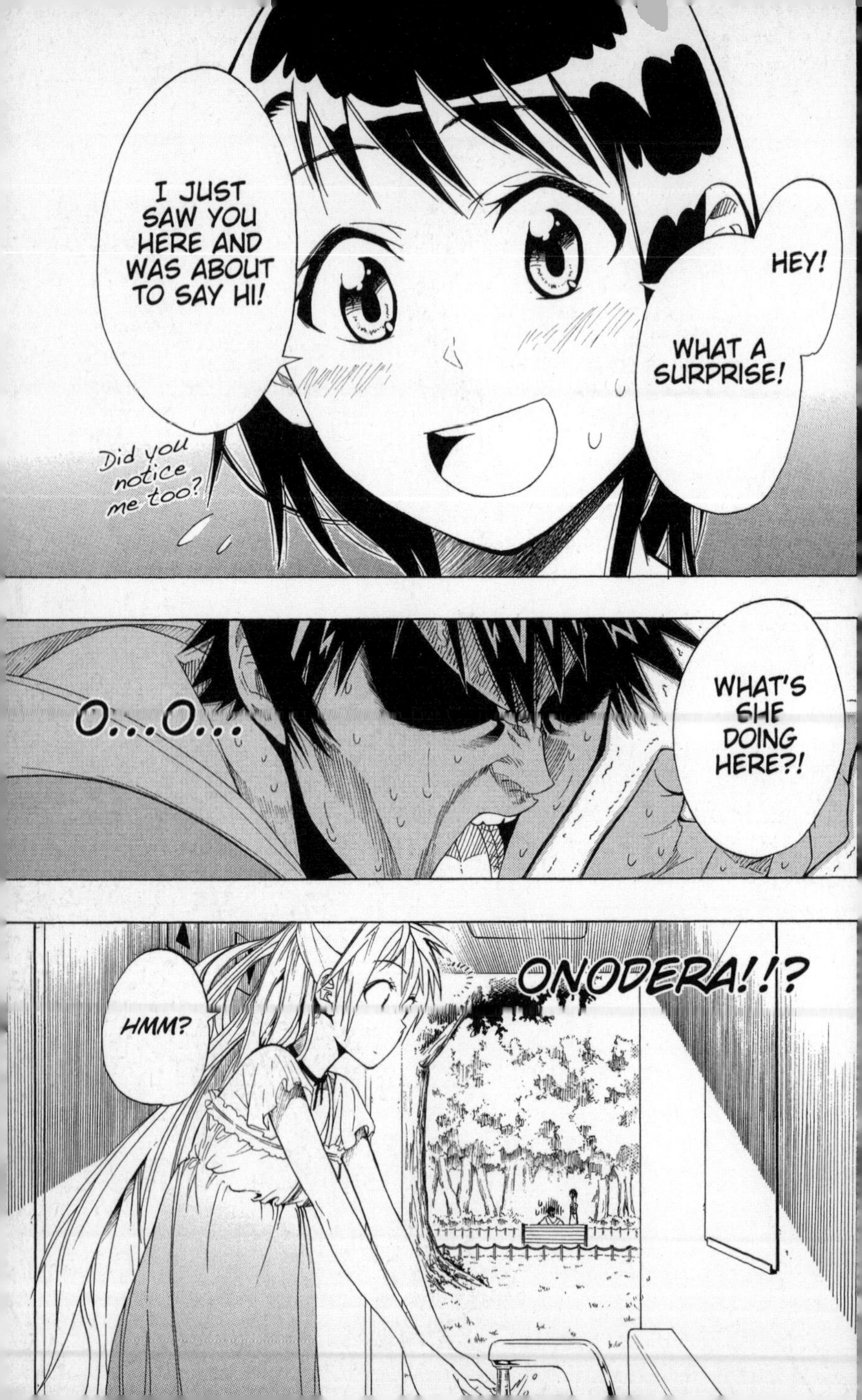
HEY!
WHAT A SURPRISE!
I JUST SAW YOU HERE AND WAS ABOUT TO SAY HI!
Did you notice me too?
WHAT'S SHE DOING HERE?!
O...O...
ONODERA!!?
HMM?

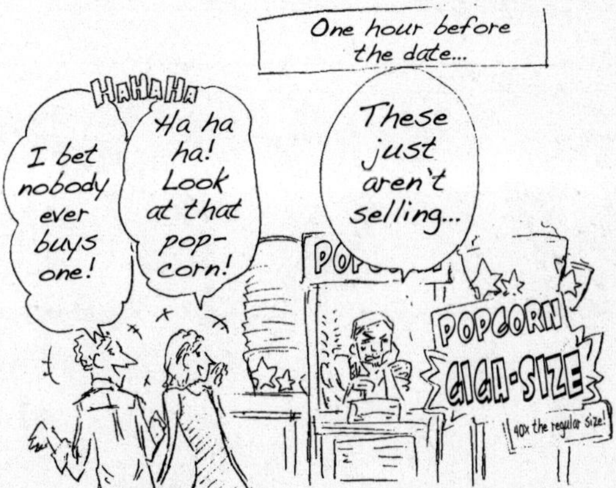
One hour before the date...
These just aren't selling...
POPCORN
GIGA-SIZE
40x the regular size!
HaHaHa
Ha ha ha! Look at that pop-corn!
I bet nobody ever buys one!

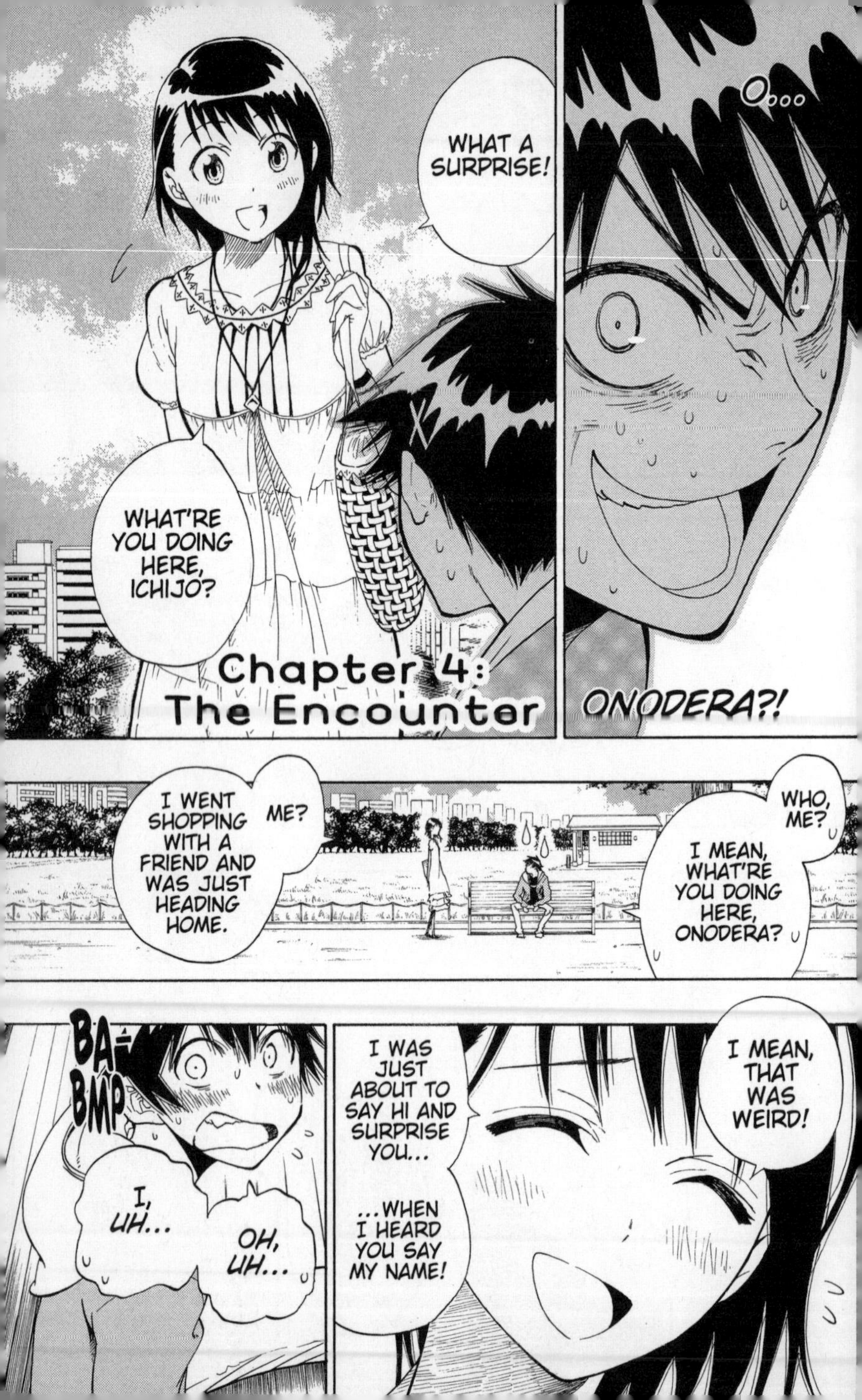
Oooo
ONODERA?!
WHAT A SURPRISE!
WHAT'RE YOU DOING HERE, ICHIJO?
Chapter 4: The Encounter
WHO, ME?
I MEAN, WHAT'RE YOU DOING HERE, ONODERA?
ME?
I WENT SHOPPING WITH A FRIEND AND WAS JUST HEADING HOME.
I MEAN, THAT WAS WEIRD!
I WAS JUST ABOUT TO SAY HI AND SURPRISE YOU...
...WHEN I HEARD YOU SAY MY NAME!
BA-BMP
OH, UH...
I, UH...

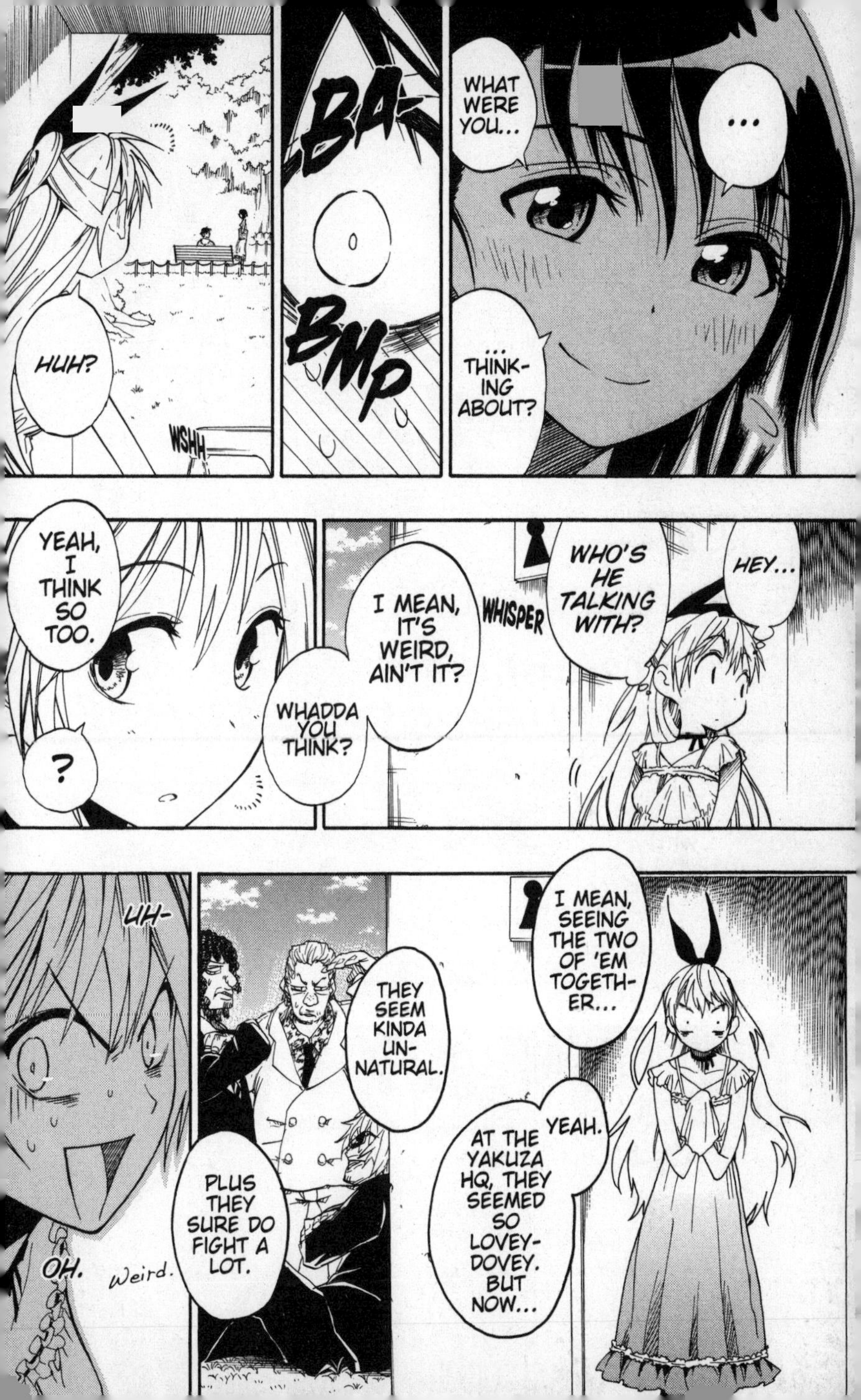
...
WHAT WERE YOU...
...THINKING ABOUT?
BA-
BMP
HUH?
WSHH
HEY...
WHO'S HE TALKING WITH?
WHISPER
I MEAN, IT'S WEIRD, AIN'T IT?
WHADDA YOU THINK?
YEAH, I THINK SO TOO.
?
I MEAN, SEEING THE TWO OF 'EM TOGETHER...
YEAH.
AT THE YAKUZA HQ, THEY SEEMED SO LOVEY-DOVEY. BUT NOW...
THEY SEEM KINDA UNNATURAL.
PLUS THEY SURE DO FIGHT A LOT.
UH-
OH.
Weird.

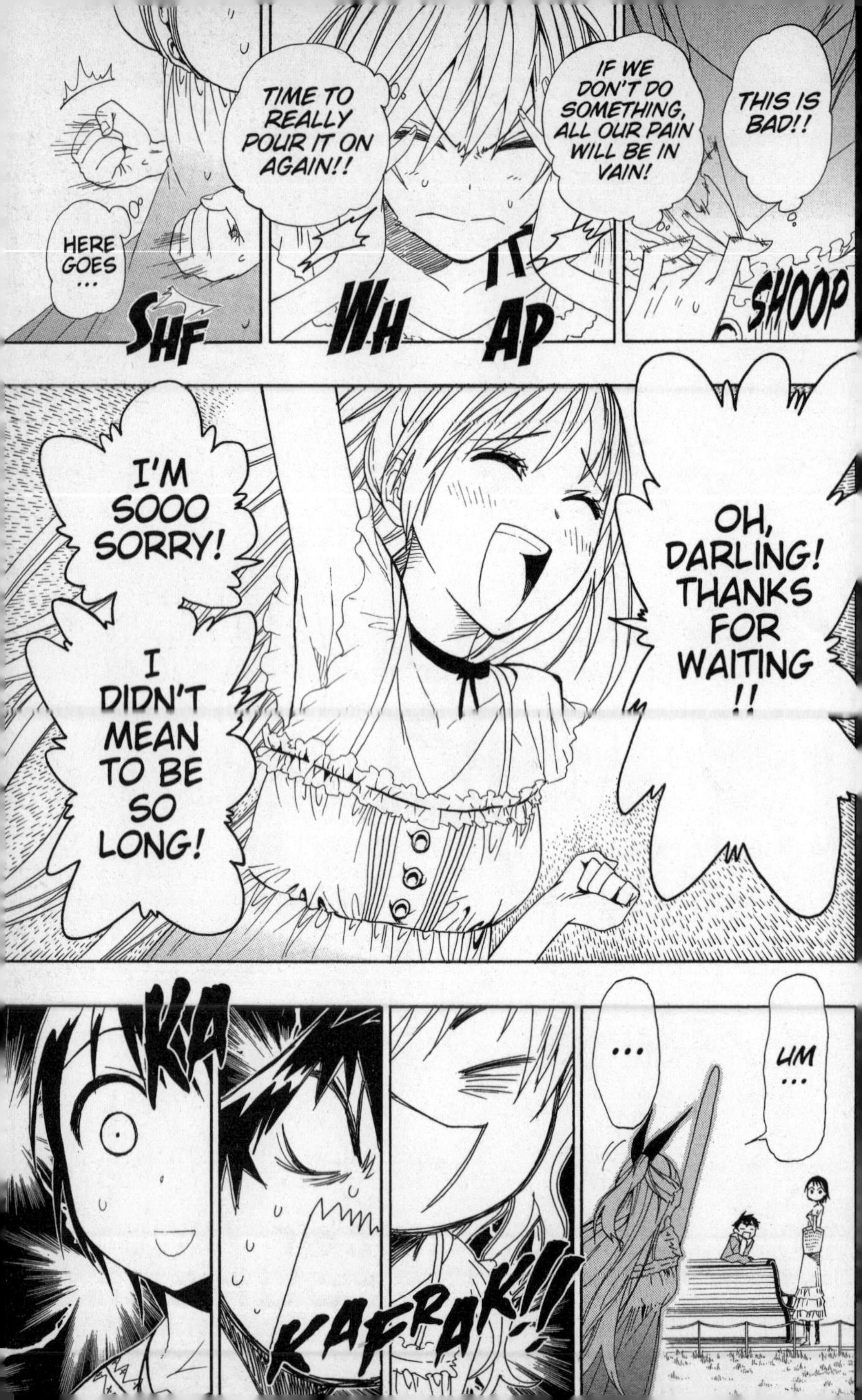
THIS IS BAD!!
IF WE DON'T DO SOMETHING, ALL OUR PAIN WILL BE IN VAIN!
SHOOP
TIME TO REALLY POUR IT ON AGAIN!!
WHAP
HERE GOES ...
SHF
OH, DARLING! THANKS FOR WAITING!!
I'M SOOO SORRY!
I DIDN'T MEAN TO BE SO LONG!
UM ...
...
KAFRAK!!
KA

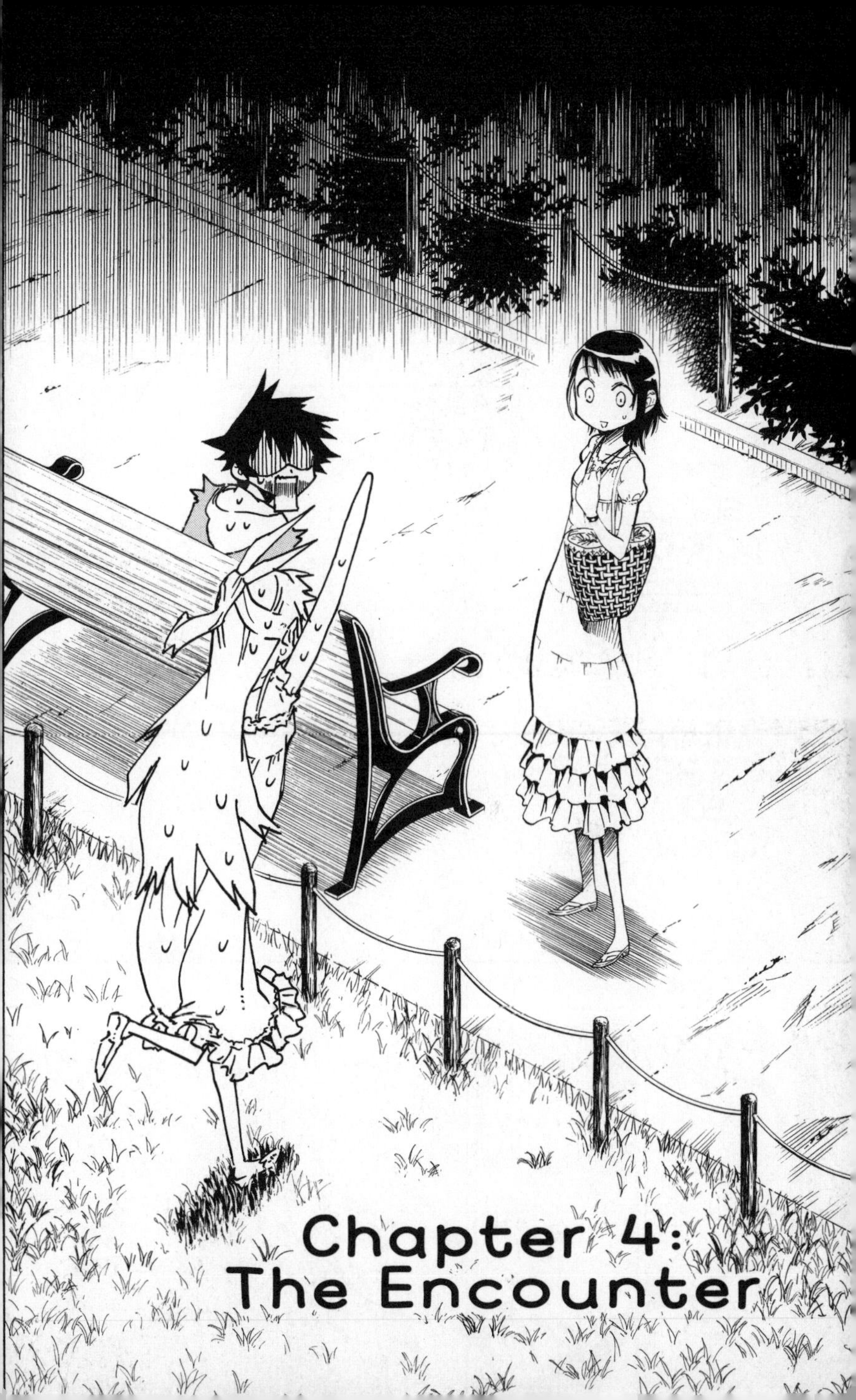
Chapter 4:
The Encounter

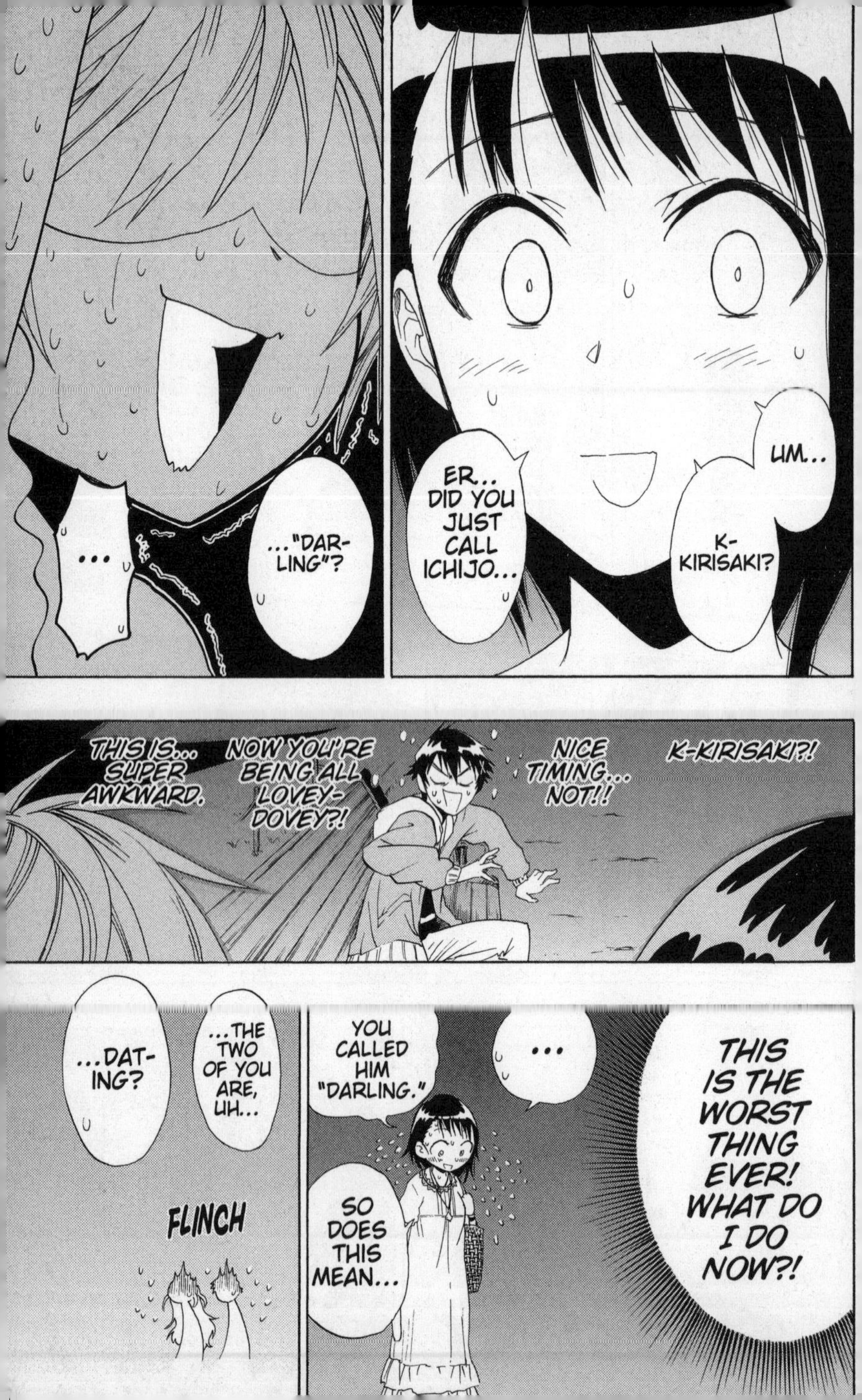
UM...
K-KIRISAKI?
ER.. DID YOU JUST CALL ICHIJO...
..."DAR-LING"?
...
K-KIRISAKI?!
NICE TIMING... NOT!!
NOW YOU'RE BEING ALL LOVEY-DOVEY?!
THIS IS... SUPER AWKWARD.
THIS IS THE WORST THING EVER! WHAT DO I DO NOW?!
...
YOU CALLED HIM "DARLING."
SO DOES THIS MEAN...
...THE TWO OF YOU ARE, UH...
...DAT-ING?
FLINCH

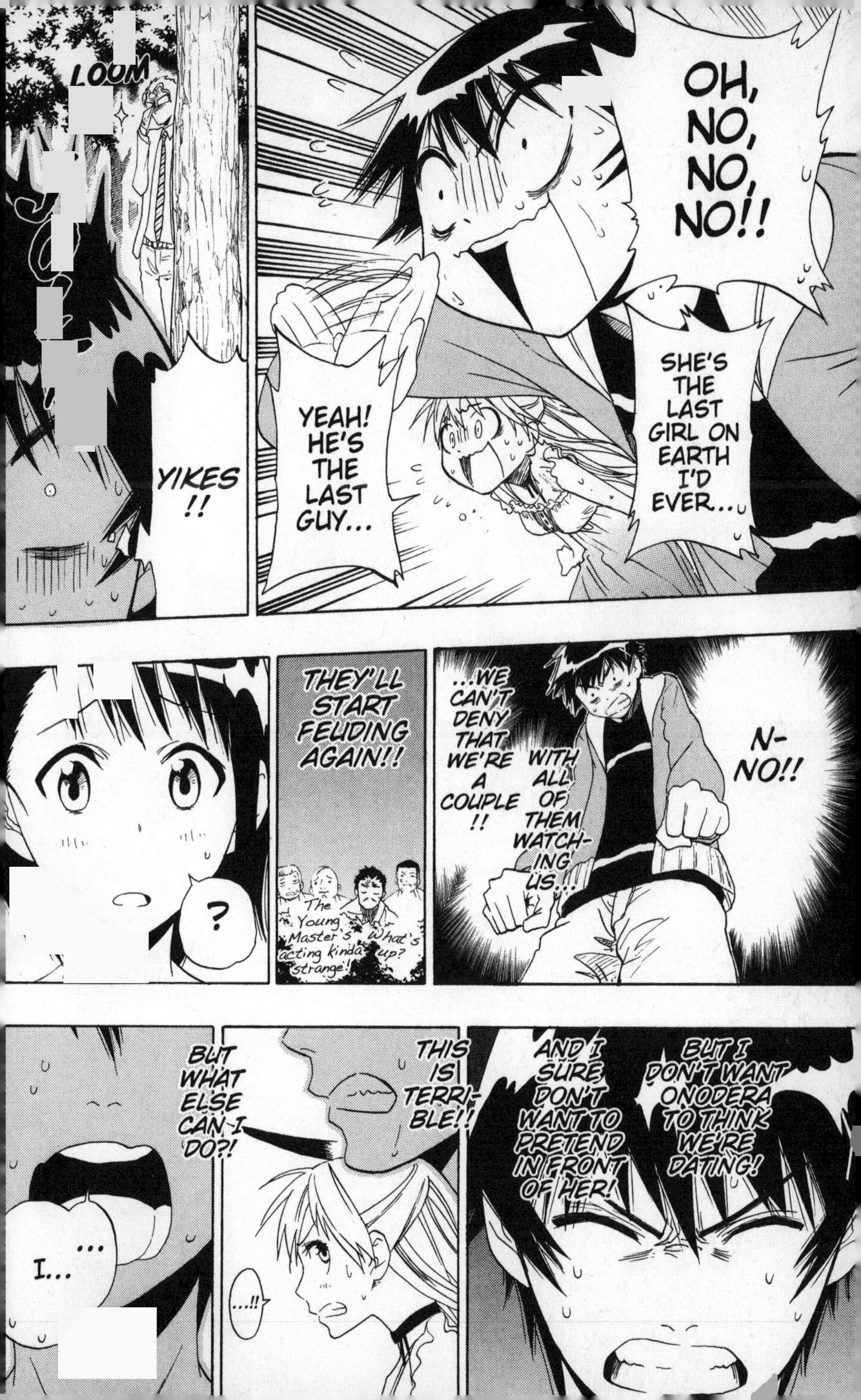
OH, NO, NO, NO!!
SHE'S THE LAST GIRL ON EARTH I'D EVER...
YEAH! HE'S THE LAST GUY...
LOOM
YIKES!!
N-NO!!
...WE CAN'T DENY THAT WE'RE A COUPLE!!
WITH ALL OF THEM WATCHING US...
THEY'LL START FEUDING AGAIN!!
The Young Master's acting kinda strange!
What's up?
?
BUT I DON'T WANT ONODERA TO THINK WE'RE DATING!
AND I SURE DON'T WANT TO PRETEND IN FRONT OF HER!
THIS IS TERRIBLE!!
...!!
BUT WHAT ELSE CAN I DO?!
...
I...

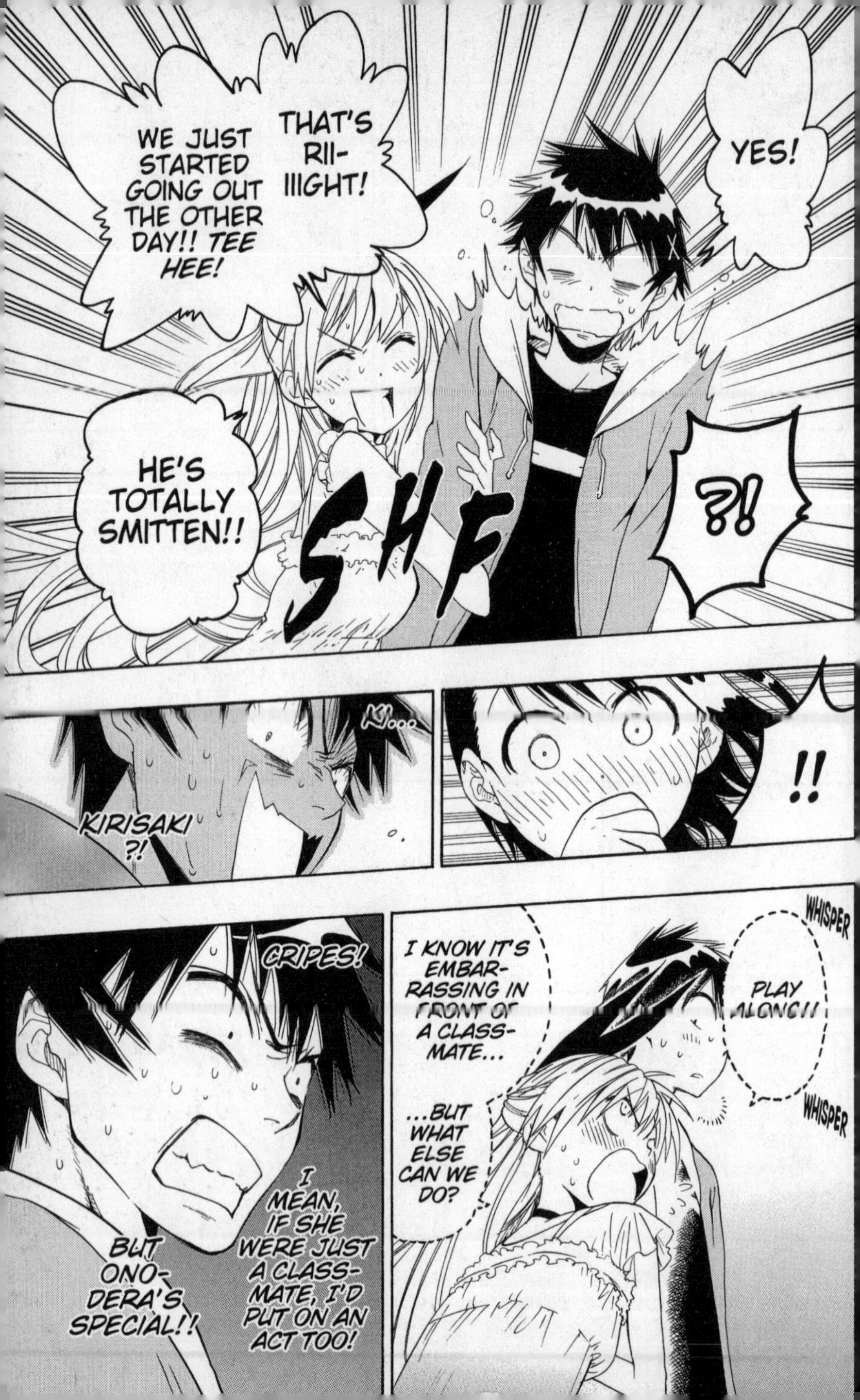
YES!
THAT'S RII-IIIGHT!
WE JUST STARTED GOING OUT THE OTHER DAY!! TEE HEE!
?!
HE'S TOTALLY SMITTEN!!
SHF
!!
KI...
KIRISAKI ?!
WHISPER
PLAY ALONG!!
WHISPER
I KNOW IT'S EMBARRASSING IN FRONT OF A CLASSMATE...
...BUT WHAT ELSE CAN WE DO?
CRIPES!
I MEAN, IF SHE WERE JUST A CLASSMATE, I'D PUT ON AN ACT TOO!
BUT ONODERA'S SPECIAL!!

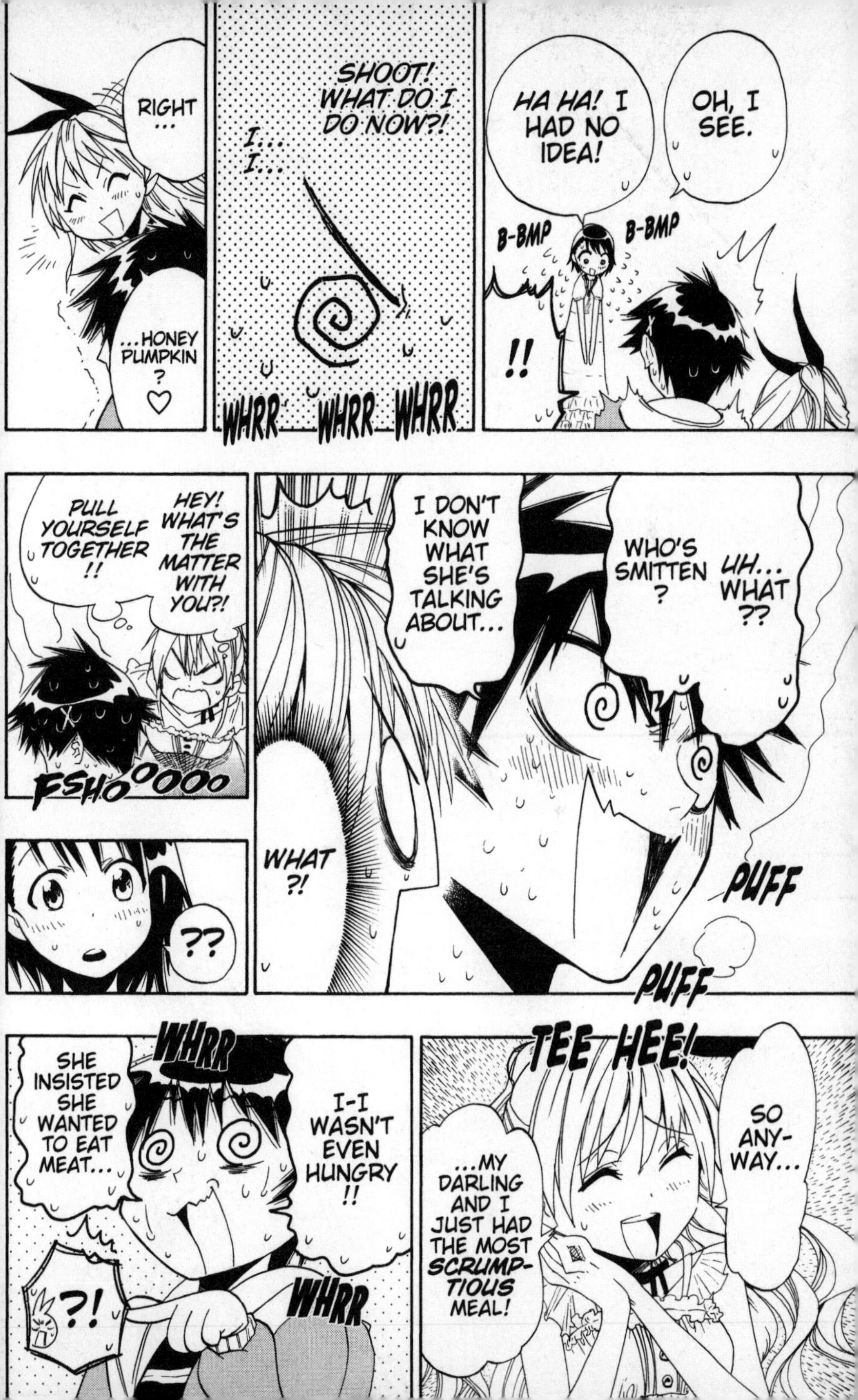
OH, I SEE.
HA HA! I HAD NO IDEA!
B-BMP
B-BMP
!!
SHOOT! WHAT DO I DO NOW?!
I... I...
WHRR
WHRR
WHRR
RIGHT...
...HONEY PUMPKIN? ♡
UH... WHAT??
WHO'S SMITTEN?
I DON'T KNOW WHAT SHE'S TALKING ABOUT...
WHAT?!
PUFF
PUFF
HEY! WHAT'S THE MATTER WITH YOU?!
PULL YOURSELF TOGETHER!!
FSHOOOOO
??
TEE HEE!
SO ANY-WAY...
...MY DARLING AND I JUST HAD THE MOST SCRUMPTIOUS MEAL!
WHRR
I-I WASN'T EVEN HUNGRY!!
SHE INSISTED SHE WANTED TO EAT MEAT...
WHRR
?!

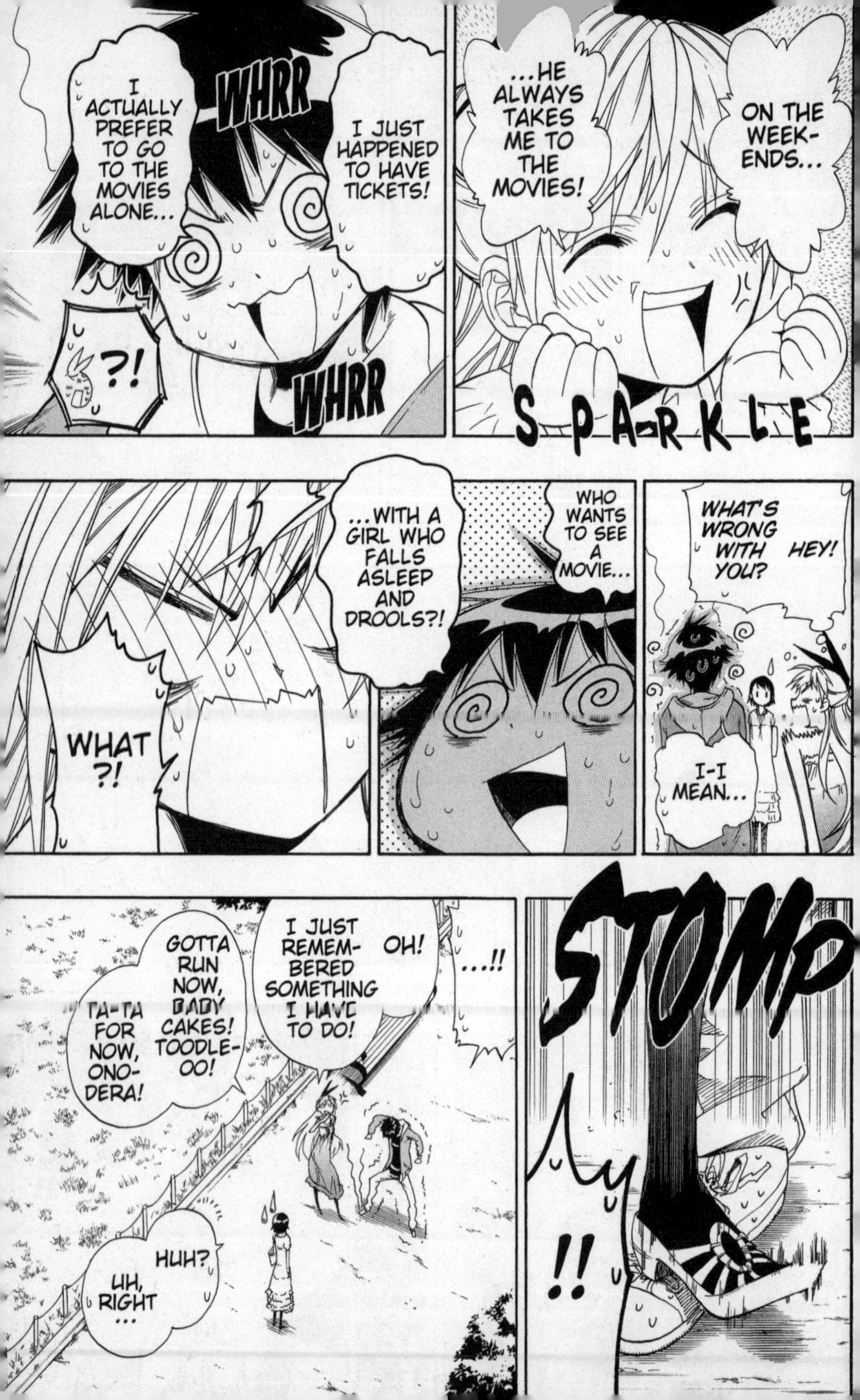
ON THE WEEK-ENDS...
...HE ALWAYS TAKES ME TO THE MOVIES!
SPARKLE
I JUST HAPPENED TO HAVE TICKETS!
WHRR
I ACTUALLY PREFER TO GO TO THE MOVIES ALONE...
WHRR
?!
HEY!
WHAT'S WRONG WITH YOU?
I-I MEAN...
WHO WANTS TO SEE A MOVIE...
...WITH A GIRL WHO FALLS ASLEEP AND DROOLS?!
WHAT ?!
STOMP
!!
...!!
OH!
I JUST REMEM-BERED SOMETHING I HAVE TO DO!
GOTTA RUN NOW, BABY CAKES! TOODLE-OO!
TA-TA FOR NOW, ONO-DERA!
HUH?
UH, RIGHT ...

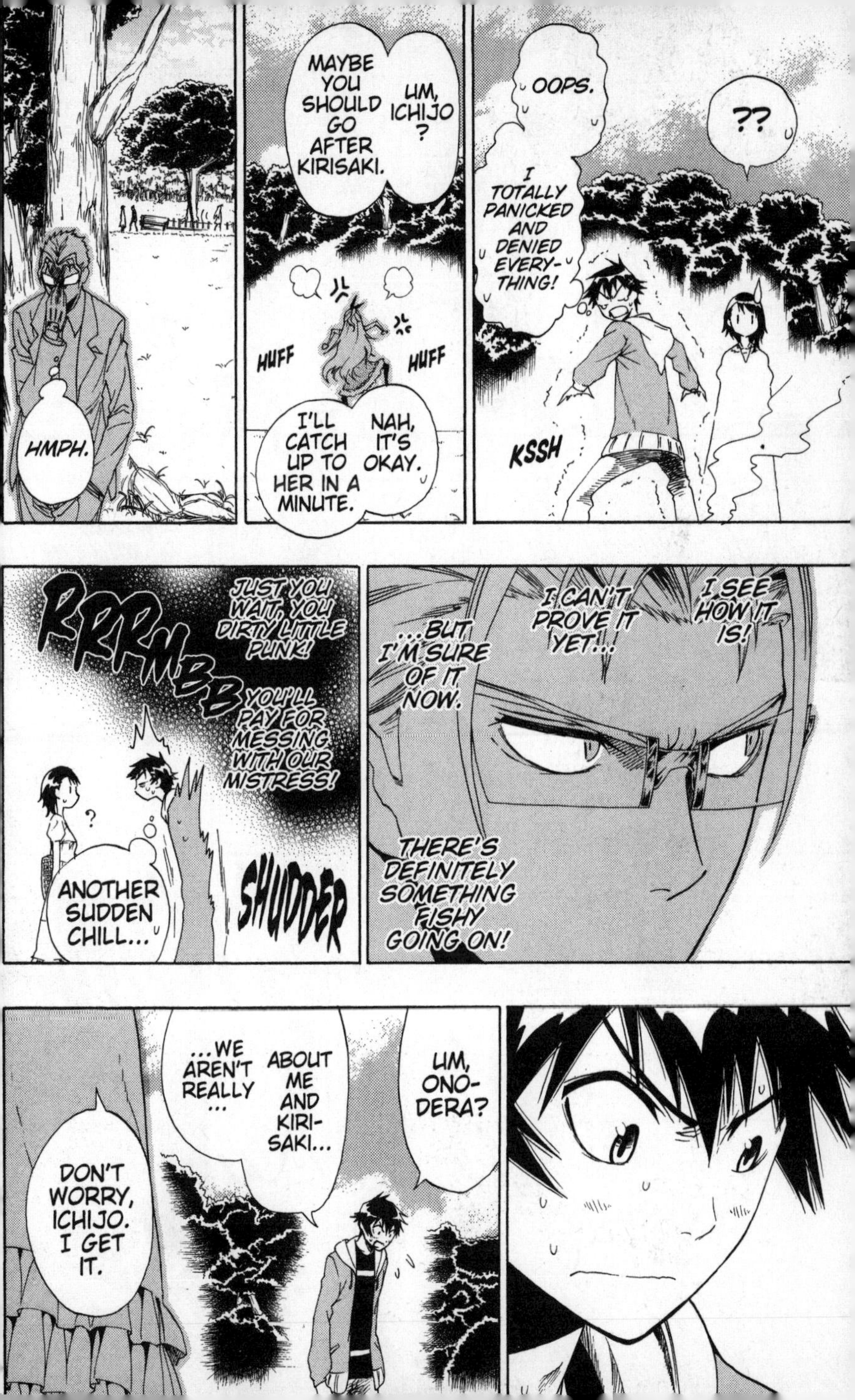
??
OOPS.
I TOTALLY PANICKED AND DENIED EVERY-THING!
KSSH
UM, ICHIJO?
MAYBE YOU SHOULD GO AFTER KIRISAKI.
HUFF
HUFF
NAH, IT'S OKAY.
I'LL CATCH UP TO HER IN A MINUTE.
HMPH.
I SEE HOW IT IS!
I CAN'T PROVE IT YET...
...BUT I'M SURE OF IT NOW.
THERE'S DEFINITELY SOMETHING FISHY GOING ON!
RRRMBB
JUST YOU WAIT, YOU DIRTY LITTLE PUNK!
YOU'LL PAY FOR MESSING WITH OUR MISTRESS!
?
SHUDDER
ANOTHER SUDDEN CHILL...
UM, ONO-DERA?
ABOUT ME AND KIRI-SAKI...
...WE AREN'T REALLY...
DON'T WORRY, ICHIJO. I GET IT.

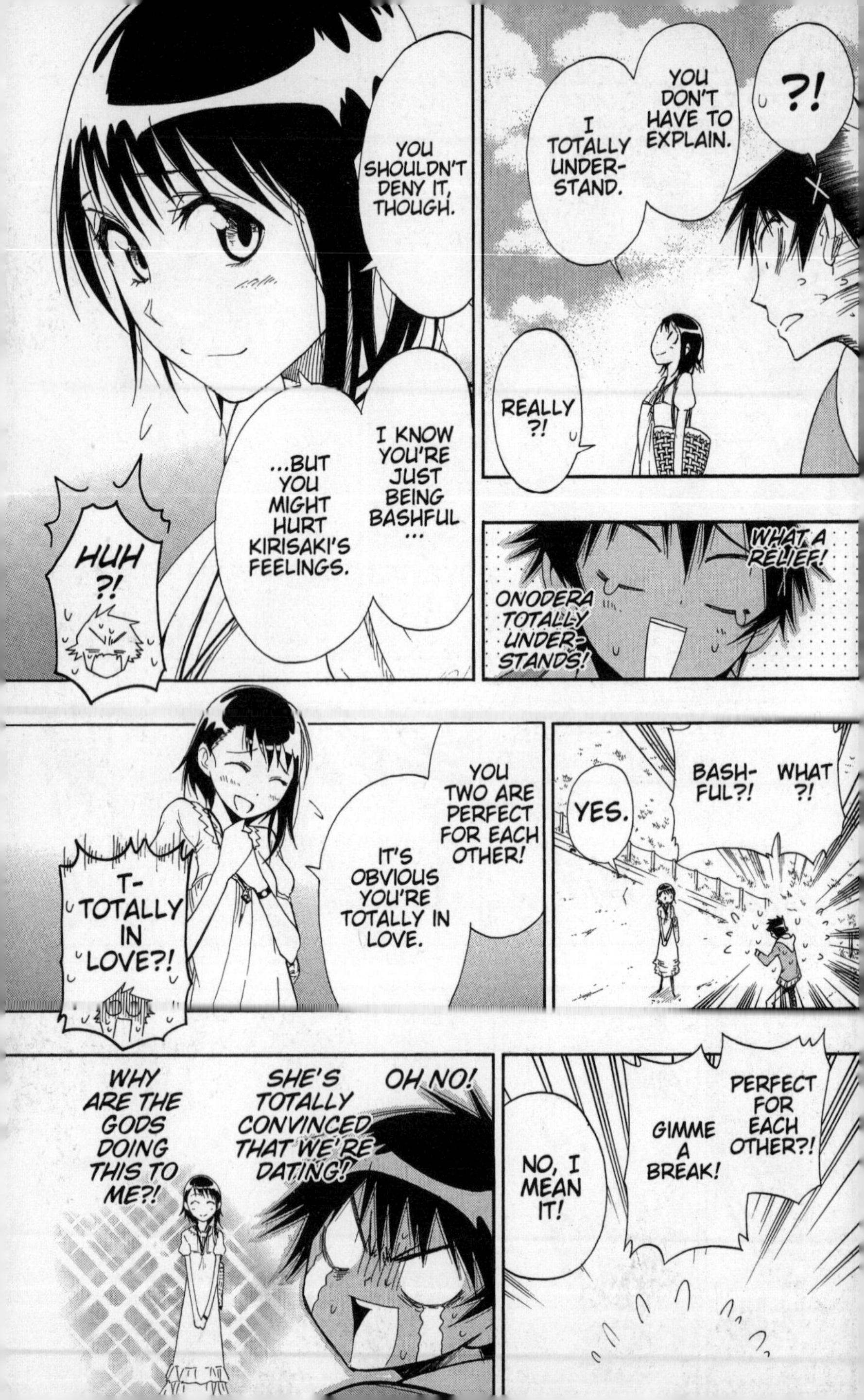
?!
YOU DON'T HAVE TO EXPLAIN.
I TOTALLY UNDER-STAND.
REALLY ?!
WHAT A RELIEF!
ONODERA TOTALLY UNDER-STANDS!
YOU SHOULDN'T DENY IT, THOUGH.
I KNOW YOU'RE JUST BEING BASHFUL ...
...BUT YOU MIGHT HURT KIRISAKI'S FEELINGS.
HUH ?!
WHAT ?!
BASH-FUL?!
YES.
YOU TWO ARE PERFECT FOR EACH OTHER!
IT'S OBVIOUS YOU'RE TOTALLY IN LOVE.
T-TOTALLY IN LOVE?!
PERFECT FOR EACH OTHER?!
GIMME A BREAK!
NO, I MEAN IT!
OH NO!
SHE'S TOTALLY CONVINCED THAT WE'RE DATING!
WHY ARE THE GODS DOING THIS TO ME?!

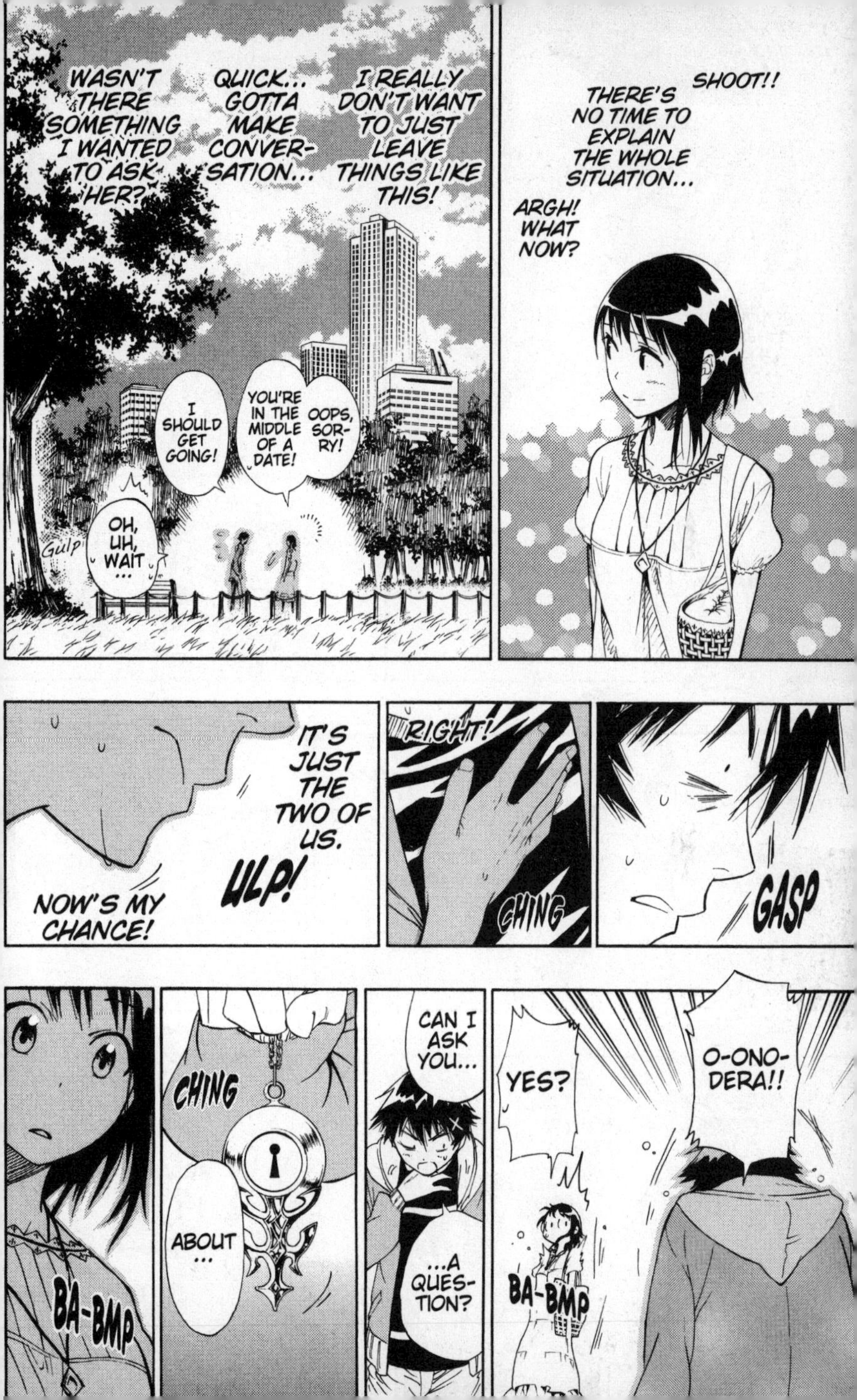
SHOOT!!
THERE'S NO TIME TO EXPLAIN THE WHOLE SITUATION...
ARGH! WHAT NOW?
I REALLY DON'T WANT TO JUST LEAVE THINGS LIKE THIS!
QUICK... GOTTA MAKE CONVER-SATION...
WASN'T THERE SOMETHING I WANTED TO ASK HER?
OOPS, SORRY!
YOU'RE IN THE MIDDLE OF A DATE!
I SHOULD GET GOING!
OH, UH, WAIT ...
Gulp
GASP
RIGHT!
CHING
IT'S JUST THE TWO OF US.
ULP!
NOW'S MY CHANCE!
O-ONO-DERA!!
YES?
BA-BMP
CAN I ASK YOU...
...A QUES-TION?
CHING
ABOUT ...
BA-BMP

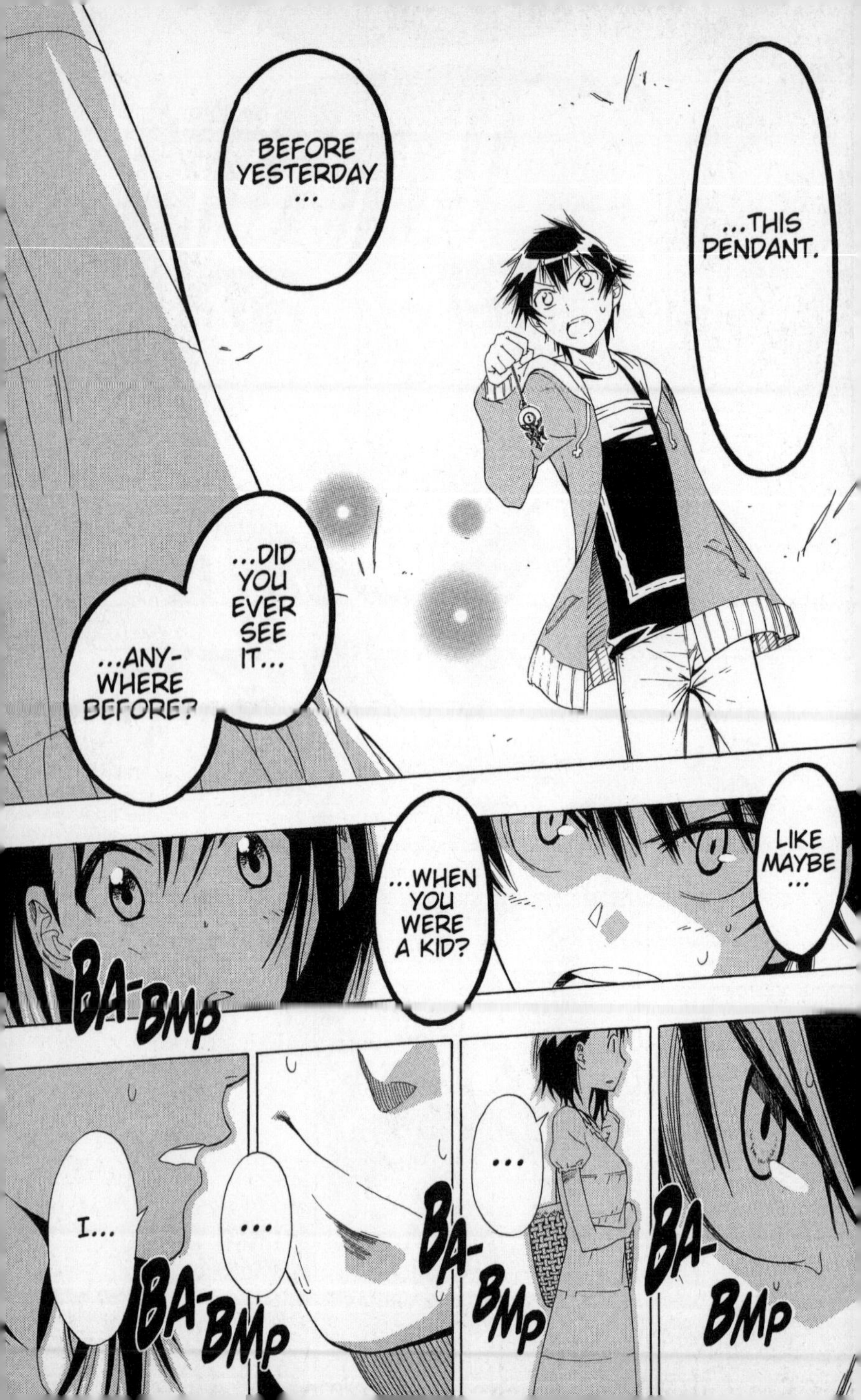
...THIS PENDANT.
BEFORE YESTERDAY...
...DID YOU EVER SEE IT...
...ANY-WHERE BEFORE?
LIKE MAYBE...
...WHEN YOU WERE A KID?
BA-BMP
BA-BMP
...
BA-BMP
...
I...
BA-BMP

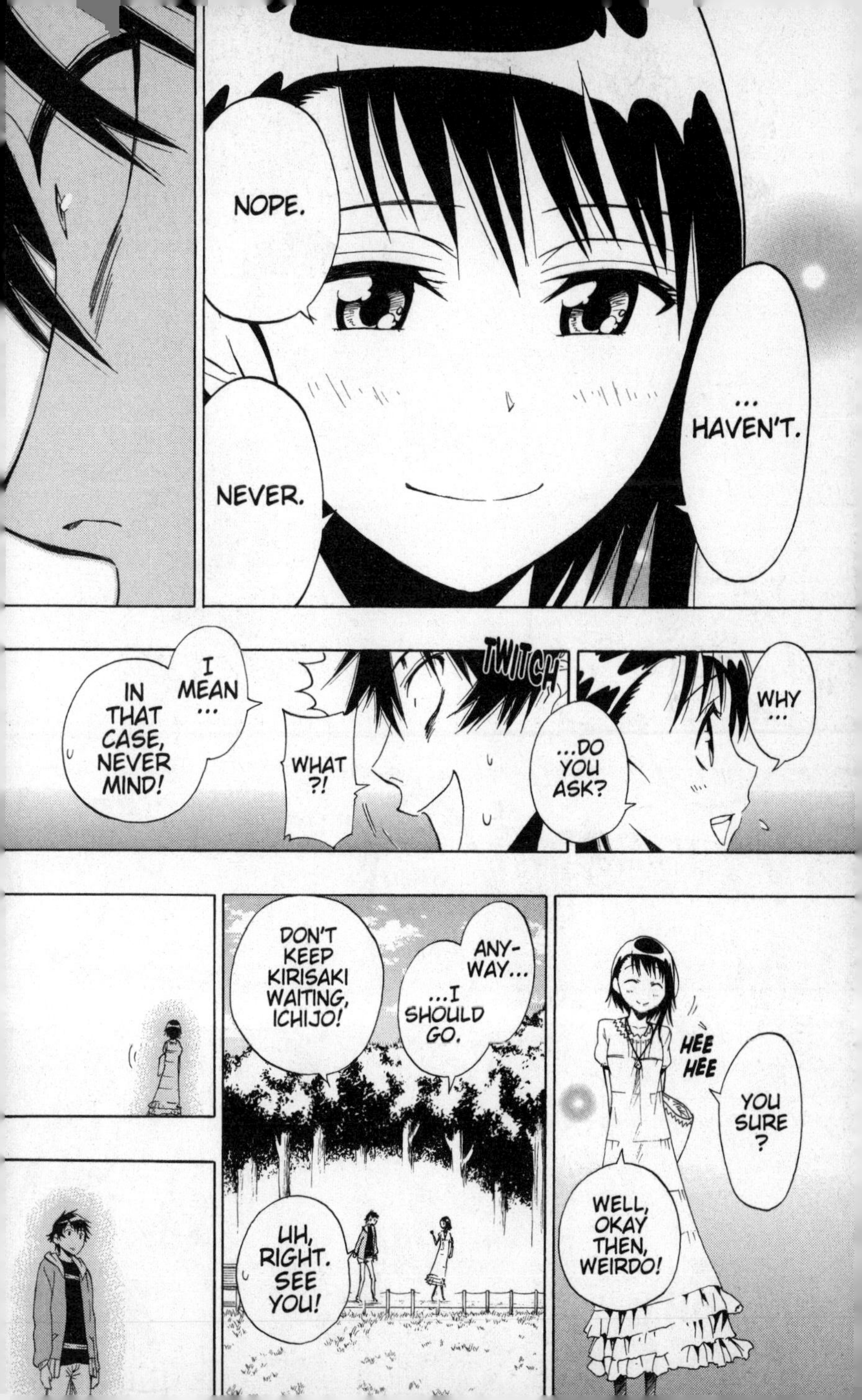
NOPE.
NEVER.
...HAVEN'T.
WHY...
...DO YOU ASK?
TWITCH
WHAT?!
I MEAN...
IN THAT CASE, NEVER MIND!
HEE HEE
YOU SURE?
WELL, OKAY THEN, WEIRDO!
ANY-WAY...
...I SHOULD GO.
DON'T KEEP KIRISAKI WAITING, ICHIJO!
UH, RIGHT. SEE YOU!

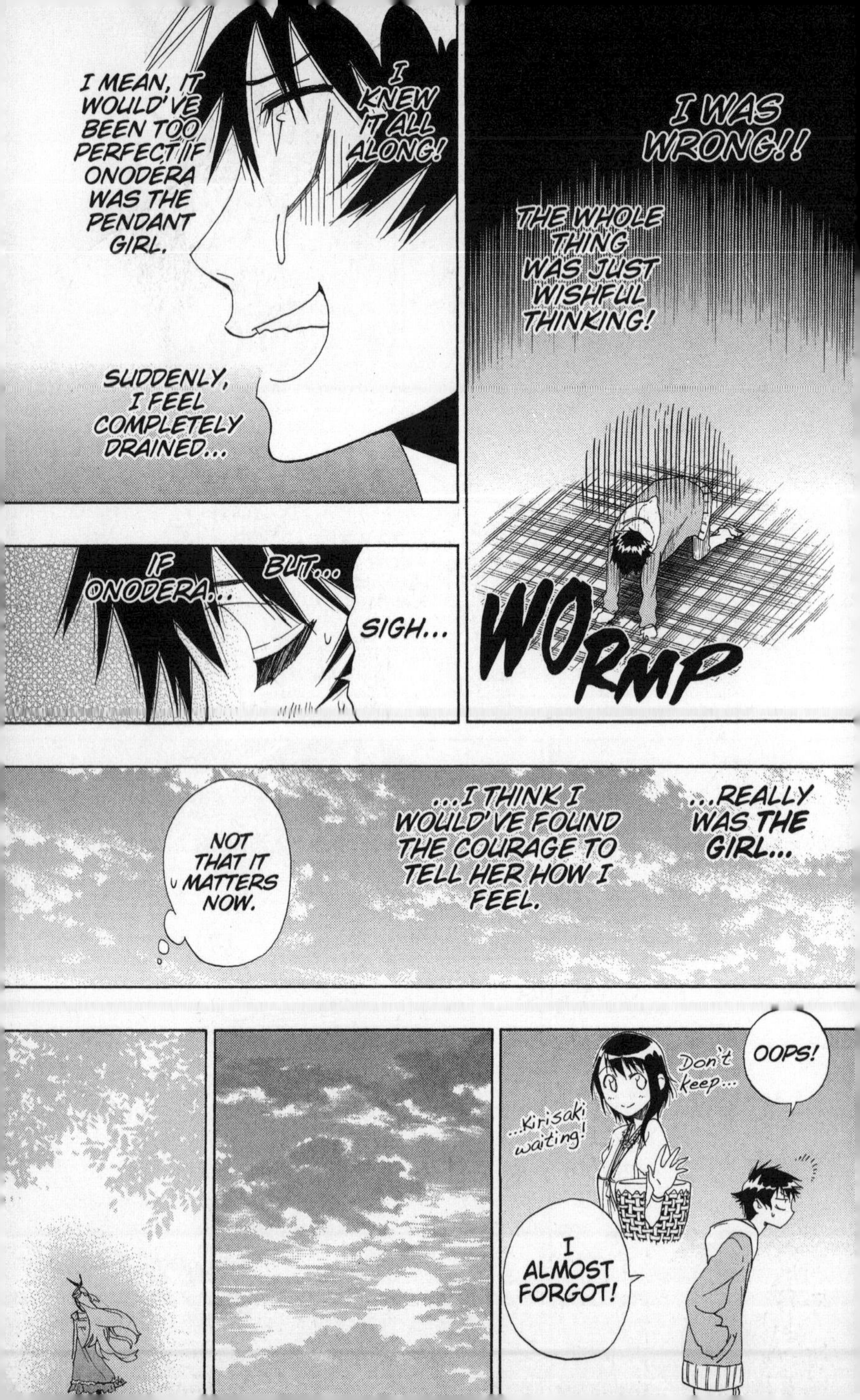
I WAS WRONG!!
THE WHOLE THING WAS JUST WISHFUL THINKING!
WORMP
I KNEW IT ALL ALONG!
I MEAN, IT WOULD'VE BEEN TOO PERFECT IF ONODERA WAS THE PENDANT GIRL.
SUDDENLY, I FEEL COMPLETELY DRAINED...
BUT...
IF ONODERA...
SIGH...
...REALLY WAS THE GIRL...
...I THINK I WOULD'VE FOUND THE COURAGE TO TELL HER HOW I FEEL.
NOT THAT IT MATTERS NOW.
OOPS!
Don't keep...
...Kirisaki waiting!
I ALMOST FORGOT!

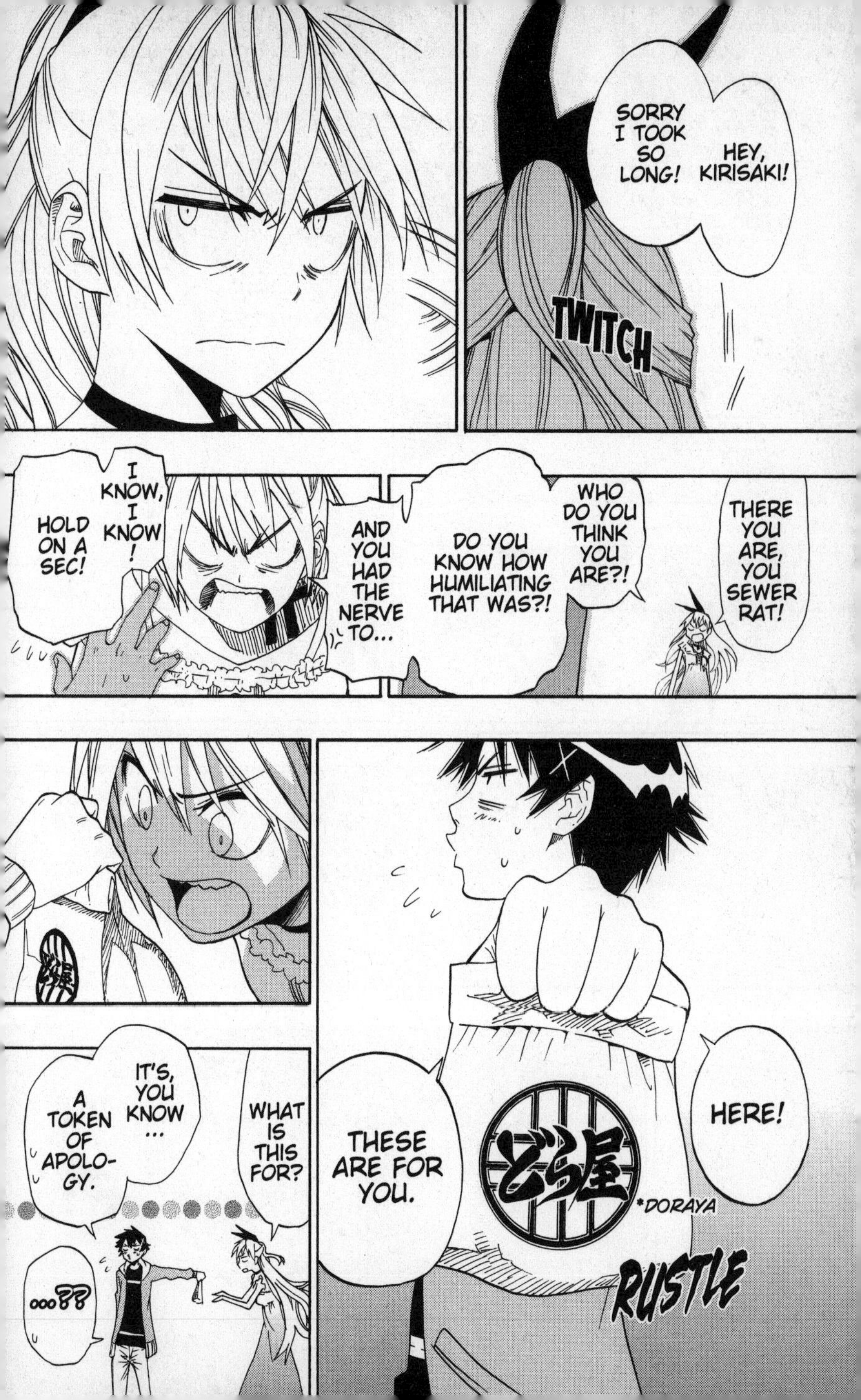

HEY, KIRISAKI!
SORRY I TOOK SO LONG!
TWITCH
THERE YOU ARE, YOU SEWER RAT!
WHO DO YOU THINK YOU ARE?!
DO YOU KNOW HOW HUMILIATING THAT WAS?!
AND YOU HAD THE NERVE TO...
I KNOW, I KNOW!
HOLD ON A SEC!
HERE!
どら屋
*DORAYA
RUSTLE
THESE ARE FOR YOU.
WHAT IS THIS FOR?
IT'S, YOU KNOW...
A TOKEN OF APOLOGY.
...??

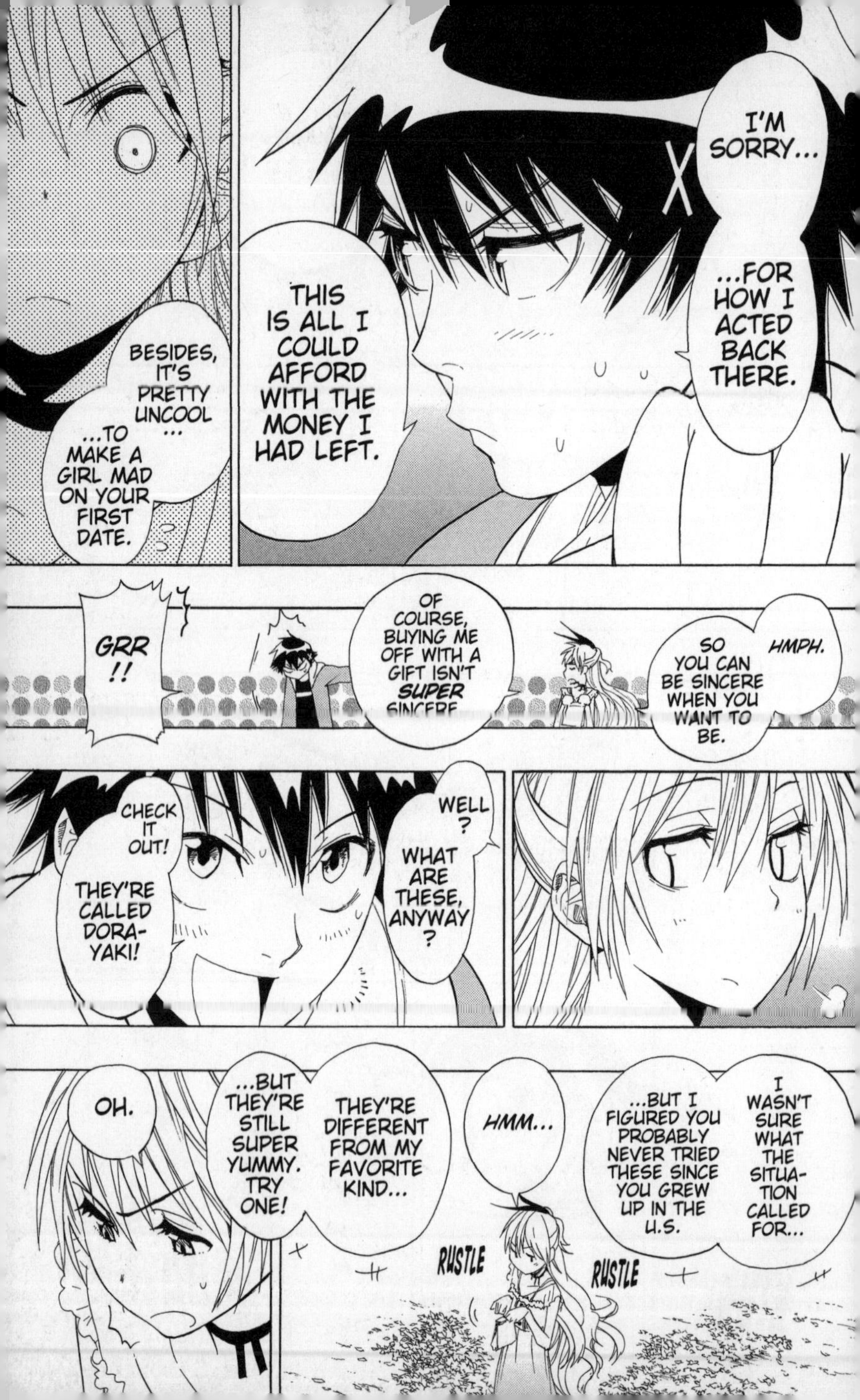
I'M SORRY...
...FOR HOW I ACTED BACK THERE.
THIS IS ALL I COULD AFFORD WITH THE MONEY I HAD LEFT.
BESIDES, IT'S PRETTY UNCOOL...
...TO MAKE A GIRL MAD ON YOUR FIRST DATE.
HMPH.
SO YOU CAN BE SINCERE WHEN YOU WANT TO BE.
OF COURSE, BUYING ME OFF WITH A GIFT ISN'T SUPER SINCERE...
GRR!!
WELL? WHAT ARE THESE, ANYWAY?
CHECK IT OUT!
THEY'RE CALLED DORA-YAKI!
I WASN'T SURE WHAT THE SITUATION CALLED FOR...
...BUT I FIGURED YOU PROBABLY NEVER TRIED THESE SINCE YOU GREW UP IN THE U.S.
HMM...
RUSTLE
RUSTLE
THEY'RE DIFFERENT FROM MY FAVORITE KIND...
...BUT THEY'RE STILL SUPER YUMMY. TRY ONE!
OH.

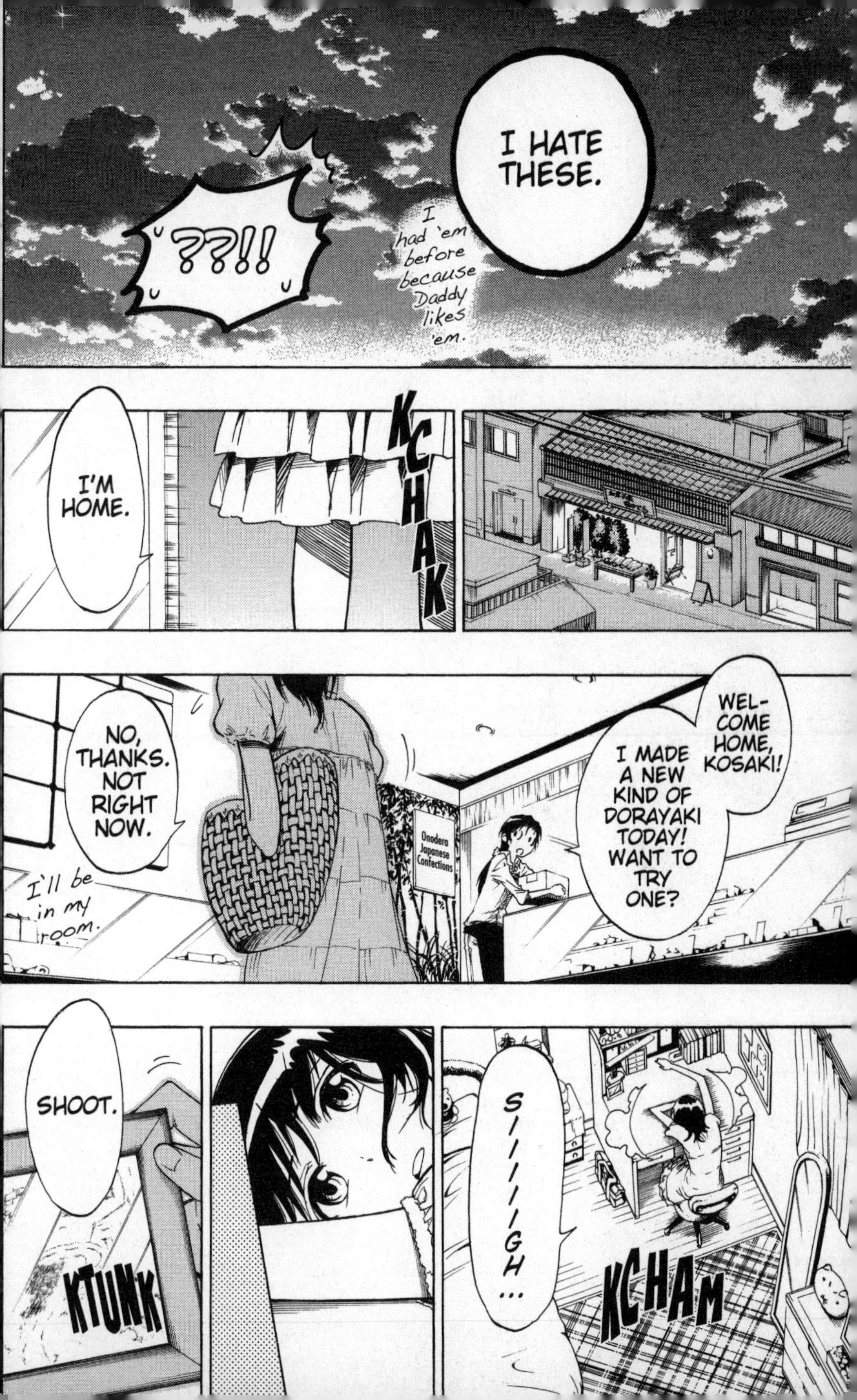
I HATE THESE.
I had 'em before because Daddy likes 'em.
??!!
KCHAK
I'M HOME.
WEL-COME HOME, KOSAKI!
I MADE A NEW KIND OF DORAYAKI TODAY! WANT TO TRY ONE?
Onodera Japanese Confections
NO, THANKS. NOT RIGHT NOW.
I'll be in my room.
SI////GH...
KCHAM
SHOOT.
KTUNK

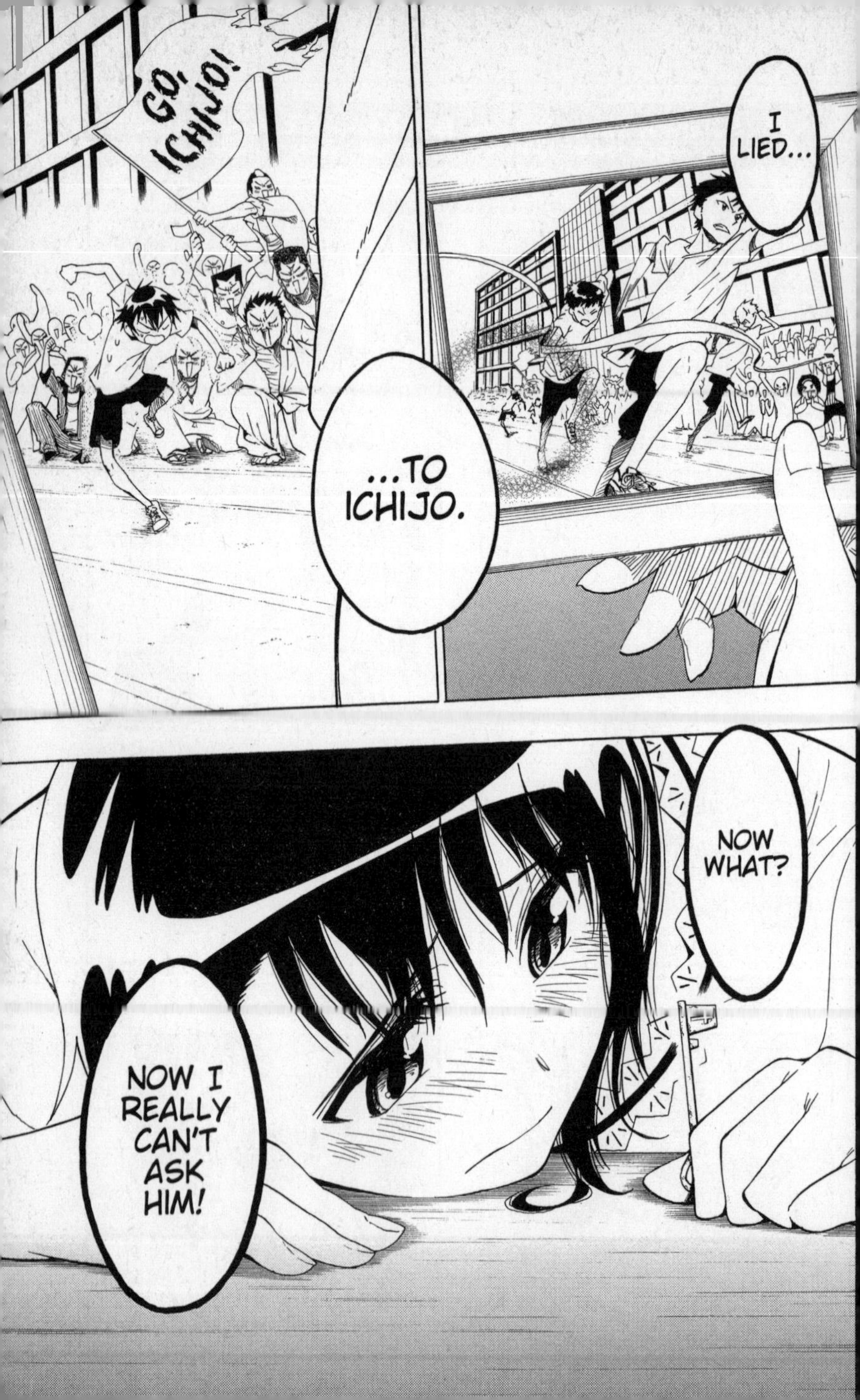
I LIED...
...TO ICHIJO.
GO, ICHIJO!
NOW WHAT?
NOW I REALLY CAN'T ASK HIM!

A Day in the Life of Ichijo

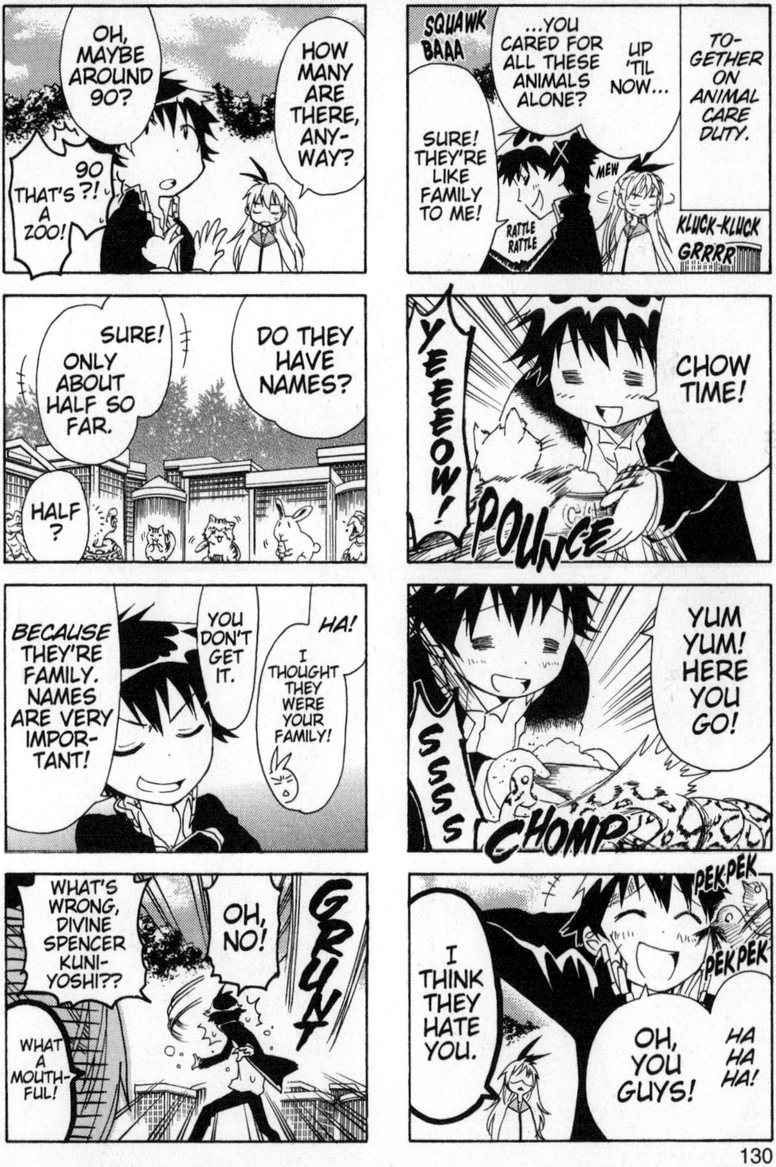
TOGETHER ON ANIMAL CARE DUTY.
UP 'TIL NOW...
...YOU CARED FOR ALL THESE ANIMALS ALONE?
SQUAWK
BAAA
SURE! THEY'RE LIKE FAMILY TO ME!
MEW
RATTLE RATTLE
KLUCK-KLUCK
GRRRR
CHOW TIME!
YEEEEOW!
POUNCE
YUM YUM! HERE YOU GO!
SSSS
CHOMP
PEKPEK
PEKPEK
HA HA HA!
OH, YOU GUYS!
I THINK THEY HATE YOU.
HOW MANY ARE THERE, ANYWAY?
OH, MAYBE AROUND 90?
90?! THAT'S A ZOO!
DO THEY HAVE NAMES?
SURE! ONLY ABOUT HALF SO FAR.
HALF?
HA! I THOUGHT THEY WERE YOUR FAMILY!
YOU DON'T GET IT.
BECAUSE THEY'RE FAMILY. NAMES ARE VERY IMPORTANT!
GRUNT
OH, NO!
WHAT'S WRONG, DIVINE SPENCER KUNIYOSHI??
WHAT A MOUTHFUL!

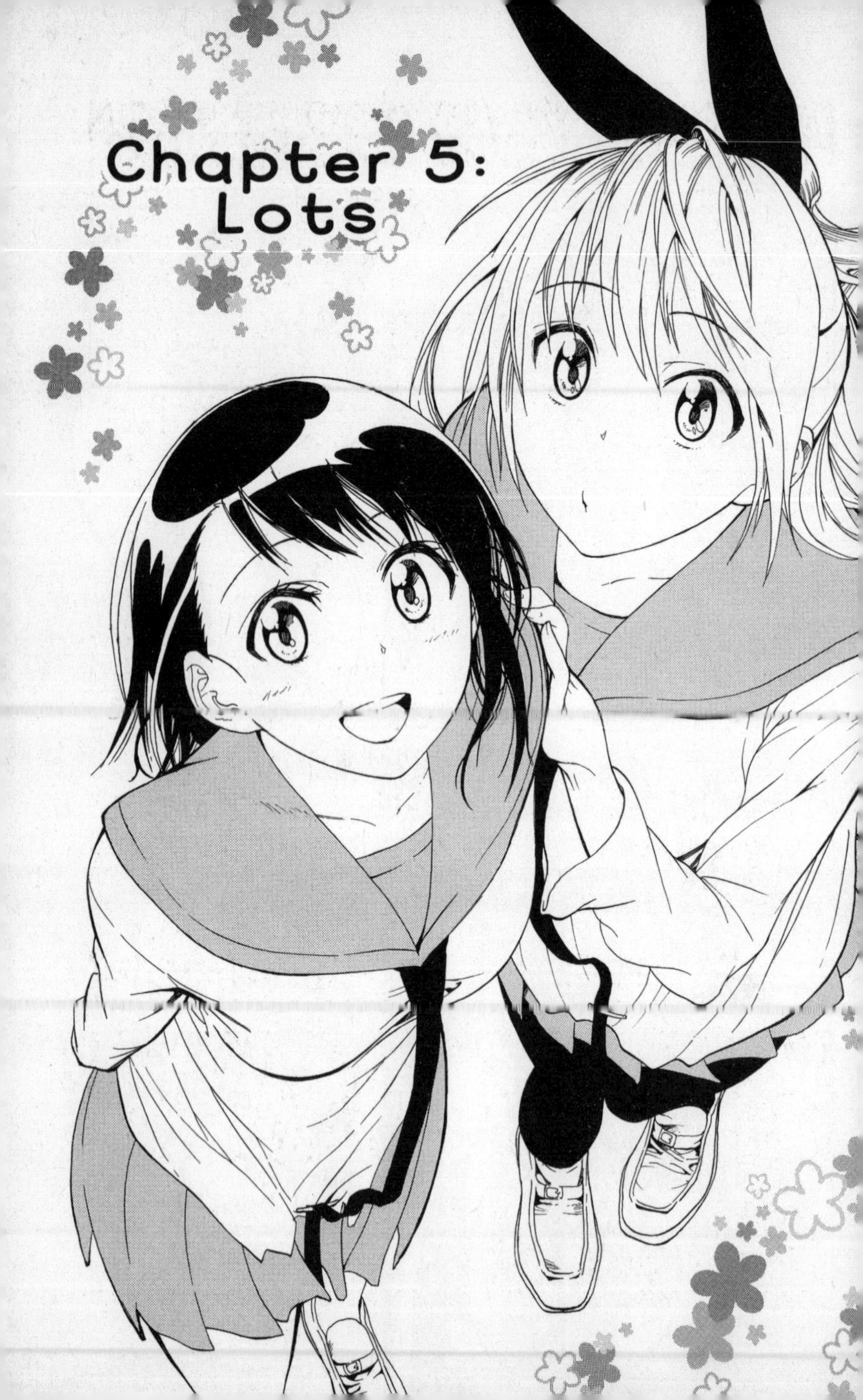
Chapter 5:
Lots

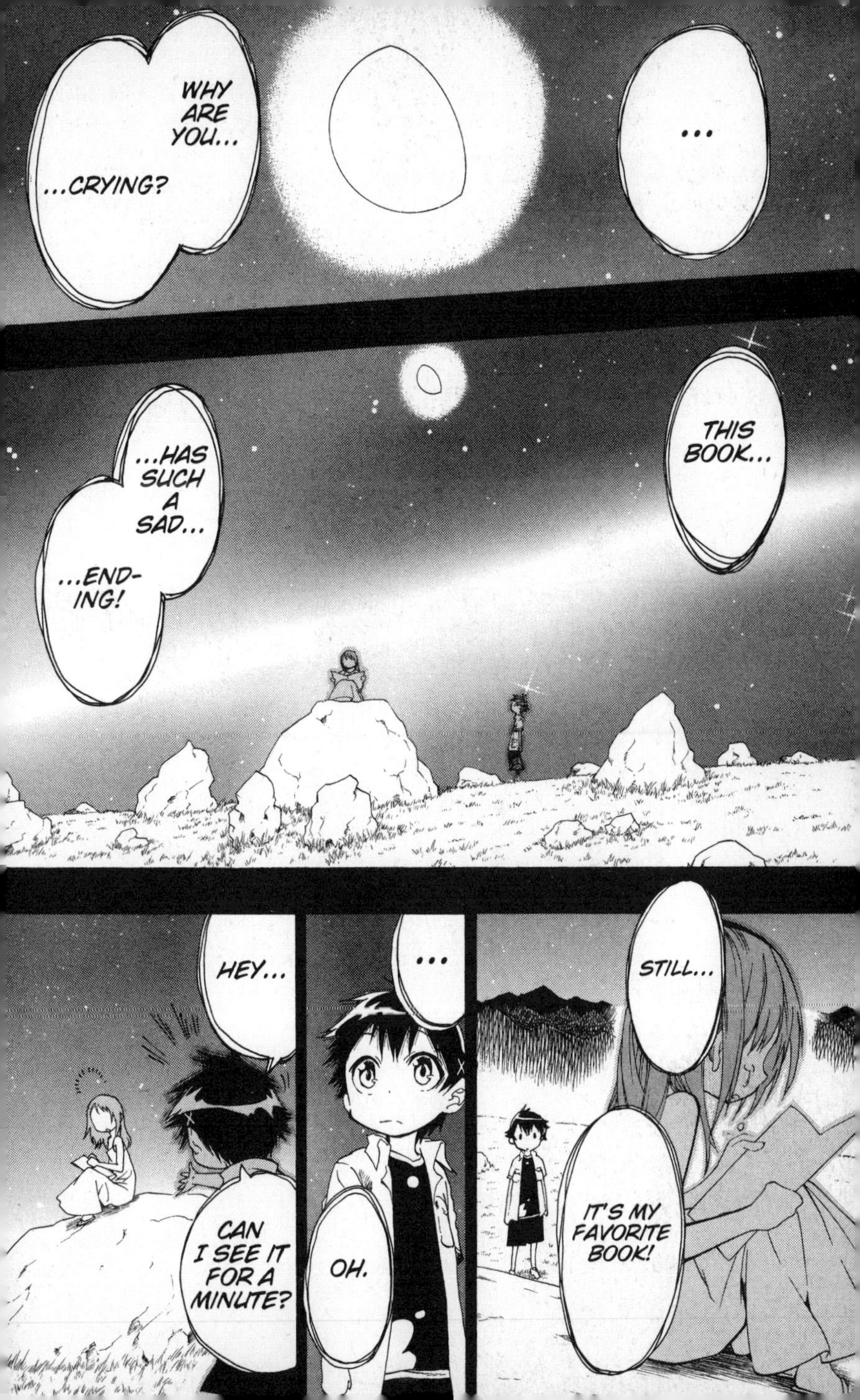
...
WHY ARE YOU... ...CRYING?
THIS BOOK...
...HAS SUCH A SAD... ...END-ING!
STILL...
IT'S MY FAVORITE BOOK!
...
OH.
HEY...
CAN I SEE IT FOR A MINUTE?

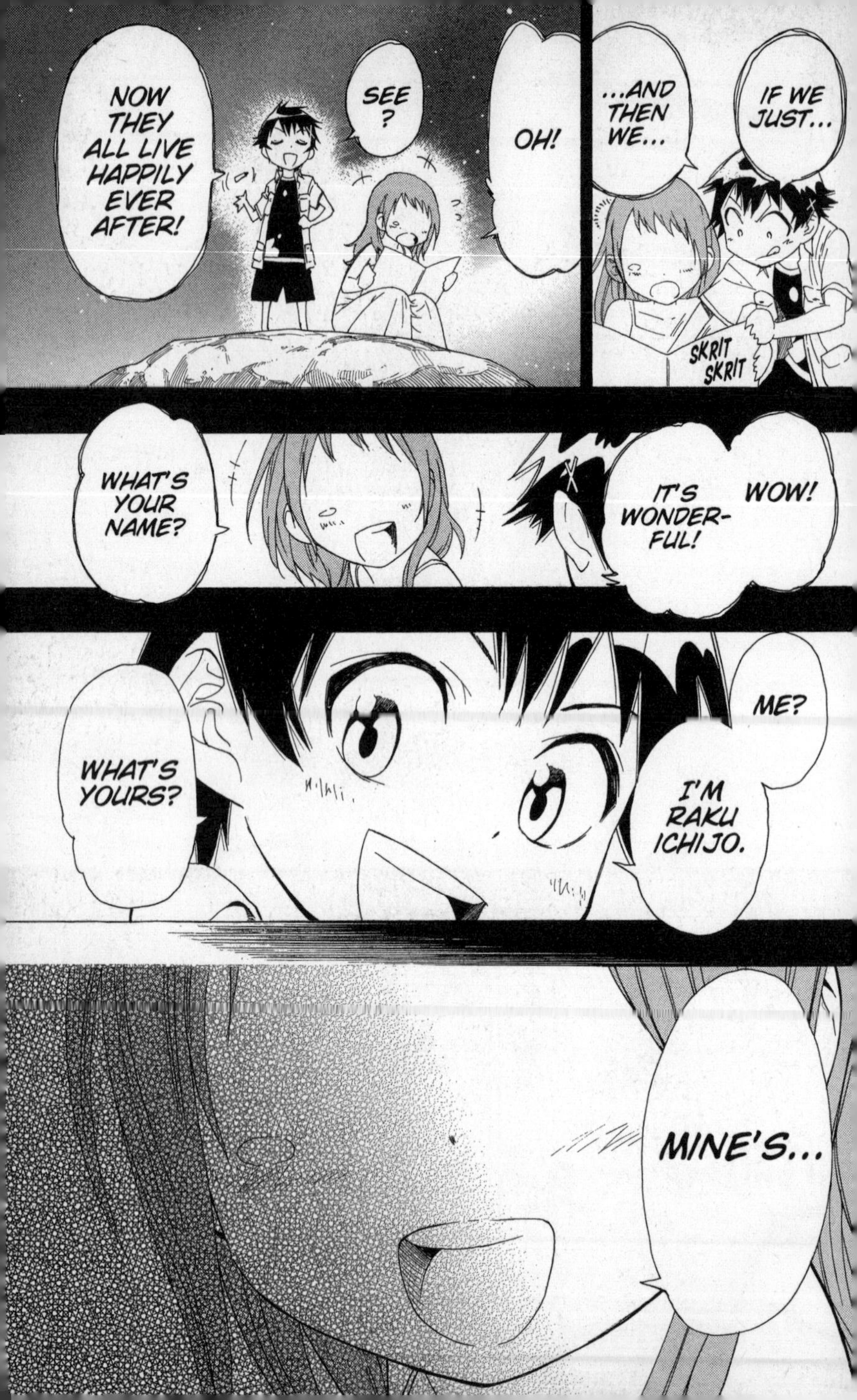
IF WE JUST...
...AND THEN WE...
SKRIT SKRIT
OH!
SEE?
NOW THEY ALL LIVE HAPPILY EVER AFTER!
WOW! IT'S WONDERFUL!
WHAT'S YOUR NAME?
ME? I'M RAKU ICHIJO.
WHAT'S YOURS?
MINE'S...

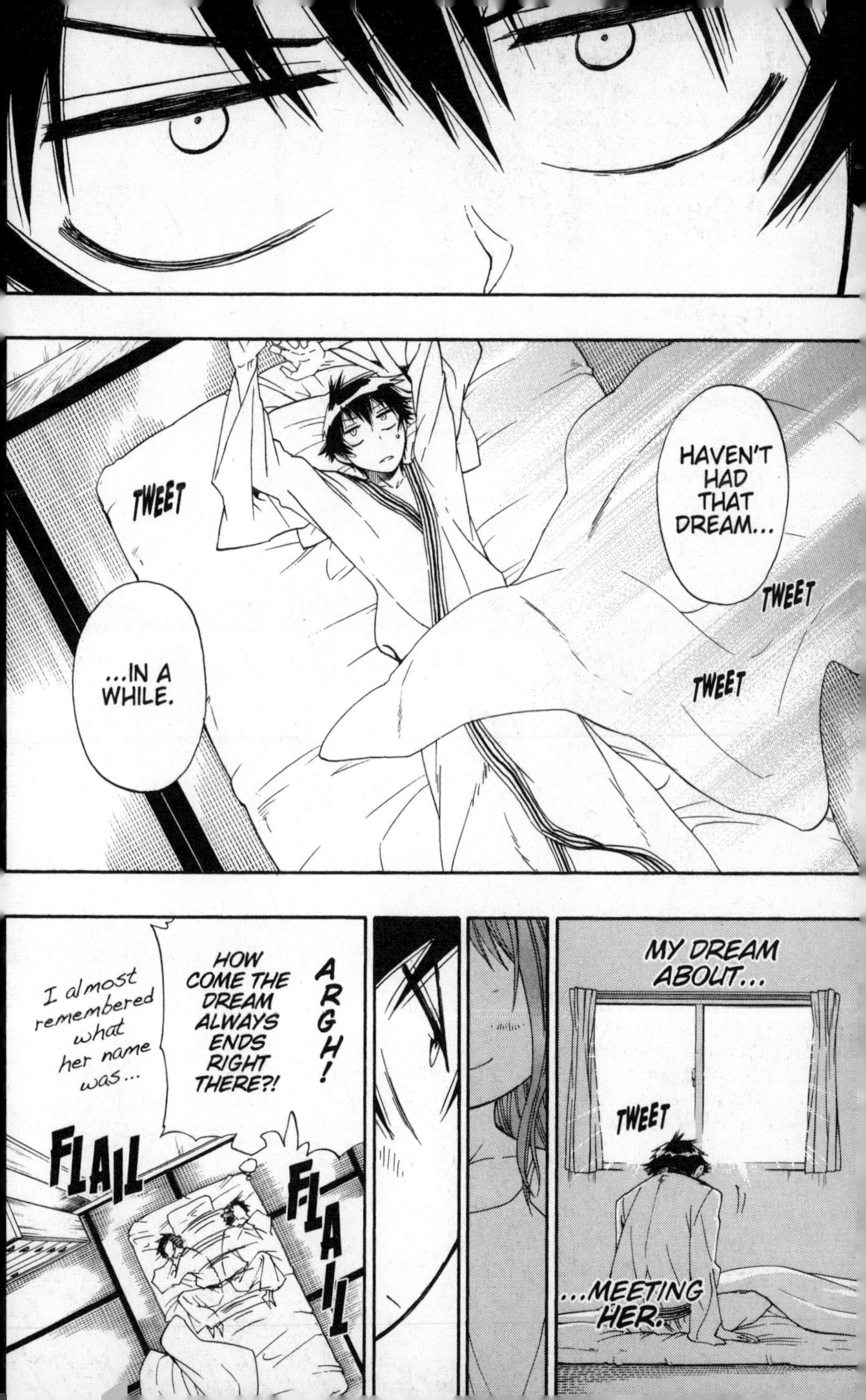
HAVEN'T HAD THAT DREAM...
TWEET
TWEET
TWEET
...IN A WHILE.
MY DREAM ABOUT...
TWEET
...MEETING HER.
ARGH!
HOW COME THE DREAM ALWAYS ENDS RIGHT THERE?!
I almost remembered what her name was...
FLAIL
FLAIL

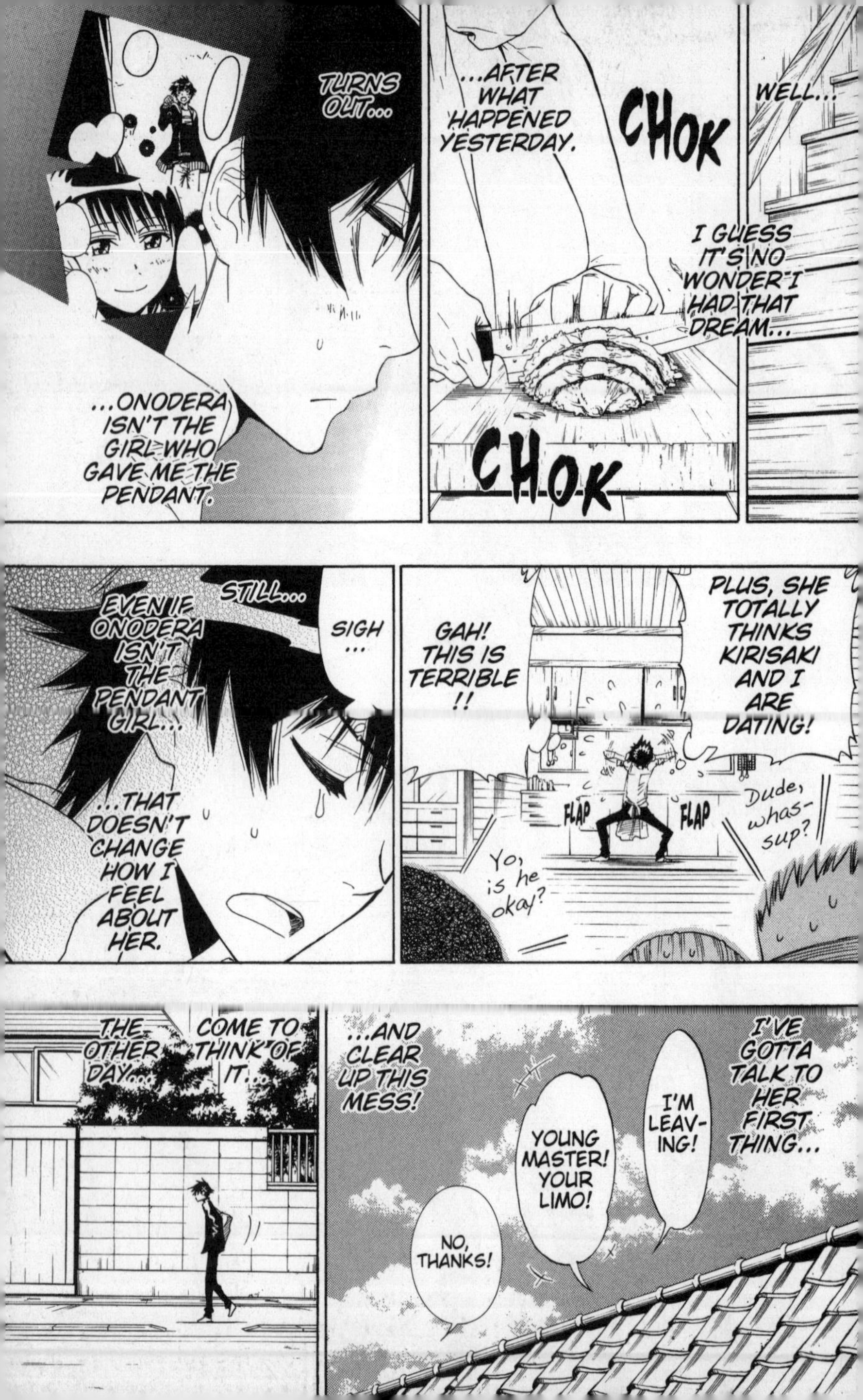
WELL...
I GUESS IT'S NO WONDER I HAD THAT DREAM...
...AFTER WHAT HAPPENED YESTERDAY.
CHOK
CHOK
TURNS OUT...
...ONODERA ISN'T THE GIRL WHO GAVE ME THE PENDANT.
PLUS, SHE TOTALLY THINKS KIRISAKI AND I ARE DATING!
GAH! THIS IS TERRIBLE!!
FLAP
FLAP
Dude, whassup?
Yo, is he okay?
STILL...
SIGH...
EVEN IF ONODERA ISN'T THE PENDANT GIRL...
...THAT DOESN'T CHANGE HOW I FEEL ABOUT HER.
I'VE GOTTA TALK TO HER FIRST THING...
...AND CLEAR UP THIS MESS!
I'M LEAVING!
YOUNG MASTER! YOUR LIMO!
NO, THANKS!
COME TO THINK OF IT...
THE OTHER DAY...

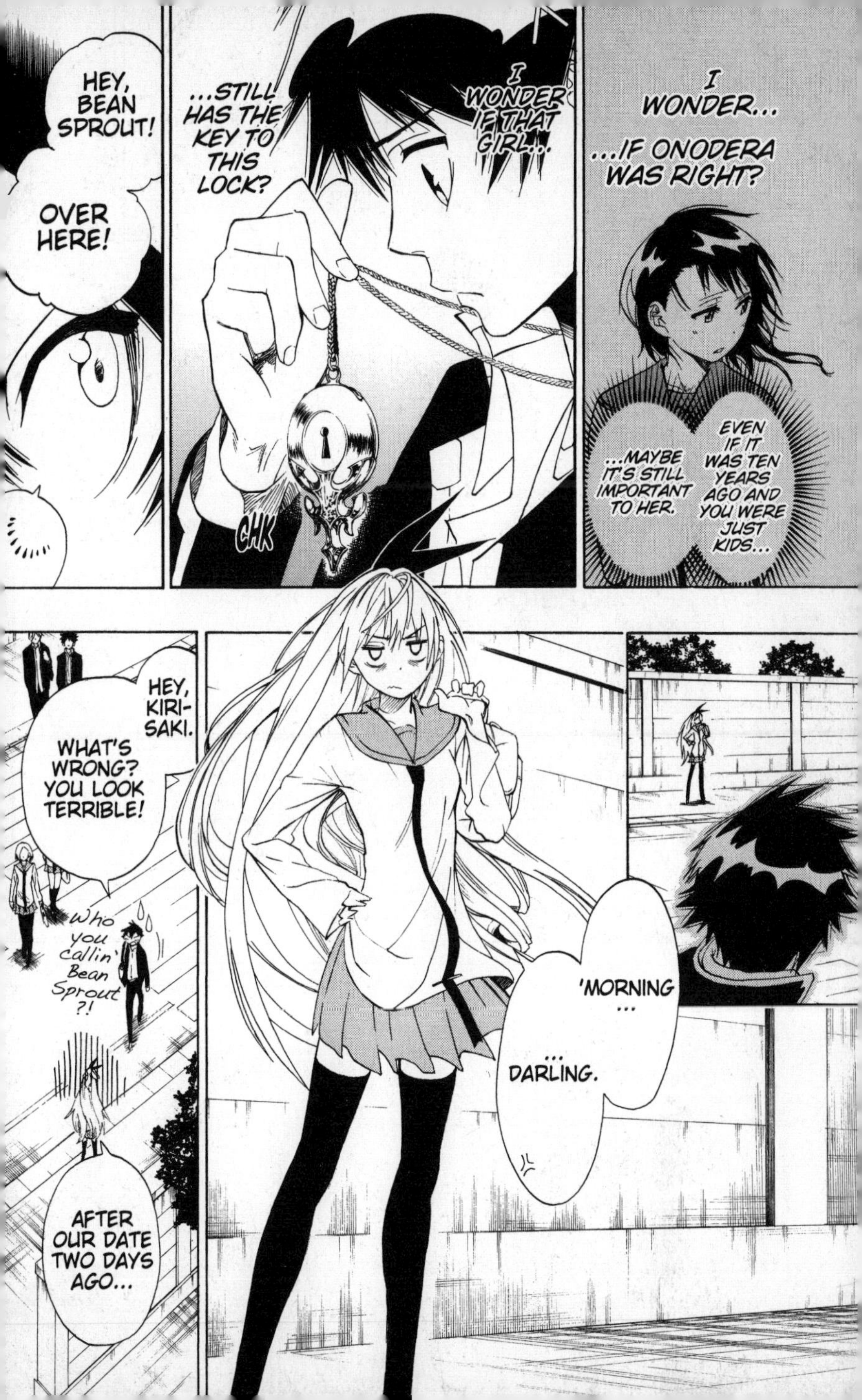

I WONDER...
...IF ONODERA WAS RIGHT?
EVEN IF IT WAS TEN YEARS AGO AND YOU WERE JUST KIDS...
...MAYBE IT'S STILL IMPORTANT TO HER.
I WONDER IF THAT GIRL...
...STILL HAS THE KEY TO THIS LOCK?
CHK
HEY, BEAN SPROUT!
OVER HERE!
'MORNING...
...DARLING.
HEY, KIRI-SAKI.
WHAT'S WRONG? YOU LOOK TERRIBLE!
Who you callin' Bean Sprout?!
AFTER OUR DATE TWO DAYS AGO...

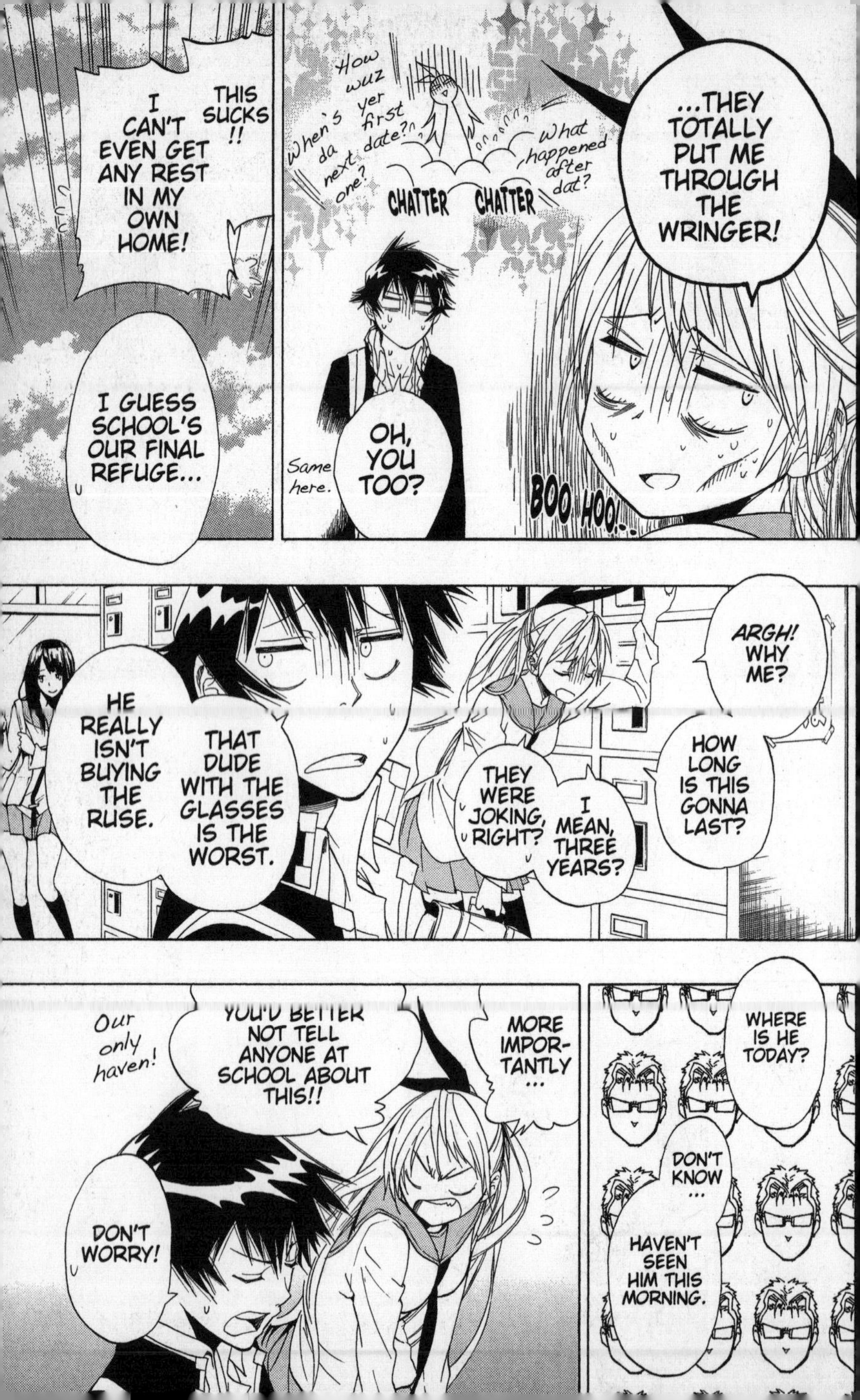
...THEY TOTALLY PUT ME THROUGH THE WRINGER!
How wuz yer first date?
When's da next one?
What happened after dat?
CHATTER CHATTER
BOO HOO!..
OH, YOU TOO?
Same here.
THIS SUCKS!!
I CAN'T EVEN GET ANY REST IN MY OWN HOME!
I GUESS SCHOOL'S OUR FINAL REFUGE...
ARGH! WHY ME?
HOW LONG IS THIS GONNA LAST?
THEY WERE JOKING, RIGHT?
I MEAN, THREE YEARS?
THAT DUDE WITH THE GLASSES IS THE WORST.
HE REALLY ISN'T BUYING THE RUSE.
WHERE IS HE TODAY?
DON'T KNOW...
HAVEN'T SEEN HIM THIS MORNING.
MORE IMPORTANTLY...
YOU'D BETTER NOT TELL ANYONE AT SCHOOL ABOUT THIS!!
Our only haven!
DON'T WORRY!

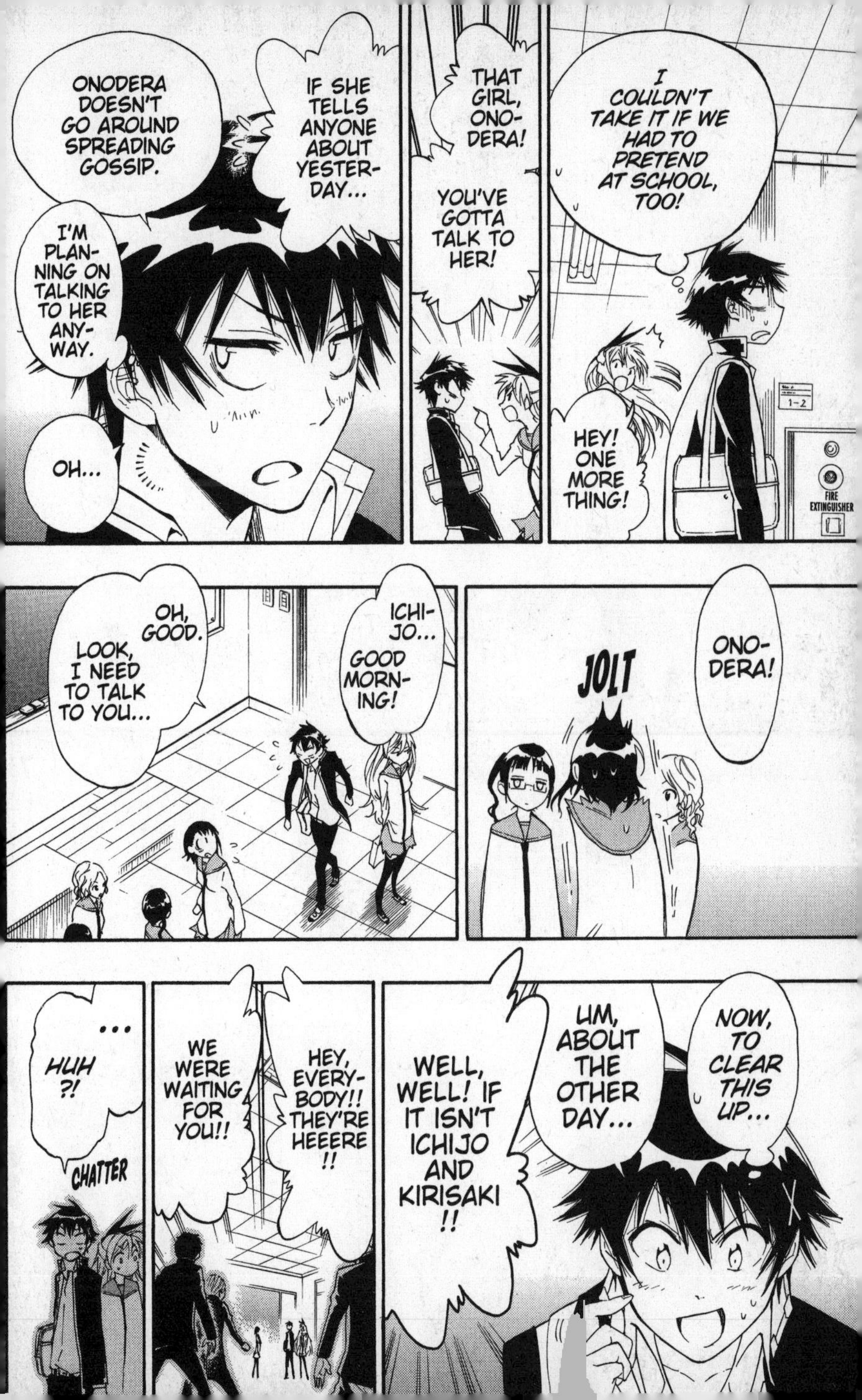
I COULDN'T TAKE IT IF WE HAD TO PRETEND AT SCHOOL, TOO!
1-2
FIRE EXTINGUISHER
HEY! ONE MORE THING!
THAT GIRL, ONO-DERA!
YOU'VE GOTTA TALK TO HER!
IF SHE TELLS ANYONE ABOUT YESTER-DAY...
ONODERA DOESN'T GO AROUND SPREADING GOSSIP.
I'M PLAN-NING ON TALKING TO HER ANY-WAY.
OH...
ONO-DERA!
JOLT
ICHI-JO...
GOOD MORN-ING!
OH, GOOD.
LOOK, I NEED TO TALK TO YOU...
NOW, TO CLEAR THIS UP...
UM, ABOUT THE OTHER DAY...
WELL, WELL! IF IT ISN'T ICHIJO AND KIRISAKI!!
HEY, EVERY-BODY!! THEY'RE HEEERE!!
WE WERE WAITING FOR YOU!!
...
HUH?!
CHATTER

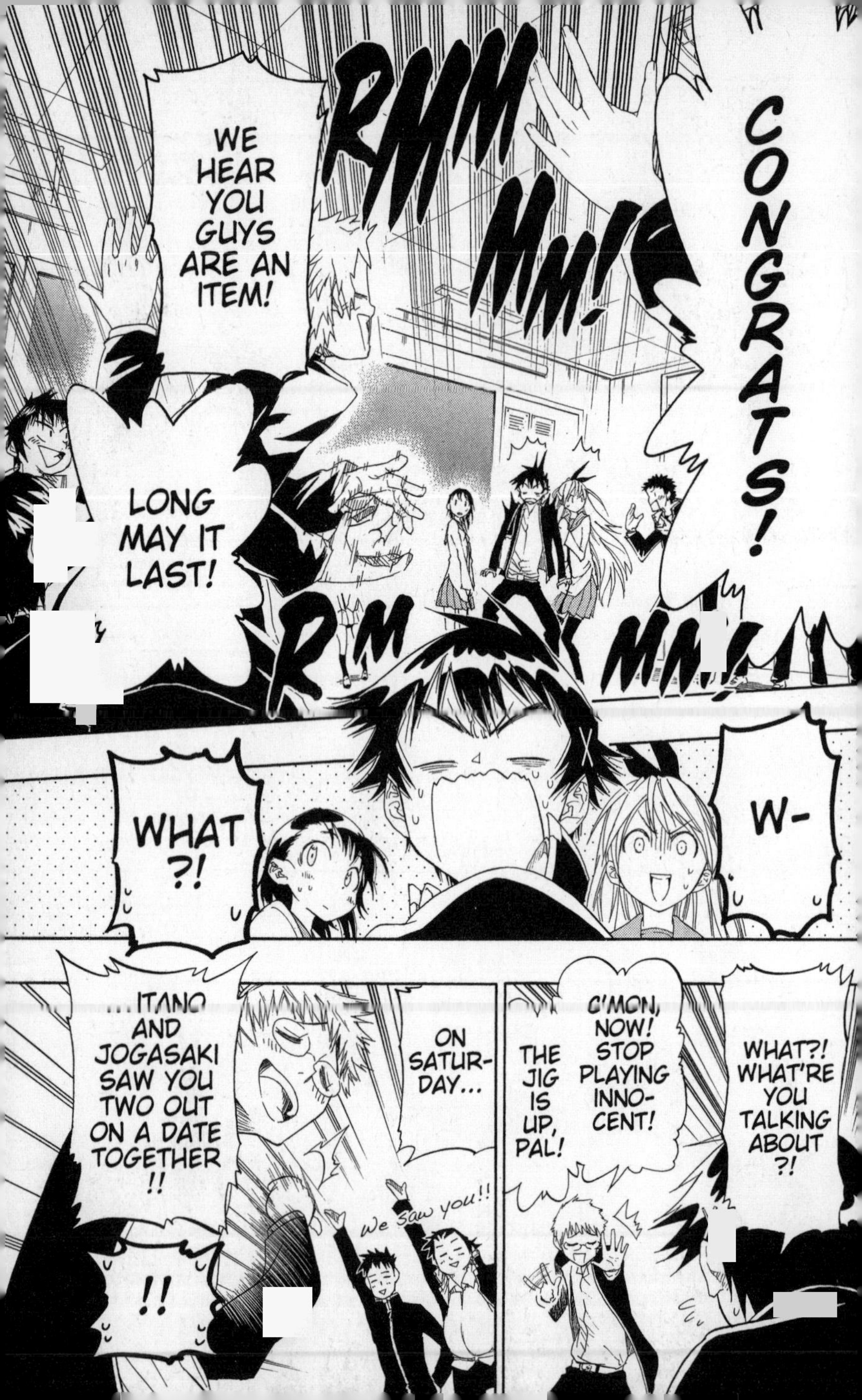
CONGRATS!
RAMMMM!
WE HEAR YOU GUYS ARE AN ITEM!
LONG MAY IT LAST!
W-
WHAT?!
WHAT?! WHAT'RE YOU TALKING ABOUT?!
C'MON, NOW! STOP PLAYING INNO-CENT!
THE JIG IS UP, PAL!
ON SATUR-DAY...
...ITANO AND JOGASAKI SAW YOU TWO OUT ON A DATE TOGETHER!!
We saw you!!
!!

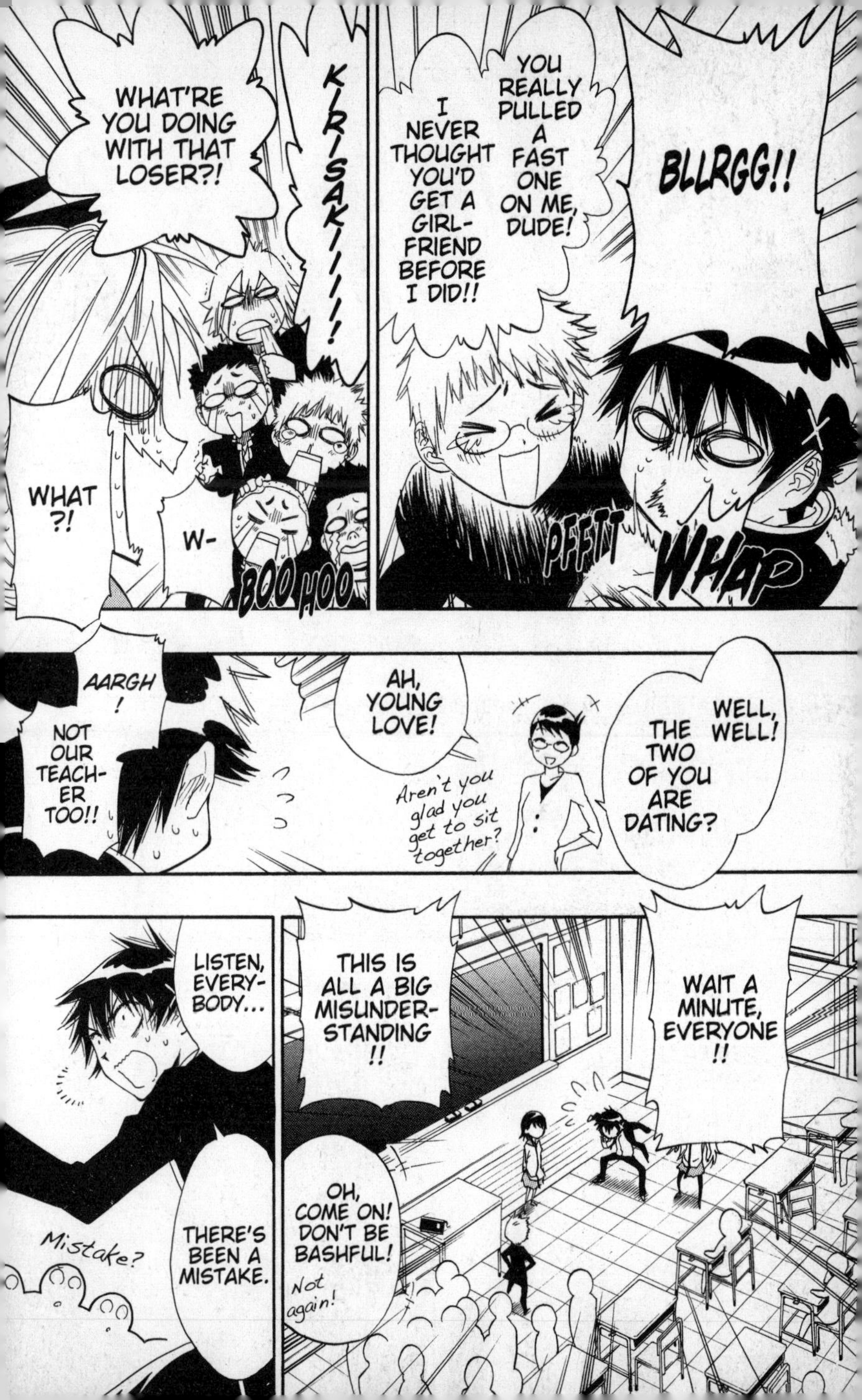
BLLRGG!!
YOU REALLY PULLED A FAST ONE ON ME, DUDE!
I NEVER THOUGHT YOU'D GET A GIRL-FRIEND BEFORE I DID!!
PFFTT
WHAP
KIRISAKI!!!!!!
WHAT'RE YOU DOING WITH THAT LOSER?!
W-
WHAT?!
BOO HOO
WELL, WELL! THE TWO OF YOU ARE DATING?
Aren't you glad you get to sit together?
AH, YOUNG LOVE!
AARGH! NOT OUR TEACH-ER TOO!!
WAIT A MINUTE, EVERYONE!!
THIS IS ALL A BIG MISUNDER-STANDING!!
OH, COME ON! DON'T BE BASHFUL!
Not again!
LISTEN, EVERY-BODY...
THERE'S BEEN A MISTAKE.
Mistake?

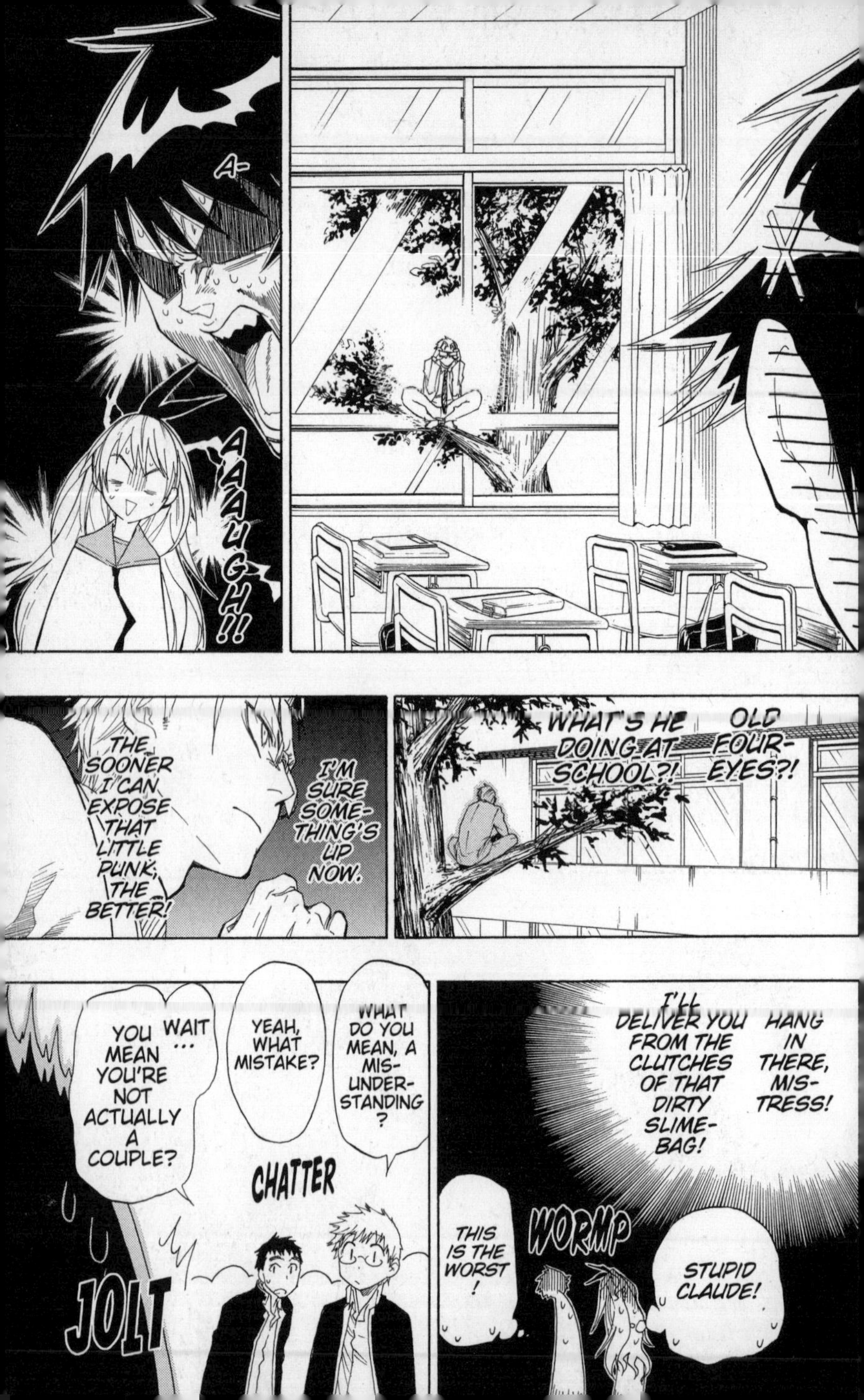
A-
AAAUGH!!
OLD FOUR-EYES?!
WHAT'S HE DOING AT SCHOOL?!
I'M SURE SOMETHING'S UP NOW.
THE SOONER I CAN EXPOSE THAT LITTLE PUNK, THE BETTER!
HANG IN THERE, MISTRESS!
I'LL DELIVER YOU FROM THE CLUTCHES OF THAT DIRTY SLIMEBAG!
STUPID CLAUDE!
WORMP
THIS IS THE WORST!
WHAT DO YOU MEAN, A MISUNDERSTANDING?
YEAH, WHAT MISTAKE?
CHATTER
WAIT...
YOU MEAN YOU'RE NOT ACTUALLY A COUPLE?
JOLT

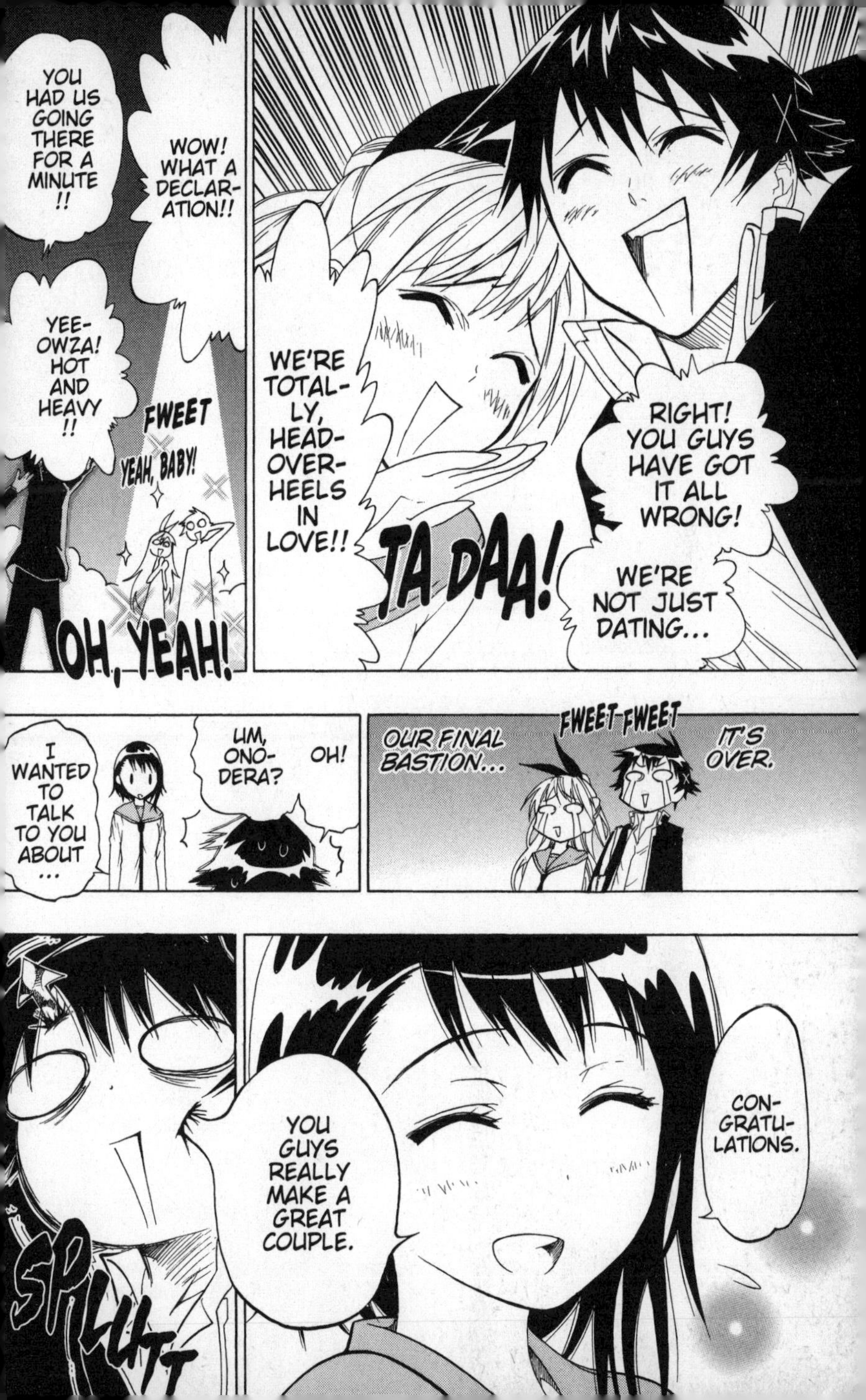
RIGHT! YOU GUYS HAVE GOT IT ALL WRONG!
WE'RE NOT JUST DATING...
TA DAA!
WE'RE TOTALLY, HEAD-OVER-HEELS IN LOVE!!
WOW! WHAT A DECLARATION!!
YOU HAD US GOING THERE FOR A MINUTE!!
YEE-OWZA! HOT AND HEAVY!!
FWEET
YEAH, BABY!
OH, YEAH!
FWEET FWEET
IT'S OVER.
OUR FINAL BASTION...
OH!
UM, ONODERA?
I WANTED TO TALK TO YOU ABOUT...
CONGRATULATIONS.
YOU GUYS REALLY MAKE A GREAT COUPLE.
SPLUTT

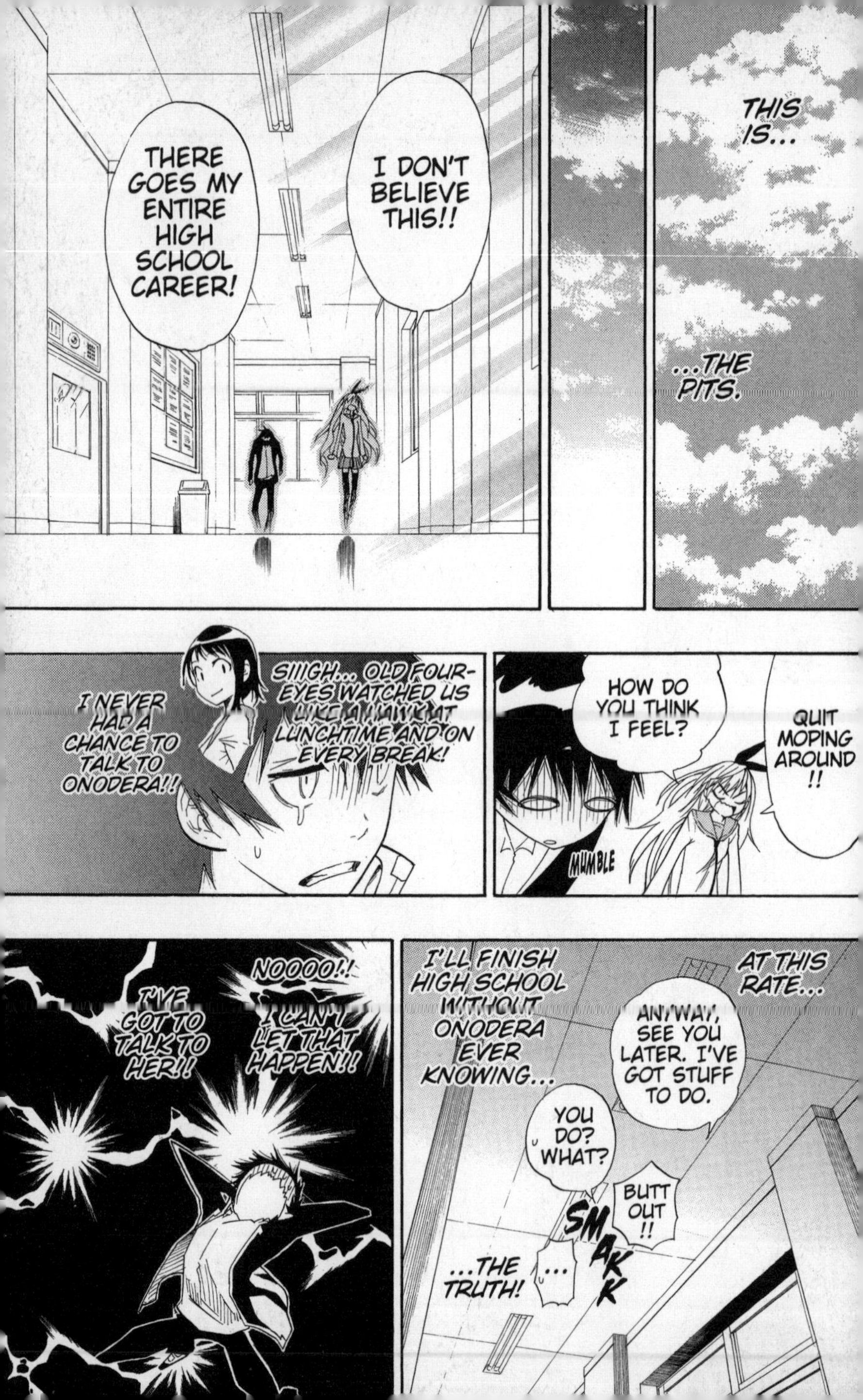
THIS IS...
...THE PITS.
I DON'T BELIEVE THIS!!
THERE GOES MY ENTIRE HIGH SCHOOL CAREER!
QUIT MOPING AROUND!!
HOW DO YOU THINK I FEEL?
MUMBLE
SIIIGH... OLD FOUR-EYES WATCHED US LIKE A HAWK AT LUNCHTIME AND ON EVERY BREAK!
I NEVER HAD A CHANCE TO TALK TO ONODERA!!
AT THIS RATE...
I'LL FINISH HIGH SCHOOL WITHOUT ONODERA EVER KNOWING...
ANYWAY, SEE YOU LATER. I'VE GOT STUFF TO DO.
YOU DO? WHAT?
BUTT OUT!!
SMAKK
...
...THE TRUTH!
NOOOO!!
I CAN'T LET THAT HAPPEN!!
I'VE GOT TO TALK TO HER!!

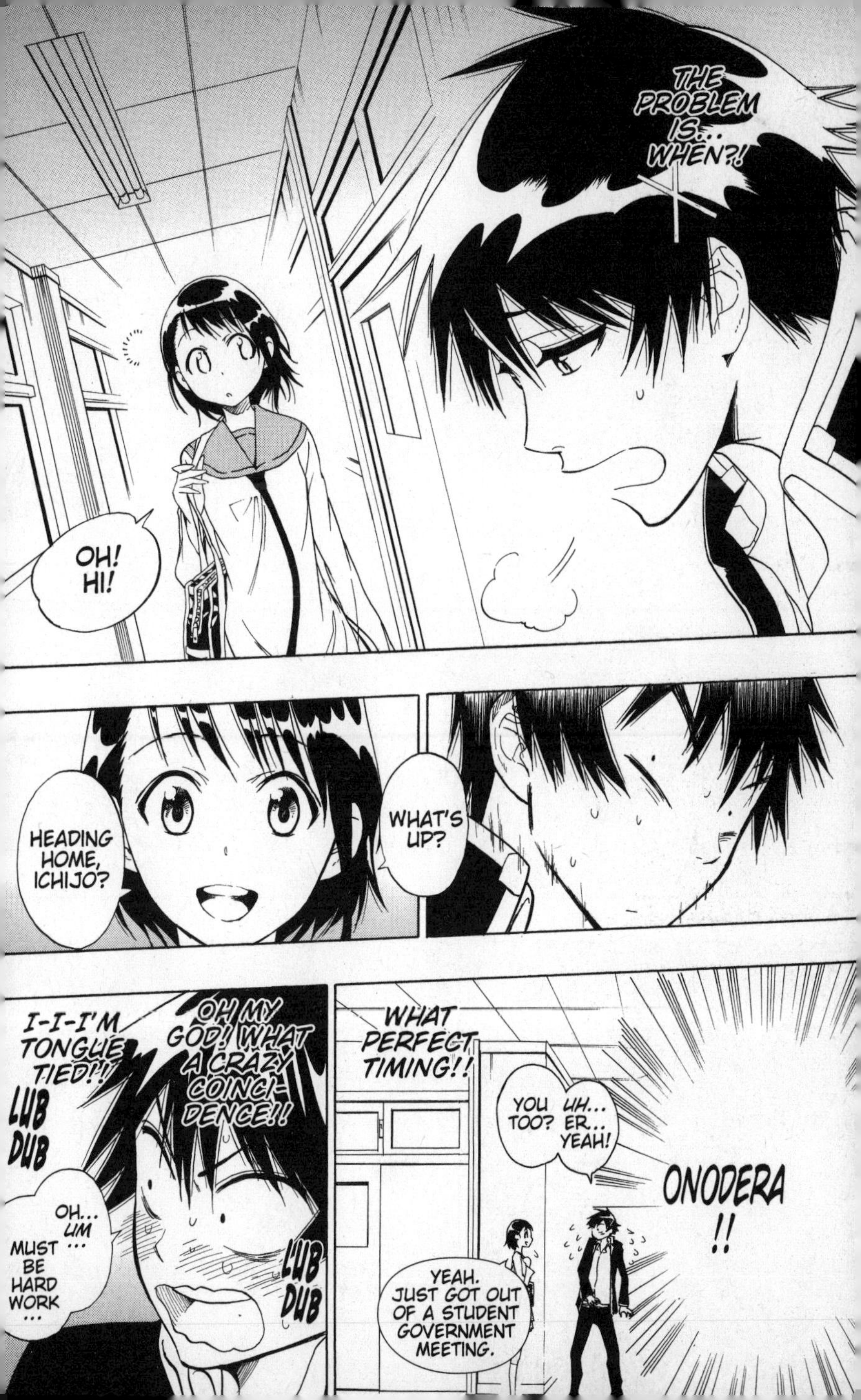
THE PROBLEM IS... WHEN?!
OH! HI!
WHAT'S UP?
HEADING HOME, ICHIJO?
ONODERA!!
UH... ER... YEAH!
YOU TOO?
WHAT PERFECT TIMING!!
YEAH. JUST GOT OUT OF A STUDENT GOVERNMENT MEETING.
OH MY GOD! WHAT A CRAZY COINCI-DENCE!!
I-I-I'M TONGUE TIED!!
LUB DUB
OH... UM...
MUST BE HARD WORK...
LUB DUB

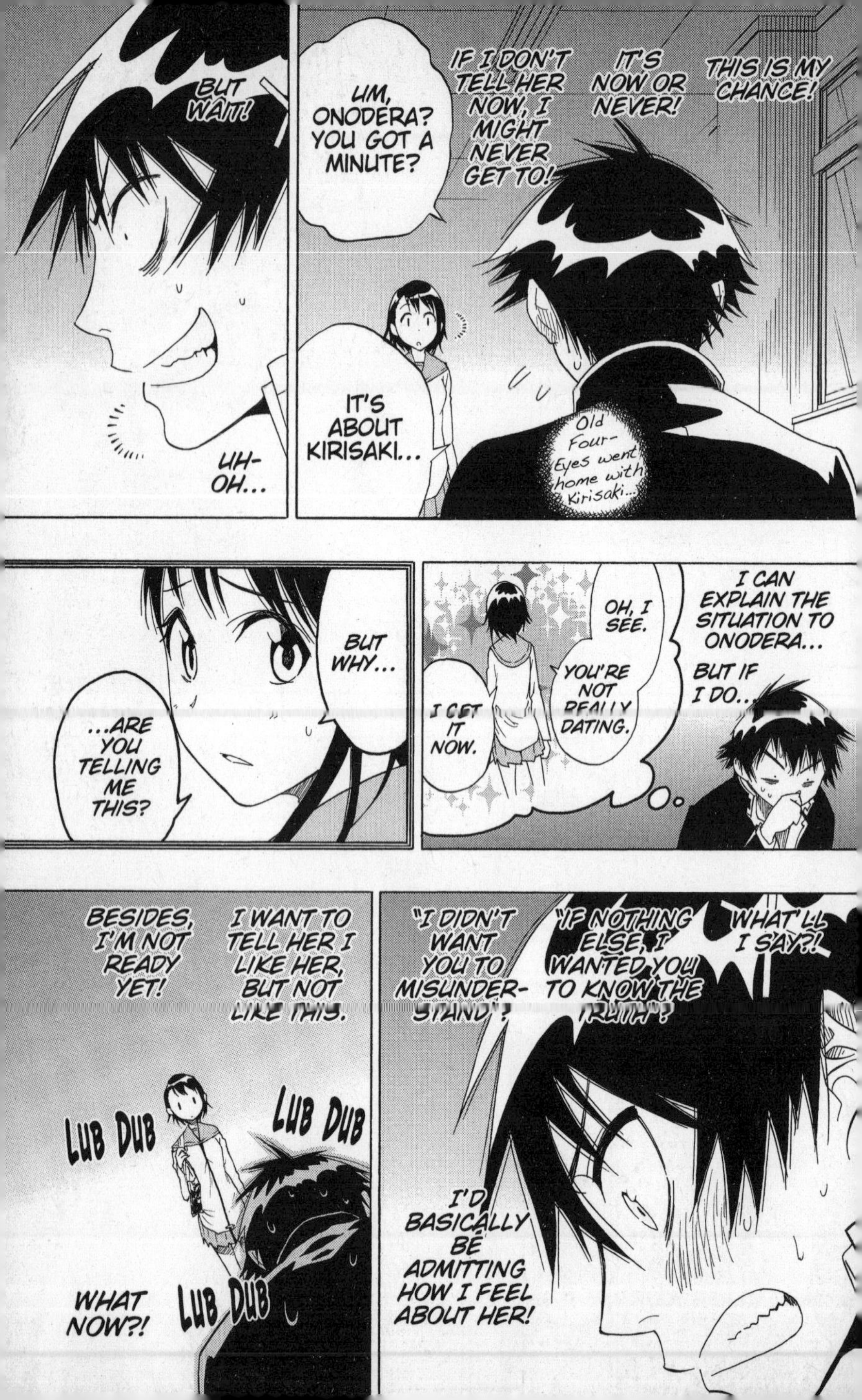
THIS IS MY CHANCE!
IT'S NOW OR NEVER!
IF I DON'T TELL HER NOW, I MIGHT NEVER GET TO!
UM, ONODERA? YOU GOT A MINUTE?
IT'S ABOUT KIRISAKI...
Old Four-Eyes went home with Kirisaki...
BUT WAIT!
UH-OH...
I CAN EXPLAIN THE SITUATION TO ONODERA...
BUT IF I DO...
OH, I SEE.
YOU'RE NOT REALLY DATING.
I GET IT NOW.
BUT WHY...
...ARE YOU TELLING ME THIS?
WHAT'LL I SAY?!
"IF NOTHING ELSE, I WANTED YOU TO KNOW THE TRUTH"?
"I DIDN'T WANT YOU TO MISUNDERSTAND"?
I'D BASICALLY BE ADMITTING HOW I FEEL ABOUT HER!
I WANT TO TELL HER I LIKE HER, BUT NOT LIKE THIS.
BESIDES, I'M NOT READY YET!
LUB DUB
LUB DUB
WHAT NOW?!
LUB DUB

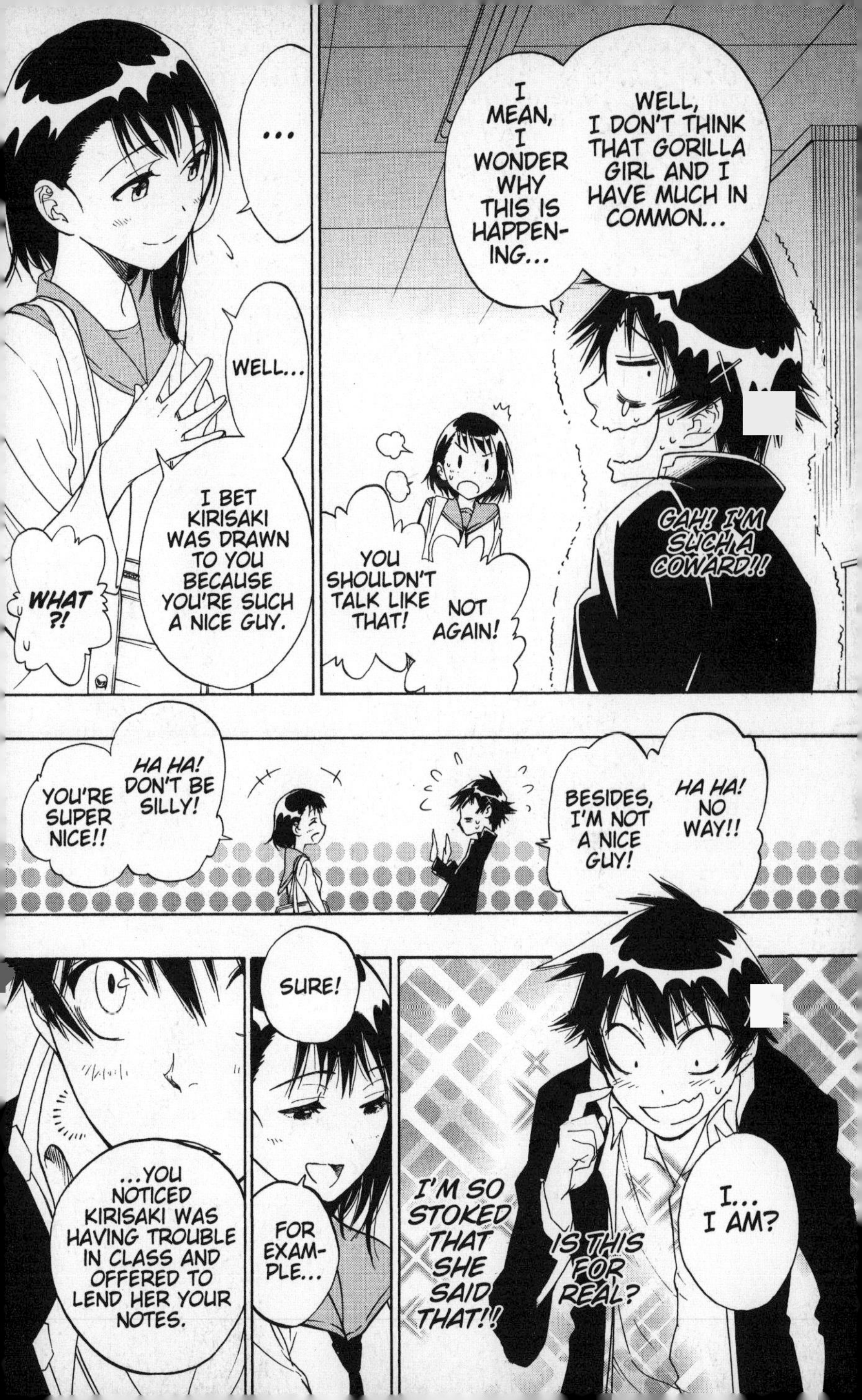
WELL, I DON'T THINK THAT GORILLA GIRL AND I HAVE MUCH IN COMMON...
I MEAN, I WONDER WHY THIS IS HAPPENING...
GAH! I'M SUCH A COWARD!!
NOT AGAIN!
YOU SHOULDN'T TALK LIKE THAT!
...
WELL...
I BET KIRISAKI WAS DRAWN TO YOU BECAUSE YOU'RE SUCH A NICE GUY.
WHAT?!
HA HA! NO WAY!!
BESIDES, I'M NOT A NICE GUY!
HA HA! DON'T BE SILLY!
YOU'RE SUPER NICE!!
I... I AM?
IS THIS FOR REAL?
I'M SO STOKED THAT SHE SAID THAT!!
SURE!
FOR EXAMPLE...
...YOU NOTICED KIRISAKI WAS HAVING TROUBLE IN CLASS AND OFFERED TO LEND HER YOUR NOTES.

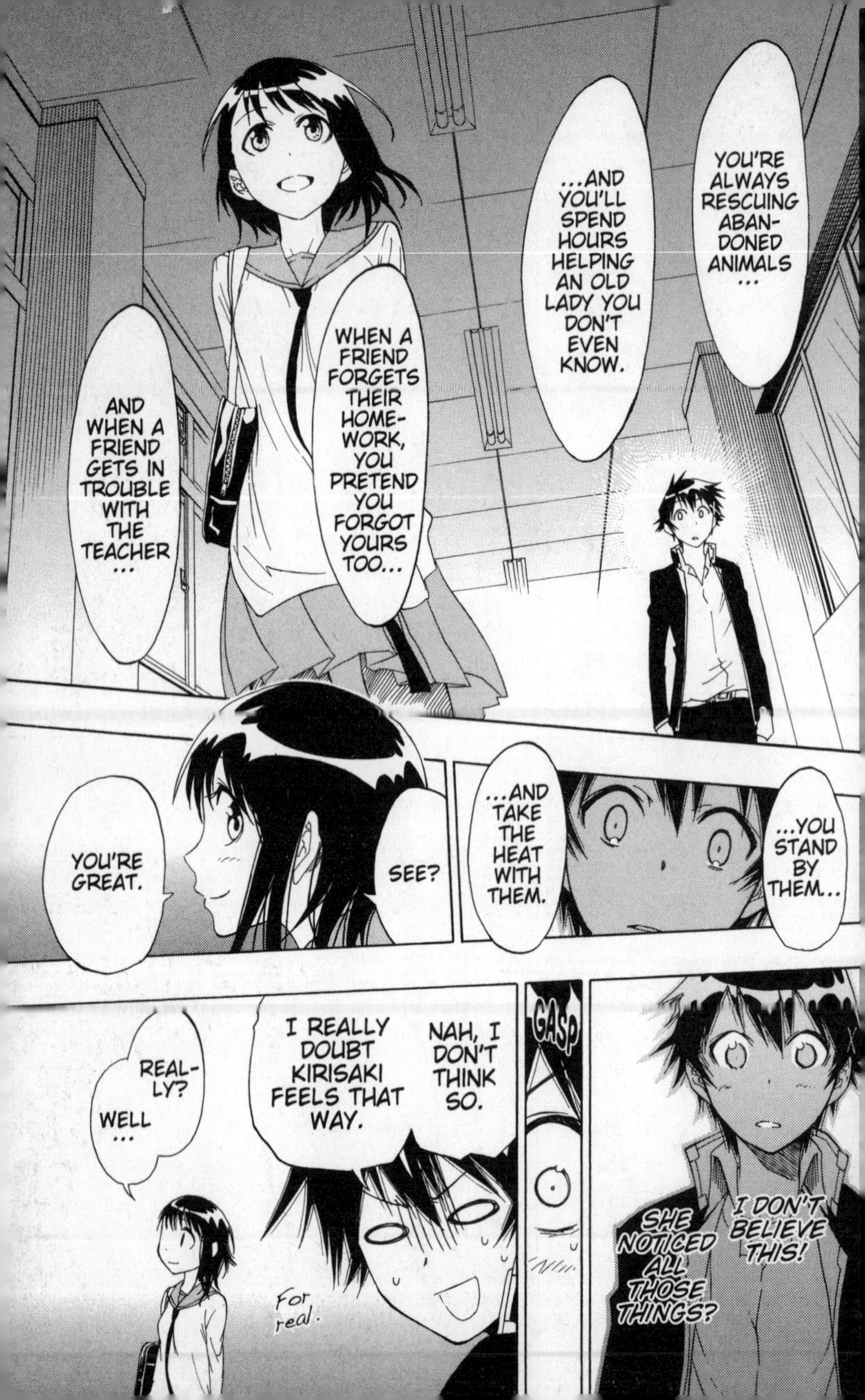
YOU'RE ALWAYS RESCUING ABAN-DONED ANIMALS...
...AND YOU'LL SPEND HOURS HELPING AN OLD LADY YOU DON'T EVEN KNOW.
WHEN A FRIEND FORGETS THEIR HOME-WORK, YOU PRETEND YOU FORGOT YOURS TOO...
AND WHEN A FRIEND GETS IN TROUBLE WITH THE TEACHER...
...YOU STAND BY THEM...
...AND TAKE THE HEAT WITH THEM.
SEE?
YOU'RE GREAT.
I DON'T BELIEVE THIS!
SHE NOTICED ALL THOSE THINGS?
GASP
NAH, I DON'T THINK SO.
I REALLY DOUBT KIRISAKI FEELS THAT WAY.
For real.
REAL-LY? WELL...

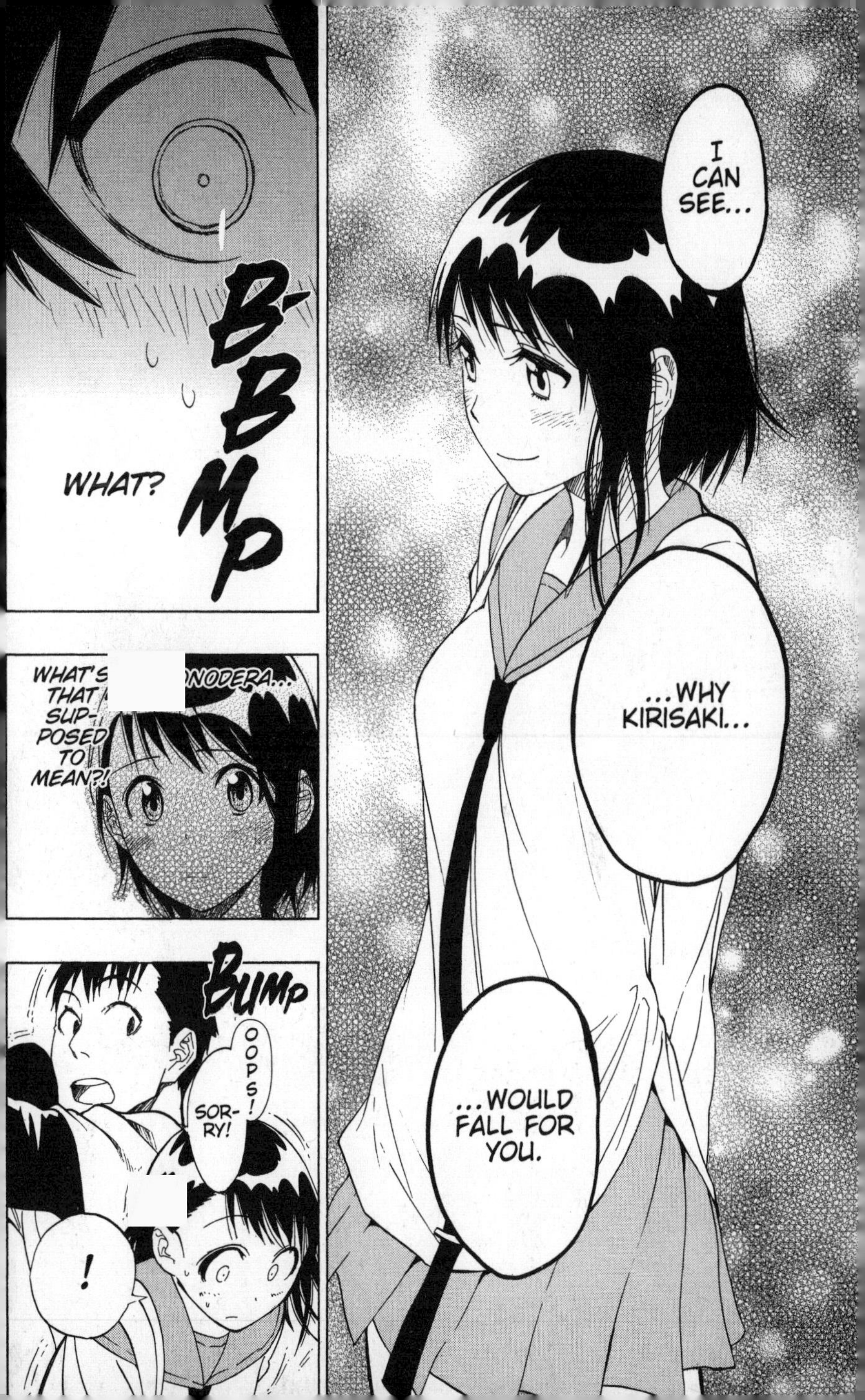
I CAN SEE...
...WHY KIRISAKI...
...WOULD FALL FOR YOU.
B-BMP
WHAT?
WHAT'S ONODERA... THAT SUP-POSED TO MEAN?!
BUMP
OOPS!
SOR-RY!
!

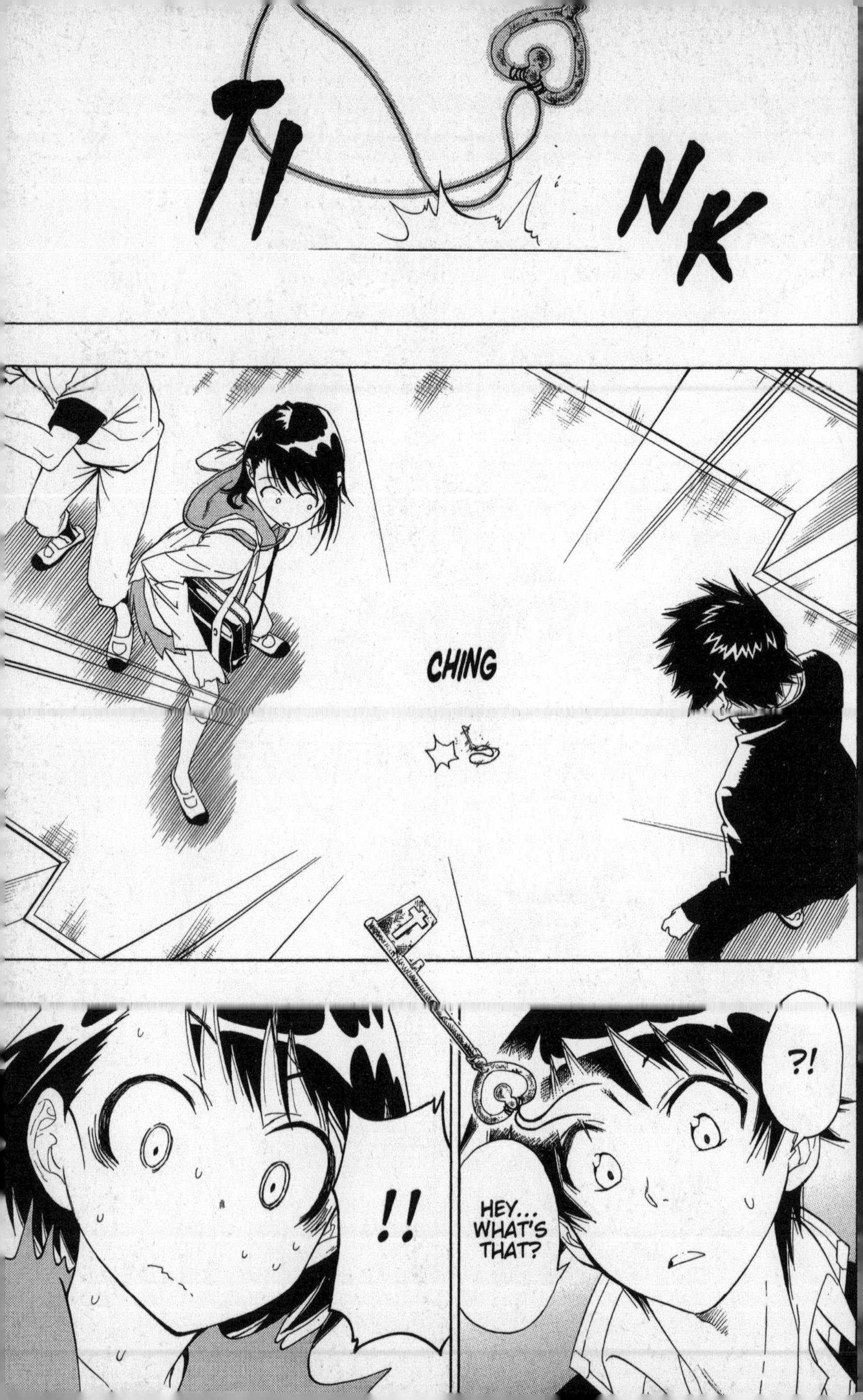
TINK
CHING
?!
HEY... WHAT'S THAT?
!!

A Day in the Life of Kirisaki

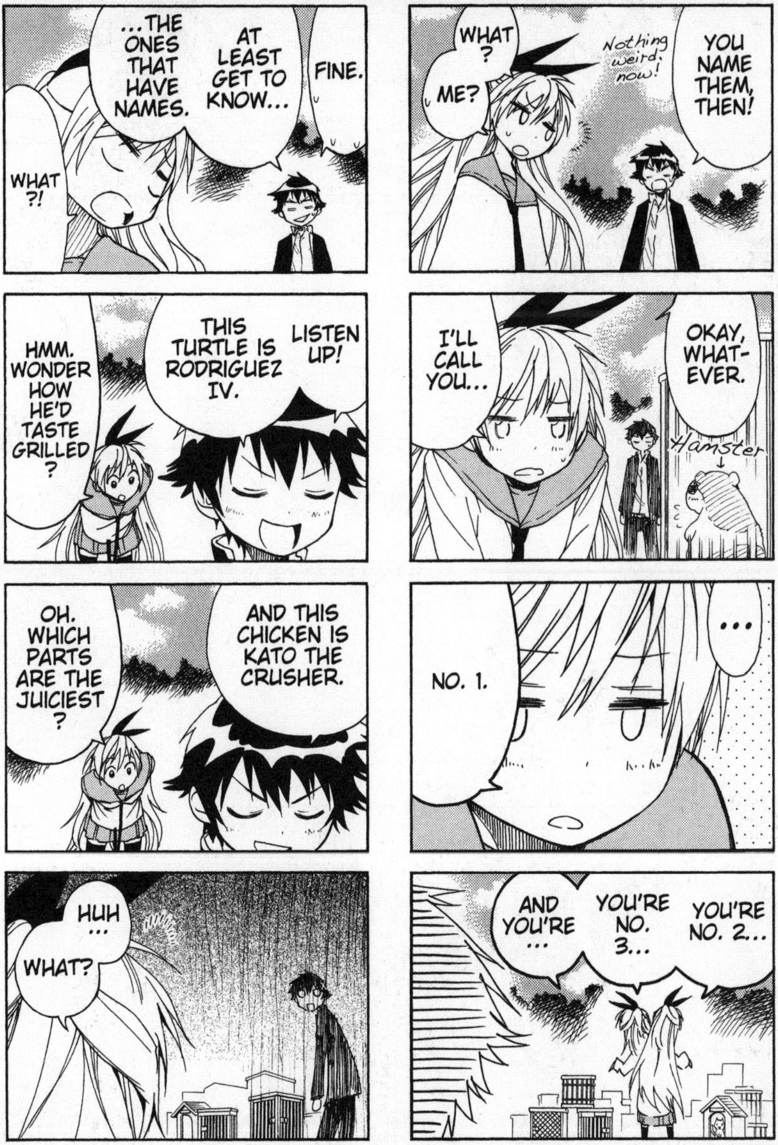
YOU NAME THEM, THEN!
Nothing weird now!
WHAT? ME?
OKAY, WHAT-EVER.
I'LL CALL YOU...
Hamster
...
NO. 1.
YOU'RE NO. 2...
YOU'RE NO. 3...
AND YOU'RE...
FINE.
AT LEAST GET TO KNOW...
...THE ONES THAT HAVE NAMES.
WHAT?!
LISTEN UP!
THIS TURTLE IS RODRIGUEZ IV.
HMM. WONDER HOW HE'D TASTE GRILLED?
AND THIS CHICKEN IS KATO THE CRUSHER.
OH. WHICH PARTS ARE THE JUICIEST?
HUH...
WHAT?

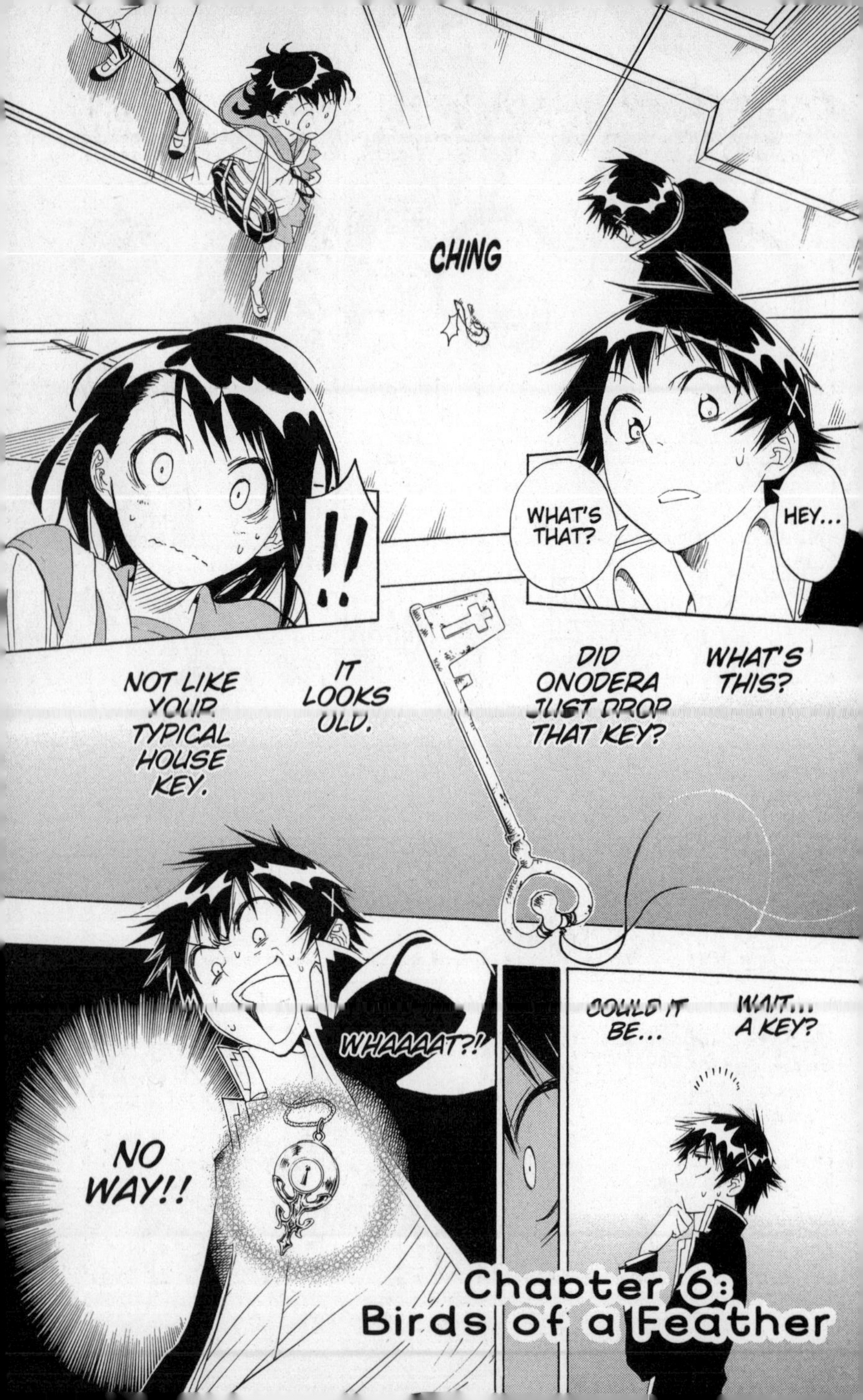
CHING
HEY...
WHAT'S THAT?
!!
WHAT'S THIS?
DID ONODERA JUST DROP THAT KEY?
IT LOOKS OLD.
NOT LIKE YOUR TYPICAL HOUSE KEY.
WAIT... A KEY?
COULD IT BE...
WHAAAAT?!
NO WAY!!
Chapter 6: Birds of a Feather

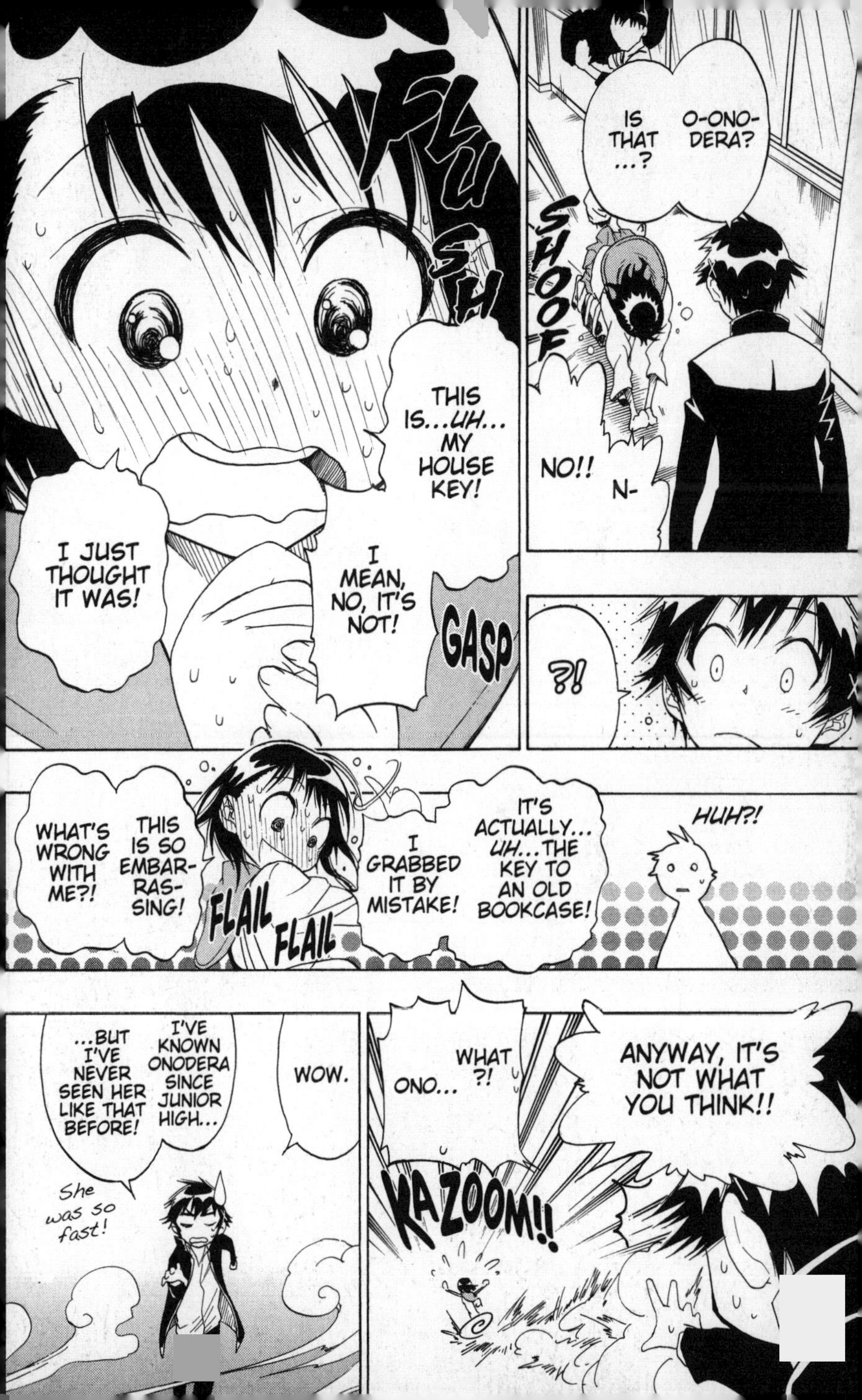
O-ONO-DERA? IS THAT ...?
SHOOF
N-
NO!!
?!
FLUSH
THIS IS...UH... MY HOUSE KEY!
I MEAN, NO, IT'S NOT!
GASP
I JUST THOUGHT IT WAS!
HUH?!
IT'S ACTUALLY... UH... THE KEY TO AN OLD BOOKCASE!
I GRABBED IT BY MISTAKE!
FLAIL FLAIL
THIS IS SO EMBAR-RAS-SING!
WHAT'S WRONG WITH ME?!
ANYWAY, IT'S NOT WHAT YOU THINK!!
WHAT ?!
ONO...
KAZOOM!!
WOW.
I'VE KNOWN ONODERA SINCE JUNIOR HIGH...
...BUT I'VE NEVER SEEN HER LIKE THAT BEFORE!
She was so fast!

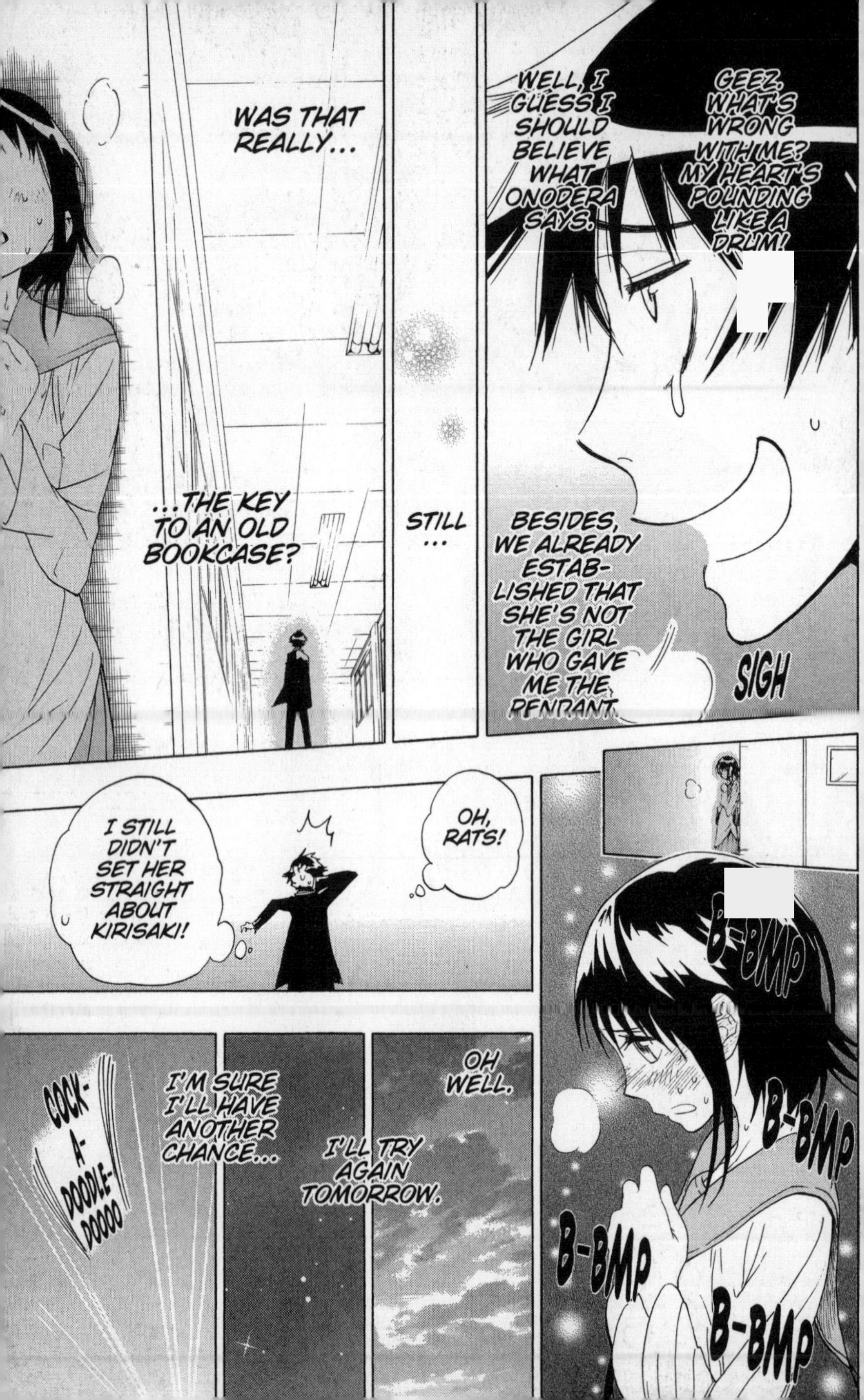
GEEZ. WHAT'S WRONG WITH ME? MY HEART'S POUNDING LIKE A DRUM!
WELL, I GUESS I SHOULD BELIEVE WHAT ONODERA SAYS.
BESIDES, WE ALREADY ESTABLISHED THAT SHE'S NOT THE GIRL WHO GAVE ME THE PENDANT.
SIGH
STILL ...
WAS THAT REALLY...
...THE KEY TO AN OLD BOOKCASE?
B-BMP
B-BMP
B-BMP
B-BMP
OH, RATS!
I STILL DIDN'T SET HER STRAIGHT ABOUT KIRISAKI!
OH WELL.
I'LL TRY AGAIN TOMORROW.
I'M SURE I'LL HAVE ANOTHER CHANCE...
COCK-A-DOODLE-DOOOO

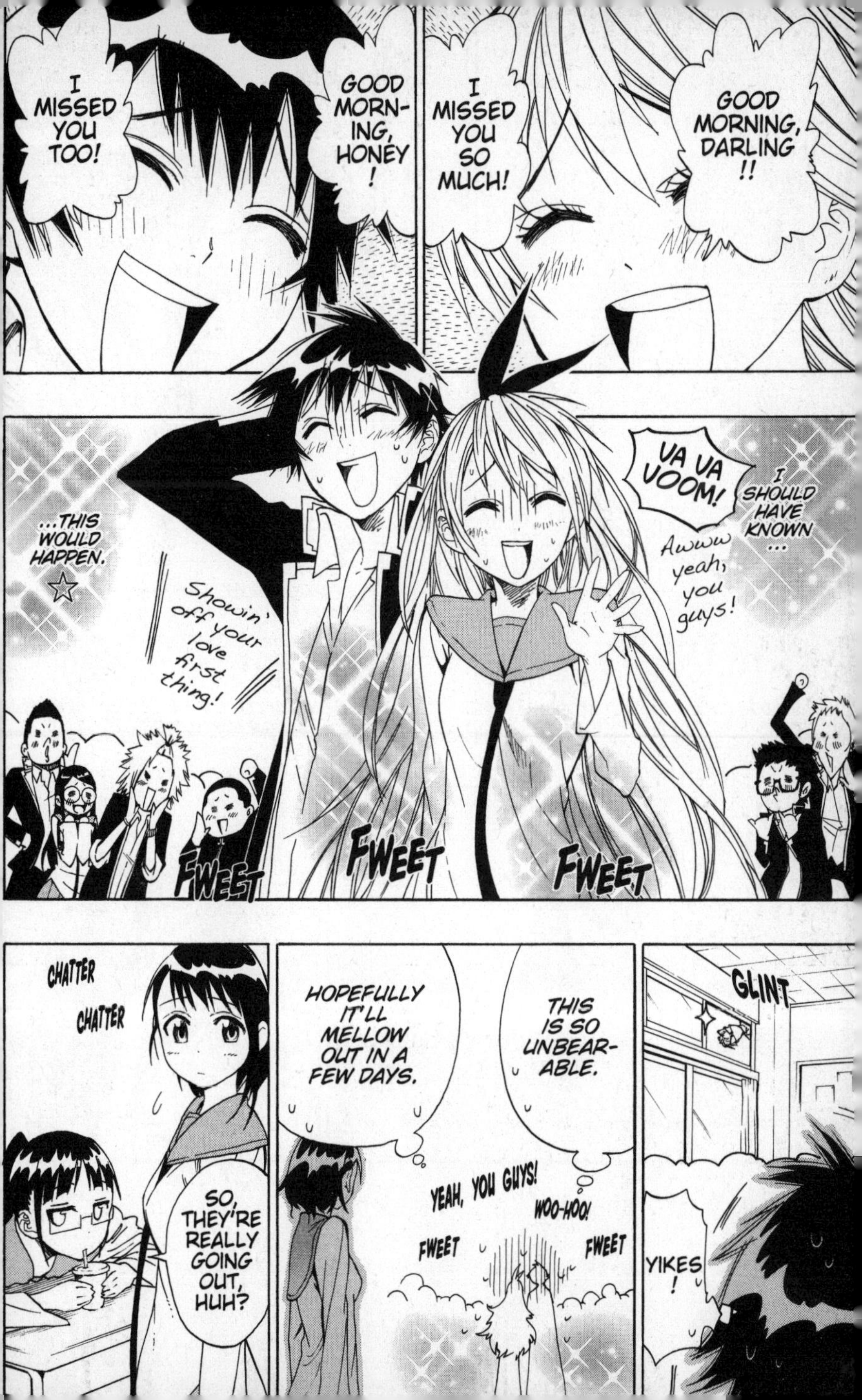
GOOD MORNING, DARLING!!
I MISSED YOU SO MUCH!
GOOD MORNING, HONEY!
I MISSED YOU TOO!
VA VA VOOM!
I SHOULD HAVE KNOWN...
Awww yeah, you guys!
...THIS WOULD HAPPEN. ☆
Showin' off your love first thing!
FWEET
FWEET
FWEET
GLINT
YIKES!
THIS IS SO UNBEARABLE.
HOPEFULLY IT'LL MELLOW OUT IN A FEW DAYS.
WOO-HOO!
YEAH, YOU GUYS!
FWEET
FWEET
CHATTER
CHATTER
SO, THEY'RE REALLY GOING OUT, HUH?

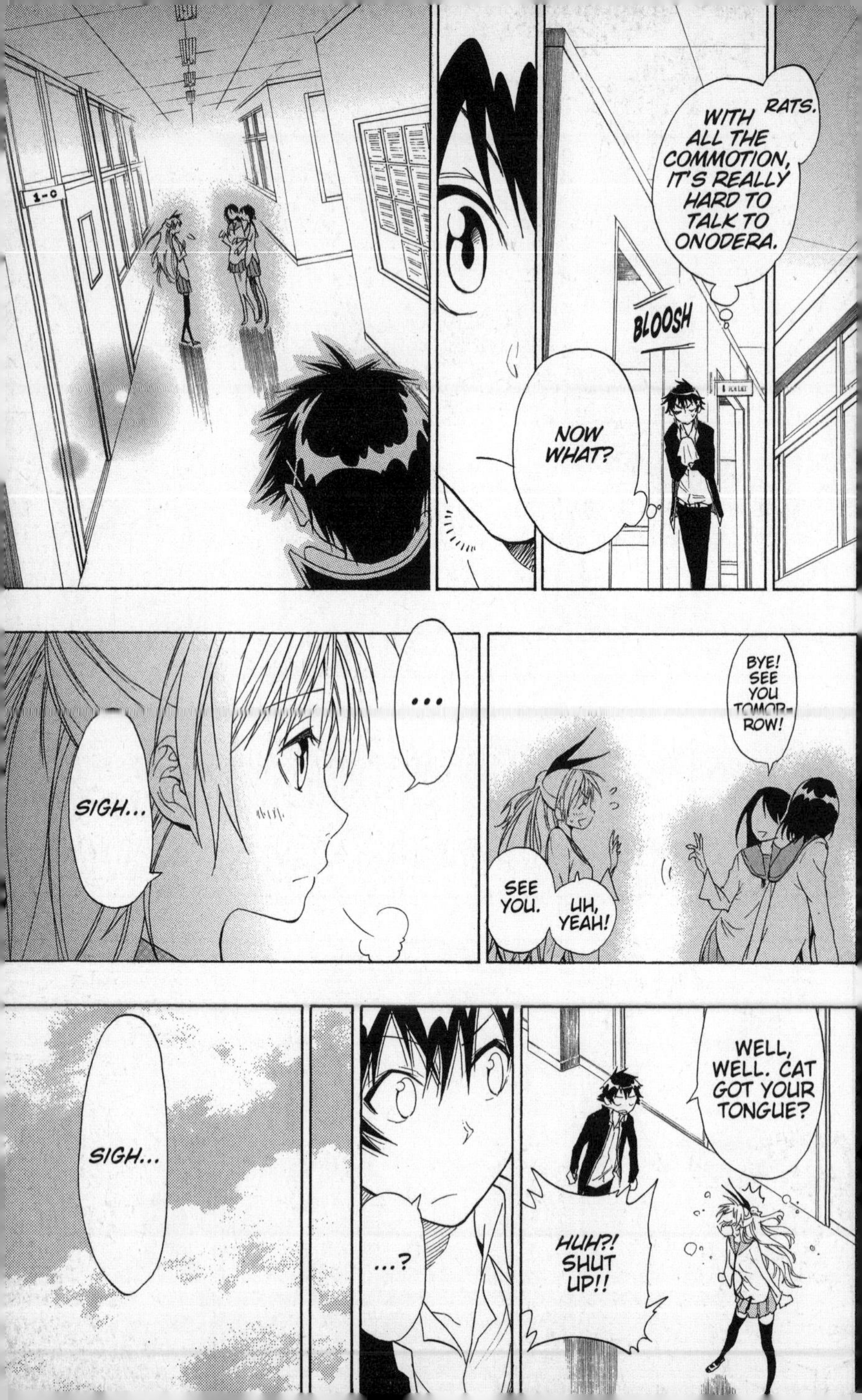
RATS. WITH ALL THE COMMOTION, IT'S REALLY HARD TO TALK TO ONODERA.
BLOOSH
NOW WHAT?
BYE! SEE YOU TOMORROW!
UH, YEAH!
SEE YOU.
...
SIGH...
WELL, WELL. CAT GOT YOUR TONGUE?
HUH?! SHUT UP!!
...?
SIGH...

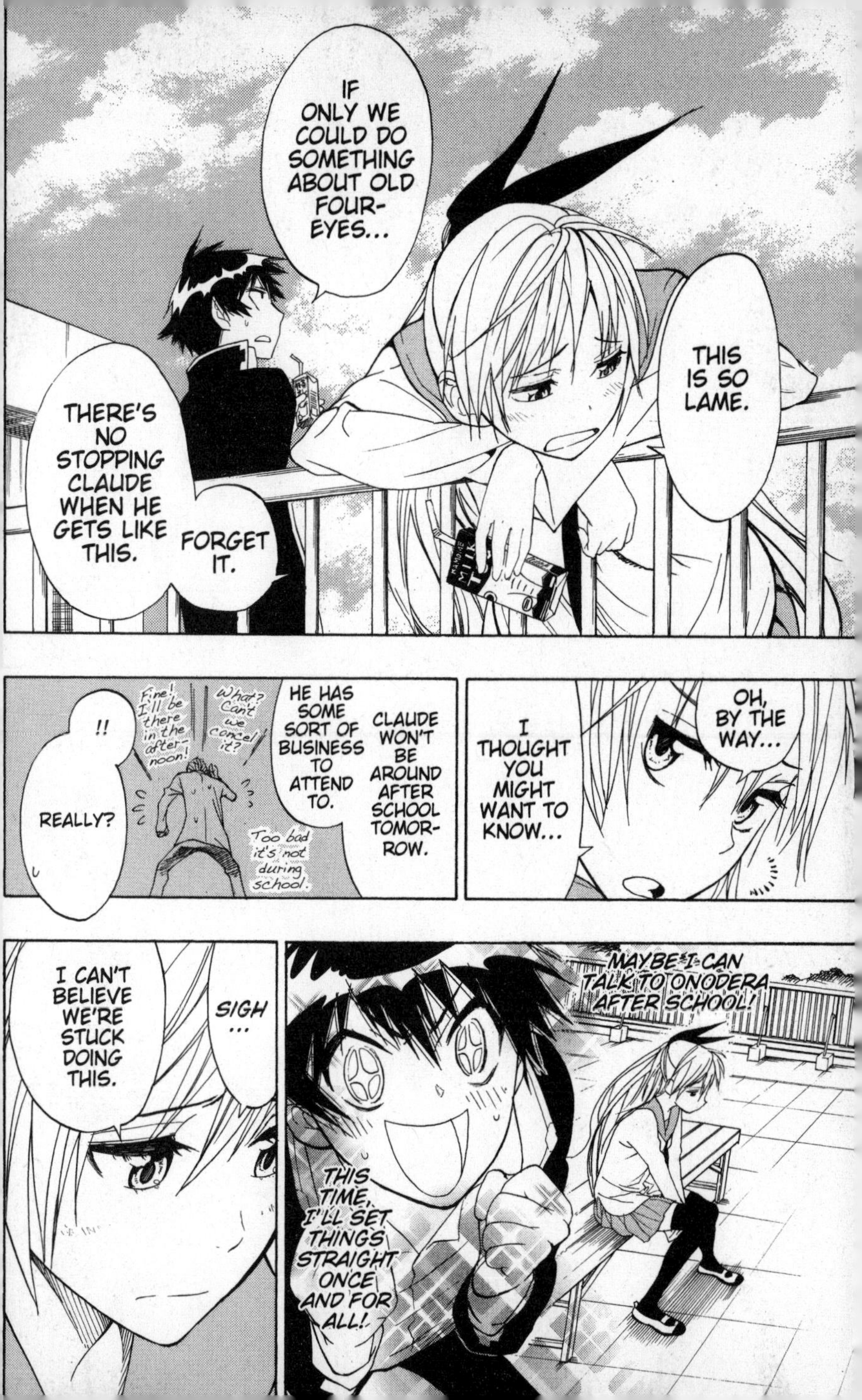
THIS IS SO LAME.
IF ONLY WE COULD DO SOMETHING ABOUT OLD FOUR-EYES...
FORGET IT.
THERE'S NO STOPPING CLAUDE WHEN HE GETS LIKE THIS.
OH, BY THE WAY...
I THOUGHT YOU MIGHT WANT TO KNOW...
CLAUDE WON'T BE AROUND AFTER SCHOOL TOMORROW.
HE HAS SOME SORT OF BUSINESS TO ATTEND TO.
Too bad it's not during school.
What? Can't we cancel it?
Fine! I'll be there in the afternoon!
!!
REALLY?
MAYBE I CAN TALK TO ONODERA AFTER SCHOOL!
THIS TIME, I'LL SET THINGS STRAIGHT ONCE AND FOR ALL!
SIGH...
I CAN'T BELIEVE WE'RE STUCK DOING THIS.

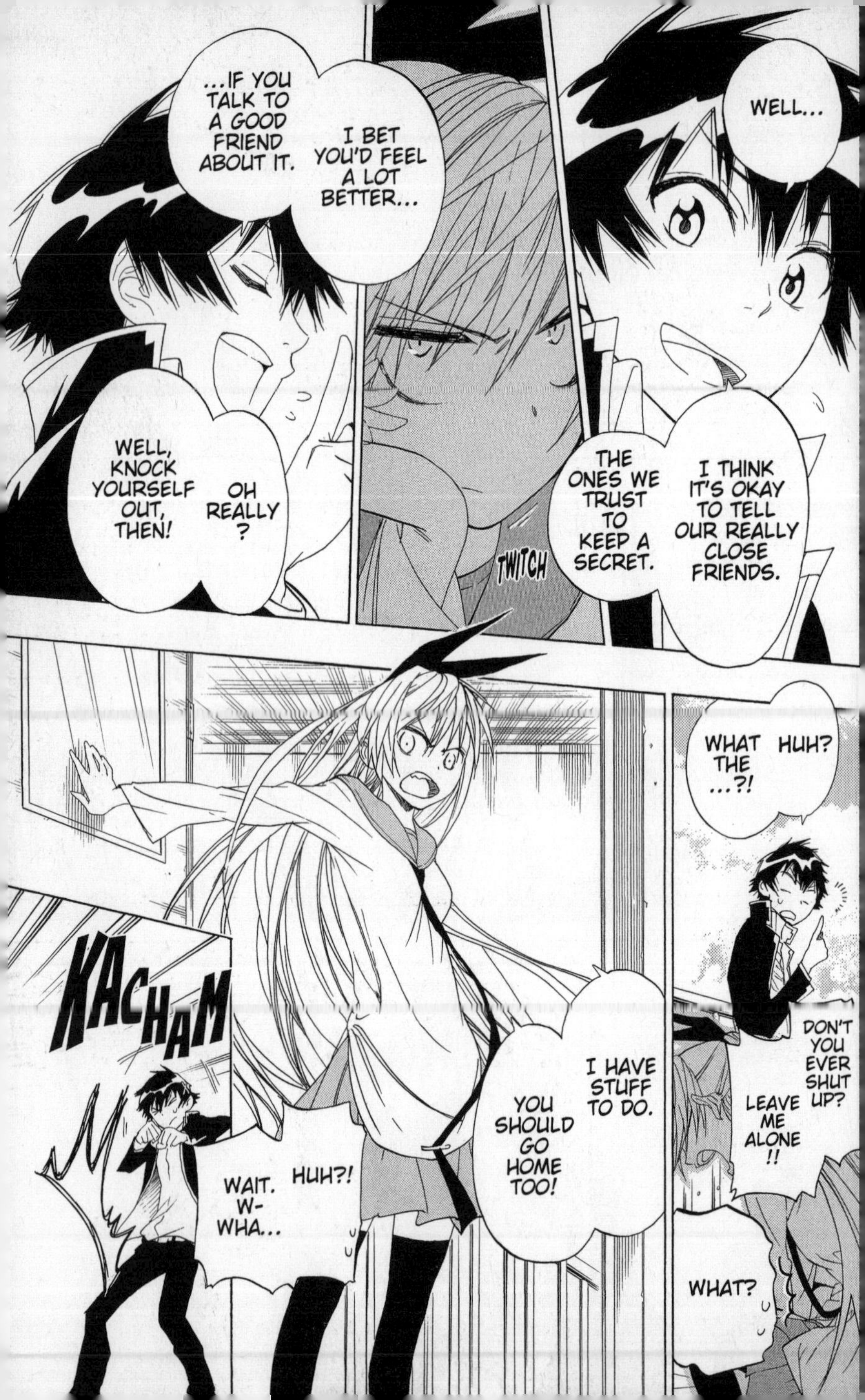
WELL...
I THINK IT'S OKAY TO TELL OUR REALLY CLOSE FRIENDS.
THE ONES WE TRUST TO KEEP A SECRET.
TWITCH
I BET YOU'D FEEL A LOT BETTER...
...IF YOU TALK TO A GOOD FRIEND ABOUT IT.
OH REALLY?
WELL, KNOCK YOURSELF OUT, THEN!
HUH?
WHAT THE ...?!
DON'T YOU EVER SHUT UP?
LEAVE ME ALONE!!
WHAT?
I HAVE STUFF TO DO.
YOU SHOULD GO HOME TOO!
KACHAM
HUH?!
WAIT. W-WHA...

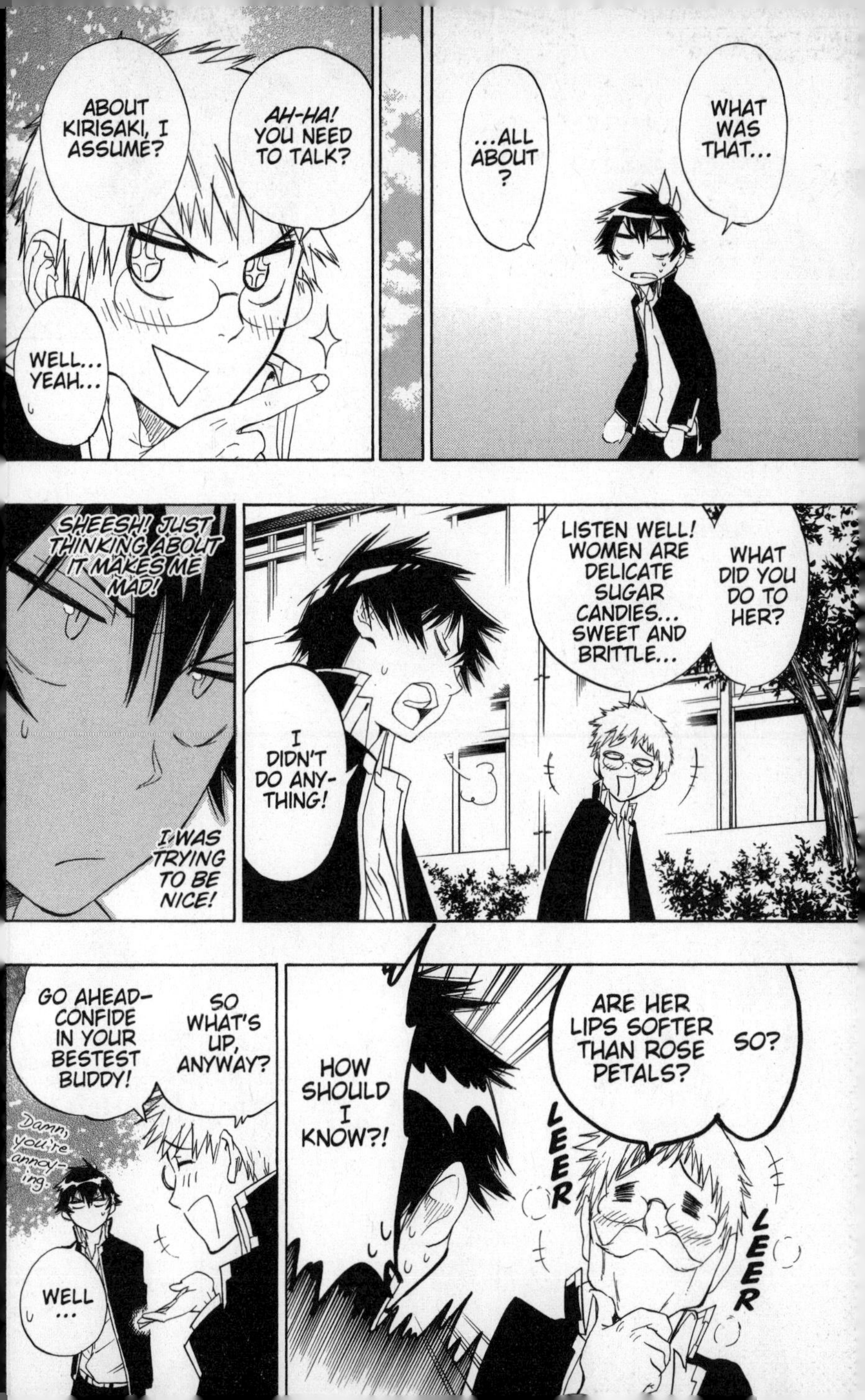
WHAT WAS THAT...
...ALL ABOUT?
AH-HA! YOU NEED TO TALK?
ABOUT KIRISAKI, I ASSUME?
WELL... YEAH...
WHAT DID YOU DO TO HER?
LISTEN WELL! WOMEN ARE DELICATE SUGAR CANDIES... SWEET AND BRITTLE...
I DIDN'T DO ANY-THING!
SHEESH! JUST THINKING ABOUT IT MAKES ME MAD!
I WAS TRYING TO BE NICE!
SO?
ARE HER LIPS SOFTER THAN ROSE PETALS?
LEER
LEER
HOW SHOULD I KNOW?!
SO WHAT'S UP, ANYWAY?
GO AHEAD-CONFIDE IN YOUR BESTEST BUDDY!
Damn, you're annoy-ing.
WELL ...

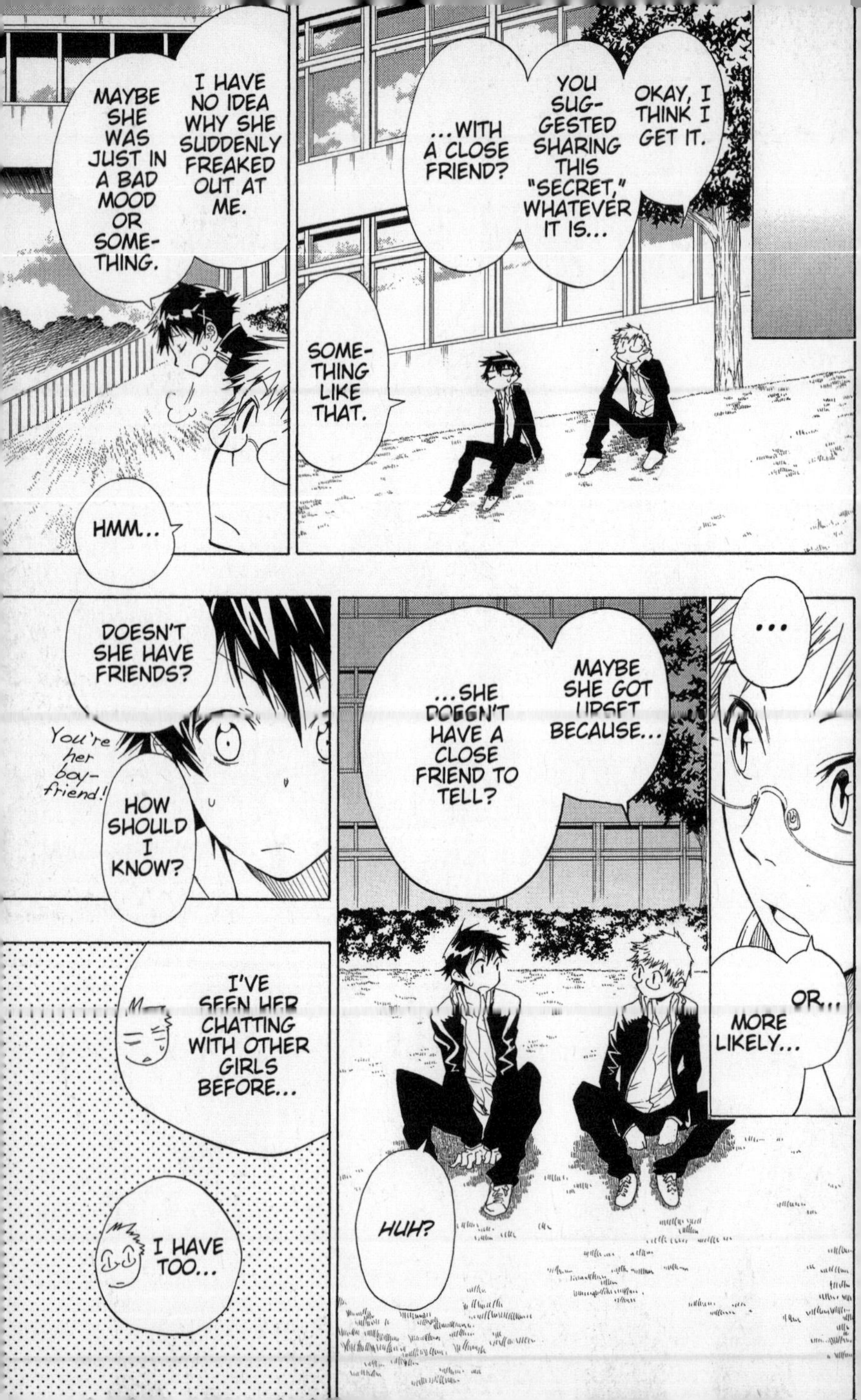
OKAY, I THINK I GET IT.
YOU SUG-GESTED SHARING THIS "SECRET," WHATEVER IT IS...
...WITH A CLOSE FRIEND?
SOME-THING LIKE THAT.
I HAVE NO IDEA WHY SHE SUDDENLY FREAKED OUT AT ME.
MAYBE SHE WAS JUST IN A BAD MOOD OR SOME-THING.
HMM..
...
OR... MORE LIKELY...
MAYBE SHE GOT UPSET BECAUSE...
...SHE DOESN'T HAVE A CLOSE FRIEND TO TELL?
HUH?
DOESN'T SHE HAVE FRIENDS?
HOW SHOULD I KNOW?
You're her boy-friend!
I'VE SEEN HER CHATTING WITH OTHER GIRLS BEFORE...
I HAVE TOO...

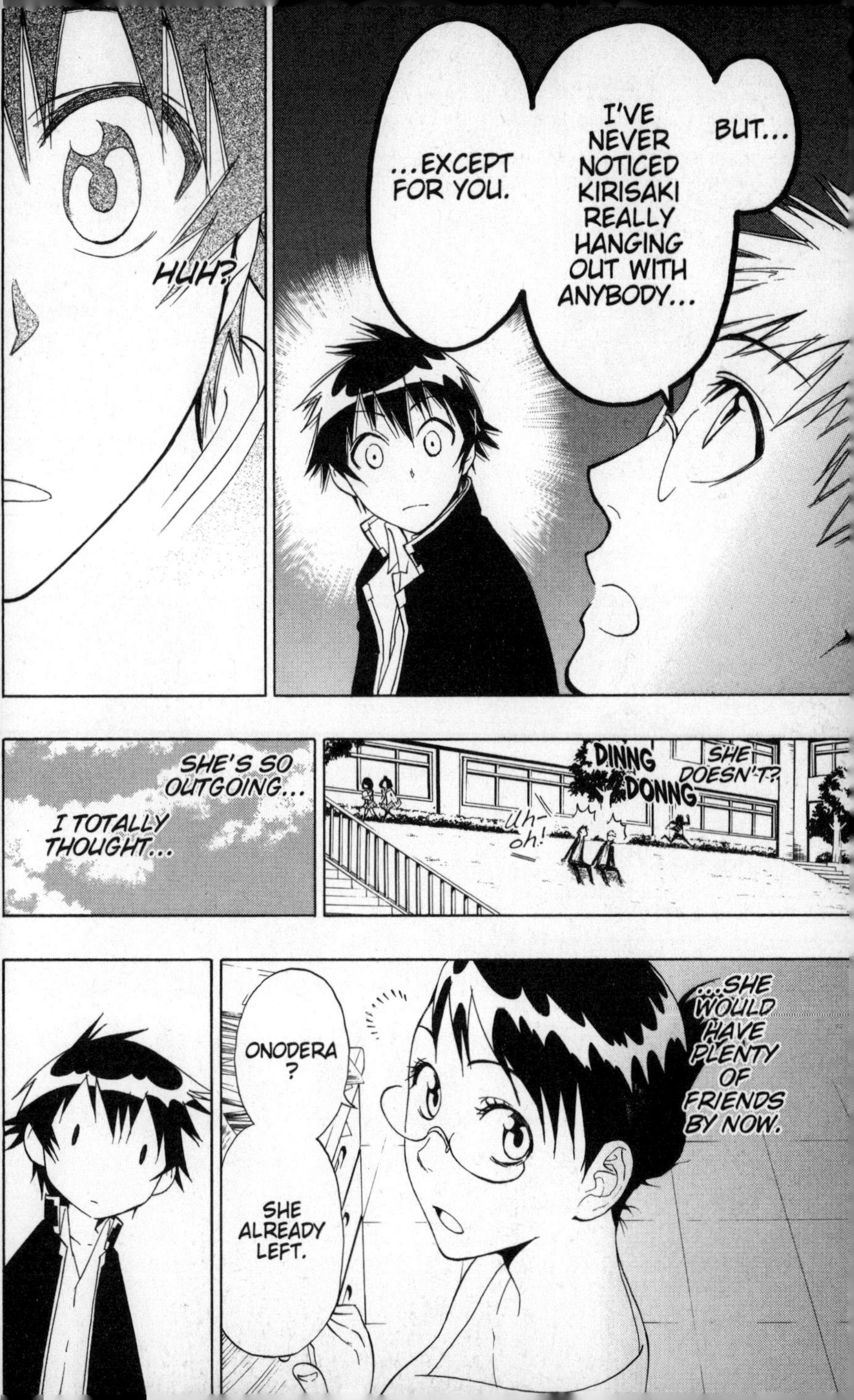
BUT...
I'VE NEVER NOTICED KIRISAKI REALLY HANGING OUT WITH ANYBODY...
...EXCEPT FOR YOU.
HUH?
SHE DOESN'T?
DINNG DONNG
Uh-oh!
SHE'S SO OUTGOING...
I TOTALLY THOUGHT...
...SHE WOULD HAVE PLENTY OF FRIENDS BY NOW.
ONODERA?
SHE ALREADY LEFT.

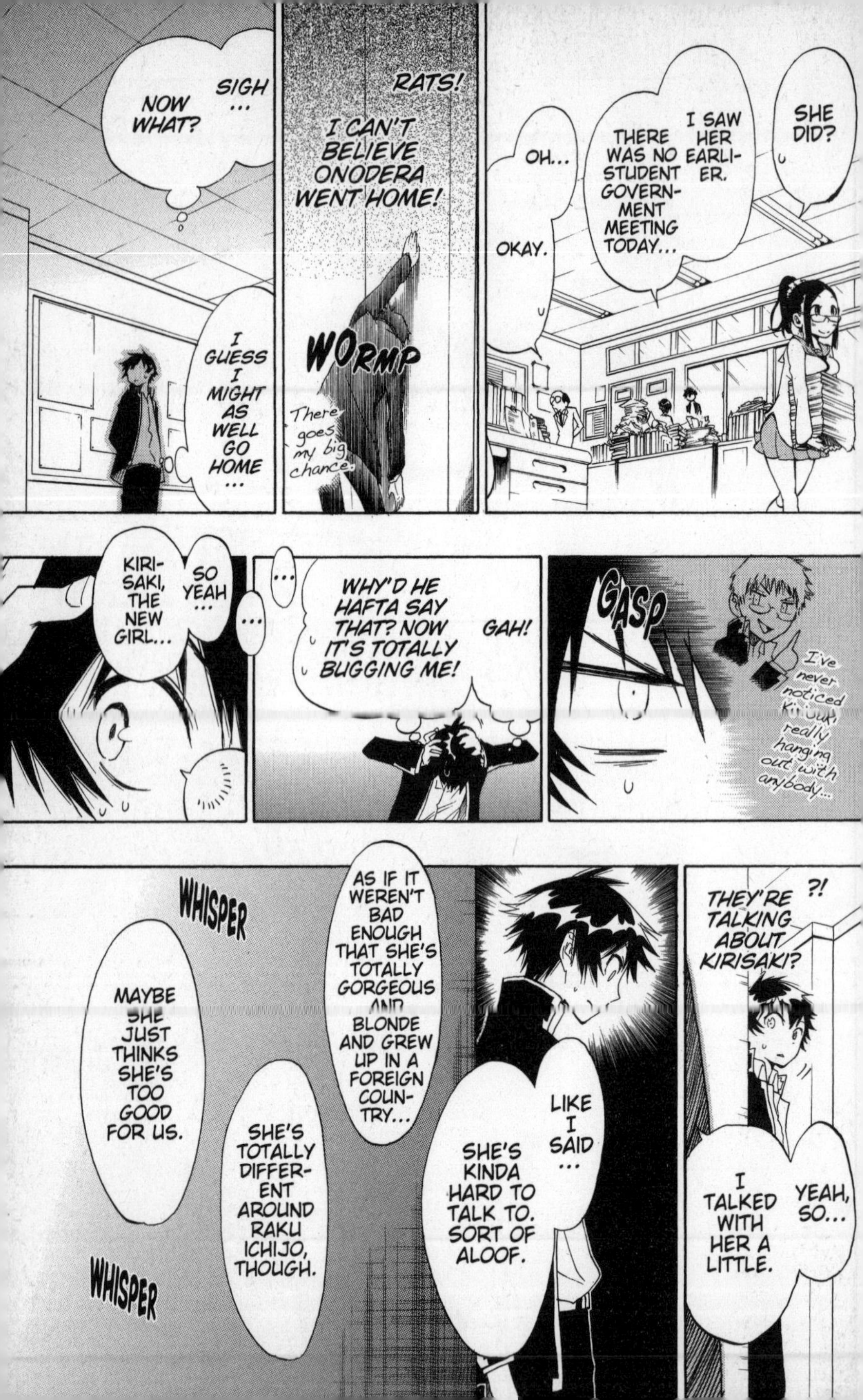
SHE DID?
I SAW HER EARLIER.
THERE WAS NO STUDENT GOVERNMENT MEETING TODAY...
OH... OKAY.
RATS!
I CAN'T BELIEVE ONODERA WENT HOME!
WORMP
There goes my big chance.
SIGH...
NOW WHAT?
I GUESS I MIGHT AS WELL GO HOME...
GASP
I've never noticed Ki[illegible] really hanging out with anybody...
...
...
WHY'D HE HAFTA SAY THAT? NOW IT'S TOTALLY BUGGING ME!
GAH!
SO YEAH...
KIRISAKI, THE NEW GIRL...
?!
THEY'RE TALKING ABOUT KIRISAKI?
YEAH, SO...
I TALKED WITH HER A LITTLE.
LIKE I SAID...
SHE'S KINDA HARD TO TALK TO. SORT OF ALOOF.
AS IF IT WEREN'T BAD ENOUGH THAT SHE'S TOTALLY GORGEOUS AND BLONDE AND GREW UP IN A FOREIGN COUNTRY...
SHE'S TOTALLY DIFFERENT AROUND RAKU ICHIJO, THOUGH.
WHISPER
MAYBE SHE JUST THINKS SHE'S TOO GOOD FOR US.
WHISPER

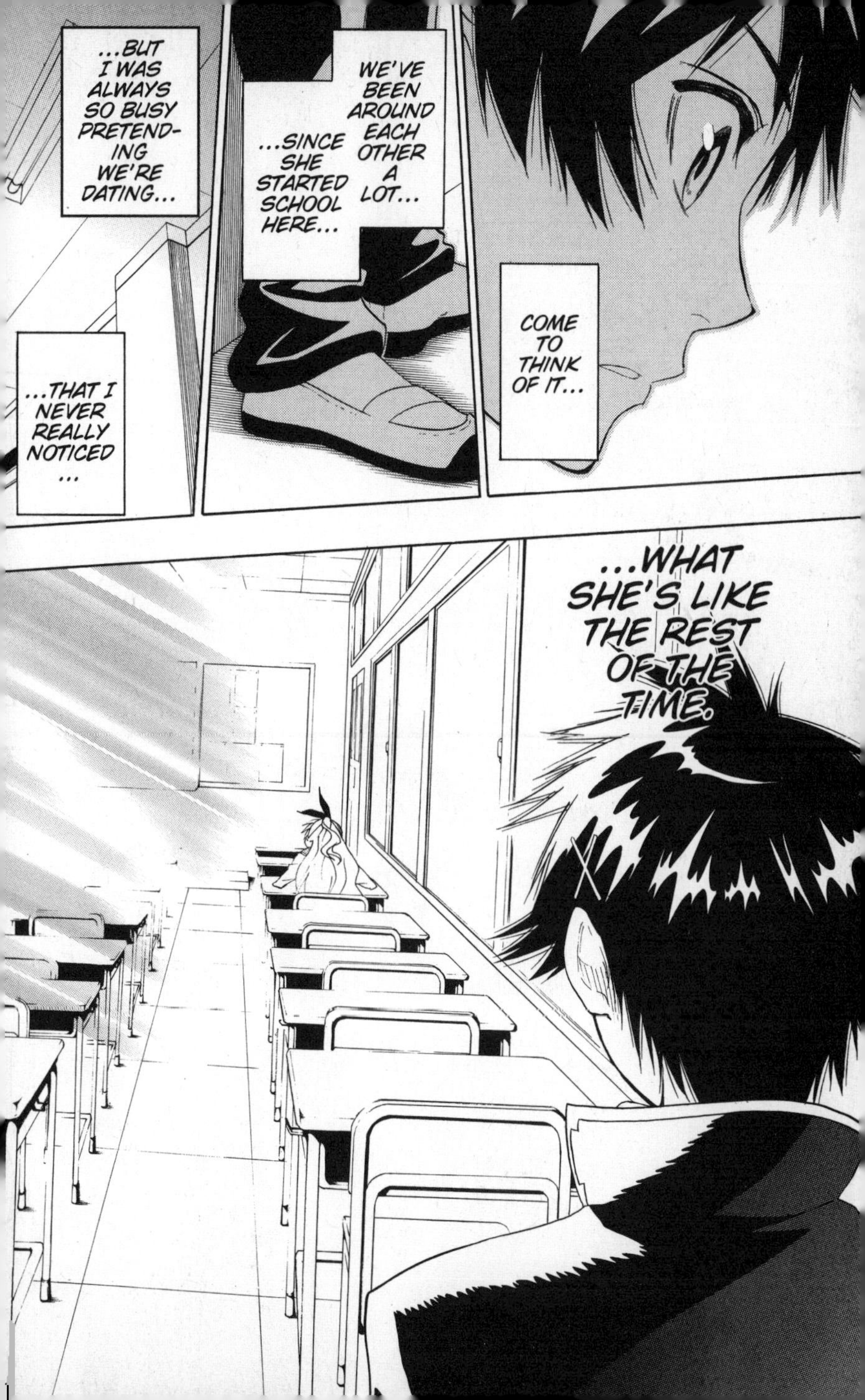
COME TO THINK OF IT...
WE'VE BEEN AROUND EACH OTHER A LOT...
...SINCE SHE STARTED SCHOOL HERE...
...BUT I WAS ALWAYS SO BUSY PRETEND-ING WE'RE DATING...
...THAT I NEVER REALLY NOTICED...
...WHAT SHE'S LIKE THE REST OF THE TIME.

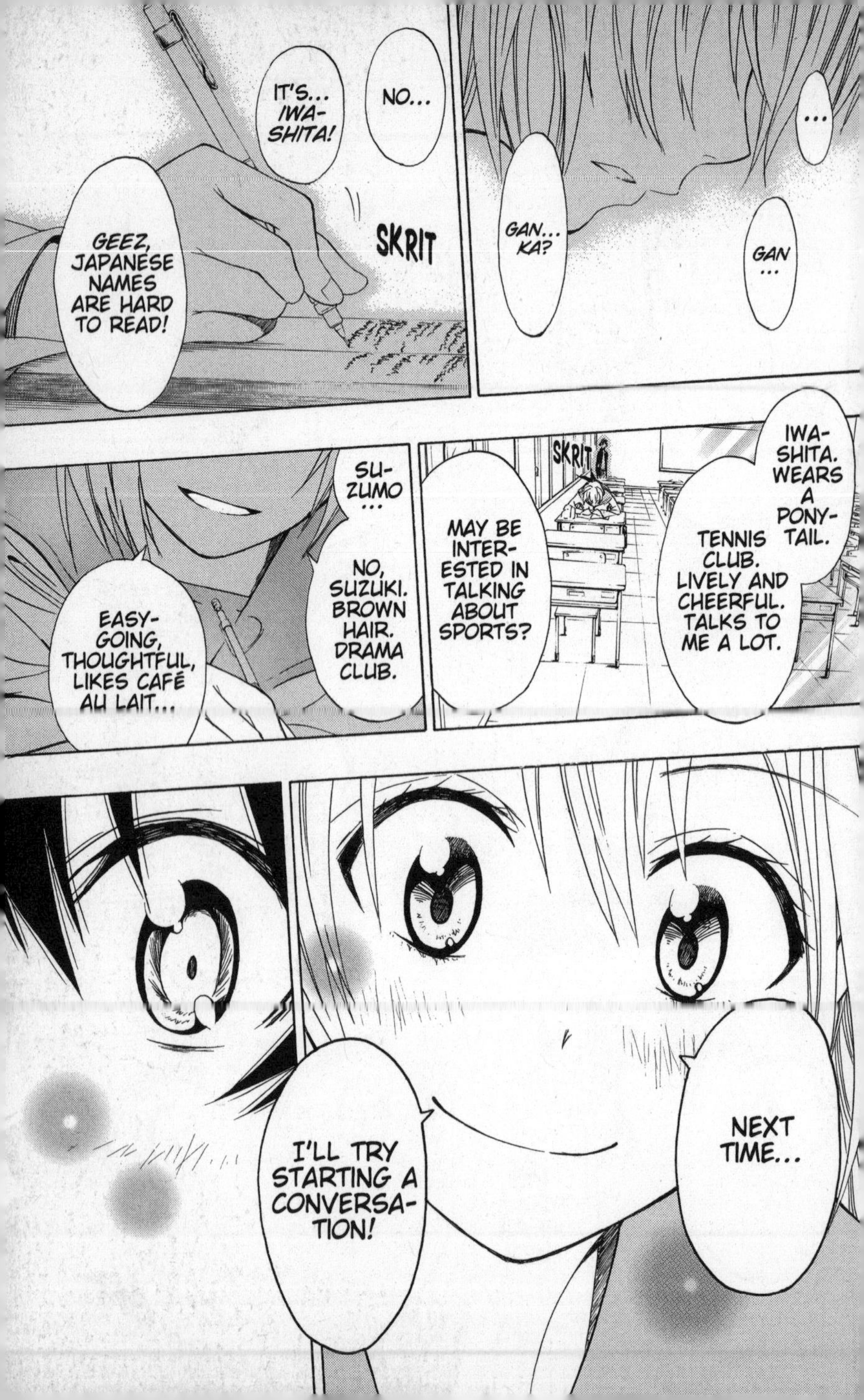
...
GAN ...
GAN... KA?
NO...
IT'S... IWA-SHITA!
SKRIT
GEEZ, JAPANESE NAMES ARE HARD TO READ!
IWA-SHITA. WEARS A PONY-TAIL.
TENNIS CLUB. LIVELY AND CHEERFUL. TALKS TO ME A LOT.
SKRIT
MAY BE INTER-ESTED IN TALKING ABOUT SPORTS?
SU-ZUMO ...
NO, SUZUKI. BROWN HAIR. DRAMA CLUB.
EASY-GOING, THOUGHTFUL, LIKES CAFÉ AU LAIT...
NEXT TIME...
I'LL TRY STARTING A CONVERSA-TION!

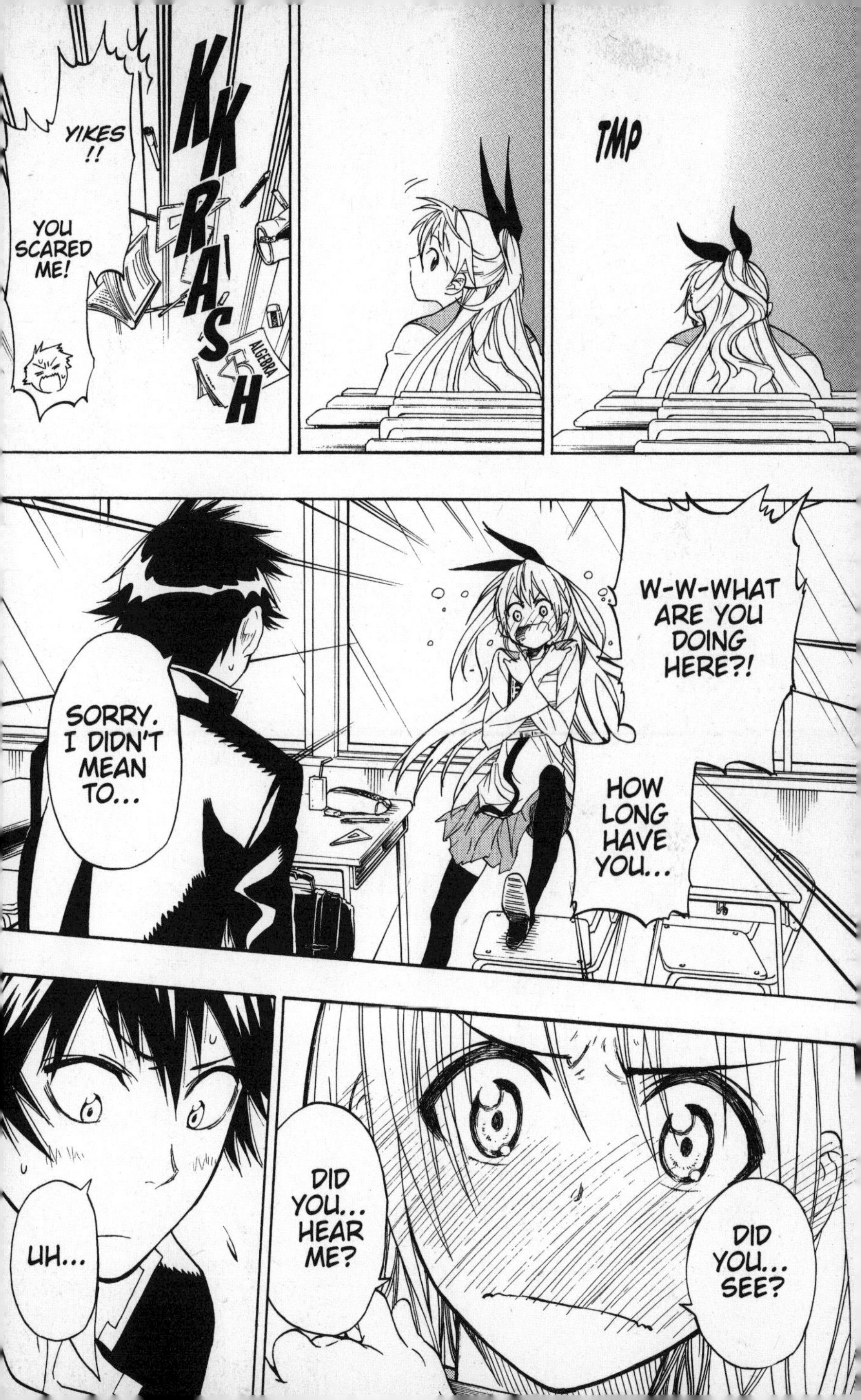
TMP
KKRASH
YIKES!!
YOU SCARED ME!
ALGEBRA
W-W-WHAT ARE YOU DOING HERE?!
HOW LONG HAVE YOU...
SORRY. I DIDN'T MEAN TO...
DID YOU... SEE?
DID YOU... HEAR ME?
UH...

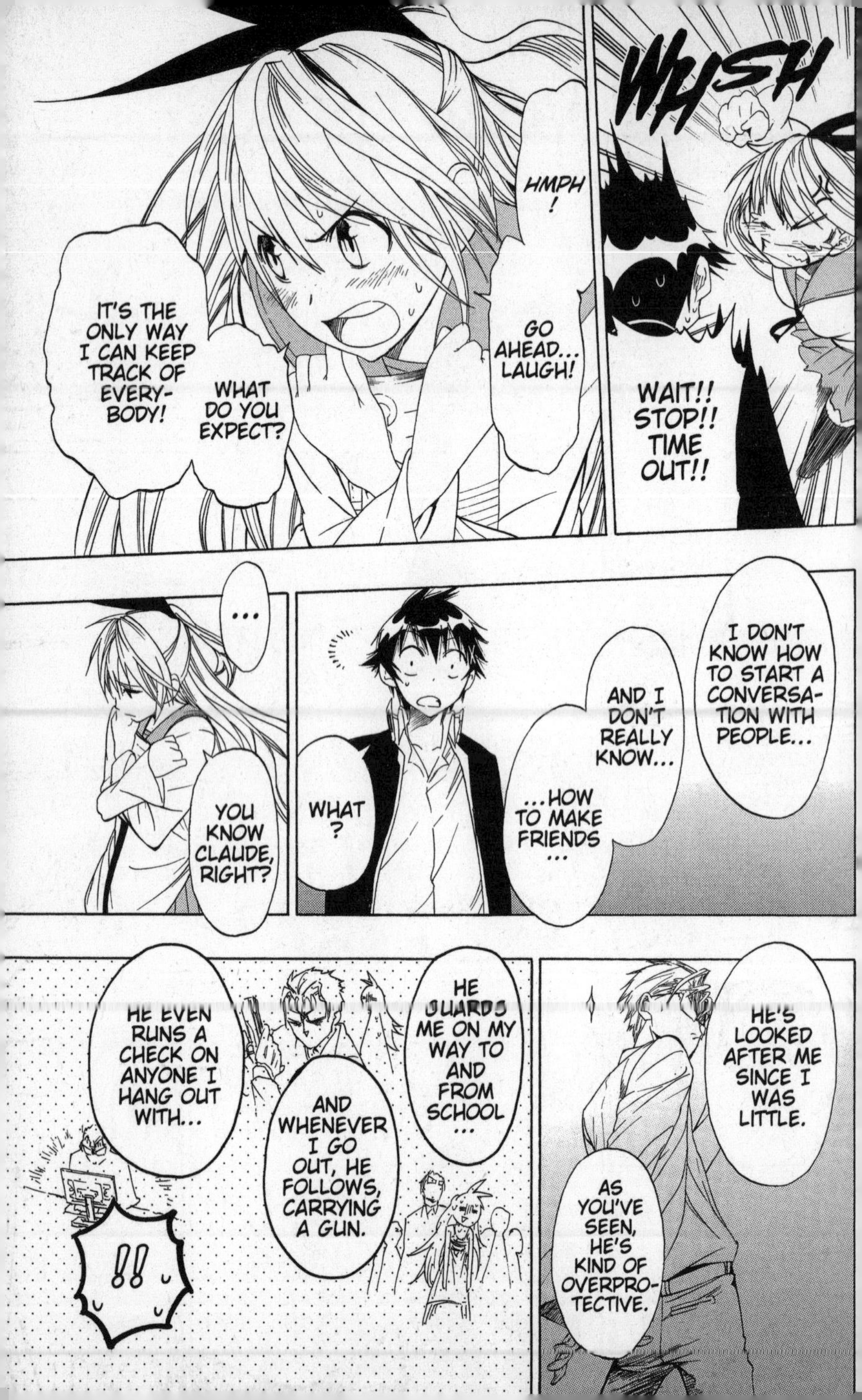
WHSH
WAIT!! STOP!! TIME OUT!!
HMPH!
GO AHEAD... LAUGH!
WHAT DO YOU EXPECT?
IT'S THE ONLY WAY I CAN KEEP TRACK OF EVERY-BODY!
I DON'T KNOW HOW TO START A CONVERSA-TION WITH PEOPLE...
AND I DON'T REALLY KNOW...
...HOW TO MAKE FRIENDS...
WHAT?
...
YOU KNOW CLAUDE, RIGHT?
HE'S LOOKED AFTER ME SINCE I WAS LITTLE.
AS YOU'VE SEEN, HE'S KIND OF OVERPRO-TECTIVE.
HE GUARDS ME ON MY WAY TO AND FROM SCHOOL...
AND WHENEVER I GO OUT, HE FOLLOWS, CARRYING A GUN.
HE EVEN RUNS A CHECK ON ANYONE I HANG OUT WITH...
!!

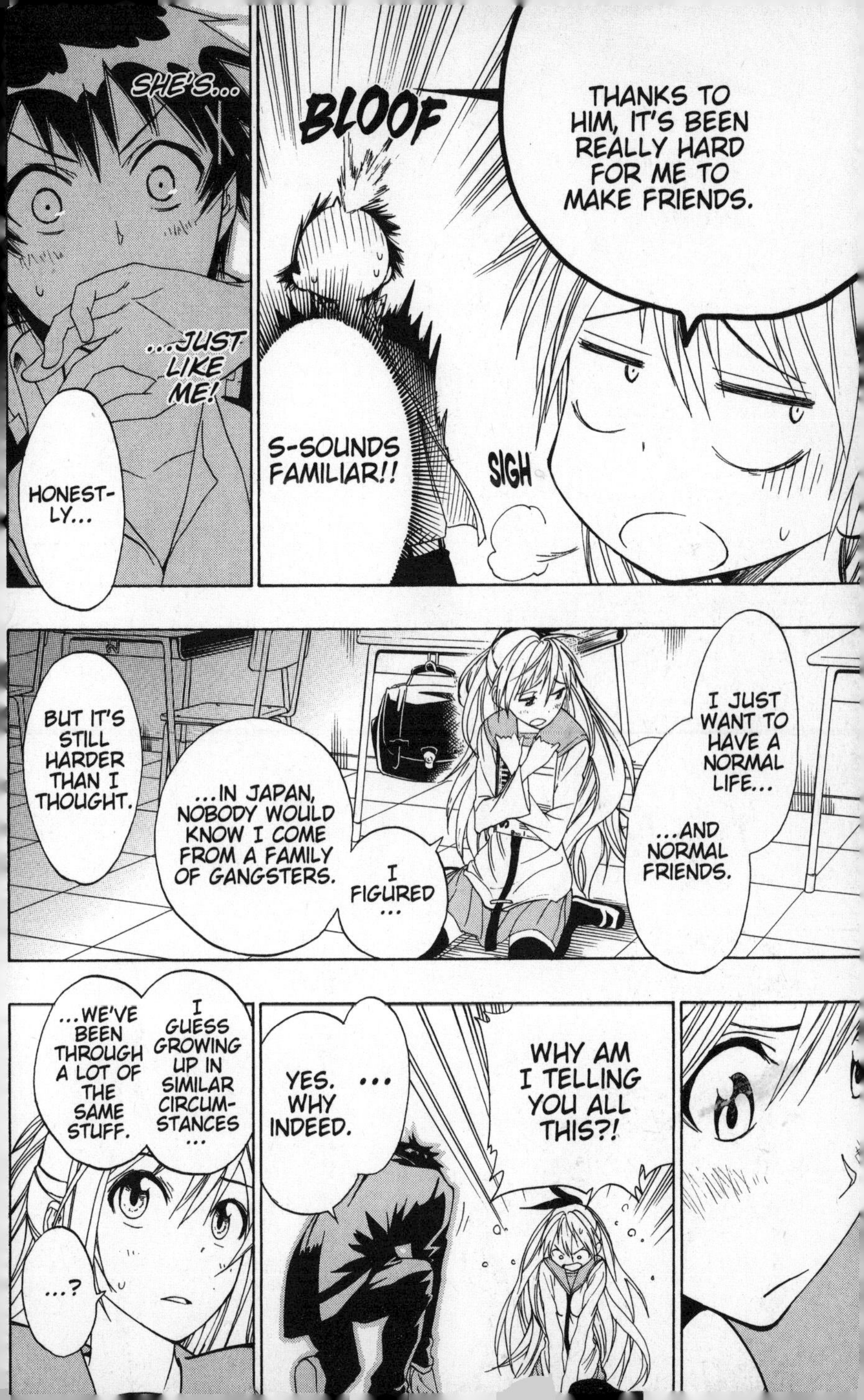
THANKS TO HIM, IT'S BEEN REALLY HARD FOR ME TO MAKE FRIENDS.
SIGH
BLOOF
S-SOUNDS FAMILIAR!!
SHE'S...
...JUST LIKE ME!
HONEST-LY...
I JUST WANT TO HAVE A NORMAL LIFE...
...AND NORMAL FRIENDS.
I FIGURED...
...IN JAPAN, NOBODY WOULD KNOW I COME FROM A FAMILY OF GANGSTERS.
BUT IT'S STILL HARDER THAN I THOUGHT.
WHY AM I TELLING YOU ALL THIS?!
...
YES. WHY INDEED.
I GUESS GROWING UP IN SIMILAR CIRCUM-STANCES...
...WE'VE BEEN THROUGH A LOT OF THE SAME STUFF.
...?

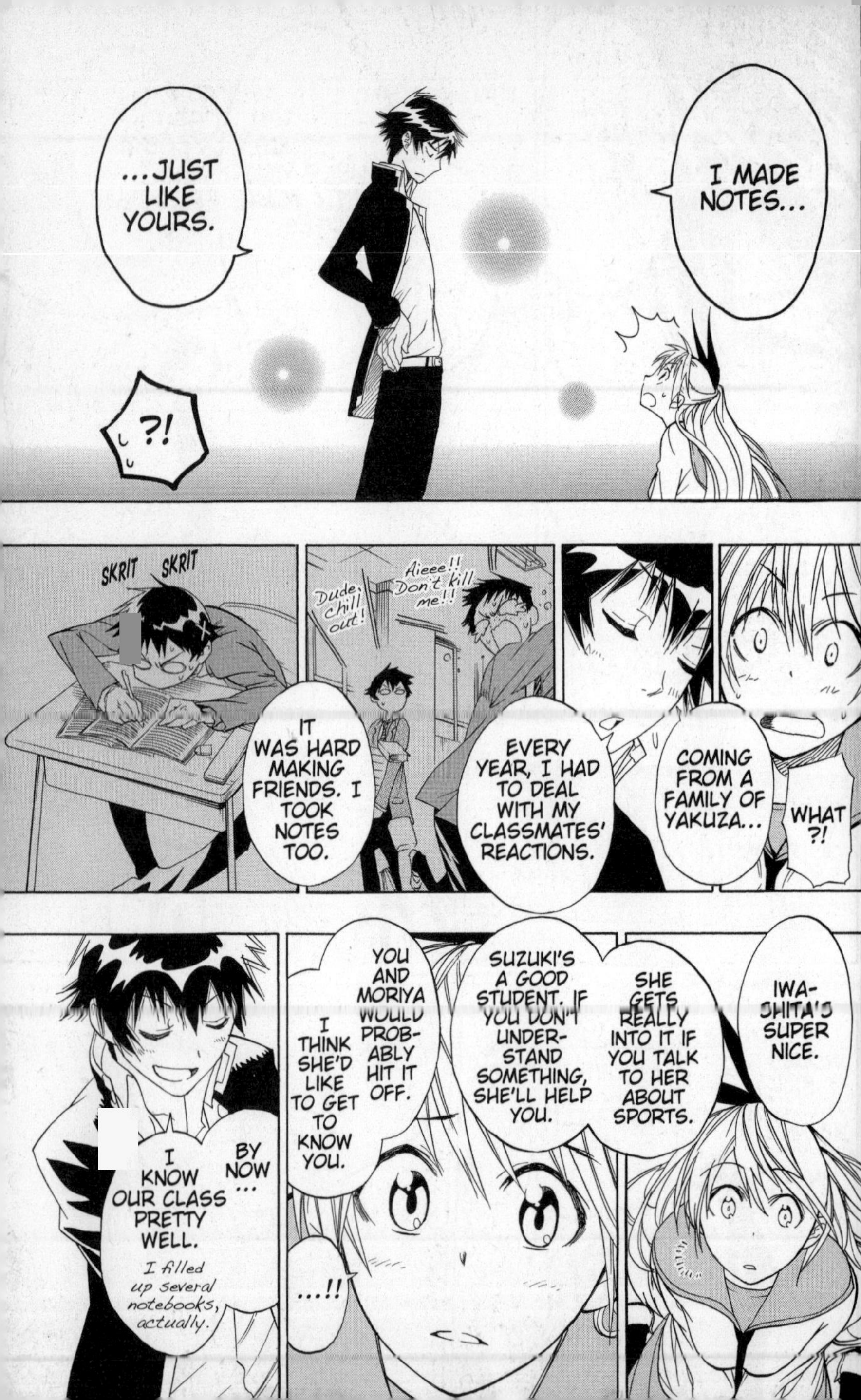
I MADE NOTES...
...JUST LIKE YOURS.
?!
WHAT ?!
COMING FROM A FAMILY OF YAKUZA...
EVERY YEAR, I HAD TO DEAL WITH MY CLASSMATES' REACTIONS.
Aieee!! Don't kill me!!
Dude, chill out!
IT WAS HARD MAKING FRIENDS. I TOOK NOTES TOO.
SKRIT SKRIT
IWA-SHITA'S SUPER NICE.
SHE GETS REALLY INTO IT IF YOU TALK TO HER ABOUT SPORTS.
SUZUKI'S A GOOD STUDENT. IF YOU DON'T UNDER-STAND SOMETHING, SHE'LL HELP YOU.
YOU AND MORIYA WOULD PROB-ABLY HIT IT OFF.
I THINK SHE'D LIKE TO GET TO KNOW YOU.
...!!
BY NOW...
I KNOW OUR CLASS PRETTY WELL.
I filled up several notebooks, actually.

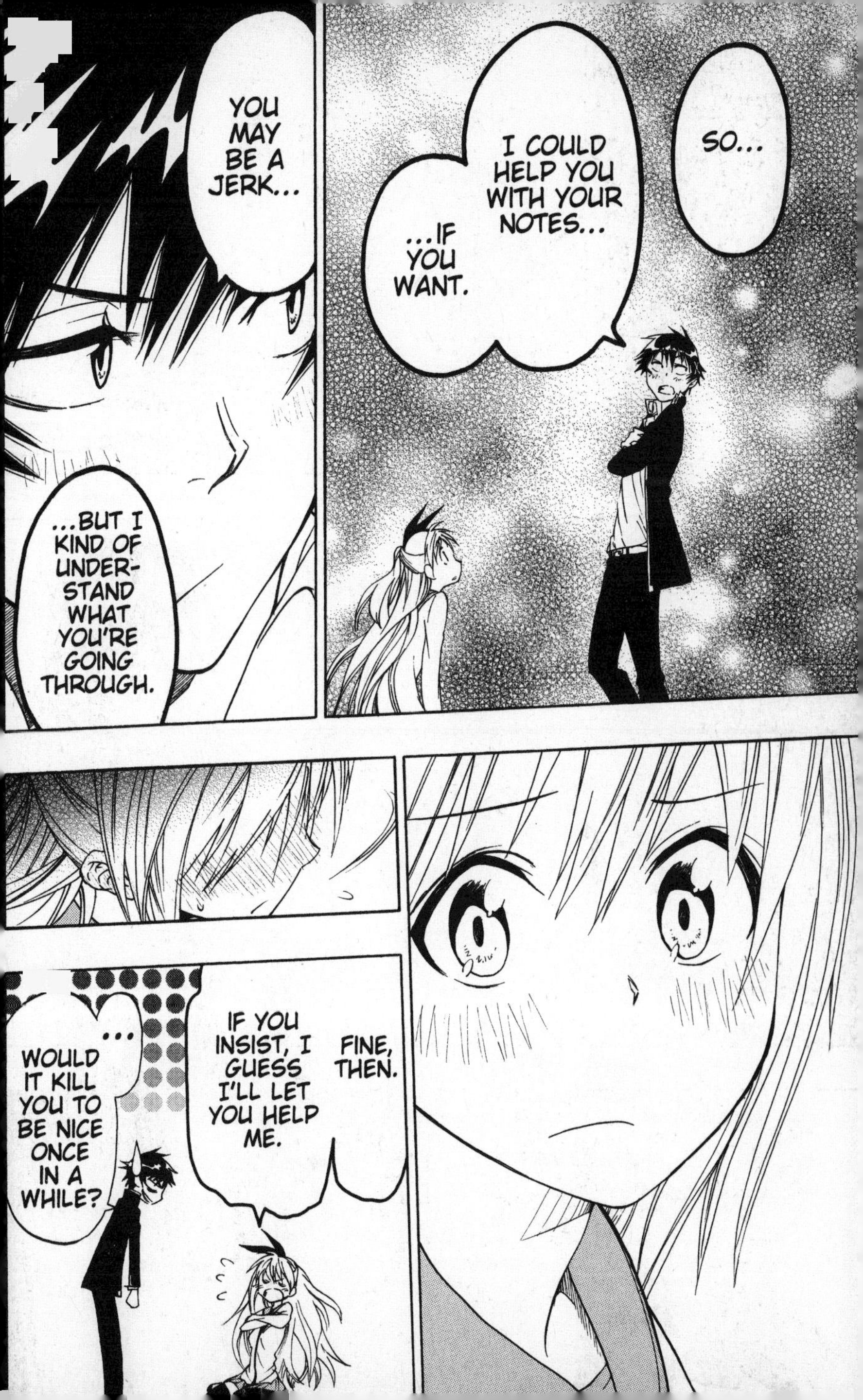
SO...
I COULD HELP YOU WITH YOUR NOTES...
...IF YOU WANT.
YOU MAY BE A JERK...
...BUT I KIND OF UNDER-STAND WHAT YOU'RE GOING THROUGH.
FINE, THEN.
IF YOU INSIST, I GUESS I'LL LET YOU HELP ME.
...
WOULD IT KILL YOU TO BE NICE ONCE IN A WHILE?

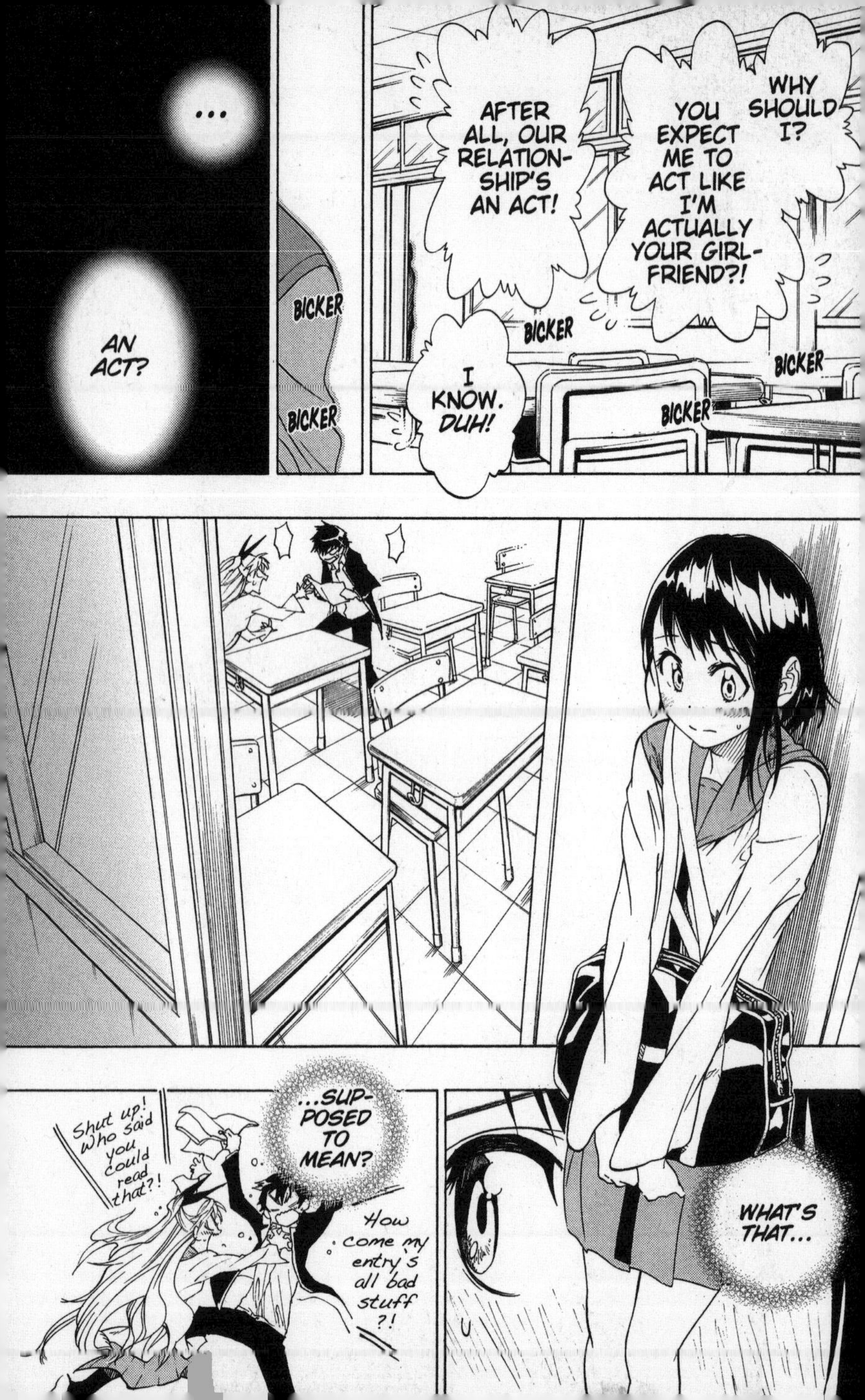
WHY SHOULD I?
YOU EXPECT ME TO ACT LIKE I'M ACTUALLY YOUR GIRL-FRIEND?!
AFTER ALL, OUR RELATION-SHIP'S AN ACT!
BICKER
BICKER
BICKER
BICKER
I KNOW. DUH!
BICKER
...
AN ACT?
WHAT'S THAT...
...SUP-POSED TO MEAN?
How come my entry's all bad stuff?!
Shut up! Who said you could read that?!

A Day in the Life of Onodera

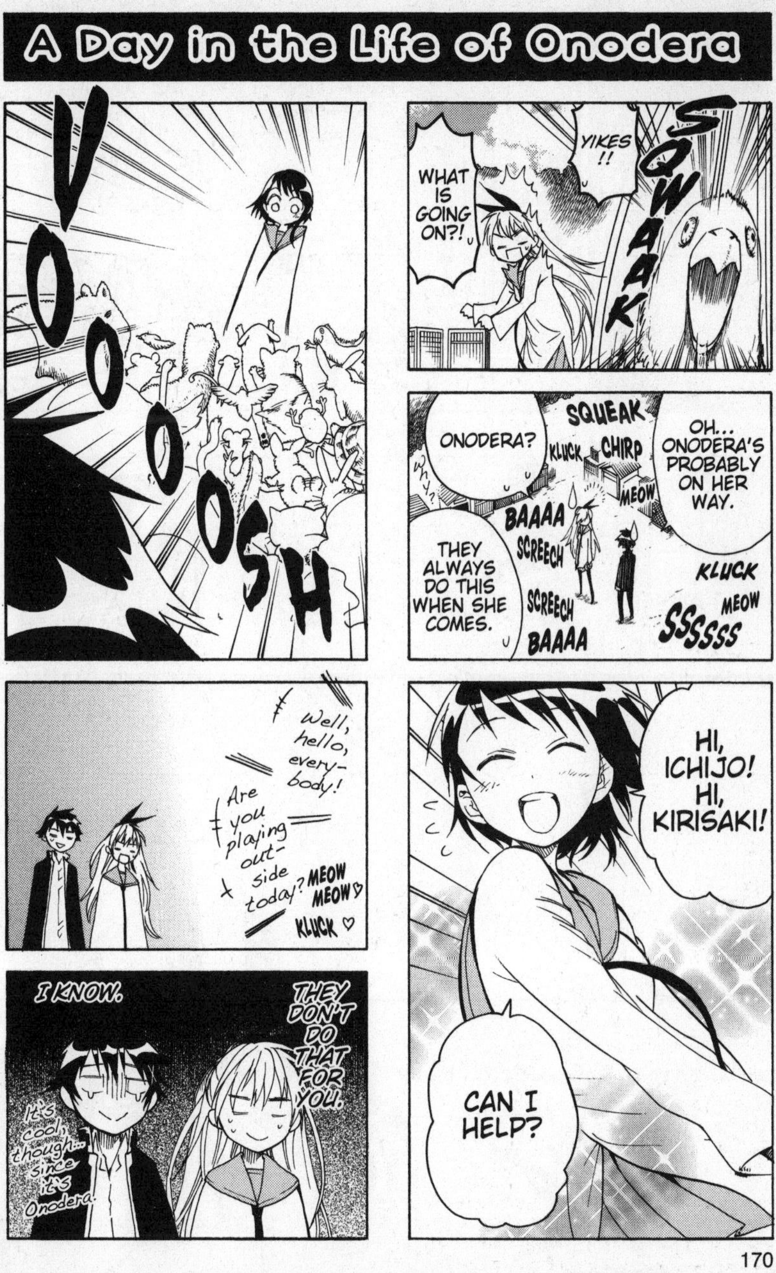
SQWAAK
YIKES!!
WHAT IS GOING ON?!
OH... ONODERA'S PROBABLY ON HER WAY.
SQUEAK
CHIRP
KLUCK
ONODERA?
MEOW
BAAAA
SCREECH
THEY ALWAYS DO THIS WHEN SHE COMES.
KLUCK
MEOW
SSSSSS
SCREECH
BAAAA
VOOOOOSH
HI, ICHIJO! HI, KIRISAKI!
CAN I HELP?
Well, hello, every-body!
Are you playing out-side today?
MEOW MEOW♡
KLUCK♡
THEY DON'T DO THAT FOR YOU.
I KNOW.
It's cool, though... since it's Onodera.

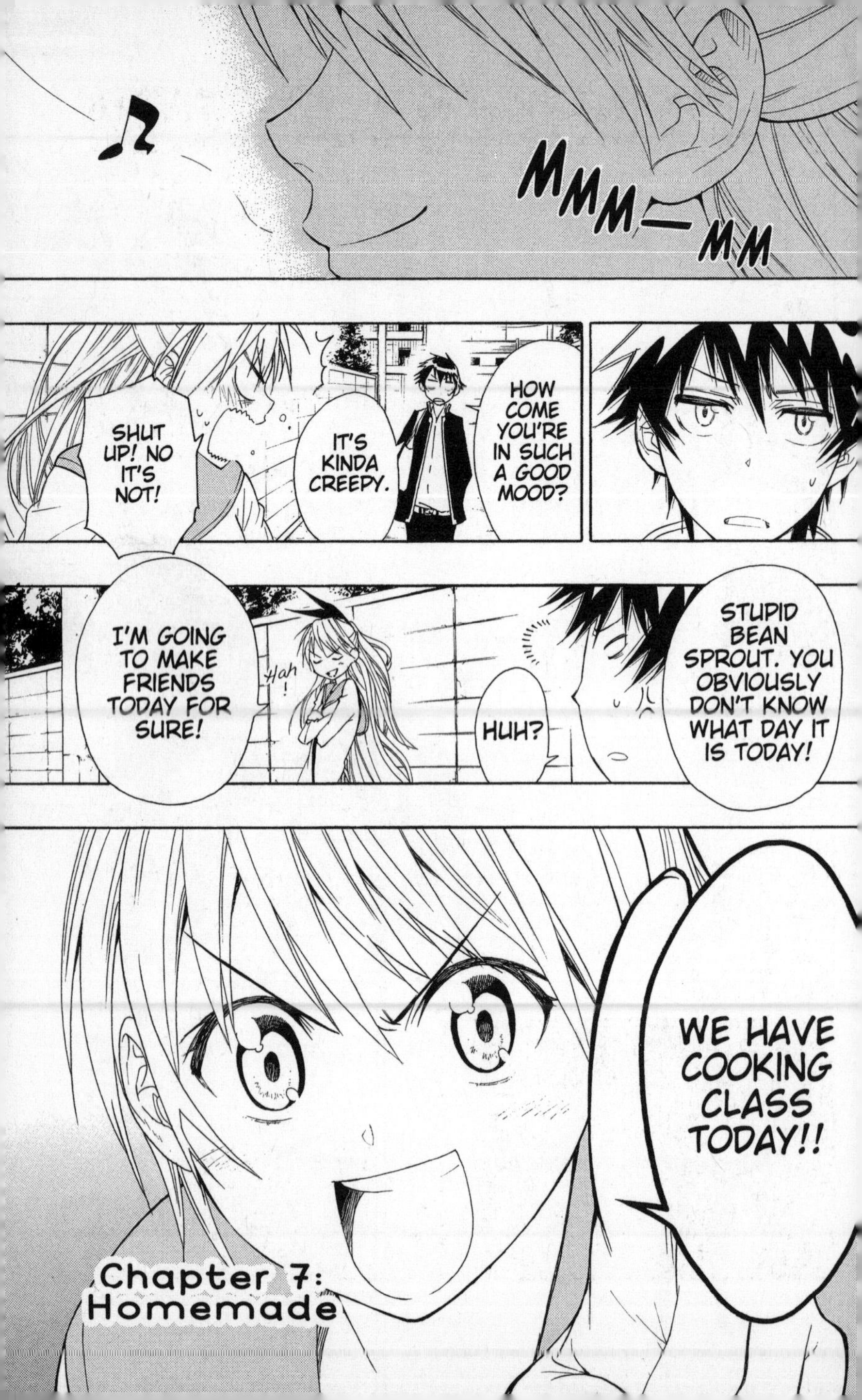
MMM—MM
HOW COME YOU'RE IN SUCH A GOOD MOOD?
IT'S KINDA CREEPY.
SHUT UP! NO IT'S NOT!
STUPID BEAN SPROUT. YOU OBVIOUSLY DON'T KNOW WHAT DAY IT IS TODAY!
HUH?
Hah!
I'M GOING TO MAKE FRIENDS TODAY FOR SURE!
WE HAVE COOKING CLASS TODAY!!
Chapter 7: Homemade

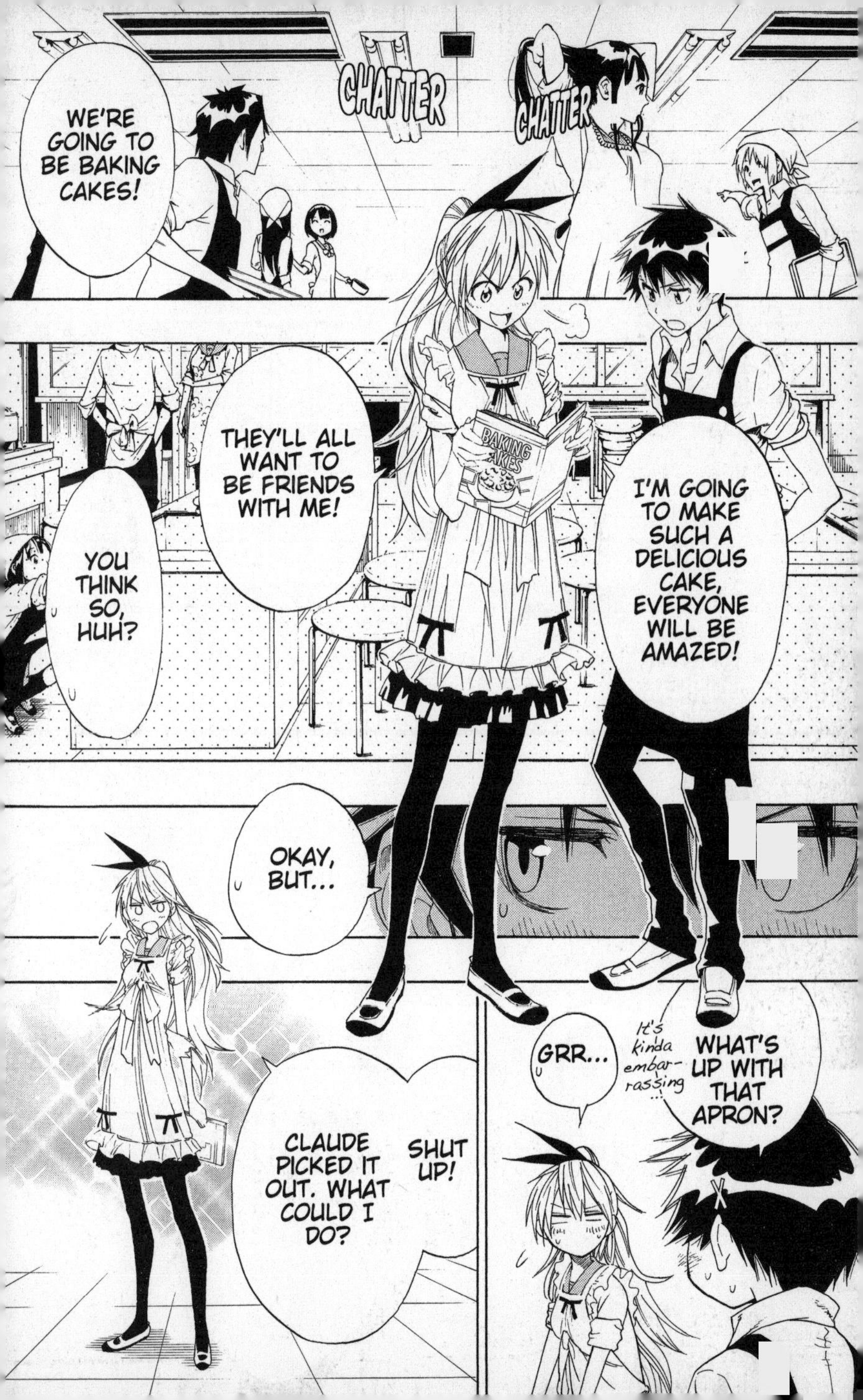
CHATTER
CHATTER
WE'RE GOING TO BE BAKING CAKES!
BAKING CAKES
I'M GOING TO MAKE SUCH A DELICIOUS CAKE, EVERYONE WILL BE AMAZED!
THEY'LL ALL WANT TO BE FRIENDS WITH ME!
YOU THINK SO, HUH?
OKAY, BUT...
WHAT'S UP WITH THAT APRON?
It's kinda embarrassing..!
GRR...
SHUT UP!
CLAUDE PICKED IT OUT. WHAT COULD I DO?

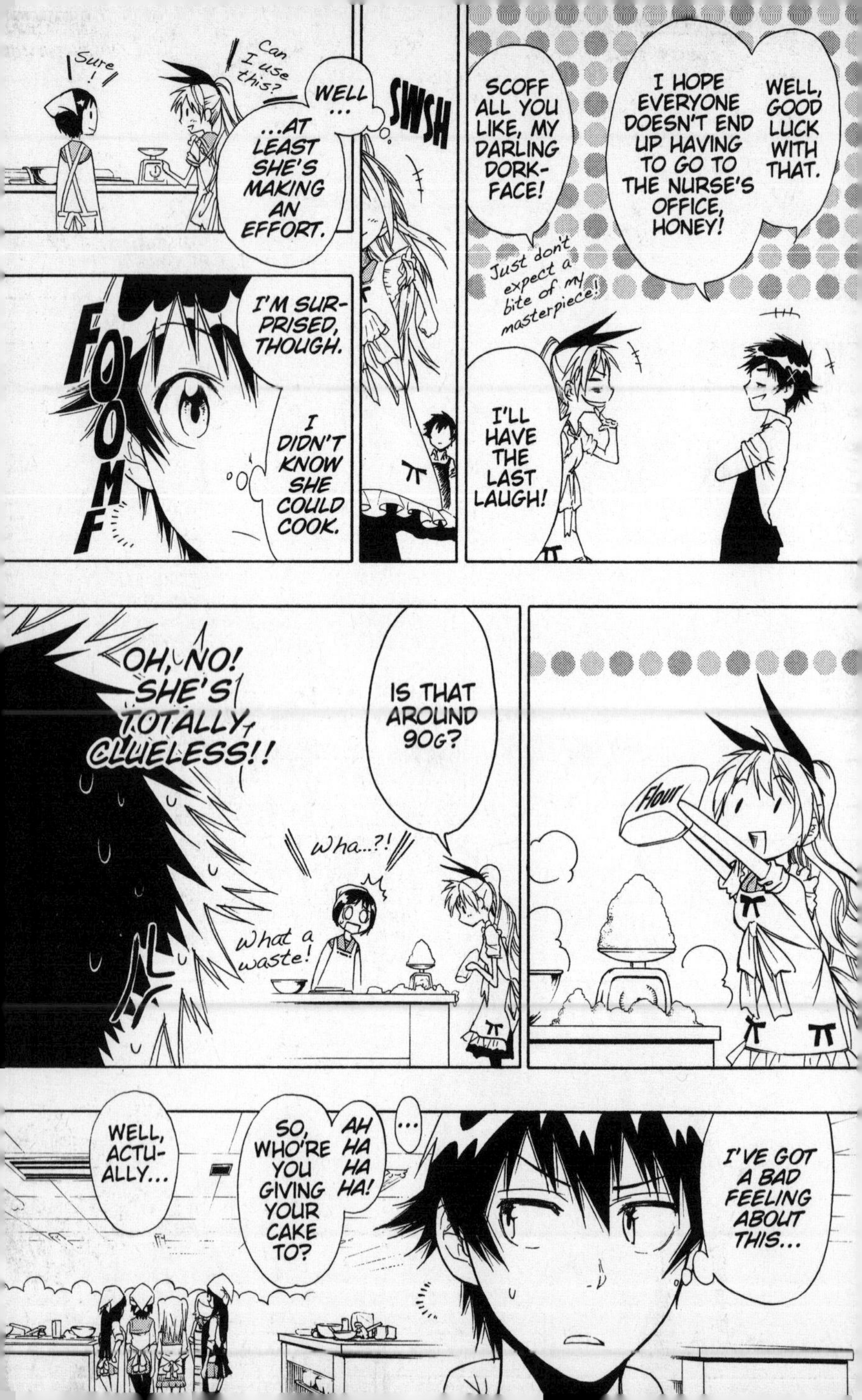
WELL, GOOD LUCK WITH THAT.
I HOPE EVERYONE DOESN'T END UP HAVING TO GO TO THE NURSE'S OFFICE, HONEY!
SCOFF ALL YOU LIKE, MY DARLING DORK-FACE!
Just don't expect a bite of my masterpiece!
I'LL HAVE THE LAST LAUGH!
SWSH
WELL...
...AT LEAST SHE'S MAKING AN EFFORT.
Can I use this?
Sure!
I'M SUR-PRISED, THOUGH.
I DIDN'T KNOW SHE COULD COOK.
FOOOMF
Flour
IS THAT AROUND 90G?
Wha...?!
What a waste!
OH, NO! SHE'S TOTALLY CLUELESS!!
I'VE GOT A BAD FEELING ABOUT THIS...
...
AH HA HA HA!
SO, WHO'RE YOU GIVING YOUR CAKE TO?
WELL, ACTU-ALLY...

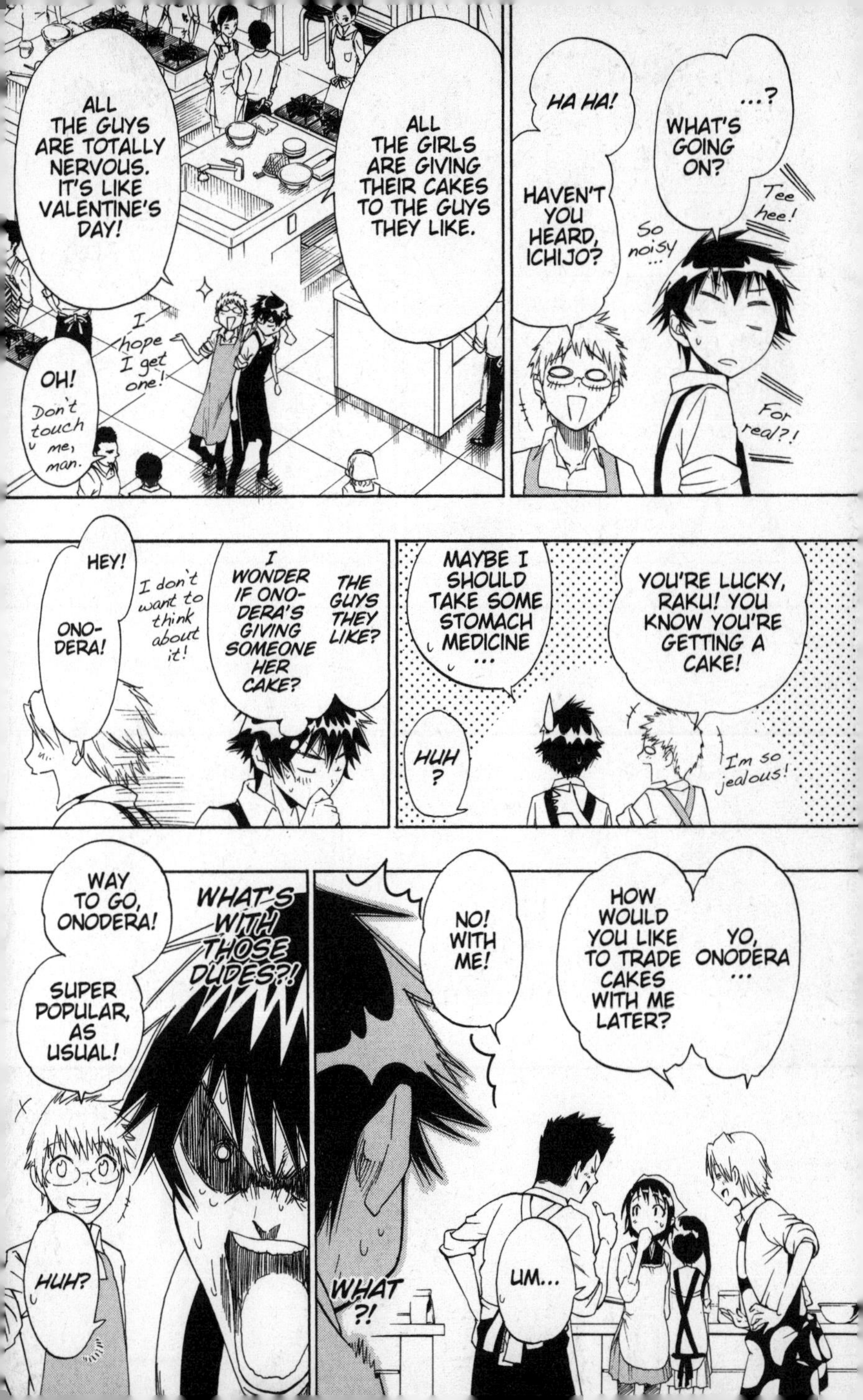
...? WHAT'S GOING ON?
Tee hee!
So noisy...
HA HA! HAVEN'T YOU HEARD, ICHIJO?
For real?!
ALL THE GIRLS ARE GIVING THEIR CAKES TO THE GUYS THEY LIKE.
ALL THE GUYS ARE TOTALLY NERVOUS. IT'S LIKE VALENTINE'S DAY!
I hope I get one!
OH! Don't touch me, man.
YOU'RE LUCKY, RAKU! YOU KNOW YOU'RE GETTING A CAKE!
MAYBE I SHOULD TAKE SOME STOMACH MEDICINE...
I'm so jealous!
HUH?
THE GUYS THEY LIKE?
I WONDER IF ONODERA'S GIVING SOMEONE HER CAKE?
I don't want to think about it!
HEY! ONODERA!
YO, ONODERA...
HOW WOULD YOU LIKE TO TRADE CAKES WITH ME LATER?
NO! WITH ME!
UM...
WHAT?!
WAY TO GO, ONODERA!
SUPER POPULAR, AS USUAL!
WHAT'S WITH THOSE DUDES?!
HUH?

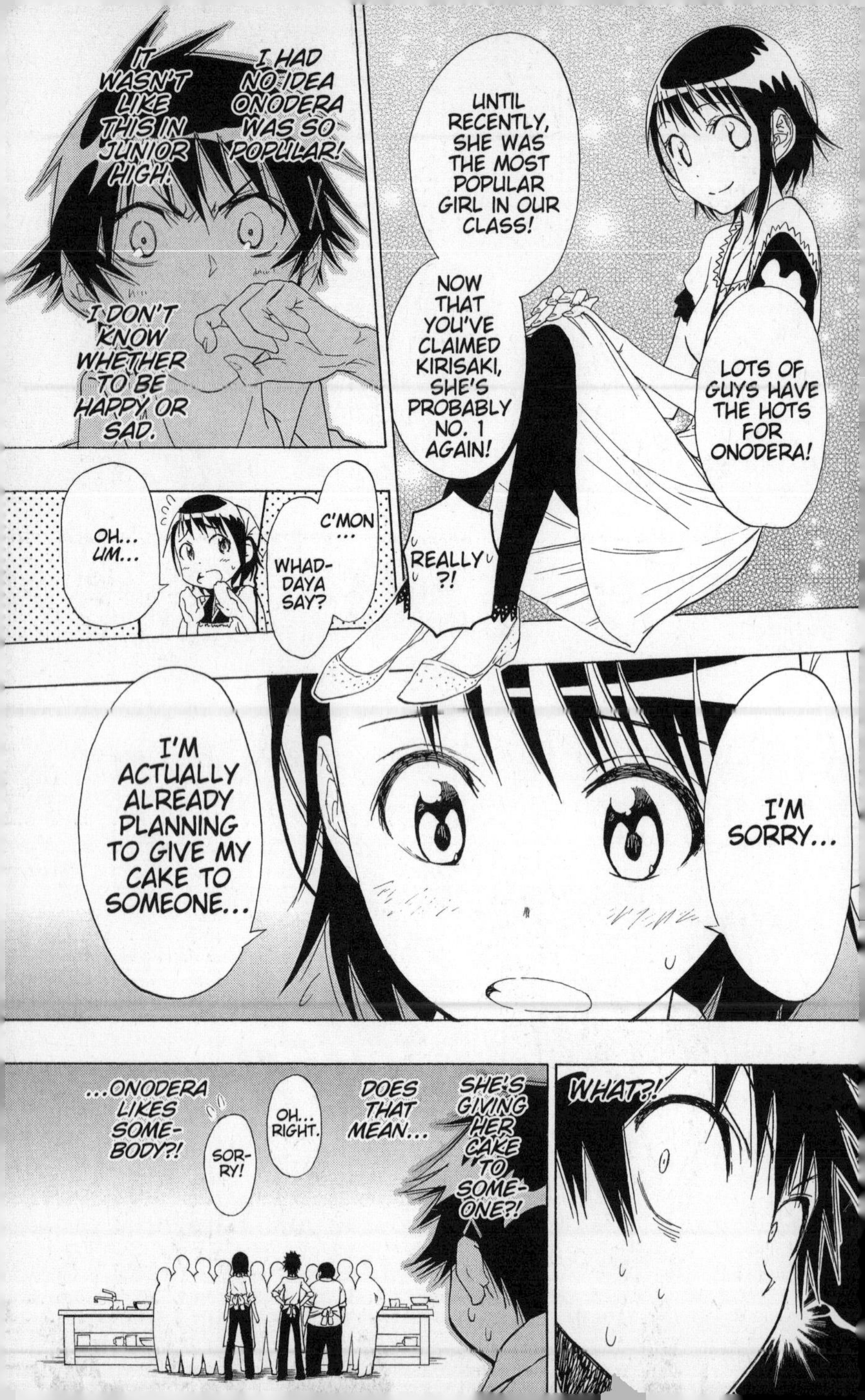
LOTS OF GUYS HAVE THE HOTS FOR ONODERA!
UNTIL RECENTLY, SHE WAS THE MOST POPULAR GIRL IN OUR CLASS!
NOW THAT YOU'VE CLAIMED KIRISAKI, SHE'S PROBABLY NO. 1 AGAIN!
REALLY?!
I HAD NO IDEA ONODERA WAS SO POPULAR!
IT WASN'T LIKE THIS IN JUNIOR HIGH.
I DON'T KNOW WHETHER TO BE HAPPY OR SAD.
C'MON... WHAD-DAYA SAY?
OH... UM...
I'M SORRY...
I'M ACTUALLY ALREADY PLANNING TO GIVE MY CAKE TO SOMEONE...
WHAT?!
SHE'S GIVING HER CAKE TO SOME-ONE?!
DOES THAT MEAN...
OH... RIGHT.
SOR-RY!
...ONODERA LIKES SOME-BODY?!

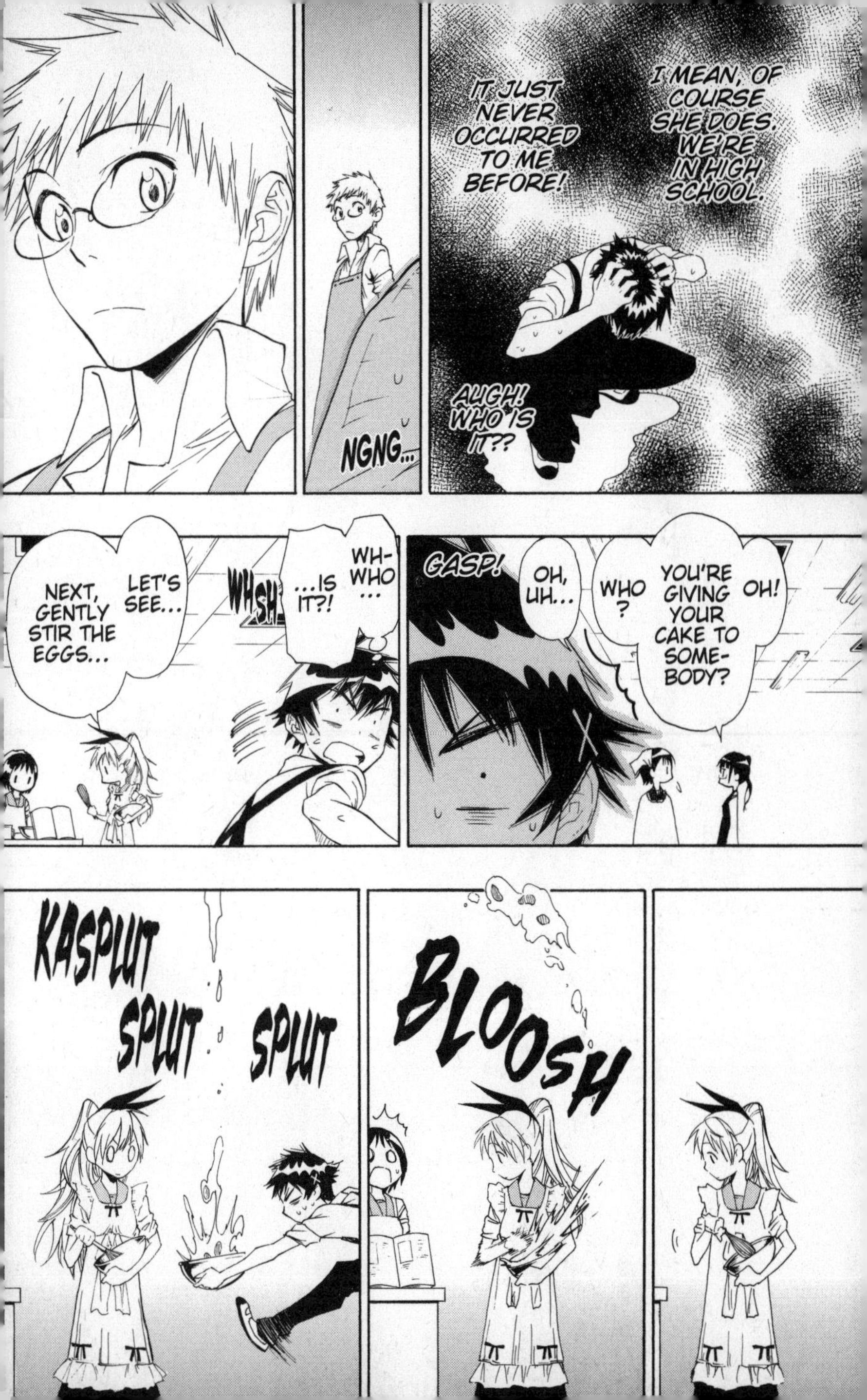
I MEAN, OF COURSE SHE DOES. WE'RE IN HIGH SCHOOL.
IT JUST NEVER OCCURRED TO ME BEFORE!
AUGH! WHO IS IT??
NGNG...
OH!
YOU'RE GIVING YOUR CAKE TO SOMEBODY?
WHO?
OH, UH...
GASP!
WH-WHO...
...IS IT?!
WHSH
LET'S SEE...
NEXT, GENTLY STIR THE EGGS...
BLOOSH
KASPLUT
SPLUT
SPLUT

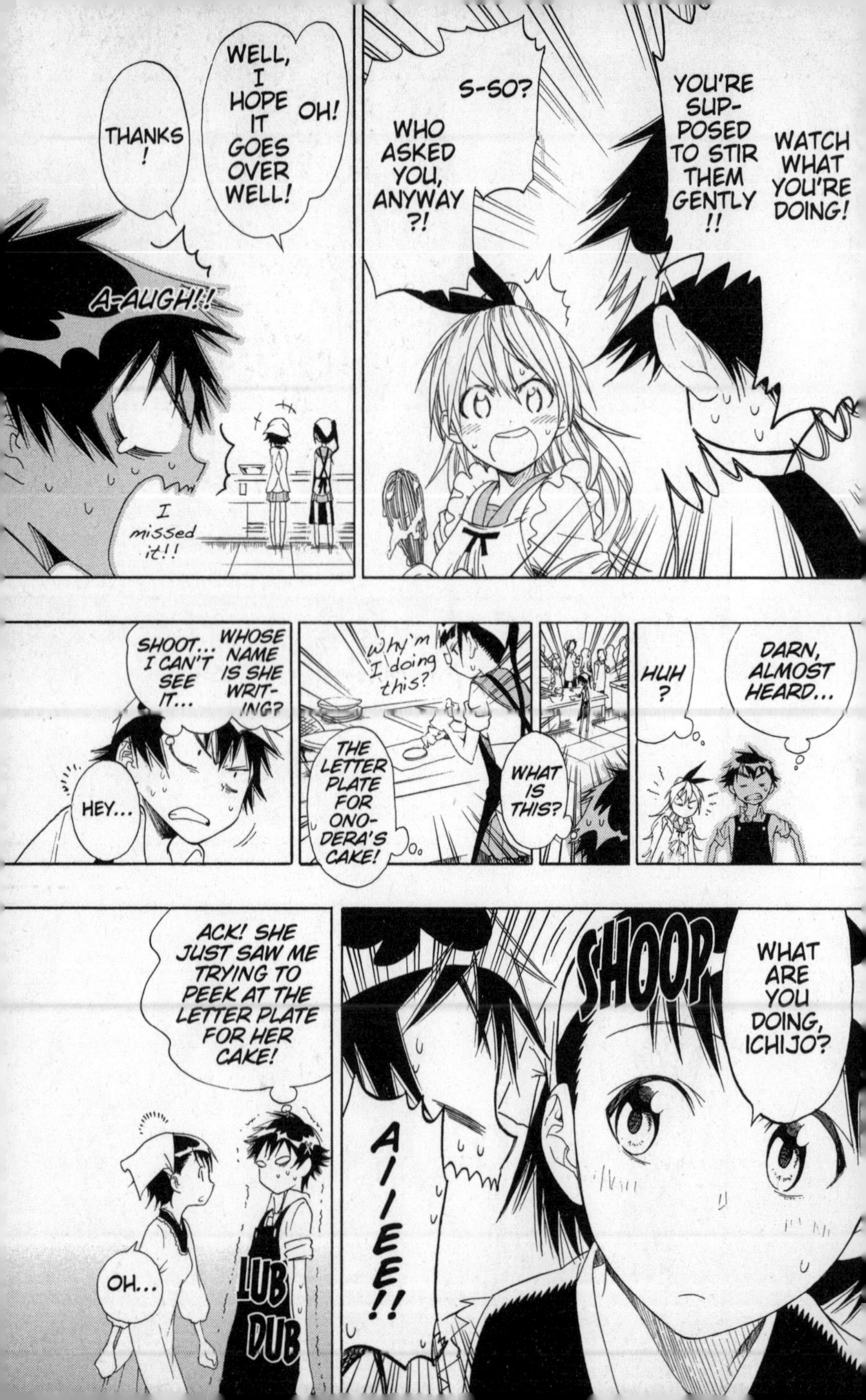
WATCH WHAT YOU'RE DOING!
YOU'RE SUP-POSED TO STIR THEM GENTLY!!
S-SO?
WHO ASKED YOU, ANYWAY?!
OH!
WELL, I HOPE IT GOES OVER WELL!
THANKS!
A-AUGH!!
I missed it!!
DARN, ALMOST HEARD...
HUH?
WHAT IS THIS?
Why'm I doing this?
THE LETTER PLATE FOR ONO-DERA'S CAKE!
WHOSE NAME IS SHE WRIT-ING?
SHOOT... I CAN'T SEE IT...
HEY...
SHOOP
WHAT ARE YOU DOING, ICHIJO?
AIIEE!!
ACK! SHE JUST SAW ME TRYING TO PEEK AT THE LETTER PLATE FOR HER CAKE!
OH...
LUB DUB

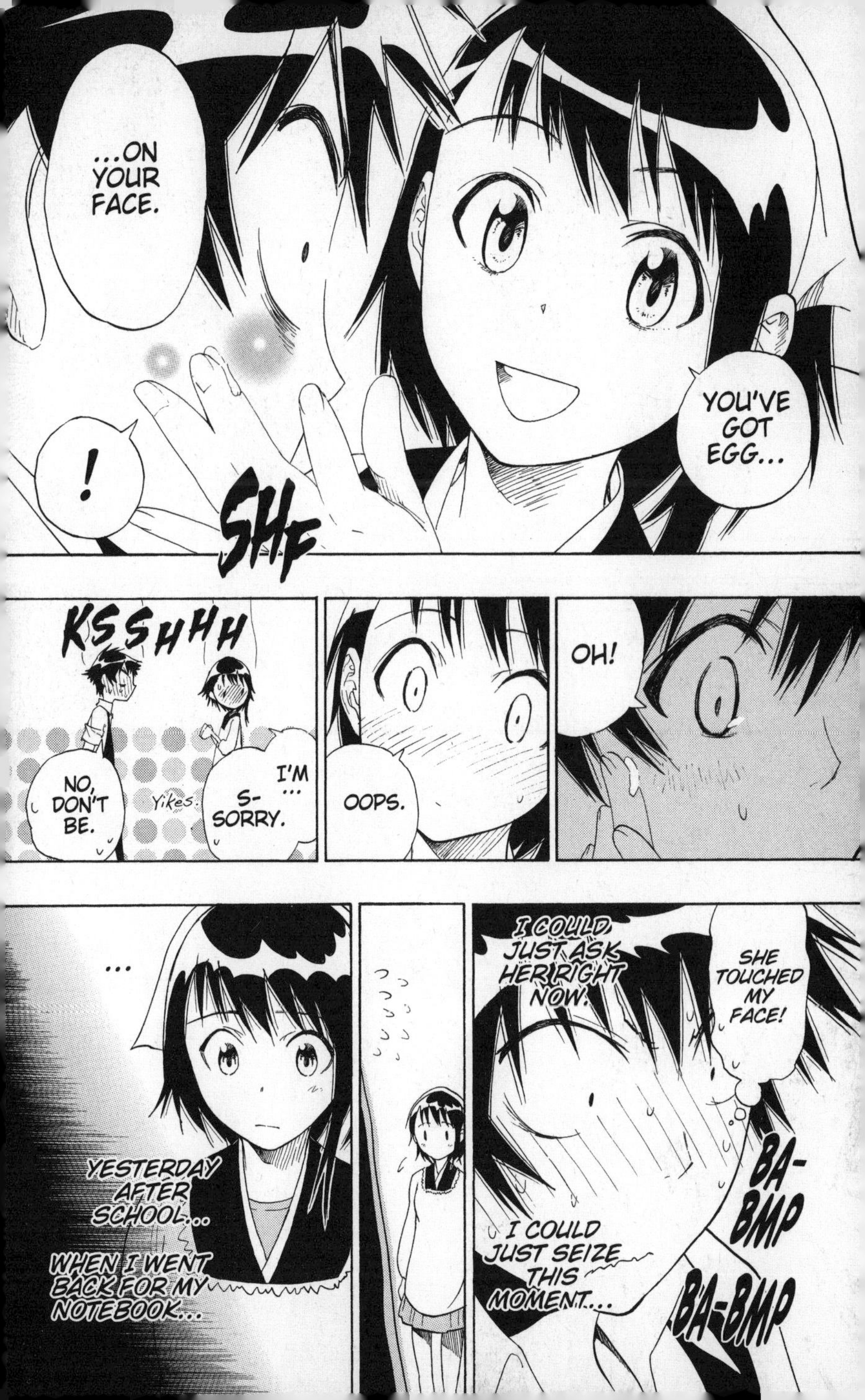
YOU'VE GOT EGG...
...ON YOUR FACE.
SHF
!
OH!
OOPS.
KSSHHH
I'M ... S-SORRY.
Yikes.
NO, DON'T BE.
SHE TOUCHED MY FACE!
I COULD JUST ASK HER RIGHT NOW.
BA-BMP
I COULD JUST SEIZE THIS MOMENT...
BA-BMP
...
YESTERDAY AFTER SCHOOL...
WHEN I WENT BACK FOR MY NOTEBOOK...

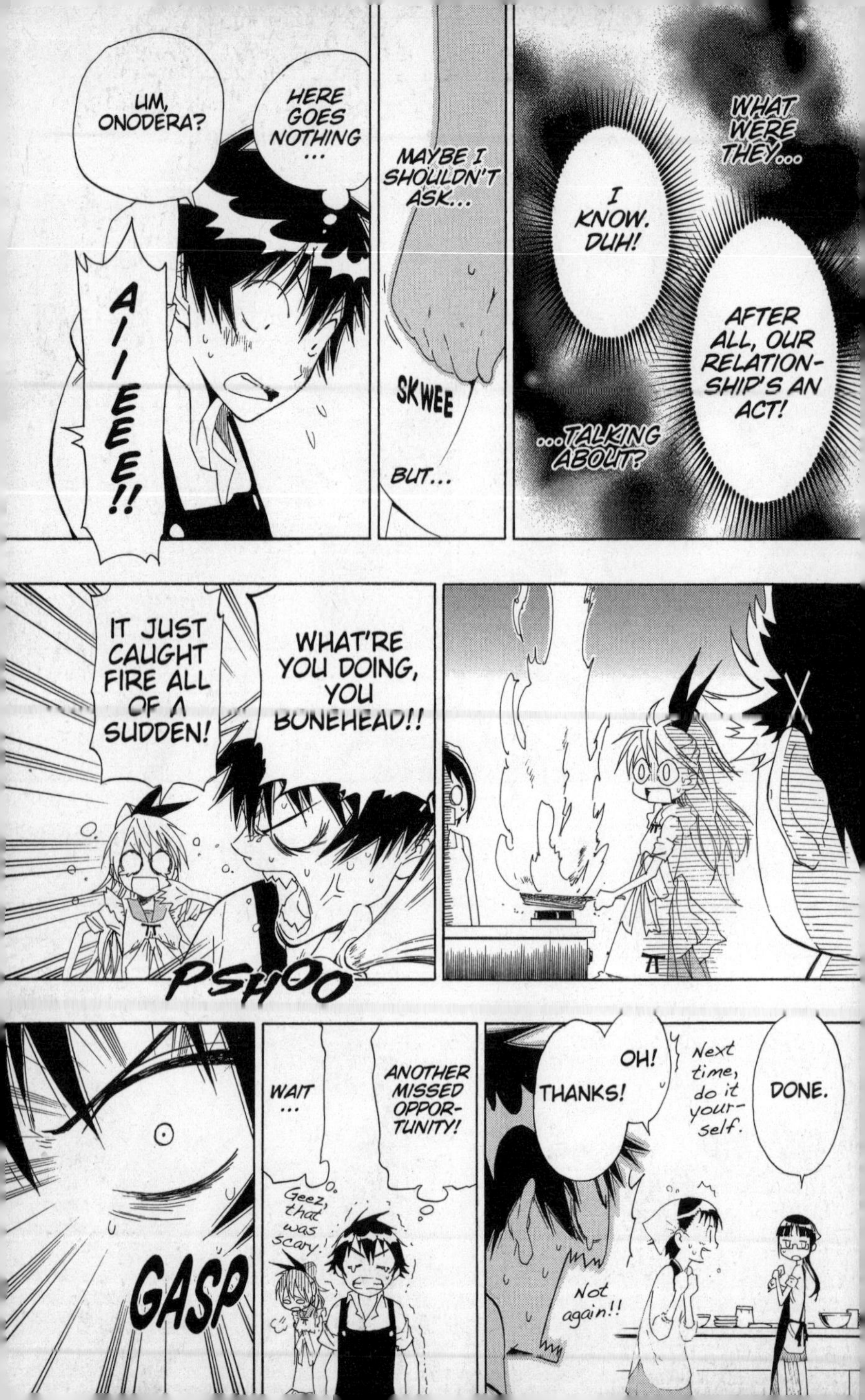
WHAT WERE THEY...
...TALKING ABOUT?
I KNOW. DUH!
AFTER ALL, OUR RELATIONSHIP'S AN ACT!
MAYBE I SHOULDN'T ASK...
SKWEE
BUT...
HERE GOES NOTHING...
UM, ONODERA?
AIIEEEE!!
WHAT'RE YOU DOING, YOU BONEHEAD!!
IT JUST CAUGHT FIRE ALL OF A SUDDEN!
PSHOO
DONE.
Next time, do it yourself.
OH! THANKS!
Not again!!
ANOTHER MISSED OPPORTUNITY!
WAIT...
Geez, that was scary.
GASP

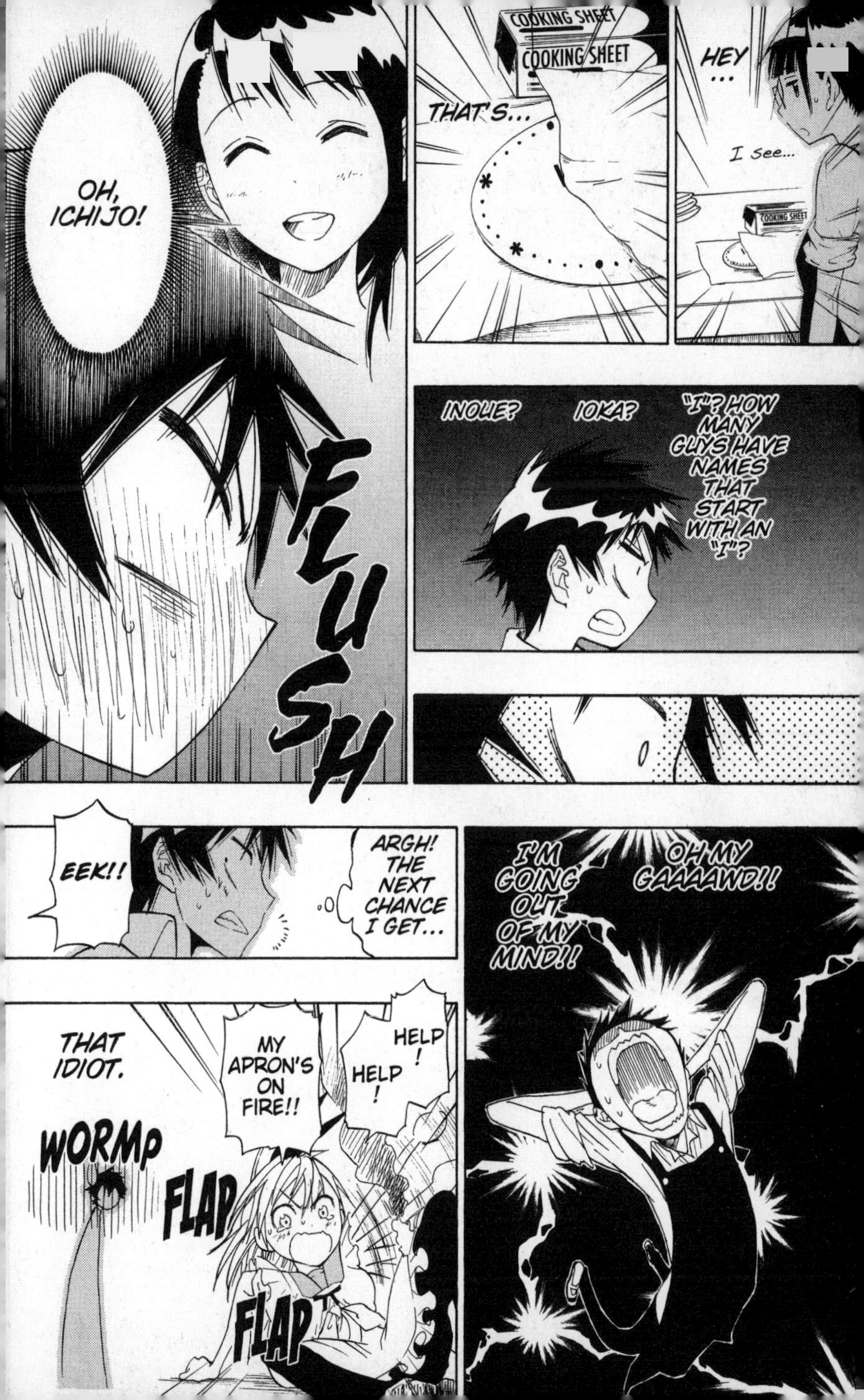
HEY ...
I see...
THAT'S...
COOKING SHEET
INOUE?
IOKA?
"I"? HOW MANY GUYS HAVE NAMES THAT START WITH AN "I"?
OH, ICHIJO!
FLUSH
OH MY GAAAAWD!!
I'M GOING OUT OF MY MIND!!
ARGH! THE NEXT CHANCE I GET...
EEK!!
HELP! HELP!
MY APRON'S ON FIRE!!
THAT IDIOT.
WORMP
FLAP
FLAP

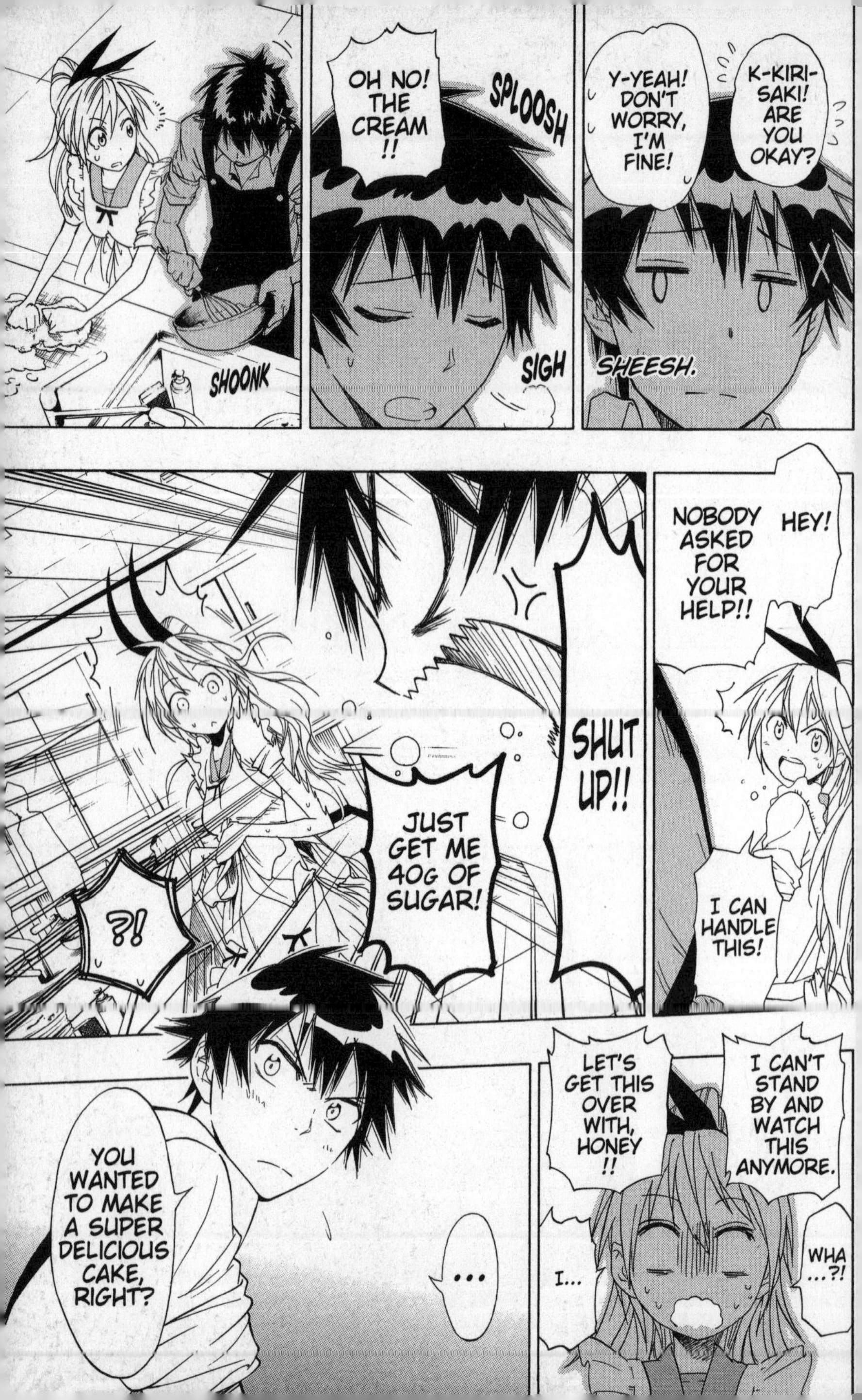

K-KIRI-SAKI! ARE YOU OKAY?
Y-YEAH! DON'T WORRY, I'M FINE!
SHEESH.
OH NO! THE CREAM!!
SPLOOSH
SIGH
SHOONK
HEY!
NOBODY ASKED FOR YOUR HELP!!
I CAN HANDLE THIS!
SHUT UP!!
JUST GET ME 40g OF SUGAR!
?!
WHA ...?!
I CAN'T STAND BY AND WATCH THIS ANYMORE.
LET'S GET THIS OVER WITH, HONEY!!
I...
...
YOU WANTED TO MAKE A SUPER DELICIOUS CAKE, RIGHT?

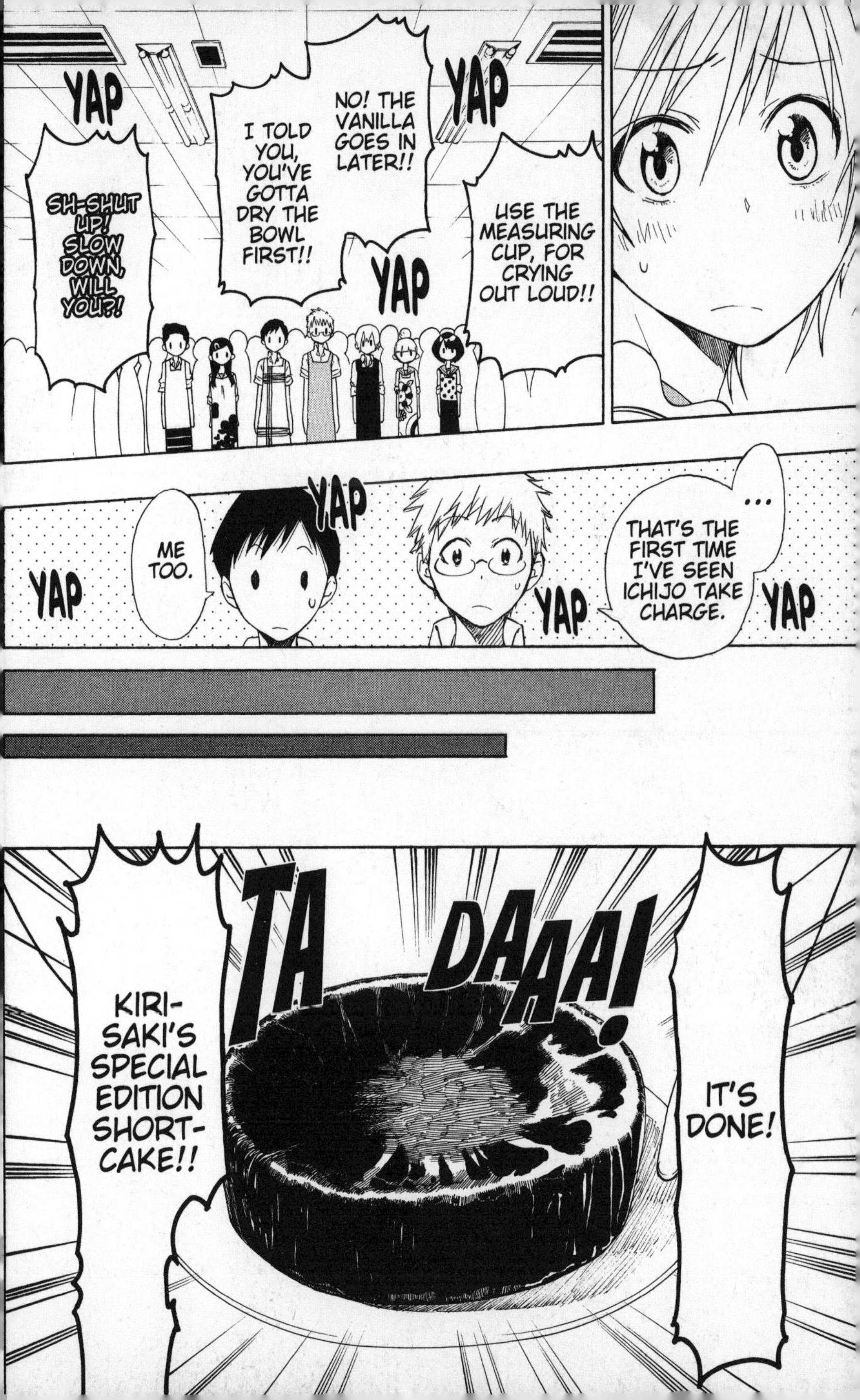
YAP
USE THE MEASURING CUP, FOR CRYING OUT LOUD!!
NO! THE VANILLA GOES IN LATER!!
YAP
I TOLD YOU, YOU'VE GOTTA DRY THE BOWL FIRST!!
YAP
SH-SHUT UP! SLOW DOWN, WILL YOU?!
...
THAT'S THE FIRST TIME I'VE SEEN ICHIJO TAKE CHARGE.
YAP
YAP
YAP
ME TOO.
YAP
IT'S DONE!
TA DAAA!
KIRI-SAKI'S SPECIAL EDITION SHORT-CAKE!!

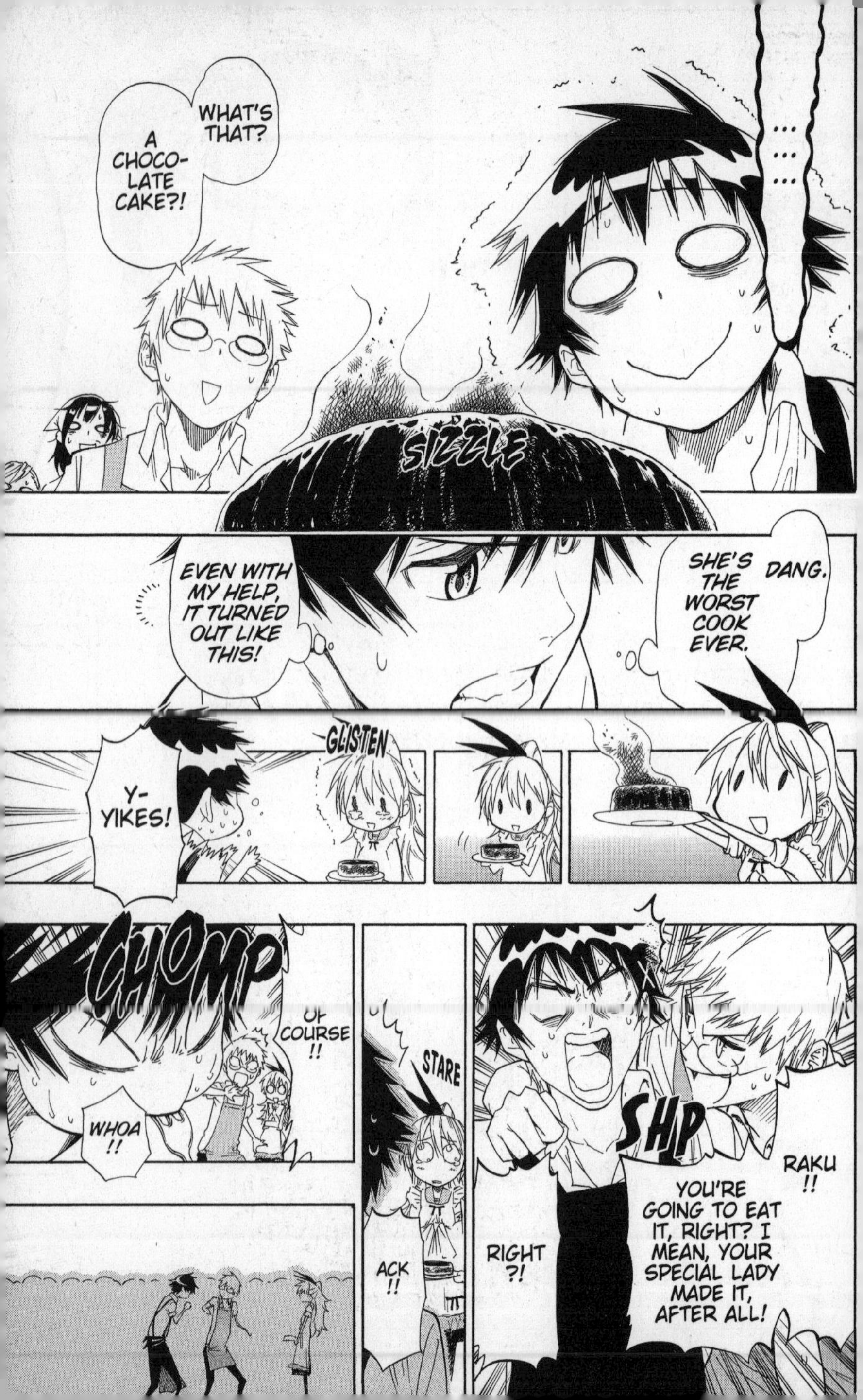
......
WHAT'S THAT?
A CHOCOLATE CAKE?!
SIZZLE
DANG.
SHE'S THE WORST COOK EVER.
EVEN WITH MY HELP, IT TURNED OUT LIKE THIS!
GLISTEN
Y-YIKES!
RAKU!!
YOU'RE GOING TO EAT IT, RIGHT? I MEAN, YOUR SPECIAL LADY MADE IT, AFTER ALL!
SHP
RIGHT?!
STARE
ACK!!
CHOMP
OF COURSE!!
WHOA!!

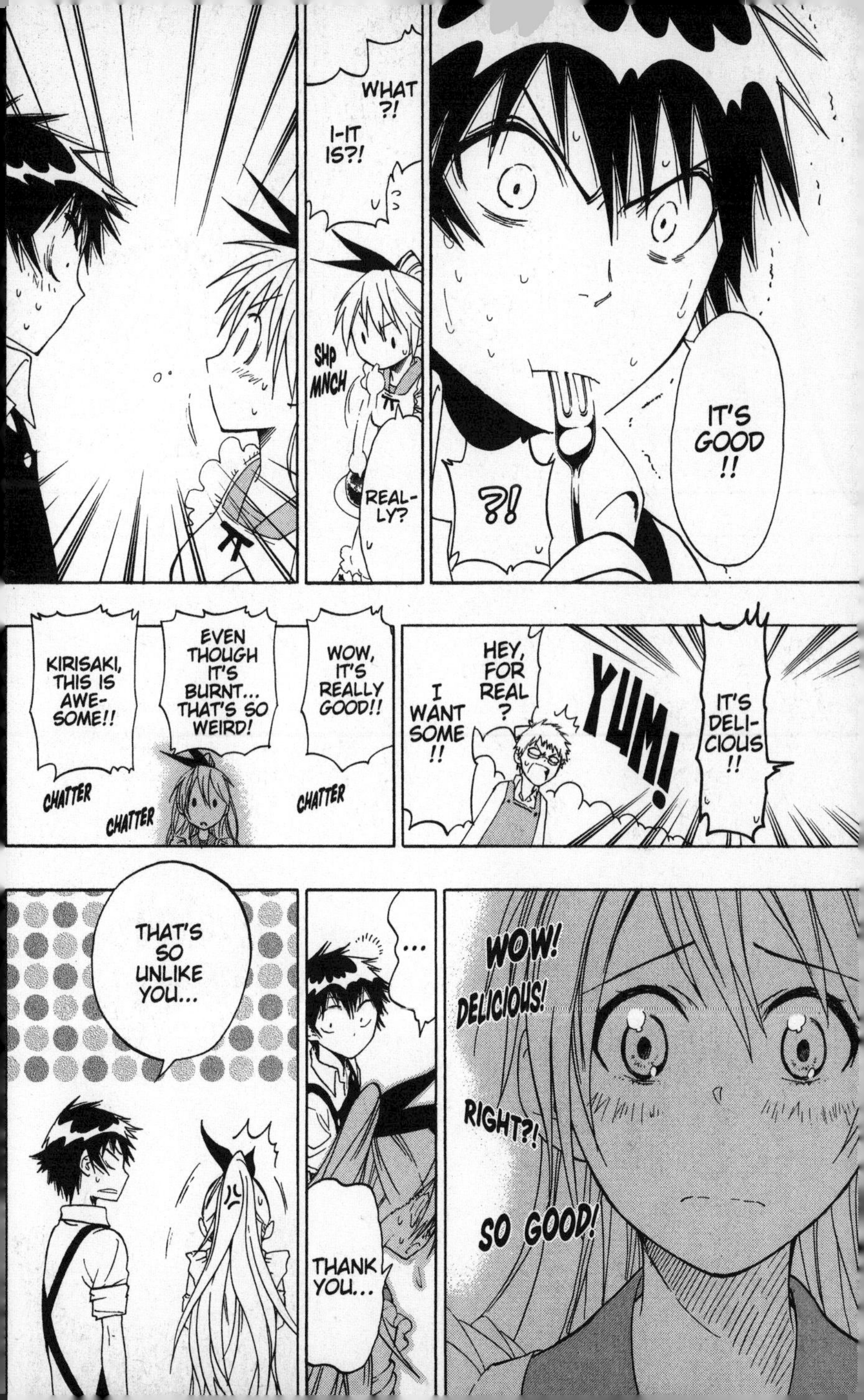
IT'S GOOD!!
?!
WHAT?!
I-IT IS?!
SHP MNCH
REAL-LY?
IT'S DELI-CIOUS!!
YUM!
HEY, FOR REAL?
I WANT SOME!!
WOW, IT'S REALLY GOOD!!
CHATTER
EVEN THOUGH IT'S BURNT... THAT'S SO WEIRD!
CHATTER
KIRISAKI, THIS IS AWE-SOME!!
CHATTER
WOW! DELICIOUS!
RIGHT?!
SO GOOD!
...
THANK YOU...
THAT'S SO UNLIKE YOU...

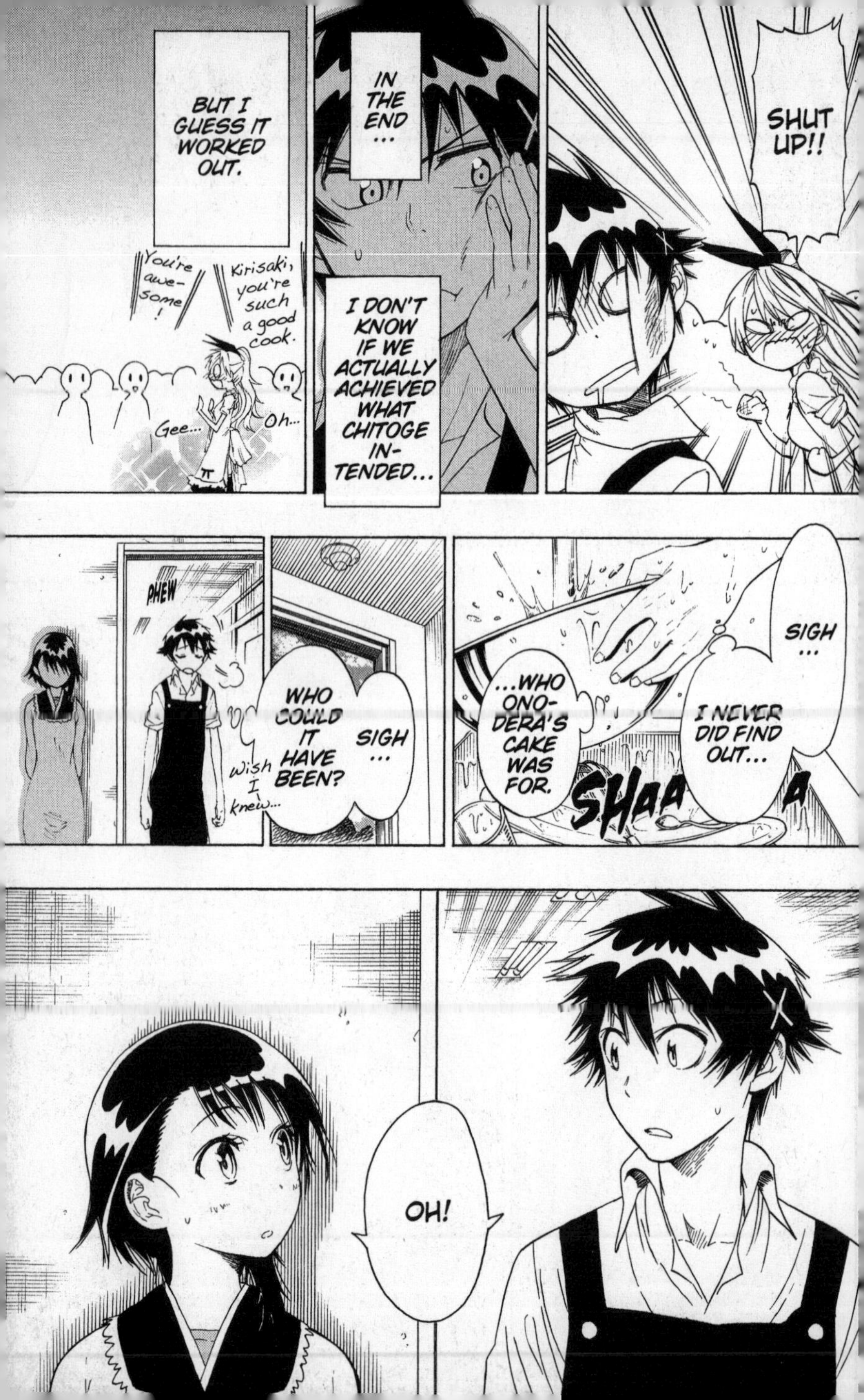

SHUT UP!!
IN THE END...
I DON'T KNOW IF WE ACTUALLY ACHIEVED WHAT CHITOGE IN-TENDED...
BUT I GUESS IT WORKED OUT.
Kirisaki, you're such a good cook.
You're awe-some!
Oh...
Gee...
SIGH...
I NEVER DID FIND OUT...
...WHO ONO-DERA'S CAKE WAS FOR.
SHAA A
SIGH...
WHO COULD IT HAVE BEEN?
Wish I knew...
PHEW
OH!

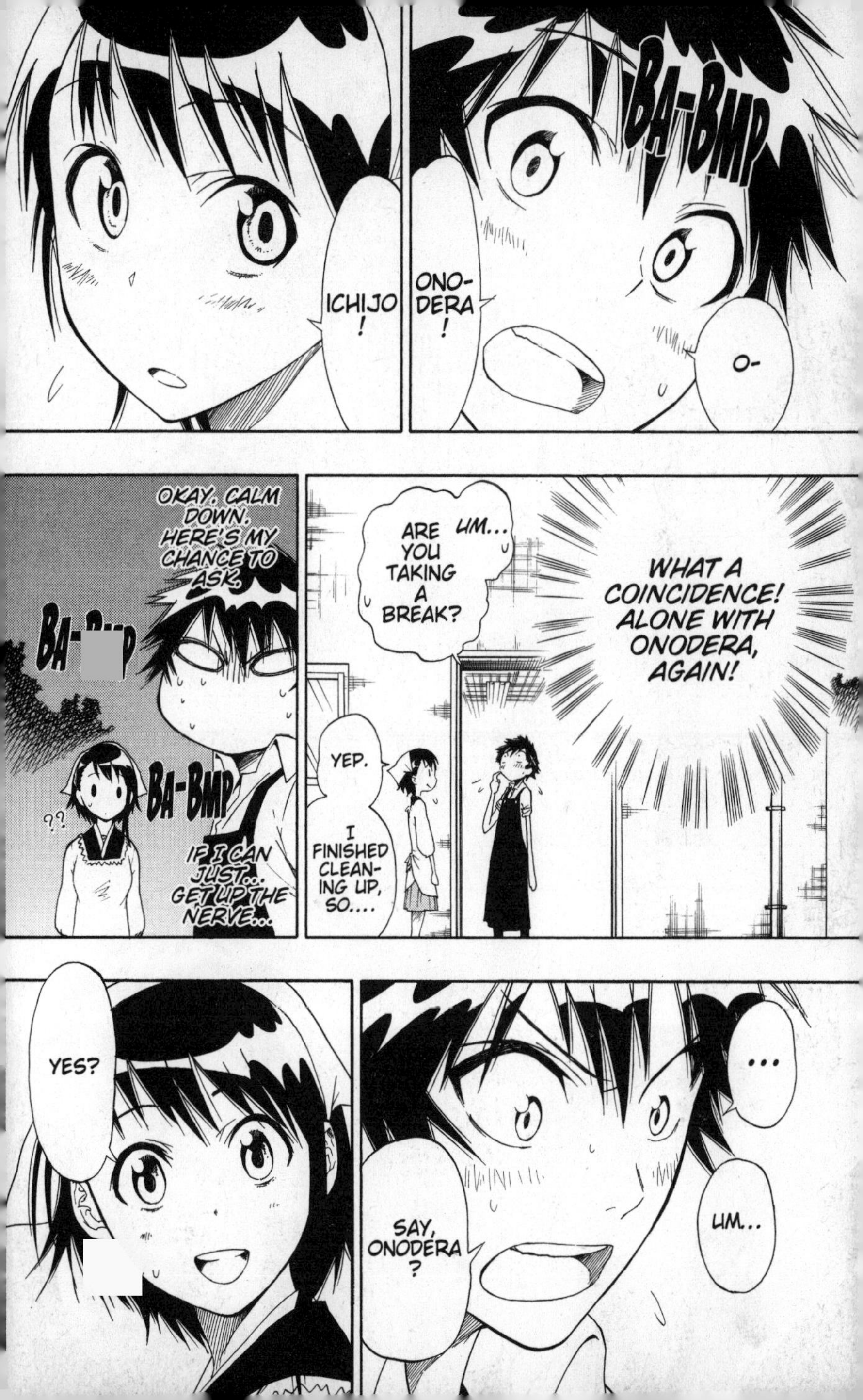
BA-BMP
O-
ONO-DERA!
ICHIJO!
WHAT A COINCIDENCE! ALONE WITH ONODERA, AGAIN!
UM...
ARE YOU TAKING A BREAK?
YEP.
I FINISHED CLEAN-ING UP, SO....
OKAY. CALM DOWN. HERE'S MY CHANCE TO ASK.
BA-BMP
IF I CAN JUST... GET UP THE NERVE...
??
...
UM..
SAY, ONODERA?
YES?

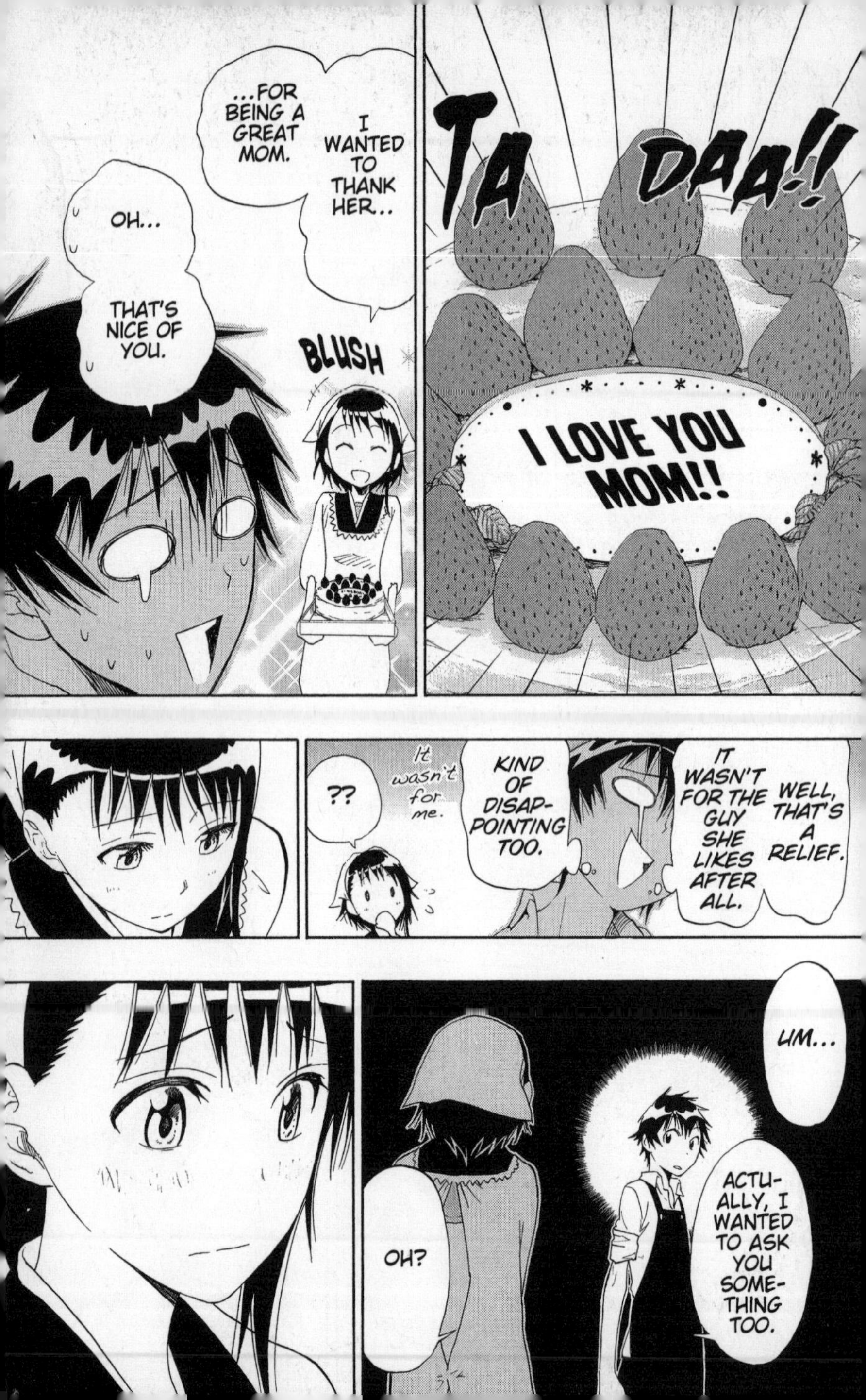
TA DAA!!
I LOVE YOU MOM!!
I WANTED TO THANK HER...
...FOR BEING A GREAT MOM.
BLUSH
OH...
THAT'S NICE OF YOU.
WELL, THAT'S A RELIEF.
IT WASN'T FOR THE GUY SHE LIKES AFTER ALL.
KIND OF DISAPPOINTING TOO.
It wasn't for me.
??
UM...
ACTUALLY, I WANTED TO ASK YOU SOMETHING TOO.
OH?

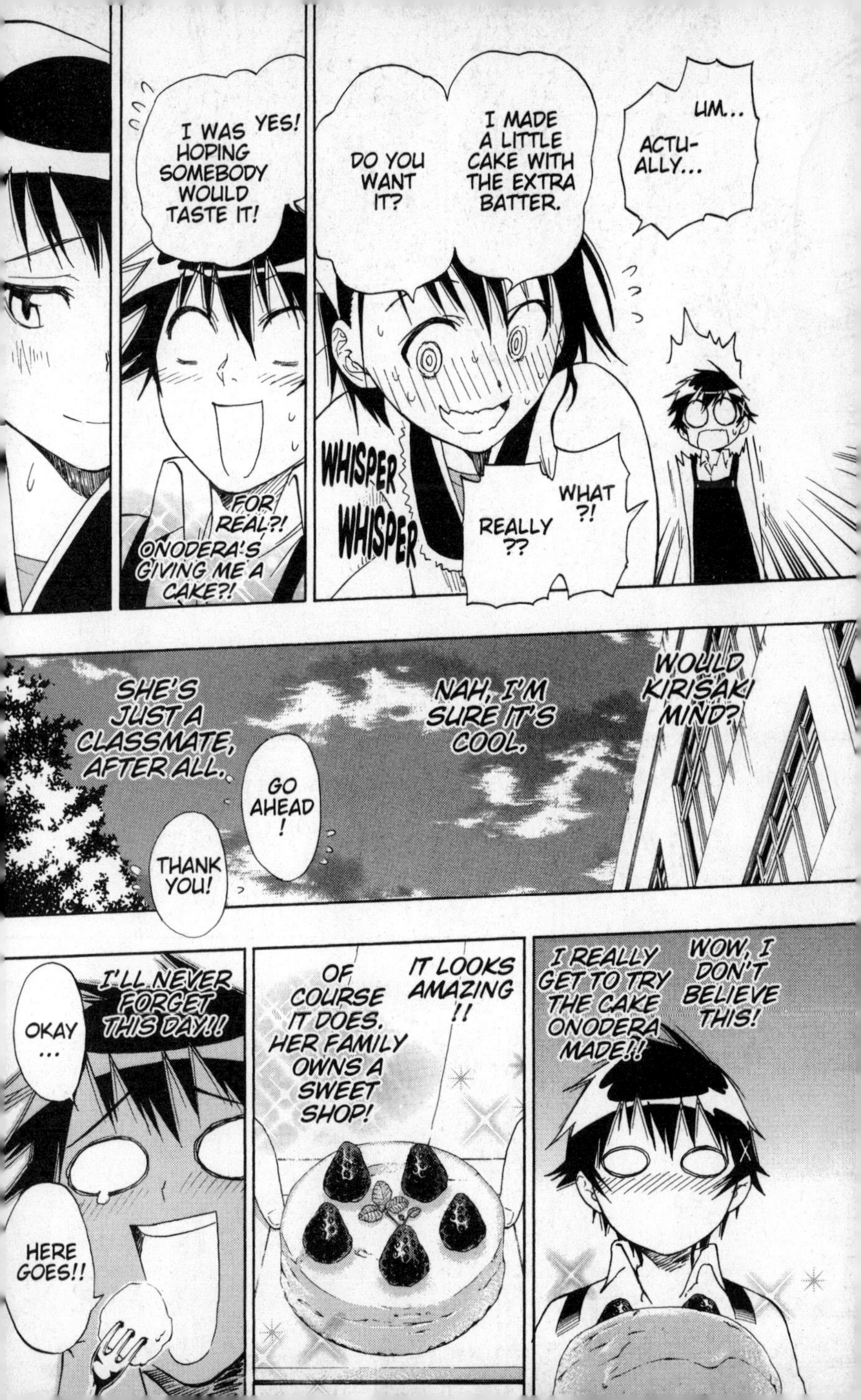
UM... ACTUALLY...
I MADE A LITTLE CAKE WITH THE EXTRA BATTER.
DO YOU WANT IT?
WHISPER WHISPER
WHAT?!
REALLY??
YES! I WAS HOPING SOMEBODY WOULD TASTE IT!
FOR REAL?! ONODERA'S GIVING ME A CAKE?!
WOULD KIRISAKI MIND?
NAH, I'M SURE IT'S COOL.
SHE'S JUST A CLASSMATE, AFTER ALL.
GO AHEAD!
THANK YOU!
WOW, I DON'T BELIEVE THIS!
I REALLY GET TO TRY THE CAKE ONODERA MADE!!
IT LOOKS AMAZING!!
OF COURSE IT DOES. HER FAMILY OWNS A SWEET SHOP!
I'LL NEVER FORGET THIS DAY!!
OKAY...
HERE GOES!!

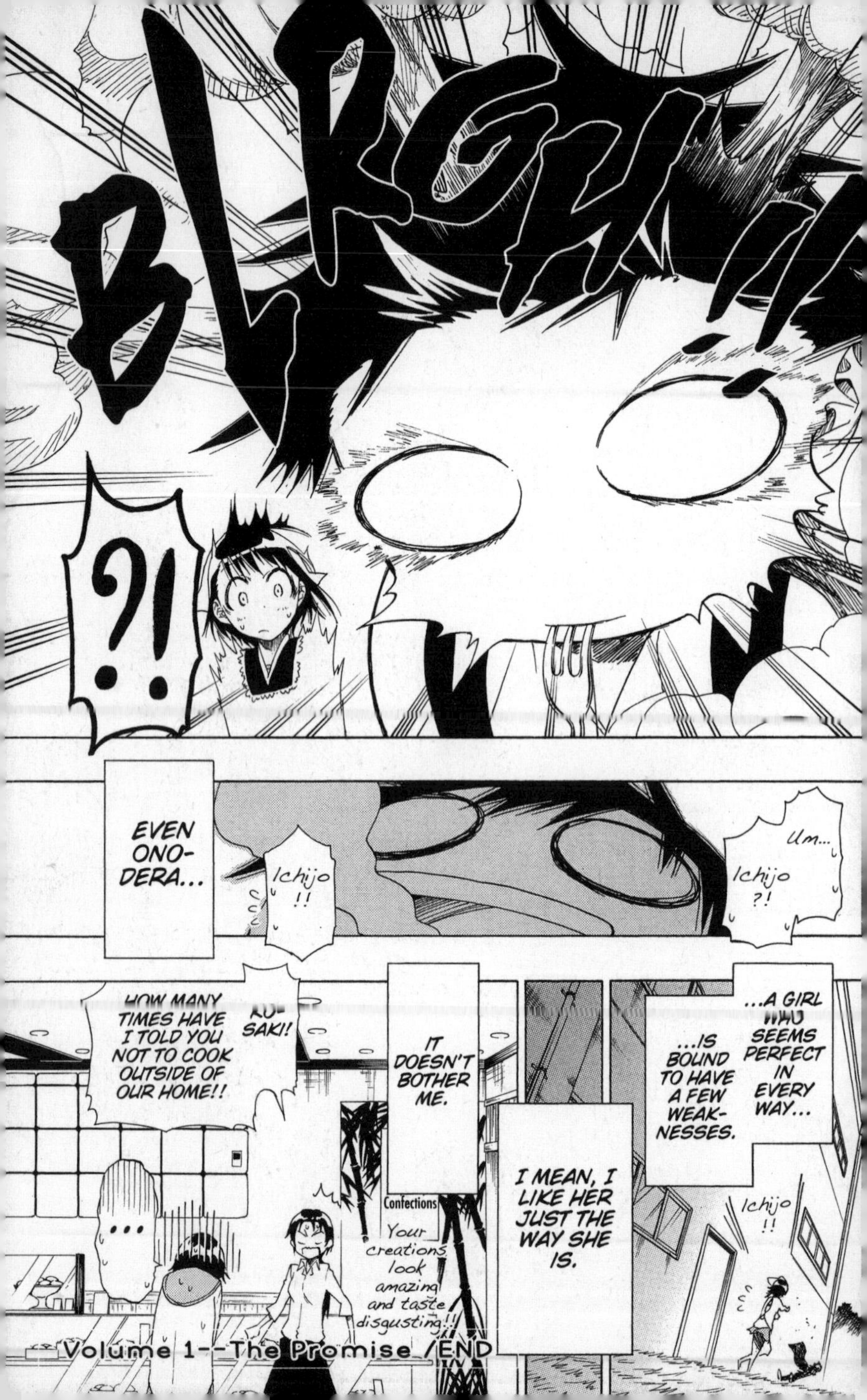
BLRGUH!!
?!
Um... Ichijo ?!
Ichijo !!
EVEN ONODERA...
...A GIRL WHO SEEMS PERFECT IN EVERY WAY...
...IS BOUND TO HAVE A FEW WEAKNESSES.
Ichijo !!
I MEAN, I LIKE HER JUST THE WAY SHE IS.
IT DOESN'T BOTHER ME.
KOSAKI!
HOW MANY TIMES HAVE I TOLD YOU NOT TO COOK OUTSIDE OF OUR HOME!!
Your creations look amazing and taste disgusting!!
Confections
...
Volume 1 -- The Promise /END

Bonus Comic

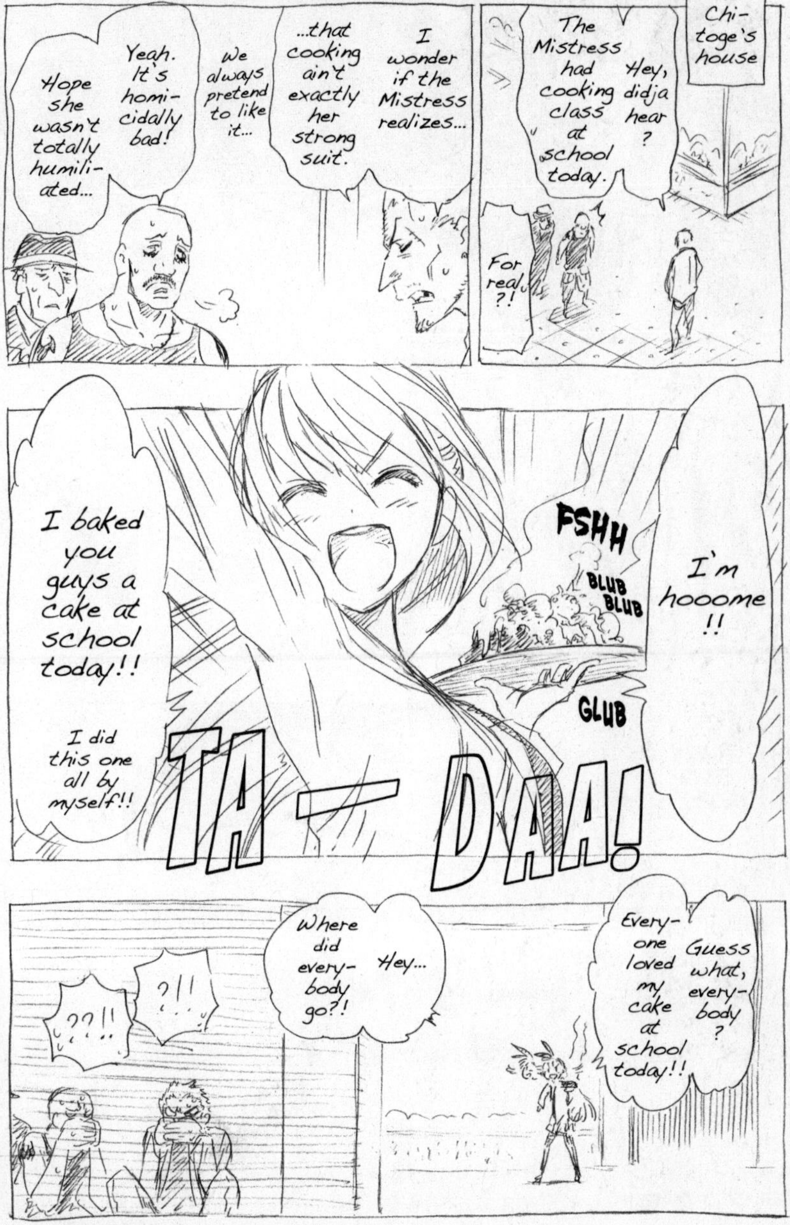
At Chitoge's house
Hey, didja hear?
The Mistress had cooking class at school today.
For real?!
I wonder if the Mistress realizes...
...that cooking ain't exactly her strong suit.
We always pretend to like it...
Yeah. It's homicidally bad!
Hope she wasn't totally humiliated...
I'm hooome!!
FSHH
BLUB BLUB
GLUB
TA-DAA!
I baked you guys a cake at school today!!
I did this one all by myself!!
Guess what, everybody?
Everyone loved my cake at school today!!
Hey...
Where did everybody go?!
?!!
??!!

THE END

Talent

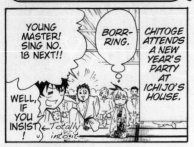

CHITOGE ATTENDS A NEW YEAR'S PARTY AT ICHIJO'S HOUSE.
BORR-RING.
YOUNG MASTER! SING NO. 18 NEXT!!
WELL, IF YOU INSIST!
Totally into it
WHOA, HE'S GOOD!!
JAPANESE FOLK SONGS ONLY.

PUBLISHED IN DOUBLE ISSUE #5-6, 2012 OF WEEKLY SHONEN JUMP

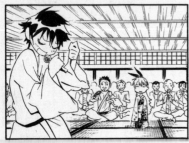

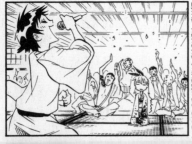

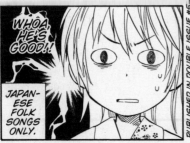

You're Reading the WRONG WAY!

1
2
1
3
4
2
5
6
3
7
8
4
9
5
142

NISEKOI reads from right to left, starting in the upper-right corner. Japanese is read from right to left, meaning that action, sound effects, and word-balloon order are completely reversed from English order.

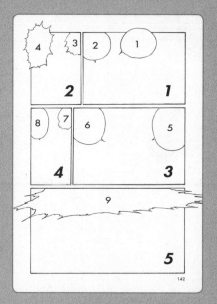

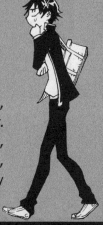